SETTING
NATIONAL
PRIORITIES
The 1978 Budget

JOSEPH A. PECHMAN, *Editor*

SETTING NATIONAL PRIORITIES
The 1978 Budget

Barry M. Blechman and Others
George J. Carcagno and Walter S. Corson
Robert W. Hartman
Herbert Kaufman
Joseph J. Minarik
Alicia H. Munnell
Richard P. Nathan and Paul R. Dommel
John L. Palmer
Joseph A. Pechman
Louise B. Russell
Milton Russell

THE BROOKINGS INSTITUTION
Washington, D.C.

THE BROOKINGS INSTITUTION is an independent organization devoted to nonpartisan research, education, and publication in economics, government, foreign policy, and the social sciences generally. Its principal purposes are to aid in the development of sound public policies and to promote public understanding of issues of national importance.

The Institution was founded on December 8, 1927, to merge the activities of the Institute for Government Research, founded in 1916, the Institute of Economics, founded in 1922, and the Robert Brookings Graduate School of Economics and Government, founded in 1924.

The Board of Trustees is responsible for the general administration of the Institution, while the immediate direction of the policies, program, and staff is vested in the President, assisted by an advisory committee of the officers and staff. The by-laws of the Institution state: "It is the function of the Trustees to make possible the conduct of scientific research, and publication, under the most favorable conditions, and to safeguard the independence of the research staff in the pursuit of their studies and in the publication of the results of such studies. It is not a part of their function to determine, control, or influence the conduct of particular investigations or the conclusions reached."

The President bears final responsibility for the decision to publish a manuscript as a Brookings book. In reaching his judgment on the competence, accuracy, and objectivity of each study, the President is advised by the director of the appropriate research program and weighs the views of a panel of expert outside readers who report to him in confidence on the quality of the work. Publication of a work signifies that it is deemed a competent treatment worthy of public consideration but does not imply endorsement of conclusions or recommendations.

The Institution maintains its position of neutrality on issues of public policy in order to safeguard the intellectual freedom of the staff. Hence interpretations or conclusions in Brookings publications should be understood to be solely those of the authors and should not be attributed to the Institution, to its trustees, officers, or other staff members, or to the organizations that support its research.

Foreword

THE ANNUAL BUDGET is the basic planning document of the federal government. In it, the President lists all the outlays to be made in the coming fiscal year and the ways in which these outlays will be financed. He also makes detailed recommendations about the changes that should be made in federal expenditure and tax programs. Inevitably, these proposals reflect only the final decisions reached by the President after considering the options available to him. The public is rarely informed of alternative ways of achieving the government's objectives, or the reasons for discarding them. Another obstacle to public awareness of the budget process is that the budget document itself is complicated and not easy to understand.

The purpose of this series of annual volumes, which was initiated seven years ago, is to explain the President's budget, examine alternative policies, and evaluate the budgetary implications of the various options for the short and long run. Because 1976 was an election year, last year's volume examined a number of major long-run foreign and domestic policy issues, only some of which had significant budgetary implications. This year's volume returns to the earlier format, which emphasizes issues and problems of more immediate budgetary significance.

This volume is the first in the series to deal with a budget that was prepared by one administration and revised by a newly elected president shortly after he assumed office. The book takes advantage of the opportunity thus offered to compare the choices made by successive presidents from the two major political parties. The authors compare the policies of Presidents Ford and Carter and evaluate their implications for the budget and for the economy. They also discuss the proposals made by President Carter in a succession of messages submitted to the Congress in his first 100 days in office.

The volume describes and analyzes the budget as a whole, explains its fiscal implications, and provides estimates of the margin that will be available for spending or tax reductions in future years. In addition, it deals in depth with several issues of major significance for this year and next: defense, employment and training programs, control of medical costs, social security, welfare reform, programs for the cities, energy, and government reorganization.

The research and preparation of this volume were undertaken jointly by the three main research programs of the Brookings Institution. Joseph A. Pechman is director, and Robert W. Hartman, Joseph J. Minarik, John L. Palmer, and Louise B. Russell are members of the staff, of the Economics Studies program. Herbert Kaufman, Richard P. Nathan, and Paul R. Dommel are members of the staff of the Governmental Studies program. Barry M. Blechman and his associates are members of the defense analysis staff of the Foreign Policy Studies program. Alicia H. Munnell is an assistant vice president and economist for the Federal Reserve Bank of Boston. George J. Carcagno is senior vice president, and Walter S. Corson is a member of the staff, of Mathematica Policy Research. Milton Russell is a member of the staff of Resources for the Future. The risk of factual error was minimized by the work of Evelyn P. Fisher. Ellen Alston edited the manuscript and prepared the book for publication. The index was prepared by Florence Robinson.

The work on this volume was supported by grants from the Ford Foundation and Carnegie Corporation of New York. Research underlying the chapters on the defense budget, on medical care costs, and on the revenue implications of the income tax proposals analyzed in the fiscal policy chapter was supported by grants from the Ford Foundation, the Directorate for Scientific, Technological and International Affairs of the National Science Foundation, and the RANN program of the National Science Foundation, respectively. The Brookings Institution is grateful to these foundations for their support and to the Federal Reserve Bank of Boston, Mathematica Policy Research, and Resources for the Future for permitting members of their staffs to collaborate in the preparation of this volume.

The views expressed here are those of the authors and should not be attributed to any of the persons whose assistance is acknowledged in the various chapters; to the trustees, officers, or other staff members of the Brookings Institution; or to the foundations and organizations that contributed to the support of this volume.

BRUCE K. MAC LAURY
President

July 1977
Washington, D.C.

Contents

4. The Defense Budget   81
Barry M. Blechman and Others

5. Employment and Training Assistance   143
John L. Palmer

6. Medical Care Costs   177
Louise B. Russell

7. Social Security   207
Alicia H. Munnell

8. Welfare Reform   249
George J. Carcagno and Walter S. Corson

Text Tables

Contents

Appendix Tables

CHAPTER ONE

Introduction and Summary

JOSEPH A. PECHMAN

THE BUDGET for the fiscal year beginning October 1, 1977, and ending September 30, 1978, which was formulated by President Ford and revised by President Carter, contains an amalgam of programs reflecting their very different budget philosophies. The major policy issues in the budget reflect the particular circumstances in which it was developed. The nation was still in the early stages of a business recovery and remained far more depressed than in any other recovery since the end of World War II. The unemployment rate was close to 8 percent when President Carter took office, and manufacturing industries were operating at about 80 percent of full capacity. At the same time, inflation was running at an annual rate of 5 to 6 percent— much lower than the double-digit rate of 1974, but much higher than the nation had ever experienced except during booms of economic activity. In these circumstances, both Presidents planned to stimulate the economy in the short run at a rate that would not exacerbate inflation and to bring the budget into balance within three or four years.

The budget strategies of the two Presidents differed sharply, however. President Ford believed that federal expenditures were much too high and placed the highest priority on curtailing them. His 1978 budget called for a substantial deficit generated by permanent tax and expenditure reductions. The tax reductions were intended not only to stimulate the economy in the short run but also to leave less room in the budget for future expenditure increases. Since President

1

Carter came into office with plans to expand a number of social programs as revenues permitted, he emphasized countercyclical expenditure programs and temporary tax cuts that would phase out as the economy improved. Both as a matter of fiscal prudence and to combat inflation, both Presidents believed that the budget must be brought into balance when the economy reached full employment.

Although economic considerations usually dominate public discussions of the budget, other major policy issues are addressed either directly or indirectly by a president's expenditure and tax decisions. The defense budget is rising in both real and money terms, after a long period of major reductions. Nondefense spending is also increasing, particularly for employment and training programs, public works, health care, income security for the aged, the poor, and the unemployed, energy, and grants-in-aid to state and local governments. Even though the 1978 budget is a transition budget between two administrations, congressional decisions on these and other matters will have a major impact on federal spending for years to come.

The Budget and the Economy

President Ford made two attempts to curtail the growth of federal expenditures. His budget for fiscal year 1977, submitted in January 1976, proposed cuts in several social programs coupled with a permanent reduction in individual and corporation income taxes and an increase in payroll taxes for social security and unemployment insurance. Congress restored most of the expenditure cuts and rejected the income and social security tax proposals, though the unemployment insurance tax proposal survived. In his 1978 budget, President Ford repeated his recommendation for major expenditure and income tax cuts. This time, President Carter reversed most of the cutbacks and added a stimulus program of his own (see chapters 2 and 3).

The Carter stimulus package included outlays for job creation programs and tax cuts. Additional outlays on other ongoing federal programs were limited because such increases, once undertaken, would be hard to stop; Carter's goal of financing a number of major new expenditure programs and of reaching a balanced budget by fiscal year 1981 would be impossible to achieve if existing programs were allowed to grow excessively. Instead, he proposed substantial expansions of public jobs programs, including accelerated public works and public service employment for the long-run unemployed and disadvantaged. These expanded programs were expected to begin in fiscal year 1977, reach a peak in 1978, and then taper off as the economy improved and unemployment declined. In addition, outlays for the countercyclical revenue sharing program, which was scheduled to terminate in September 1977, were to be increased and extended through 1982.

On the tax side, the President proposed an immediate rebate of $50 per person for calendar year 1976 income taxes, with $50 payments to most nontaxed persons. The rebate, which was to be paid in the spring of 1977, was designed to provide immediate stimulation for consumer spending to prepare the way for the slow-starting jobs programs. To provide an additional stimulus and simplify the income tax for low- and middle-income taxpayers, the President also proposed a permanent increase in the standard deduction for 1977 and beyond. A 2 percent increase in the investment tax credit or an optional credit of 4 percent of employers' social security payroll taxes against business income taxes were added to stimulate investment and reduce labor costs, respectively.

The rebate ran into business and congressional resistance and, during the delay, the economic indicators showed signs of faster growth in consumer demand and more inflation. Political pressures mounted as the President anticipated confrontations with Congress over water resource projects and energy. Accordingly, he withdrew the 1976 income tax rebate and the business tax cuts from his stimulus proposal. Congress concurred on the rebate and the investment credit, but formulated its own version of a temporary employment tax credit in place of the administration's original social security payroll tax credit.

Ironically, in view of the positions of the candidates on the economic issues during the 1976 campaign, President Carter's fiscal 1977 budget turned out to be somewhat less stimulative than President Ford's. On the other hand, the Carter 1978 budget will be substantially more stimulative than the Ford budget, assuming that the jobs programs move into high gear, as expected, early in the fiscal year.

Thus, the degree of fiscal stimulus to the economy under President Carter is approximately the same as it would have been under President Ford until about October 1977. Whether the withdrawal of the rebate, which would have given a boost to consumer spending in the spring and summer of 1977, was a wise decision depends on developments in the private sector. There is a risk that private demand will not be buoyant enough to reduce unemployment significantly during the remainder of 1977. Proponents of the rebate argued that the additional stimulus would keep the recovery going at a satisfactory rate without running the risk of generating greater inflationary pressures at this stage of the cycle. Opponents of the rebate argued that the additional stimulus was unnecessary and that more moderate growth was desirable in the interest of holding down inflation.

The employment outlook for fiscal 1978 depends on the speed with which the jobs programs is implemented. The expansion of the public service employment program may take longer than expected. Public works programs are always slow in building up steam, despite the assurances of federal and state and local officials that there is a large backlog of projects available for immediate activation. For these reasons, it is entirely possible that the stimulus planned for early fiscal 1978 may not be felt in full force until later. If President Carter's assumption of a vigorous recovery in 1977 (which led to the withdrawal of the rebate) is correct, the economy may be able to wait for the additional boost; but a slowdown in growth could leave the economy and the unemployment rate at unsatisfactory levels well into 1978. The odds are, however, that the economy will continue to recover at a moderate rate in 1977 and 1978.

In contrast, the outlook for inflation is not encouraging. The deepest and longest recession since 1938 has not reduced the underlying inflation rate of 5–6 percent a year. The evidence suggests that this inflation is a continuation of the rapid inflation of the last several years and is largely unrelated to the current level of aggregate demand. President Carter has announced that his goal is to reduce inflation to 4 percent by the end of 1979, not by intervention in price and wage decisions, but by relying on such long-run policies as deregulation, antitrust enforcement, lower price supports, and import competition to hold down prices. Even if successful, these policies will have an effect only gradually. Moreover, the energy program will inevitably have the effect of raising prices. In all likelihood, therefore, the general rate of inflation will not be greatly moderated by the policies proposed by the new administration.

The Budget Outlook

During his election campaign, President Carter promised to balance the budget by fiscal year 1981, with outlays limited to about 21 percent of the gross national product in a fully employed economy. Such a strategy was claimed to be consistent with undertaking new commitments in domestic programs, as well as with significant tax reductions, because economic recovery would generate the necessary margin of additional receipts over built-in expenditure increases.

These campaign promises clearly affected the budget proposals submitted by President Carter in February 1977. The immediate need for a fiscal stimulus to put the economy on a full-employment track, combined with the longer-term need to preserve room for future spending initiatives and tax reductions, dictated the shape of his budget. The stimulus package used up only a small fraction of the fiscal year 1981 budget margin. Nonetheless, other budget revisions —notably the reversal of most of President Ford's proposed cutbacks in health, income security, and manpower programs, as well as the absence of significant cuts in the outgoing administration's defense plans—had the effect of increasing the fiscal year 1981 spending projection by nearly $25 billion. On the tax side, the new administration's tax proposals would add about $6 billion to 1981 receipts— $11 billion from social security taxes less a $5 billion revenue loss resulting from the increase in the standard deduction.

Our analysis of the outlook for fiscal year 1981 indicates that, although the budget margin has narrowed considerably from earlier estimates, President Carter can still look forward to having some leeway for new spending programs and for tax cuts. If the unemployment rate drops to 4.8 percent by fiscal year 1981 and if inflation slows to about 5 percent by that year, limiting spending and taxes to 21 percent of the gross national product would imply outlays and receipts of $582 billion. This would allow $30 billion in spending above projected current program levels and a $21 billion tax cut. The spending leeway is shaved to $15 billion if all existing programs are fully adjusted for inflation. However, another $20 billion would be available for added spending and tax cuts under more optimistic growth projections (see chapter 11).

Doubts may be raised, however, about the economic assumptions underlying the budget projections. Inflation may not drop to 5 percent by fiscal year 1981, much less to 4 percent as the new administration hopes. Achieving an unemployment rate under 5 percent while tightening fiscal policy requires much more vigorous real growth in private investment than has occurred in the recent sluggish performance of that sector.

If economic policy turns restrictive too quickly, the economy will falter and none of the Carter administration's long-run goals will be realized. This is likely to happen if no new expenditure programs or tax reductions are undertaken and the budget is held to current service levels, or if monetary policy prematurely tightens and retards private spending. On the other hand, if federal spending accelerates too much or excessive permanent tax cuts are enacted, another episode of rapid inflation (which will raise receipts more than outlays and thus help to balance the budget) followed by a recession (which will generate huge deficits) is in the cards. While inflation does increase the government's share of the gross national product, it will almost certainly generate reactions in both the public and private sectors that will ultimately reduce the resources available to both.

The limited budget margin available for fiscal year 1981 offers a challenge to the Carter administration. The $30 billion above current program levels is probably inadequate to fulfill all President Carter's campaign pledges on aiding the cities, reforming welfare, expanding education programs, and the like. But it does provide enough extra resources for the administration to achieve many of its social goals, particularly if it is able to combine some cutbacks in existing programs with the additional fiscal resources that will be generated by economic recovery. Similarly, the more than $20 billion of revenues available for tax reduction could be the "sweetener" offered to Congress to make tax reform palatable. These reform plans could be phased in over the period 1979–81, with the phase-in rate determined by the state of the economy.

Economic forecasting is in no position now to predict how strong the economy will be or what the price level will be by 1981. If the administration proceeds according to a realistic—though by no means assured—set of economic assumptions and remains flexible enough to change course if needed, it would be doing as much as can be expected from responsible leadership. Extreme positions—such as "there is no way to balance the budget by 1981," "budget balance is the number one priority and requires that no new programs be started," or "more federal spending will pay for itself by generating new revenues"—simply distort the picture. Consequently, it would be inadvisable for the administration to lock itself into fulfillment of a rigid budgetary goal irrespective of economic developments. At the same time, there is no reason, so far, to shift course.

The Defense Budget

Defense spending is again scheduled to increase in fiscal year 1978, continuing a trend that started in 1975 (see chapter 4). In that year, apprehension about the continuing growth in Soviet military power brought about a major turning point in U.S. defense policy. Real defense spending and military force levels had been declining steadily from the Vietnam War peak in 1968, and there was public and congressional pressure to cut programs even further. But in 1975, policies were adopted that would expand general-purpose force levels (that is, army divisions, navy ships, and air force tactical squadrons) and would accelerate the pace at which new weapons, both general purpose and strategic, were being developed and introduced into deployed units. Despite some savings from measures to improve efficiency in defense management, these programs turned the defense budget around, and real spending obligations began to rise rapidly.

The fiscal year 1978 budget submitted by President Ford continued on this course. He proposed to obligate $123 billion for defense in fiscal 1978—$13 billion more than the previous year, for a real increase of $7 billion, or 6 percent. Further annual real increases of 3 percent were projected for fiscal years 1979 through 1982. The Ford 1978 defense budget represented a real growth of $16.5 billion from 1975 levels, with most of the increase earmarked for new military hardware and to expand research and development. Growth in the cost of defense manpower, however, which put substantial upward pressure on the defense budget in the first half of the 1970s, has largely been brought under control.

President Carter's amendments to the Ford budget included reductions in defense obligations totaling $2.8 billion, leaving real growth of about 3 percent. As compared to the Ford program, the Carter budget places less emphasis on strategic nuclear weapons and more emphasis on the readiness of military units for combat, requires tighter scrutiny of the cost of the most expensive aircraft and missile systems, shifts from nuclear to conventional power for surface warships, and reflects a continued determination to strengthen U.S. military capabilities in Europe. Still, the Carter changes were not substantial enough to indicate clear directions in the new administration's defense program. Most weapons programs that were modified were slowed down rather than terminated, and major reforms in defense manpower policy, which had been promised during the campaign, have yet to be unveiled.

The basic elements of the U.S. military posture are now being reviewed by the new administration. Over the past dozen years, Soviet defense outlays have increased more than 40 percent in real terms. How the United States assesses the extent, direction, and significance of the Soviet military buildup will determine the future course of its defense policy.

Not all aspects of the Soviet military buildup threaten significant U.S. interests. Indeed, in some ways and in some regions the West has kept pace with advances in Soviet capabilities. Nevertheless, recent and prospective Soviet gains cannot be ignored. The most important concerns for the West are how to improve NATO's capability to fight a conventional war on short warning on the central front of Europe and the United States' ability unilaterally to deter, or if necessary, to defeat any Soviet attempt to intervene in the Middle East with combat forces. These are not the only ways in which the Soviet buildup threatens Western interests, but they are by far the most significant and should receive highest priority in allocating U.S. defense resources.

The budgetary implications of this assessment cannot be measured precisely, but some real growth in the defense budget, though less than that envisioned in the Ford budget, probably will be necessary. It would be possible to moderate this growth by further improving the efficiency of the defense work force. Immediate measures include reform of the methods by which blue-collar wage rates are set each year, reductions in the average grade of white-collar civilian personnel, and reductions in the number of people in the military pipeline (those in classrooms or between assignments). Longer-range measures, such as reforming the system of compensation (including the retirement system) and rationalizing the military base structure, would have far-reaching budgetary implications.

To reverse the upward trend in the defense budget would require greater cooperation between the United States and the Soviet Union. Only when the two superpowers recognize the self-defeating nature of the competition in which they have been engaged, on and off, for thirty years, can defense spending be reduced significantly without danger to the nation's security.

Employment and Training

In contrast to President Ford, President Carter has put major emphasis on employment programs to speed recovery in 1977 and 1978 (see chapter 5). President Ford recommended that the temporary public service employment program be phased out in 1978 and expenditures under the Comprehensive Employment and Training Act be reduced to approximately the level that prevailed before the recent recession. He also opposed the use of public works and employment tax credits to combat unemployment. President Carter requested instead an increase in budget authority of about $10 billion for employment and training assistance and $4 billion for public works over fiscal years 1977 and 1978. The employment and training assistance increases are concentrated primarily in the public service employment program ($7 billion in new budget authority) and new national work experience programs for unemployed youth ($1.5 billion in budget authority). There is also a smaller increase (nearly $1 billion in new budget authority) for intensive skill training programs, including the Job Corps.

Congress has accepted the general thrust of President Carter's proposals; but it is clear that the Democratic majority prefers even larger expenditures on direct job-creating measures. This explains its rejection of the proposed social security tax credit (which the President subsequently withdrew) in favor of a much larger employment tax credit designed to encourage additional employment of low-wage workers.

While these decisions are motivated in part by a desire to reduce cyclical unemployment, most of the new programs are intended to help reduce structural unemployment by more than would be expected from a general stimulus of the same magnitude. Thus, the youth programs and the employment tax credit are directed at unskilled workers; and all new temporary public service employment jobs are to go to members of low-income families who have been unemployed for several months or are welfare recipients. This focus on structural unemployment in a high-unemployment economy is based on the belief that such federal policies have the potential to reduce the inflationary pressure associated with given levels of output and employment, as well as to promote the long-term employment prospects of the chronically unemployed. In the long run, these policies could contribute to the achievement of lower aggregate unemployment rates, lower inflation rates, and a more equitable distribution of job opportunities.

Unfortunately, the requirements of structural and countercyclical programs are very different. The latter must be capable of rapid implementation and quick phase-out in order to meet macroeconomic policy needs, whereas the former should be carefully designed and implemented since their objectives are inherently more difficult to achieve. For example, if the temporary public service employment program is to promote its structural goal, the following are necessary prerequisites. All potential applicants should be screened to ensure that they meet the target group requirements. State and local governments must identify and initiate new services, or review and select project proposals by local nonprofit organizations to provide such services. A strategy must be developed to use a heterogeneous and predominantly low-skilled and inexperienced labor force. The selected projects must not substitute for services that otherwise would have been provided by the public or private sectors, yet must be of substantial social value and must train workers for positions in the regular labor market. Finally, the programs must develop techniques to help participants make the transition to regular employment. These steps all take time.

The mixing of structural and countercyclical objectives in the stimulus package is a risky strategy and the result could easily be that neither objective will be well served. One alternative would have been to place greater reliance on general tax cuts and spending measures to provide the immediate countercyclical stimulus. This would have provided an opportunity to expand the employment and training programs slowly and carefully in conformity with structural goals. The general measures would impart an immediate stimulus to the economy, while the employment and training programs would become fully effective when most of the unemployment was structural in nature.

There is an additional argument for a cautious approach to many of these programs. In at least three cases—public service employment, youth work experience, and employment tax credits—the policies favored by Congress represent significant departures from previous efforts. There is little prior experience or analysis to suggest how such programs should be designed and on how large a scale they can operate effectively. Consequently, the experience of the next two or three years should be viewed largely as a series of experiments and the programs should be structured to provide basic information on their operations and results. Approached in this manner, these activities could help to provide guidance for future employment policy. But this necessitates a much stronger commitment to careful program planning, administration, and analysis than is now in evidence.

Medical Care Costs

In fiscal year 1976 the United States spent $139 billion on medical care—8.6 percent of the GNP, and more than triple the amount spent in 1965. Hospital costs are the fastest growing component of the total: the average cost of a day in the hospital rose from $40 to $147 over the period. The rapid increases in costs and expenditures have created great financial problems for federal health programs. The two largest, Medicare and Medicaid, will cost the federal government $37 billion in fiscal year 1978, up from $7 billion in 1968, their second full year of operation, and far above the initial cost estimates for these programs.

Both Ford and Carter proposed cost control programs in their 1978 budgets (see chapter 6). President Ford would have placed a limit of 7 percent on increases in payments to hospitals and physicians under Medicare and Medicaid. President Carter has proposed a program that would apply to all hospital costs; it is intended as the first step in the development of a more permanent system of cost controls. For 1978 the program would limit increases in inpatient revenues from all payers—not just Medicare and Medicaid—to 9 percent. The specific mechanisms proposed for enforcing the 9 percent limit, and the desirability of setting such a limit, are being debated by the administration, the Congress, and hospital groups.

The fundamental problem any control mechanism must deal with is that the increases in medical care costs have not been primarily a matter of inflation—that is, rising prices for the same goods and services. The growth of third-party financing (a term that includes private health insurance as well as public programs like Medicare and Medicaid) over the last twenty-five years has radically altered the structure of the medical care industry. With third-party financing now paying 90 percent of the average hospital bill, the direct cost to those making decisions about medical care resources—the cost that the patient must pay out of his own pocket—is virtually zero. This means that doctors and patients can act as though resources are free, and use them accordingly. The result has been a phenomenal increase in the resources used in medical care. For example, over the last ten years the resources—space, labor, equipment and supplies—used per day of hospital care have increased almost 80 percent.

The methods proposed to deal with the cost problem include some that would change the economic incentives of the industry and others that would impose direct controls on the amounts of resources used and the services produced by the industry. The history of the last several decades, during which the level of third-party financing has risen to its present heights, indicates that introducing substantial rates of copayment for patients might be an effective way to control costs. Most people are already paying a large part of their incomes to support the medical care system—over 10 percent for a family with the median income—and these costs would not be more burdensome on the average if less were paid through premiums and taxes and more through direct payments. Protection against unusually high expenses in relation to income could be provided by a catastrophic insurance plan. Special provisions would need to be made for the very poor, who cannot afford to make any payments for medical care.

Health maintenance organizations (HMOs), which provide comprehensive medical care in return for a fixed annual fee, have been suggested as another means of cost control. In the prepaid group practice form, HMOs have demonstrated a marked ability to reduce hospital use, although their success in reducing the total costs of medical care has been less consistent. Unfortunately, the reasons for their frequent successes are not clear: for example, other forms of HMOs, which also face whatever incentives are inherent in fixed annual fees, have not reduced hospital use. Until these reasons are well enough understood to allow the best results from HMOs to be replicated with reasonable certainty, HMOs cannot be relied upon as a major element in a cost-control program.

The other major cost-control mechanisms that have been proposed —prospective reimbursement, certificate-of-need reviews of new investment, and professional standards review organizations—amount in fact, if not always in name, to direct regulation, either of the rates paid medical care providers or of the quantities of resources used or services produced by the industry. None of these has yet proved effective in controlling costs, and studies of industries that are subject to permanent regulation show that regulation has not reduced prices below the levels that would prevail in the absence of regulation. Nor is the fact that permanently regulated industries are growing at rates much slower than that of the medical care industry any evidence that regulation can successfully place limits on medical care spending. The limits on other industries are the natural result of the fact that most of their customers must pay the full price for their goods and services; third-party payment has removed these economic limits on the size of the medical care industry.

The cost problem in medical care is thus not a short-term problem of inflation. It is a long-term problem concerning the way the nation wants to allocate its resources among different uses. Third-party payment has created an incentive structure with an unlimited potential for drawing resources into medical care. This incentive structure is at the heart of the cost problem, and will continue to be whether third-party payments are channeled through a national health insurance plan or through the network of programs that exists today. The choice between a public and a private, or largely private, system must then be based on other considerations, such as the distribution of benefits and costs and the ability of the system to respond as conditions change in the future, and on the values the nation attaches to them.

Social Security

Social security today is an enormous program, covering over 90 percent of the working population. The system has received considerable attention of late because a shortfall in revenues has created the danger that the trust funds may soon be exhausted; the long-run financial viability of the system has also been questioned. Many institutional and demographic changes have coincided with the emergence of the short- and long-run deficits, extending the issues beyond purely financial considerations. The problems are manageable, but Congress must make some difficult decisions and act soon.

Social security benefits are financed out of current payroll taxes. In normal times, the trust funds should have enough accumulated assets to pay about one-half of a year's benefits. Since the government can raise future tax payments, if necessary, the fact that social security, unlike private pension plans does not have a large trust fund is not a matter of great concern. But in a recession, when receipts fall and benefit payments rise, the trust fund balances can run down quickly. Over the longer term, problems arise if there is an increase in the ratio of beneficiaries to workers or if prospective benefits are too generous in relation to projected tax receipts.

The sharp reduction in payroll tax receipts during the 1974–75 recession and its aftermath has led to a shortfall in trust fund revenues. Corrective action is needed immediately to bolster the disability insurance trust fund, which will be exhausted in 1979. Although a simple transfer of revenues between trust funds or a small increase in the disability insurance tax would solve the immediate problem, a longer-term solution will be needed by 1982 when the combined old age, survivors, and disability insurance trust funds would be depleted under present law.

President Ford recommended increases in the payroll tax rate to restore the necessary balances in the trust funds. President Carter has proposed that the revenue shortfall attributable to the recession be made up by transfers from general revenues to the trust funds. For the future, he proposes to eliminate the ceiling on the taxable wage base for the employer's portion of the payroll tax, raise the ceiling for the employee's portion by $2,400 in four installments from 1979 to 1985 (in addition to the automatic adjustments that are made annually for wage growth), accelerate scheduled payroll tax rate increases by one-quarter of one percent in 1985 and by three-quarters of one percent in 1990, and shift scheduled hospital insurance tax increases of two-tenths of one percent in 1978 and 1981 to the old age, survivors, and disability funds (see chapter 7).

The appropriate solution depends on a resolution of the philosophical question whether social security should be strictly a wage-related annuity program, with benefits geared to past contributions, or a part of the government's transfer system designed to bring about some income redistribution. Since the present system is really a compromise between these two views, supplementing the payroll tax with general revenues to finance the current deficits may be an acceptable solution.

Another consideration is that the payroll tax places a particularly heavy burden on low-wage workers. Although the earned income tax credit has alleviated this burden for poor workers with families, increasing the payroll tax rate still aggravates the regressivity of the tax system. Raising the ceiling on taxable wages is preferable on distributional grounds; but, because benefits are related to the employee's taxable wage base, it creates higher future benefits that could as well be financed out of private saving. To limit the increase in future benefit liabilities, President Carter has opted for a modest increase in the ceiling on taxable wages for the employee's portion of the payroll tax and complete removal of the ceiling for the employer's portion.

The Social Security Administration projects a huge increase in social security expenditures as a percentage of taxable payrolls after the year 2000. This increase is attributable to two major factors. The first, responsible for about one-half of the projected increase, is the changing demographic structure of the population. Today, there are about thirty beneficiaries for each one hundred workers; in 2055, there will be almost fifty for each one hundred workers. With a pay-as-you-go system, an increase in the ratio of beneficiaries to workers implies an inevitable matching increase in costs. Of course, the higher ratio of retired people to active workers will impose a cost on the nation, regardless of how social security may be altered.

The other half of the forecasted deficit results from a feature of the 1972 social security legislation that introduced an unintended double adjustment for inflation into the benefit formula. This happens because the same formula is used for both currently retired and still active workers, creating what is known as a "coupled" system. Future retirees receive a double inflation adjustment: first, from the cost-of-living adjustment of the benefit formula and, second, from the higher wages that compensate for the effect of inflation and the automatic adjustment of the taxable base for the growth in average wages. This technical flaw makes future replacement rates (the ratio of benefits to preretirement earnings) highly dependent on the exact pattern of future wages and prices.

Fortunately, it is possible to modify the system to yield predictable replacement rates and avoid excessive long-run cost increases. The most significant difference among alternative schemes is whether the inflation adjustment is accomplished by adjusting the benefit formula for wages or prices. Wage indexing, which has been endorsed by both the Ford and Carter administrations, would produce constant replacement rates, while price indexing would generate gradually declining rates. Thus, in choosing among alternatives, it will be necessary to decide explicitly what share of resources to commit to future retirement benefits. Wage indexing will cost more than price indexing (although both will be less costly than the present coupled system). How replacement rates should behave over time is a complex issue, but some action is needed soon to avoid an unnecessary increase in long-run costs.

Welfare Reform

In May 1977, President Carter outlined the main principles that would guide the administration in implementing his campaign promise to reform the welfare system. Among these were adequacy and equity of benefits, allowances for regional cost-of-living differences, work incentives to encourage employment, assured jobs for those who cannot find work in the private sector, fiscal relief for states and local governments, and improvements in administration. These principles are not new and there is little disagreement over their desirability, although the degree of emphasis on any one principle will vary among different groups. Nevertheless, welfare reform continues to be extremely difficult to achieve, mainly because there is no agreement on two key issues. These are, first, what form should work incentives in a welfare program take; and, second, should the low-income population be divided into categories to be served by separate programs (see chapter 8)?

There are numerous plans to satisfy the work objective. One plan involves structuring the program so that there are sufficient rewards from work (by avoiding high tax rates on the earnings of persons receiving benefits) and pursuing macroeconomic policies that restore high employment. This two-pronged approach is based on the notion that most people want to work and that it should be possible to ensure an adequate supply of jobs. Another plan is to deny cash assistance to able-bodied persons but guarantee them a job if they cannot find one. This approach presumes that cash assistance inevitably reduces the attractiveness of work and that it will be difficult to ensure an adequate supply of "desirable" jobs in the private sector for the population in question.

In the short run, neither of these approaches is realistic and some compromise will have to be worked out. Cash assistance and a jobs program will both be components of a revised welfare system; the relevant issues are how the funds will be allocated between the two, how the two components will relate to each other, and whether an effective employment and training program can be designed for the low-income population.

The issue of categorization concerns the extent to which separate programs should be used to differentiate among the needs of different groups in the low-income population. The present welfare system is highly categorical, with many programs administered by numerous agencies. Such differentiation leads to inequitable treatment of recipients and contributes to administrative inefficiency.

The various proposals for welfare reform can be divided into three groups: those calling for minor restructuring, incremental reforms, and comprehensive reforms. Minor restructuring would work within the existing program structure, seeking to improve management efficiency and to redirect benefits to those most in need. The difficulty with this approach is that it does not alleviate the major defects of the current system; the complexities, inequities, and weak work incentives would remain. Incrementalism involves streamlining existing programs and adding new ones to fill the gaps in the welfare system. While regarded by many as the most politically feasible possibility, the incremental approach can be as expensive as, and even more complicated than, comprehensive reform. Some of the component programs would require substantial alterations, and the addition of new programs without eliminating existing ones would make administration of the system even more complex. Incremental reform may thus be no more feasible than other approaches.

The comprehensive approach would rely on the consolidation of all cash assistance programs and would combine this with training and jobs programs. Cash assistance would be paid to those who are not expected to work, and the earnings of those who work but have low incomes would be supplemented. Aid to families with dependent children, supplemental security income for the aged and disabled, and the food stamp programs would be eliminated. If the jobs component went so far as to guarantee employment to all those who are expected to work, it would require the establishment of several million jobs (estimates range from 2 to 5 million).

As desirable as the employment approach might appear, there is considerable doubt whether enough really useful jobs—not simply make-work—can be created in the immediate future for the entire employable poverty population. Moreover, the impact of a guaranteed jobs program on wages and on the attractiveness of jobs in the private sector is largely unknown. Thus, a consolidated cash assistance program with a modest jobs component offers the best hope of meeting the welfare objectives in the short run. Nevertheless, the efforts now under way to learn how to train unskilled workers and create jobs for them should be encouraged so that the government will some day be in a position to offer a dignified alternative to welfare for all those who are able to work.

President Carter hopes to accomplish his welfare objective without adding to the costs now borne by the federal government. It is not clear whether the costs he refers to include the $5.9 billion of outlays for the public service jobs program in 1978. Even if these expenditures are devoted to welfare, however, it will be difficult to finance a reform program that meets his principles without spending more money.

The Cities

Federal grants to local governments, particularly to cities, have become factors of considerable significance in the budget calculations of both national and local decisionmakers. The federal government distributed fourteen times as much money to local governments in 1975 as it did in 1956; the amount of federal funds relative to locally raised revenue was almost seven times higher. The Ford and Carter budgets for fiscal years 1977 and 1978 have implications of considerable importance for cities, as to both the level of support they provide and the manner in which these funds are distributed (see chapter 9).

The question of distribution—who wins and who loses—is of special importance because of the nature of urban problems in the United

States. The complex of factors that can be considered "urban crisis conditions"—relatively slow growth (or decline) of population and fiscal resources, old housing and public facilities, and high concentrations of the socially and economically disadvantaged—is not uniformly distributed throughout the country, but concentrated in a relatively few cities in the Northeast and Midwest. Many of the newer cities in the South and West, by contrast, do not appear to be experiencing particularly severe hardship, relative either to their own suburbs or to the older central cities. One of the major tasks for urban policy in the next few years, therefore, is to devise strategies for channeling federal funds more directly to those areas experiencing substantial urban hardship.

The Ford and Carter budgets present different approaches to dealing with the problems faced by cities, both in the level of funding they propose and the manner in which they would distribute the grants. The Ford budget proposed to phase out a number of public service employment and public works programs, and to reduce future commitments in other programs. While it recommended increased funding for hardship cities under the community development grants, it also continued a distributional strategy initiated under the New Federalism of the Nixon administration: the allocation of funds by formula to a relatively large number of jurisdictions, rather than by approval of individual projects submitted by local governments. This strategy has had the effect of "spreading" funds away from hardship cities to assist a larger number of smaller and suburban cities that do not face significant hardship conditions. As a result of this strategy, the share of federal funds going to the largest cities declined by almost 20 percent between 1968 and 1975, while the share received by smaller cities and other types of local governments increased appreciably.

The Carter budget proposes to increase the funds distributed to cities in 1977 and 1978 and, in some areas, to direct these funds specifically to cities that are experiencing substantial urban hardship conditions. The increases are concentrated in programs that are part of the administration's stimulus package, particularly for public service employment and local public works projects. The Carter budget also contains proposals to increase funds provided to larger, older cities—for example, by the addition of a supplemental "action grant" to the existing community development block grant program.

While President Carter's strategy would produce a substantial increase in the funds going to the older cities, it neither exhausts the range of strategies for redirecting the flow of federal funds nor avoids potential future problems. In spite of the nominally countercyclical nature of these funds, there is every reason to suspect that state and local officials will make concerted efforts to maintain the level, if not the mix, of funding past the current recovery period. If they are successful in this attempt, many cities, particularly those which perform primarily housekeeping functions, will be receiving large shares of their operating budgets from the federal government on a more or less permanent basis. This sizable claim on the Treasury may undercut the macroeconomic objectives originally envisioned and also consume funds that the federal government may wish to use for other programs.

Perhaps the most important factor governing the future of federal urban policy, however, is political. The nation's most hard-pressed cities have been losing both population and seats in the House to the South and West in recent years and seem likely to continue to do so. Whether these cities and their representatives can develop and sustain a coalition interested in channeling funds to urban areas in greatest need is a critical question for the future course of federal urban policy.

Energy

The United States faces three energy problems: possible short-run economic disruptions caused by the restriction of oil supply by foreign nations; an increase in the relative cost of energy; and the need to move, over the next several decades, from an economy based on oil and natural gas to one relying on more abundant energy sources. The goal of a federal energy policy is to minimize the effect of these problems on the security and prosperity of the nation. Reducing energy consumption, increasing domestic energy production, and reducing oil imports are the means proposed to achieve these goals.

The emphasis of President Carter's program is on conservation of energy and conversion from oil and natural gas (see chapter 10). Its cornerstone is the requirement, to be phased in gradually, that most consumers pay the replacement cost of energy. Through rising energy prices, encouragement of insulation, and an automobile tax and rebate scheme, the President hopes to lower the growth of energy consumption from the present annual rate of 3 to 4 percent to 2 percent in 1985. A standby gasoline tax increase of 5 cents a gallon for each year in which gasoline consumption increases by more than 1 percent above a target level was also proposed; it would begin in 1979 and rise to a maximum of 50 cents a gallon. The proceeds of this tax would be refunded to the population as a whole through income tax credits or other devices.

But even if the growth in demand is slowed, additional energy supplies will be required. The Carter program is based on the assumption that the additional supplies can be obtained from coal and nuclear power. These sources are also expected to substitute for some of the energy now supplied by oil and natural gas. The switch from oil and gas is to be achieved by inducing or requiring industry and electric utilities to convert to coal, and by encouraging utilities to bring more nuclear power on line, primarily by reducing licensing delays.

President Carter does not plan to trade environmental quality for increased energy supplies. He has promised to maintain or strengthen environmental quality and health and safety standards and to offer government support for developing clean-up technologies. The result would be a cleaner and healthier environment at the expense of delays in increasing domestic energy production and higher energy costs.

This sweeping program would be phased in gradually to avoid disrupting economic recovery. Energy prices and taxes would rise slowly over the next three years, and the decrease in energy consumption would not be fully achieved until the mid-1980s. Conversions from oil and gas will occur slowly because of lags in bringing new energy-using equipment and coal and nuclear facilities into being. The chief near-term response to the insecurity of oil import levels is to double the ultimate size and to speed the completion of the strategic petroleum reserve.

Imports provide the incremental supply of oil, and in this country, as in most of the rest of the world, oil is the major substitute for other fuels. Consequently, when the world oil price rose in 1973–74, the replacement cost of energy consumed in the United States—what must be given up to obtain an equivalent amount of energy from alternative sources—increased as well.

Domestic energy prices were controlled so as to prevent them from rising by the same amount as the rise in energy costs. This decision was made because of the fear of exacerbating inflation, the need to avoid excessive burdens on low- and middle-income groups, and the desire to limit windfall incomes of domestic energy producers. The result was that more energy was consumed, and hence more oil was imported, than would have been the case without controls. Additionally, imports supplied energy that could have been produced domestically at the same or lower cost. Thus, energy costs not covered directly by energy prices were paid through greater vulnerability to international pressure and lower output through inefficient use of energy and other resources. Nevertheless, energy policy decisions continue to be dominated by concern about the equity, employment, and inflationary effects of an immediate rise in energy prices to the replacement cost level.

It has been possible to hold down prices to domestic energy producers and consumers without rationing (except for natural gas) because oil imports have been allowed to increase. If imports are now to be reduced, the situation will change markedly. In the proposals announced so far by the Carter administration, economic incentives (differential prices, taxes, and subsidies) rather than specific rules and regulations predominate among the instruments chosen to allocate energy consumption by fuel form and end use. Some critics believe that these indirect incentives will eventually need to be supplemented by direct controls if the goals of import limitation and consumption reduction prove impossible to meet. But compared to decontrolling prices and using general energy taxes to achieve import limitation goals, the Carter program requires a substantial role for government in directing the production and consumption of energy.

Improving Government Efficiency

A major theme of President Carter's election campaign was that he would improve the efficiency of the federal government. Two methods by which he proposed to achieve this objective are zero-base budgeting and sunset laws, and government reorganization.

Zero-Base Budgeting and Sunset Laws

The 1970s will probably be remembered as the period in which the federal government's processes for handling its budget were

greatly improved. In the Congress, a new budget process was instituted in 1975, forcing consideration of the budget as a whole rather
than piece-by-piece scrutiny. In the executive branch, each year's
budget has been oriented more than before to the implications for
the long-run outlook of the annual expenditure and tax proposals.
In his budget for fiscal year 1978, President Ford set the precedent
of explicitly laying out his plans for fiscal year 1979, and contended
that his fiscal 1978 decisions were conditioned by their implications
for future years.

Zero-base budgeting will be implemented by the Carter administration during 1977 in time for the development of the fiscal year 1979
budget (see chapter 11). The new procedure requires each government unit to identify a minimum level of service below the level currently provided and display its budget request by a set of increments
above that minimum. Agencies then rank the minimums and increments in descending order of priority. Ultimately the President draws
a cutoff line on this priority list; everything above the line is the
President's budget proposal. Programs whose minimum level fall
below the line are terminated. In the course of preparing such rankings, agencies must identify outputs associated with increments in
spending, consider alternative means of producing the output, and
involve a broader array of people in the budgeting process.

Judged as a procedure for making budget decisions, zero-base
budgeting has some merits and some drawbacks. No one can be
against careful study of results in relation to costs, assessment of
alternatives, or involving those in government who have field experience in the key budget decisions. The process also forces agencies
to examine reductions as well as increases in funding. These features,
though by no means unique to zero-base budgeting, constitute its
major virtues.

On the other hand, zero-base budgeting seems poorly structured to
deal with most of the federal budget, especially with rapidly growing
transfer payment and grant-in-aid programs. These functions, which
make up 55 percent of outlays, are characterized by interdepen-
dence; how much education funds to allocate to states, for example,
is related to how much they are to receive in health and welfare grants.
By forcing individual program units to rank increments of spending
independently, zero-base budgeting overlooks this interrelationship.

But the most important criticism of zero-base budgeting is what must be given up because of it. Zero-base budgeting is an entirely new procedure for federal bureaucrats, and it focuses exclusively on the upcoming budget year. It will, therefore, divert energy, time, and thought away from fashioning multiyear budgets. This diversion is especially to be regretted because it is likely that major cutbacks in old programs can be sold only as part of a package involving expansion in new programs. Multiyear budgets can carry such a message to the Congress and the public; zero-base budgets cannot.

Sunset laws require the Congress to review every federal activity at least once every five years. If any activity is not reendorsed, it terminates automatically. The reviews are to be conducted by joint examination of all spending and taxing programs in a particular subfunction (such as public assistance) in one year. Like zero-base budgeting, the motive behind the sunset laws is laudable; nothing should stay on the books just because it was put there many years ago. But most federal spending programs are already subject to frequent reauthorization and review, so the gains from the comprehensive functional overview must be weighed against the torrent of paperwork and time spent in trying to review everything. A good case can be made for a selective approach to the sunset idea: setting out a few areas of spending, regulation, and tax law for intensive scrutiny over the next few years. If such reviews prove fruitful, more areas could be added later.

Such selectivity would have been well advised for the executive branch's adoption of zero-base budgeting. If zero-base budgeting could have been restricted to operating programs with identifiable outputs, and suitably modified in each case (such as, in defense, to emphasize long-term plans), something positive may have come of it. As it stands, pouring national defense, transfers, grants, and national parks into one mold is not likely to produce useful analytical results. Its comprehensiveness may, however, aid President Carter in justifying changes he wants to make by creating the impression of a fair, evenhanded budget process.

Government Reorganization

President Carter further proposes to reduce inefficiency by reorganizing and cutting the number of federal agencies (see chapter 12). Inefficiency is abhorrent in and of itself, but it is an especially salient target when an administration hopes to find funds for new programs without cutting old ones, raising taxes, or incurring large deficits.

Reorganization is not a very promising means to this end. The strategies for simplifying and rationalizing the executive branch and making it more efficient clash with and often nullify each other or impose heavy costs. Most of the strategies are variations on one or another of the following basic prescriptions: (1) limit the number of line subordinates over whom any executive is assigned jurisdiction (commonly referred to as "the span of control"); (2) group related functions under a common command; (3) furnish executives with ample staff assistance; (4) authorize executives to reorganize fairly freely the agencies and units under their command; (5) keep politics out of administration; (6) decentralize administration; and (7) increase public participation in the administrative process. These seven objectives do not go well together.

In general, the first four push power upward in hierarchies, while the last three push it outward and downward. In addition, there are specific contradictions and costs. Trying to keep politics out of administration, for example, engenders attempts to insulate agencies from executive intervention (as in the case of the independent regulatory commissions), but this practice prevents the grouping of related functions under a common command. Increasing public participation lets politics into the administrative process. Reorganization power cannot be reconciled with agency independence. Limiting span of control produces a steeper administrative pyramid with many additional levels in it, increasing the distance between leaders and frontline workers. Grouping functions by purpose usually precludes grouping them by area or clientele served, or by process. Decentralization frequently results in reduced coordination and inconsistency of policy. The quest for efficiency and simplicity through reorganization thus turns out in most cases to resemble a zero-sum game; for every gain, there is an offsetting loss.

The real payoffs in reorganization are of a different kind. Reorganization can be used to redistribute political influence, to alter the substance of public policies, and to signal the intentions of the administration to the rest of the government and, indeed, to the country as well. For example, a separate and powerful environmental agency, consumer agency, or energy department, at the cabinet level, is almost certain to (1) increase the leverage of some groups and contain that of others; (2) raise the probability that environmental, consumer, and energy concerns will be registered a little more force-fully on policy decisions than they might otherwise be; and (3) serve notice that these values will be emphasized by the government to a greater extent than in the past. By the same token, if arms control and disarmament were assigned to inferior status in the Department of Defense, or if promotion of equal employment opportunity were left exclusively to each department and agency without any leader-ship from the center, these programs would doubtless change in char-acter and be perceived as lacking in presidential support. Such re-organizations have little net effect on efficiency, but they have considerable political consequences. The calculus of reorganization is thus the calculus of politics itself.

Whatever its intent, the administration has seized on one of the principal reorganization tools in the President's managerial toolbox —the power to propose reorganization plans that attain the force of law unless vetoed by the Congress. This authority was granted to every president from Franklin D. Roosevelt to Richard M. Nixon, under whom it lapsed. President Carter asked the Congress for a freer hand than some of his predecessors enjoyed, and while the Congress did not give him all he requested, he got most of what he wanted.

His staff has made it clear that he will go at reorganization piece-meal, relying chiefly on his own Office of Management and Budget to work up the plans, and proceeding on a long-range timetable rather than on a crash basis. In so doing, he has apparently rejected options chosen by (or imposed upon) some of his predecessors, such as a large commission of outsiders and insiders representing the legisla-tive and executive branches, a small committee of experts apart from his regular staff, or a grand design for the executive branch rather than a series of more modest steps. His proposal for a new Depart-ment of Energy is in keeping with this strategy; he elected not to wait for a complete plan for restructuring the executive branch before moving on an urgent problem.

Nobody expects any instantaneous cures for the ills of the govern-ment or the ills of the country as a result of these efforts. Reorgani-zation efforts may produce useful marginal gains, but only gradually and after countless frustrations and disappointments. The contro-versies of 1977 are merely the first skirmishes in an extended and uncertain campaign to reorganize the executive branch of the federal government.

THE AUTHORS of this book make no pretense of trying to guess what President Carter's budget may look like four years from now. That budget will embody the responses of the administration and Congress to an evolving economic picture in which output, employment, and price developments will almost surely not proceed along predicted paths. Moreover, although the new administration has in its first few months tipped its hand on a broad range of policy issues with major budgetary implications—hospital costs, employment and training, social security, welfare, and energy—an equally impressive list remains: defense, health care financing, education, aid to the cities, and tax reform.

As in the past, the choices to be made will be difficult, partly because many of the objectives, however desirable in their own right, are often in conflict. Energy conservation can conflict with lowering unemployment and retarding inflation; restraining medical costs can work against expanding access to health care; and tax reform must strike a balance among equity, economic, and administrative considerations.

The new budget procedures in both the executive and legislative branches may help. Information about the overall balance between outlays and receipts and between costs and benefits of different programs can narrow the area of conflict and suggest new ways to reach particular objectives. But conflict cannot be eliminated. The choices to be made will inevitably pit one set of values against another, and some political interest groups against others, and the battles can be expected to be heated and prolonged.

President Carter is in the tradition of those presidents who sought to use the federal budget to achieve their economic objectives and to mold and limit federal activities. He is already using budget policy to stimulate the economy in the short run and seems determined to bring the budget into balance when the economy reaches full employment. Carter's early statements and decisions suggest that, while he will be an activist in trying to solve national problems, he will be cautious in expenditure policies in order to avoid overcommitting his future budgetary resources. Whether he will achieve his economic and budget goals will depend not only on his own decisions, but also on changing circumstances both at home and abroad.

CHAPTER TWO

The Federal Budget in Review

JOSEPH A. PECHMAN

SINCE THE BUDGET in any particular year reflects to a large extent decisions made in earlier years, it is necessary to review previous developments to understand the budget for fiscal year 1978. This chapter thus begins with a brief discussion of recent budget trends; it then reviews the budget for 1977 before proceeding to an examination of the 1978 budget.[1]

Recent Budget Trends

In recent years, federal outlays have increased rapidly in dollar terms, but only moderately in relation to the size of the economy. At the same time, the major emphasis in the budget has changed drastically—from defense to nondefense spending. In addition, the federal budget has been used by the government to combat inflation and recession and to stabilize the rate of economic activity.

Size of the Budget

Between fiscal years 1955 and 1976, federal budget outlays increased from $68.5 billion to $366.5 billion, a rise of $298 billion,

The author is grateful for the suggestions of James L. Blum and Darwin Johnson, who read an early draft of this chapter, and for the research assistance of Thang Long Ton That and Nancy Osher.
1. The Congressional Budget and Impoundment Control Act of 1974 shifted the fiscal year from July–June to October–September beginning October 1, 1976. Figures for the transition quarter July 1 to September 30, 1976, are available, but they are not

or 435 percent. During this period, incomes and prices also increased, but at a less rapid pace. In relation to the gross national product (which represents the total expenditures of consumers, business, and government), federal spending was roughly stable between 1955 and 1965, and rose sharply between 1965 and 1975. It fluctuated between 18 and 19 percent in the earlier period, rose to 21.5 percent at the peak of the Vietnam War outlays in 1968, declined slightly below 20 percent in 1973 and 1974, and then rose again to a peak of 22.8 percent in 1976 (see table 2-1).[2]

These figures must be interpreted with care. Federal outlays and receipts are extremely sensitive to changes in the level of business activity. Unemployment benefits, welfare payments, and food stamp benefits rise during recessions and decline as business activity improves, while tax receipts drop during recessions and rise sharply during periods of expansion. These "built-in stabilizers" help to moderate fluctuations in private incomes and thus to stabilize private demand. To approximate the underlying budgetary trends free of swings in business activity, corrections are made to both the gross national product and the budget figures for the effect of deviations of economic activity from that rate of unemployment which is considered to represent full employment.

On the basis of an estimate of gross national product at full employment[3] that reflects the changing composition of the labor force,[3] the federal spending ratio still rose to a peak during the Vietnam War and declined thereafter. But the bulge in fiscal years 1975 and

---

referred to here since they are hard to interpret (because of seasonal problems) and shed no light on the underlying trends or policy choices.

2. State and local governments have increased their outlays much more rapidly than the federal government. For a detailed discussion of recent budget trends at all levels of government, see Henry Owen and Charles L. Schultze, eds., *Setting National Priorities: The Next Ten Years* (Brookings Institution, 1976), chaps. 8 and 9.

3. The gross national product at full employment, or "potential" GNP, depends on the labor force, the capital stock, and productivity. Until recently, it was generally assumed that full employment corresponded to an unemployment rate of 4 percent and that this rate was compatible with reasonable price stability. However, the influx of women and younger skilled workers into the labor force has raised the full-employment unemployment rate. In addition, the rate of growth of productivity has slowed in recent years. The full-employment GNP estimates used in table 2-1 assume that the unemployment rate at full employment rose from 4.0 percent in 1955 to 5.0 percent in 1976–81 and that productivity growth slowed beginning in 1969. For a discussion of the technical problems of measuring potential GNP and budget estimates for alternative potential GNP estimates, see appendix A. The full-employment figures used in this chapter are the series B estimates of appendix A.

Table 2-1. Relation of Federal Unified Budget Outlays to the Gross National Product and to Full-Employment Gross National Product in Current and Constant Dollars, Fiscal Years 1955-76

Fiscal year[a]	Budget outlays (current dollars)		Budget outlays (constant dollars)[b]	
	Percent of GNP	Percent of full-employment GNP	Percent of GNP	Percent of full-employment GNP
1955	18.0	17.6	21.2	20.7
1956	17.1	17.2	20.0	20.0
1957	17.7	17.4	20.3	20.0
1958	18.7	17.5	21.1	19.8
1959	19.5	18.5	21.8	20.7
1960	18.5	17.6	20.6	19.6
1961	19.2	17.7	21.3	19.6
1962	19.5	18.5	21.6	20.4
1963	19.3	18.4	21.0	20.0
1964	19.2	18.7	20.8	20.2
1965	18.0	17.8	19.3	19.1
1966	18.7	19.0	19.6	20.0
1967	20.4	21.0	21.3	21.9
1968	21.5	22.1	22.3	22.9
1969	20.4	21.1	20.8	21.6
1970	20.5	20.5	20.5	20.6
1971	20.7	20.1	20.5	19.9
1972	20.9	20.2	20.5	19.9
1973	19.9	19.9	19.3	19.3
1974	19.8	19.4	18.8	18.4
1975	22.4	20.2	21.2	19.0
1976	22.8	20.4	21.4	19.1

Source: *The Budget of the United States Government, Fiscal Year 1978*, pp. 435-36. Full-employment figures are author's estimates (see appendix A, series B).
a. Ending June 30 of year shown.
b. Calculated in fiscal 1972 prices.

1976, when actual outlays increased sharply as a result of the large rise in unemployment benefits, is greatly reduced by the adjustments to full employment. On this basis, the spending ratio averaged 20.3 percent in 1975–76, as compared with an average of 17.9 percent in 1955–64.

Another factor influencing the rate of growth of federal spending is inflation. In general, the prices of services tend to rise faster than the prices of goods because capital investment and technological changes improve productivity faster in the production of goods, while wages in both sets of industries (including wages of federal employees) rise at about the same rate. Moreover, in the absence of any measure of government output, the official national income accounts assume no productivity growth in the government sector. This means that all increases in wages and salaries of government employees are counted as price increases, even though part of the increases may be associated with more output. Since much of federal spending other than transfer payments is devoted to purchasing services, prices paid by the federal government tend to rise faster than the average price level. The prices of construction projects—a major outlay in the federal budget—have also risen more than other prices. In addition, federal pay scales rose rapidly in the early 1970s to catch up to private pay levels,[4] and the all-volunteer army generated a continuing escalation in military pay. Over the entire period from fiscal year 1955 to 1976, the price index for government expenditures rose 172 percent, while the price index for all goods and services included in the gross national product rose 116 percent.

The movement of the federal spending ratio in real terms is revealed by comparing budget outlays and the gross national product expressed in constant prices. As shown in table 2-1, the ratio of federal spending to the gross national product (in fiscal 1972 prices) fluctuated between 19 and 22 percent in the period 1955–76, but without a trend. In fact, the period began with a ratio of 21.2 percent and ended with 21.4 percent. Thus, virtually the entire increase in the federal spending ratio was equal to the rise in outlays resulting from the larger relative price increases paid by the federal government.

On a full-employment basis, the federal spending ratio in constant prices actually declined during the period, from 20.7 percent in 1955 to 19.1 percent in 1976, indicating that the federal government has been using fewer resources relative to the total available resources in recent years. Nevertheless, its budget in money terms has risen in relation to the rest of the economy because the government price index has risen faster than the price index for the private sector. Even if inflation is arrested, this trend will continue indefinitely so long as productivity growth in government is assumed to be zero and productivity increases in the goods-production industries continue to outstrip increases in the service industries.

4. Wages and salaries of federal civilian and military employees have been set to be comparable to those in corresponding positions in private industry since 1963 and 1967, respectively.

Composition of the Budget

The increase in the share of total federal spending relative to the gross national product in the past twenty years, though modest, has accompanied significant changes in the composition of the budget. The most pervasive development has been an almost steady decline in the portion of the budget allocated to defense, and a corresponding increase in the share going to nondefense programs. Between 1955 and 1976, the defense share declined from 58.2 percent to 24.6 per-cent (with only a temporary interruption during the Vietnam War), while the nondefense share rose from 41.8 percent to 75.5 percent (see table 2-2). Future plans call for increases in real defense spending, but the share of the budget allocated to these programs will not increase dramatically.

Large changes have also occurred within the nondefense part of the budget. The growth in nondefense spending is accounted for by four major types of programs: (1) benefit payments to individuals under social insurance programs and cash and in-kind assistance to the aged and the poor; (2) social investment programs, such as education, health, and manpower training; (3) physical investments and subsidies for natural resources and for industrial and commercial development; and (4) aid to state and local governments. Together, these four groups of programs accounted for 70.6 percent of nondefense expenditures in 1955 and 96.8 percent in 1976.

The rise in benefit payments to individuals is attributable to the expansion in the scope and coverage of a variety of programs. Social security benefits have been increased in real terms, disability insurance was introduced in 1957, and Medicare was enacted in 1965. Beginning in 1975, retirement and disability benefits under social security have been automatically adjusted to keep pace with the cost of living.[5] Unemployment insurance has expanded in coverage and provides larger real benefits as real wages increase. There were large increases in unemployment compensation payments in 1975 and 1976, but these will be reduced as the employment picture improves. Federal cash assistance to the poor has increased mainly as a result of the large rise in the proportion of eligible families claiming aid for

5. The formula actually overcorrects for inflation over the long run and should be revised to avoid placing an unnecessary burden on workers whose payroll taxes support these programs. See chapter 7 for a discussion of this and other problems in the social security benefit structure.

Table 2-2. Composition of Federal Unified Budget Outlays, Fiscal Years 1955–76

Percent of total outlays

Fiscal year	Defense	Total nondefense	Payments for individuals[a]	Social investments and services[b]	Physical investments and subsidies[c]	Other grants-in-aid[d]	Other (including net interest)	Addendum: total grants-in-aid
1955	58.2	41.8	18.9	1.1	9.3	0.2	12.3	4.7
1956	56.4	43.6	19.6	1.3	9.7	0.2	12.8	5.3
1957	55.1	44.9	20.4	1.4	9.2	0.2	13.8	5.3
1958	53.1	46.9	23.6	1.4	9.4	0.2	12.4	6.0
1959	49.9	50.1	23.0	1.6	13.5	0.2	11.8	7.0
1960	49.0	51.0	24.8	1.9	12.1	0.2	12.0	7.6
1961	47.6	52.4	26.5	2.0	11.9	0.2	11.8	7.3
1962	47.2	52.8	25.4	2.3	13.2	0.2	11.8	7.4
1963	46.3	53.7	25.7	2.6	13.8	0.2	11.3	7.7
1964	44.5	55.5	25.1	2.8	16.0	0.2	11.4	8.6
1965	41.0	59.0	25.7	3.3	17.7	0.2	12.1	9.2
1966	41.5	58.5	25.5	5.0	16.9	0.2	10.9	9.6
1967	43.7	56.3	25.3	8.1	14.9	0.2	7.9	9.6
1968	44.4	55.6	25.7	9.3	14.9	0.2	5.5	10.4
1969	43.5	56.5	28.6	10.1	13.0	0.3	4.6	11.0
1970	40.3	59.7	30.4	10.7	13.2	0.3	5.1	12.2
1971	36.3	63.7	35.3	11.2	13.0	0.3	3.9	13.3
1972	33.3	66.7	36.8	12.6	12.8	0.4	4.1	14.8
1973	30.4	69.6	38.8	12.4	12.3	3.2	2.9	16.9
1974	29.1	70.9	41.2	12.5	11.4	2.8	3.0	16.1
1975	26.6	73.4	43.7	13.2	10.9	2.4	3.2	15.2
1976	24.6	75.5	45.7	14.1	11.1	2.2	2.4	16.1

Sources: Office of Management and Budget, "Federal Government Finances" (1977: processed): *The Budget of the United States Government, Fiscal Year 1978*, pp. 435–36; and *Special Analyses, Budget of the United States Government, Fiscal Year 1978*, p. 273. Figures are rounded.

a. Payments for retirement, disability, and unemployment (principally social security, Medicare, veterans' pensions and compensation, and unemployment insurance), and low-income assistance (principally welfare, food stamps, housing, and Medicaid). Includes grants-in-aid to state and local governments.

b. Education, health, manpower training, and social services. Includes grants-in-aid to state and local governments.

c. Natural resources, environment and energy, agriculture, commerce and transportation, community and regional development, and general science, space, and technology. Includes grants-in-aid to state and local governments.

d. Grants-in-aid for international affairs, veterans' benefits and services, law enforcement and justice, general government, revenue sharing, and general-purpose fiscal assistance.

dependent children and the introduction of the supplemental security program for the aged, blind, and disabled in 1972. In addition, Medicaid and food stamps, which are of recent origin, and housing assistance to the poor have grown rapidly. The growth of payments under the social insurance programs is slowing down because they have reached a relatively mature stage. However, programs to aid the poor are still in a state of flux, so that future budgetary commitments will depend on decisions yet to be made (see chapter 8).

Numerous social programs were enacted during the Johnson administration in an effort to promote equality of opportunity, remove discrimination, and provide new skills to people who cannot find jobs. Most of these programs were initiated just before the Vietnam War and were not financed at the levels contemplated in the early legislation. Nevertheless, their share of the budget has more than tripled since 1965. Present plans call for expansion of some of these programs, particularly manpower training and public employment, to help stimulate the economy (see chapter 5). Some of the current spending for employment programs is intended to be temporary, but the trend for other social programs is uncertain.

Physical investments and subsidies rose sharply, from 9.3 percent of budget outlays in fiscal year 1955 to 17.7 percent in 1965, mainly for the interstate highway system, water resource projects, agricultural subsidies, and (after 1960) space exploration. Since the Vietnam War, these expenditures have declined in relative importance; they reached a low of 10.9 percent of budget outlays in fiscal year 1975 and then rose slightly, to 11.1 percent, in 1976. Increased outlays for research and development of energy may increase the importance of this budget category in the future (see chapter 10).

Federal payments to state and local governments have increased sharply in the last two decades. They accounted for 16.1 percent of the federal budget in 1976, as compared with 4.7 percent in 1955.[6] In the 1950s and 1960s, federal grants were on a categorical basis— that is, they were intended to finance specific programs at the state and local levels, such as highway construction, aid to the poor, and housing. In 1972, a general revenue sharing program was enacted to provide assistance to state and local governments that gave them

6. A major portion of federal grants to state and local governments is for transfer payments and other programs. Hence, there is considerable duplication between these figures and the figures for the programs just discussed (see table 2-2).

almost complete freedom on how the funds are to be spent. A temporary countercyclical revenue sharing program, also with few strings attached to the types of expenditures allowed, was adopted in 1976 to cushion the decline in the revenues of state and local governments when unemployment exceeds 6 percent of the labor force. Other recent innovations include block grants for manpower and community development programs. Consideration is now being given to new ways to assist the hard-pressed central cities, but it is uncertain whether these programs will redirect existing aid or add additional funds to the federal grant system (see chapter 9).

Fiscal Policy

The budget is used not only to finance needed government outlays but also to help stabilize the economy. The federal government exerts a considerable influence on economic activity and on the rate of growth of prices through its expenditure and tax policies. When the government runs a deficit, it is adding to the spending stream and providing a stimulus to the economy; when it runs a surplus, it is withdrawing funds from the spending stream and thus exercises a restraining influence on the economy. Deficits are appropriate when demand by consumers and businessmen is weak; surpluses are needed when private demand is strong. If, as is widely expected, private investment demand is large when the economy recovers fully from the 1974–75 recession, a budget surplus will be needed to help contain inflation and to generate enough government saving to make room (along with private saving) for the prospective level of investment.

The built-in stabilizers mentioned earlier automatically produce large changes in the budget surplus or deficit, which help to moderate fluctuations in private incomes and spending. In addition, the federal government makes discretionary changes in its expenditure and tax policies to help pull the economy out of a recession or to restrain it during boom conditions.[7] The increases in expenditures and reductions in receipts resulting from the automatic and discretionary changes in the budget generate deficits or reduce surpluses during recessions; as business activity improves, recession-induced increases in expenditures and reductions in receipts are automatically reversed

7. There have been frequent tax reductions; but, since the end of World War II, tax increases have occurred only during wartime.

and the deficits are reduced and, if the recovery goes far enough, may ultimately be eliminated.

Since 1960, the federal budget has run a surplus in only one year—1969, when there was a surplus of $3.2 billion. During the early 1960s, the deficits were confined to a range of up to $10 billion, but beginning with the Vietnam War, the deficits have been gyrating over a much larger range. In fiscal year 1976, the deficit reached $66.5 billion, or 4.1 percent of the gross national product (see table 2-3).[8]

The major explanation of these large swings in the deficit is that the economy has been exhibiting a high degree of economic instability in recent years. There was only one mild recession in the 1960s, in 1960–61. In contrast, two recessions have already occurred in the 1970s, in 1970 and 1974–75, and the second of these was the most severe since the end of World War II. To stimulate recovery, increasing use has been made of permanent and temporary tax cuts to raise consumer and business spending.[9] Taxes were reduced by $8.0 billion in 1971 and $22.8 billion in 1975;[10] another tax cut of $7.3 billion was enacted in May 1977. Expenditures are also raised—usually for temporary unemployment compensation payments, employment programs, and public works—to accelerate business recovery.

The full-employment budget helps one visualize what the balance between receipts and outlays would have been if recessions and periods of slow growth had been avoided throughout the period 1955–76. As shown in table 2-3, the federal budget would have been in balance in nine of the eleven years between 1955 and 1965, but in only one of the eleven years between 1966 and 1976. Four of the recent deficits (1966 through 1969) occurred during the Vietnam War, when surpluses were called for to prevent inflation. Four of the other six deficits (1970, 1971, 1975, and 1976) were in years of high unemployment during or immediately after recession. The only recent nonrecession, peacetime years were 1972 and 1973, and the

8. The postal service and several federal loan agencies are excluded by law from the unified budget totals, while a number of "off-budget" loan programs are in the budget. President Ford recommended that the outlays of the off-budget federal entities also be included in the budget. Alternatively, the loan programs now in the budget might be excluded. The considerations involved in this decision are discussed in appendix B.

9. The permanent personal income tax cuts have also been intended to compensate for the erosion of the personal exemptions as a result of inflation.

10. The 1975 reductions included a rebate of $8.1 billion on 1974 individual income taxes and $1.8 billion of direct payments to social security recipients.

Table 2-3. Federal Unified Budget Surplus or Deficit, Fiscal Years 1955–76

Billions of dollars

Fiscal year	Actual surplus or deficit		Full-employment surplus or deficit	
	Amount	Percent of GNP	Amount	Percent of GNP
1955	−3.0	−0.8	−1.1	−0.3
1956	4.0	1.0	3.9	1.0
1957	3.3	0.8	4.8	1.1
1958	−3.0	−0.7	2.7	0.6
1959	−12.9	−2.7	−8.2	−1.7
1960	0.3	0.1	7.7	1.5
1961	−3.4	−0.7	9.8	1.8
1962	−7.1	−1.3	3.1	0.5
1963	−4.8	−0.8	4.6	0.8
1964	−5.9	−1.0	1.5	0.2
1965	−1.6	−0.2	1.2	0.2
1966	−3.8	−0.5	−8.0	−1.1
1967	−8.7	−1.1	−13.3	−1.8
1968	−25.2	−3.0	−28.5	−3.5
1969	3.2	0.4	−5.1	−0.6
1970	−2.8	−0.3	−4.0	−0.4
1971	−23.0	−2.3	−3.9	−0.4
1972	−23.4	−2.1	−14.6	−1.3
1973	−14.8	−1.2	−10.8	−0.9
1974	−4.7	−0.3	3.1	0.2
1975	−45.1	−3.1	−11.4	−0.7
1976	−66.5	−4.1	−15.3	−0.9

Source: *The Budget of the United States Government, Fiscal Year 1978*, pp. 435, 437. Full-employment figures are author's estimates (see appendix A, series B).

full-employment budget was not in balance in either year. In retrospect, it is generally agreed that fiscal policy should have been much more restrictive, at least in 1973, when a worldwide boom and inflation developed.

For fiscal policy analysis, both the year-to-year changes and the level of the full-employment surplus or deficit are significant. Thus, the sharp increases in the full-employment deficit during the Vietnam War helped to spark the inflation that is still plaguing the economy. The reduction in the full-employment deficit from 1972 to 1973 indicates that fiscal policy was appropriately moving in a restrictive direction; but, in view of the inflationary developments in 1973, the movement did not go far enough. On the other hand, the increase in the full-employment surplus from 1960 to 1961 and the shift from a full-employment deficit in 1973 to a surplus in 1974 were unfortunate because the economy was in recession in both 1961 and 1974.

This historical record suggests that fiscal policy errors have been made in both directions: the budget has been too expansionary at some times and too restrictive at others. A major impediment to the achievement of a balanced federal budget has been the poor performance of the economy, but too much spending in relation to tax receipts is also a factor. Careful budget management is needed to keep outlays in line with the growth of full-employment receipts.

The 1977 Budget

The Congressional Budget Act of 1974 requires the Office of Management and Budget to prepare an estimate of a "current services" budget by November 15 of the year preceding the beginning of the fiscal year. This estimate indicates what would happen to the federal budget if current policies were to remain unchanged.[11] On November 10, 1975, the OMB submitted a current services estimate for fiscal year 1977 of $414.5 billion for outlays and $372.6 billion for receipts, leaving a deficit of $41.9 billion. More than seventeen months later, on April 22, 1977, the Carter administration issued a budget review that included the final estimates for fiscal year 1977. This review called for outlays of $408.2 billion, receipts of $359.5 billion, and a deficit of $48.7 billion. Although the two sets of estimates suggest that the major changes were made on the receipts side, the chief battleground in the 1977 budget was actually on the outlay side. President Ford recommended large cuts in both spending and taxes for fiscal year 1977; Congress rejected the major proposals for cutting expenditures and did not accept the Ford tax cuts. Later, ex-

11. The current services budget estimates costs of continuing into the next year existing federal programs and activities without policy changes. It takes into account mandatory inflation adjustments, previously legislated changes in the benefit base, and the anticipated number of beneficiaries for entitlement programs, such as social security; formula increases or legislative commitments for grants to state and local governments; and continuation of procurement and construction activities in an orderly fashion, consistent with current law and appropriation levels. Estimates for entitlement programs not linked to the cost of living take into account only the changes in the benefit base and in the number of those eligible. Inflation adjustments for these and other programs are not estimated in the current services budget; such adjustments are prepared by the Congressional Budget Office and are included in the "current policy" budget, which is not discussed in this chapter.

penditures were increased further as part of the economic stimulus program proposed by President Carter.

The Ford Budget

President Ford's budget for fiscal year 1977, which was submitted on January 21, 1976, proposed a sharp curtailment in the growth of federal expenditures accompanied by a permanent reduction in income taxes. The most important elements of this budget were:

1. The growth in outlays was to be held down to 5.5 percent, about half the annual growth rate in the prior ten years. Proposed outlays were $394.2, or $20.3 billion *lower* than the current services budget estimates.

2. A major shift in budget priorities was to be accomplished. An increase in real defense spending and a reduction in real nondefense spending were proposed, thus arresting the long-term decline in the proportion of the budget allowed to defense.

3. Significant reductions in several major social programs were proposed, largely by replacing numerous categorical grants-in-aid with broad block grants for health, education, school lunch, and community development programs, and reducing the total funding for these programs.

4. Permanent cuts in individual and corporation income taxes amounting to $10 billion at an annual rate were recommended.

5. Increases in social security and unemployment insurance payroll taxes were proposed, to take effect on January 1, 1977. These increases would have raised tax receipts by $5.4 billion in fiscal year 1977 and by about $8.5 billion in a full year.

The effect of the Ford proposals on the major categories of federal expenditures is summarized in table 2-4, which compares the November 1975 current services estimates for fiscal year 1977 with subsequent budget estimates for the same year. Of the total reductions below the current services level of $20.3 billion in the Ford budget, $16.5 billion are accounted for by five nondefense categories: income security ($9.0 billion),[12] health ($3.3 billion), education, training, employment, and social services ($1.8 billion) commerce and transportation ($1.6 billion), and veterans' benefits and services ($0.8

12. The income security category in table 2-4 is similar to payments for individuals in table 2-2, except that veterans' benefits and Medicare and Medicaid payments are excluded.

Table 2-4. History of Fiscal Year 1977 Budget Estimates

Billions of dollars

Functional outlay and receipts categories	Current services budget, November 1975	Ford budget estimate, January 1976	Second congressional budget resolution, September 1976	Third congressional budget resolution, March 1977	Carter budget, April 1977
Budget outlays	**414.5**	**394.2**	**413.1**	**417.4**	**408.2**
National defense	103.1	101.1	100.6	100.1	97.1
International affairs	6.4	6.8	6.9	6.8	6.6
General science, space, and technology	4.6	4.5	4.5	4.4	4.6
Natural resources, environment, and energy	14.1	13.8	16.2	17.2	16.0
Agriculture	2.2	1.7	2.2	3.0	4.5
Commerce and transportation	18.1	16.5	17.4	16.0	14.9
Community and regional development	6.2	5.5	9.0	10.6	7.7
Education, training, employment, and social services	18.4	16.6	22.2	22.7	20.7
Health	37.7	34.4	38.9	39.3	39.1
Income security	146.1	137.1	137.2	141.3	138.6
Veterans' benefits and services	18.0	17.2	19.5	18.1	18.2
Interest	41.9	41.3	39.6	38.0	37.8
Other[a]	−2.3	−2.3	−1.1	0.0	2.4
Budget receipts	**372.6**	**351.3**	**362.5**	**347.7**	**359.5**
Individual income tax	166.2	153.6	161.7	148.4	160.1
Corporation income tax	60.2	49.5	58.5	54.2	55.0
Payroll taxes[b]	108.2	113.1	107.1	108.7	108.0
Other[c]	38.1	35.1	35.2	36.4	36.3
Budget deficit	**−41.9**	**−43.0**	**−50.6**	**−69.7**	**−48.7**

Sources: Office of Management and Budget, *Current Services Estimates for Fiscal Year 1977* (November 10, 1975), pp. 12 and 22; *The Budget of the United States Government, Fiscal Year 1977*, p. 312; *Second Concurrent Resolution on the Budget, Fiscal Year 1977*, H. Rept. 94-1502, 94:2 (1976); *Third Concurrent Resolution on the Budget, Fiscal Year 1977*, H. Rept. 95-30, 95:1 (1977); Office of Management and Budget, "Current Budget Estimates, April 1977" (processed). Figures are rounded.

a. Law enforcement and justice, revenue sharing and general purpose fiscal assistance, interest, and undistributed offsetting receipts. Minus (−) sign indicates that undistributed offsetting receipts exceed expenditures for other categories in this group.

b. Includes employee contributions to federal retirement funds.

c. Includes excise taxes, customs, estate and gift taxes, and miscellaneous receipts.

billion). Most of the $9.0 billion reduction in the income security programs was the result of overestimates in the current services budget, but the remaining reductions were intended to be major cuts in ongoing programs. In addition, the estimates of interest payments on the national debt were reduced by $0.6 billion to reflect the effect of declining interest rates. Defense expenditures were also reduced $2.0 billion, but this is probably accounted for by a shortfall in these expenditures below the estimates for fiscal year 1976—a shortfall that continued into 1977.[13]

On the receipts side, President Ford's budget for fiscal year 1977 estimated total receipts of $351.3 billion, which was $21.3 billion lower than the estimate in the current services budget. The major reductions were $12.6 billion in individual income tax receipts, reflecting the proposed tax cuts of $11.2 billion; $10.7 billion in corporate income tax receipts, reflecting an overestimate of receipts in the current services budget of $8.0 billion and a $2.7 billion proposed tax cut; and a reduction in the estimates of receipts other than payroll taxes of $3 billion. These reductions were offset by an increase in payroll tax receipts of $4.9 billion, which is accounted for mainly by the proposed increases in social security and unemployment insurance taxes.

The Congressional Budget

The congressional reaction to the Ford proposals was extremely negative. With unemployment running at about 8 percent of the labor force, Congress was not prepared to reduce expenditures. It raised expenditures in most categories to the levels estimated in the current services budget or higher, added a substantial economic stimulus of its own through jobs programs, took no action on the proposed income tax cuts, and rejected the social security payroll tax increases. The increases in the congressional budget were $18.9 billion on the outlay side and $11.2 billion on the receipts side, thus raising the budget deficit by $7.6 billion (table 2-4).[14]

President Ford attempted to reduce spending by vetoing a number of bills and by recommending rescissions and deferrals of numerous authorized expenditures.[15] Although many of his vetoes were sus-

13. See the note at the end of this chapter.
14. Congress passed two resolutions in 1976 and one in early 1977 on the fiscal year 1977 budget. The first concurrent resolution, which was approved May 13, 1976, provided the initial guidelines, but this was superseded by the second resolution enacted on September 16, 1976. Since the two resolutions differed very little, the first resolution figures are omitted from table 2-4. The third resolution, which included economic stimulus proposals similar to those recommended by President Carter, is discussed below.
15. Rescissions proposed by the President may be overturned by majority vote of either house of Congress within forty-five days; deferrals are effective until overturned by either house.

tained, they had little impact on the budget. In the end, appropriations for fiscal year 1977 turned out to be more in line with the congressional budget than with the budget submitted by President Ford. Although there were no new initiatives, practically all the proposed cutbacks in social programs were restored and the accompanying tax cuts were eliminated. The result was an estimated budget of $413.1 billion—$18.9 billion higher than President Ford's budget and $1.4 billion lower than the current services budget.

The Carter Stimulus

President Ford's and the congressional budget for fiscal year 1977 assumed that the economy would be growing at high enough rates in calendar year 1976 to bring the unemployment rate down below 7 percent by the year's end. The economy was in fact extremely buoyant in the first quarter of 1976, but then slowed down considerably. In the first quarter, real gross national product grew at an annual rate of 9.2 percent; by the last quarter, the growth rate was less than 3 percent. Unemployment in the last quarter averaged 7.9 percent of the labor force.

Even before he was inaugurated, President Carter announced that he would introduce a fiscal stimulus that would be designed to raise the 1977 growth rate to 6 percent,[16] and to lower the unemployment rate to 7 percent by the end of that year. On January 31, 1977, he proposed a two-year $31.2 billion package of tax rebates, a temporary business tax incentive, an increase in the standard deduction for individuals, and expenditure increases, with the budgetary costs to be divided about equally between fiscal years 1977 and 1978. The budgetary impact of the tax cuts was concentrated mainly in fiscal year 1977, while the impact of the expenditure increases was mainly in fiscal year 1978.

The main features of the program proposed by President Carter were as follows:

1. A $50 per capita rebate on 1976 taxes and $50 payments to various transfer payment recipients, amounting to a total of $11.4 billion in fiscal year 1977.

2. An optional credit against the individual income and corporation income taxes equal to 4 percent of the social security payroll tax

16. The goal was later interpreted to mean a 6 percent growth rate from the fourth quarter of 1976 to the fourth quarter of 1977.

paid by employers, or an increase of 2 percentage points in the investment credit (from 10 to 12 percent), at a total annual cost of $2.4 billion.

3. A permanent increase in the standard deduction for the individual income tax that would cost $4 billion a year.

4. Increased authorizations of $4 billion for local public works.

5. An increase in public service employment by 415,000 jobs and in training and youth programs by 176,000 positions.

6. An extension of an increase in the countercyclical revenue sharing program designed to pay out an additional $1 billion a year at the expected 1977 levels of unemployment.

Congress incorporated the fiscal stimulus in a third concurrent budget resolution on the 1977 budget,[17] which provided new guidelines of $417.4 billion for outlays and $347.7 billion for receipts, leaving a deficit of $69.7 billion. The major changes in the congressional budget are summarized in table 2-5. On the expenditure side, the largest increases were for the rebate in excess of tax liabilities (which was counted as a budget outlay) and the payments to social security and other transfer payment recipients ($3.2 billion), public service and training programs ($1.0 billion), countercyclical revenue sharing ($0.9 billion), extension of supplemental unemployment insurance to March 31, 1978 ($0.5 billion), and public works ($0.2 billion). Receipts were lowered by $10.6 billion to reflect the effect of the tax rebate and tax reductions in fiscal year 1977, and by $4.2 billion for an overestimate resulting from lower-than-expected levels of incomes.

On April 14, 1977, President Carter withdrew his request for the tax rebate and the business tax incentive on the grounds that the economy had improved.[18] New estimates of the budget for fiscal year 1977 were issued by the Office of Management and Budget eight days later (see table 2-5). These estimates reduced budget outlays by $9.3 billion below the guidelines in the third congressional budget resolution—$3.2 billion for the withdrawal of the payments to nontaxpayers and transfer payment recipients associated with the rebate, and

17. This procedure is required because legislation that would breach the expenditure and revenue guidelines set in the second concurrent resolution would otherwise be ruled out of order. The third resolution was agreed to on March 3, 1977.

18. The improvement in business conditions was the official reason for abandoning the rebate. However, the rebate was not popular in the Senate and might well have been defeated had it come up for a vote.

Table 2-5. Adjustments in the Federal Unified Budget Made by the Third Congressional Budget Resolution and the April 1977 Budget Review, Fiscal Year 1977

Billions of dollars

Item	Amount	
Budget outlays		
Total outlays, second congressional budget resolution		**413.1**
Employment and training	+1.0	
Countercyclical revenue sharing	+0.9	
Rebates in excess of tax liabilities and payments to		
transfer payment recipients	+3.2	
Public works	+0.2	
Extension of federal supplemental unemployment benefits		
to March 31, 1978	+0.5	
Other expenditure changes and reestimates	−1.4	
Total outlays, third congressional budget resolution		**417.4**
Withdrawal of tax rebates in excess of tax liabilities and		
payments to transfer payment recipients	−3.2	
Estimated shortfall in the rate of expenditures	−7.5	
Reestimates	+1.4	
Total outlays, April 1977 budget review		**408.2**
Budget receipts		
Total receipts, second congressional budget resolution		**362.5**
Tax rebates and tax reductions	−10.6	
Reestimates	−4.2	
Total receipts, third congressional budget resolution		**347.7**
Withdrawal of tax rebates and business tax reductions	+9.1	
Reestimates	+2.7	
Total receipts, April 1977 budget review		**359.5**

Sources: *Third Concurrent Resolution on the Budget, FY 1977*, S. Rept. 95-9, 95:1 (1977); *Third Concurrent Resolution on the Budget—Fiscal Year 1977*, H. Rept. 95-12; *Third Concurrent Resolution on the Budget, Fiscal Year 1977*, H. Rept. 95-30, 95:1 (1977); and Office of Management and Budget, "Current Budget Estimates, April 1977." Figures are rounded.

$7.5 billion for the shortfall in federal spending below earlier estimates, offset by an upward adjustment of $1.4 billion for reestimates. Receipts were raised $9.1 billion as a result of the withdrawal of the tax rebate and the business tax incentive, and $2.7 billion as a result of reestimates. The revised Carter budget called for outlays of $408.2 billion, receipts of $359.5 billion, and a deficit of $48.7 billion.

Thus, the 1977 budget went through two separate transformations. First, President Ford's proposed expenditure cutbacks and tax reductions were rejected by the Congress on social policy grounds. Second, the economy turned weaker than expected and an economic stimulus was proposed by President Carter, though the 1977 stimulus was greatly reduced as a result of the withdrawal of the request for a tax rebate and a business tax incentive. These actions set the stage for the 1978 budget.

The 1978 Budget

The opening round of the debate over the fiscal year 1978 budget, which began in January 1977, was almost an exact duplicate of that in the previous year. President Ford recommended sharp expenditure and tax cuts, but his major changes were set aside by President Carter within a month after he took office. The stimulus package, which President Carter announced in January and modified in April to eliminate the temporary tax cuts, proposed increases in expenditures and tax cuts in fiscal year 1978 as well as 1977. As a result, planned 1978 budget outlays substantially exceed the level estimated in the current services budget, planned receipts are lower, and the planned deficit is much higher.

The Ford Budget

The current services budget for fiscal year 1978, estimated by President Ford when he submitted his budget on January 17, 1977, called for outlays of $445.4 billion, receipts of $407.6 billion, and a deficit of $37.8 billion. In his own budget, the President proposed outlays of $440 billion, receipts of $393 billion, and a deficit of $47 billion (see table 2-6).

President Ford's budget included an itemized account of the proposed increases and decreases in outlays from the current services budget; these changes are summarized in table 2-6. Outlay increases of $7.0 billion and reductions of $12.4 billion were proposed, leaving a net reduction of $5.4 billion. Proposed tax increases amounted to $1.7 billion, but these were more than offset by tax reductions of $16.3 billion, leaving a net reduction in receipts of $14.6 billion.

The specific reductions in the Ford spending plans were similar to those recommended a year earlier. Funds for major social programs were to be cut below the current services levels and national defense outlays were to be increased. Outlays for income security were reduced $4.0 billion; education, manpower and training, and social services, $2.0 billion; health, $2.0 billion; and veterans' benefits and services, $0.7 billion. Increases were proposed for national defense

Table 2-6. History of Fiscal Year 1978 Budget Estimates

Billions of dollars

Functional expenditure and tax categories	Current services budget, January 1977	Ford budget, January 1977	Carter budget, April 1977
Budget outlays	445.4	440.0	462.6
National defense	110.7	112.3	112.8
International affairs	6.8	7.3	7.2
General science, space, and technology	4.6	4.7	4.7
Natural resources, environment, and energy	18.6	19.7	20.9
Agriculture	2.6	2.3	4.4
Commerce and transportation	19.0	19.3	19.9
Community and regional development	7.9	7.9	9.9
Education, manpower, and social services	21.4	19.4	27.0
Health	45.2	43.2	44.6
Income security	147.9	143.9	148.7
Veterans' benefits and services	19.0	18.3	18.8
Interest	39.7	39.7	40.9
Other[a]	1.9	2.0	2.8
Budget receipts	407.6	393.0	404.7
Individual income tax	183.6	171.2	183.0
Corporation income tax	62.5	58.9	61.3
Payroll taxes	124.8	126.1	124.1
Other	36.7	36.8	36.3
Budget deficit	−37.8	−47.0	−57.9

Sources: *The Budget of the United States Government, Fiscal Year 1978*, pp. 52, 57, 65; *Fiscal Year 1978 Budget Revisions, February 1977*, pp. 21, 28; and Office of Management and Budget, "Current Budget Estimates, April 1977."

a. Law enforcement and justice, revenue sharing and general purpose fiscal assistance, interest, and undistributed offsetting receipts.

($1.6 billion); the conduct of international affairs ($0.5 billion); and natural resources, environment, and energy ($1.1 billion).

The proposed net cut of $14.6 billion in receipts was again the result of a large reduction in individual income and corporation income taxes ($16.0 billion), offset by an increase in social security taxes ($1.3 billion in fiscal year 1978, and over $6 billion in future years). President Ford also urged that net tax cuts be planned in future years, reflecting his view that the growth of federal spending should be curbed.

The Carter Budget

The Carter revisions called for increases in outlays of $22.6 billion over the Ford budget (see table 2-7). Of this total, reversal of cut-

**Table 2-7. Adjustments in the Ford Budget Made by President Carter,
Fiscal Year 1978**

Billions of dollars

Item		Amount
Budget outlays		
Total outlays in the Ford budget, January 1977		**440.0**
Reversal of cutbacks and proposed increases		+12.5
Employment and training programs	+1.3	
Countercyclical revenue sharing (extension)	+0.9	
Supplemental unemployment benefits (extension)	+0.4	
Earned income credit (extension)	+0.9	
Food stamps and child nutrition	+2.1	
Health	+1.3	
Education	+1.1	
Energy	+1.0	
Veterans' benefits	+0.6	
Commerce and transportation	+0.6	
Social services	+0.3	
Farm price supports	+2.0	
Economic stimulus package		+7.5
Public service employment	+3.4	
Training and youth programs	+1.6	
Public works	+1.8	
Countercyclical revenue sharing	+0.7	
Proposed reductions		−0.3
Water resource development	−0.3	
Reestimates		+2.0
Social security	+1.8	
Unemployment insurance	−1.0	
Interest	+1.2	
All other revisions (net)		+0.9
Total outlays in the Carter budget, April 1977		**462.6**
Budget receipts		
Total receipts in the Ford budget, January 1977		**393.0**
Removal of Ford tax proposals	+22.5	
Increase in the standard deduction	−5.9	
Extension of temporary tax reductions	−7.8	
Revised economic assumptions	+2.9	
Total receipts in the Carter budget, April 1977		**404.7**

Sources: *Fiscal Year 1978 Budget Revisions, February 1977*, p. 22; and Office of Management and Budget, "Current Budget Estimates, April 1977." Figures are rounded.

backs and some increases totaling $12.5 billion were recommended, with particular emphasis on employment, health, education, food stamps and child nutrition, countercyclical revenue sharing, and veterans' benefits. The economic stimulus package accounted for another $7.5 billion. A reduction of $0.3 billion was proposed for nineteen water resource projects regarded as economically or environmentally unsound. The result of these revisions was to reverse the cutbacks with large price tags proposed by President Ford, while most of the smaller changes were accepted. The following were the major decisions made in the Carter budget:

• Federally funded public service jobs were scheduled to increase from 310,000 at the end of fiscal year 1977 and 50,000 at the end of 1978 to 600,000 at the end of 1977 and 725,000 during 1978, at a cost of $4.5 billion over the amount recommended in the Ford 1978 budget. An additional $1.8 billion was provided for training and employment programs.

• The countercyclical revenue sharing program, which was authorized until September 30, 1977, would be extended through 1982, and a new formula was proposed to raise quarterly outlays. These changes would add $1.6 billion to 1978 outlays.

• The refundable earned income credit under the individual income tax,[19] which would have been eliminated retroactively to January 1, 1977, by President Ford, was to be extended for another year. The payments to those who are not taxable, or whose tax liability is not large enough to absorb the credit, are counted as budget outlays. This would add $0.9 billion to 1978 outlays.

• A proposed tightening of eligibility standards for food stamps ($0.9 billion) and reductions in child nutrition programs ($1.2 billion) were reversed.

• Consolidation of Medicaid and other categorical health programs into a health block grant was rejected, and a $180 million program of improvements in comprehensive health care for children in low-income families under Medicaid was added. President Ford's proposed 7 percent limit on the annual rise in payments to hospitals and doctors in 1978 was converted to a proposed limit on increases in hospital reimbursements of 9 percent. These changes would increase outlays by $1.3 billion.

• The renewed proposal for consolidating separate education grants into a block grant was dropped and cuts in the financing of education were restored, adding $1.1 billion to outlays.

• Proposed legislation for establishing a new energy independence

19. This is a credit of 10 percent of earned income up to $4,000, which is phased down to zero between $4,000 and $8,000. The credit is called "refundable" because any excess of the credit over an individual's income tax liability is refunded to him.

authority was withdrawn, and additional funds were allocated for the petroleum storage program. The net increase in outlays for energy amounted to $1.0 billion.

• Outlays for veterans' benefits were increased $0.6 billion to reflect cost-of-living increases in 1978 compensation and benefits, as well as the withdrawal of a proposal to limit the GI bill education benefits.

• Funds were added for highways and mass transit ($0.2 billion), additional railroad assistance ($0.2 billion), and the post office subsidy ($0.2 billion).

• Proposed cuts of $0.2 billion in grants for child day care and of $0.1 billion for rehabilitation services to the disabled were restored.

• Farm price support programs were expected to add $2.0 billion.

Total budget receipts were raised by President Carter from $393.0 billion to $404.7 billion, an increase of $11.7 billion. The increase reflected the removal of $22.5 billion in tax cuts by President Ford, which was only partly offset by the $5.9 billion increase in the standard deduction and $7.8 billion for a one-year extension of temporary tax cuts scheduled to expire December 31, 1977. The remaining $2.9 billion is accounted for by revisions in the economic assumptions underlying the receipts estimates.

The Full-Employment Budget

The rate of growth of federal spending will continue at a rapid pace under President Carter's budget.[20] Outlays will increase at an annual rate of 9.1 percent in fiscal year 1977,[21] but then are expected to jump by 13.3 percent in 1978. The ratio of planned outlays to the gross national product in the two years—22.3 and 22.6 percent, respectively—remain at the highest levels since 1955 (see tables 2-1 and 2-9). Although these ratios indicate that outlays are rising about in proportion to the increase in total output, they are higher than the 21 percent goal that President Carter announced during his election campaign and has frequently repeated since the election. The planned deficits for the two fiscal years total $106.6 billion, increasing fed-

20. This assumes that the shortfall in expenditures discussed in the note at the end of this chapter will be made up before the end of fiscal year 1977.

21. Outlays in 1977 will exceed those in 1976 by 11.4 percent, but since the change in fiscal year makes this an increase over fifteen months (see p. 29, note 1), 11.4 percent is converted to an annual basis, yielding 9.1 percent.

Table 2-8. Adjustments in the Federal Unified Budget for Full Employment and Temporary Programs, Fiscal Years 1977 and 1978

Billions of dollars

Adjustments	Budget receipts	Budget outlays	Surplus or deficit
1977			
Estimates at projected employment levels	359.5	408.2	−48.7
Adjustments to full employment	+37.1	−5.3	+42.4
Full-employment estimates	396.6	402.9	−6.3
Adjustments for temporary programs			
Public works	...	−0.3	+0.3
Public service employment	...	−2.5	+2.5
Countercyclical revenue sharing	...	−2.2	+2.2
Adjusted full-employment estimates	**396.6**	**397.9**	**−1.3**
1978			
Estimates at projected employment levels	404.7	462.6	−57.9
Adjustments to full employment	+34.5	−3.3	+37.8
Full-employment estimates	439.2	459.3	−20.1
Adjustments for temporary programs			
One year increase in refunds[a]	+1.5	...	+1.5
Public works	...	−3.8	+3.8
Public service employment	...	−5.9	+5.9
Countercyclical revenue sharing	...	−1.6	+1.6
Adjusted full-employment estimates	**440.7**	**448.0**	**−7.3**

Sources: *The Budget of the United States Government, Fiscal Year 1978*, p. 437; Office of Management and Budget, "Current Budget Estimates, April 1977"; adjustments are estimated by author on the basis of *Fiscal Year 1978 Budget Revisions, February 1977*, pp. 12, 13, 51, 52, 71. Figures are rounded.

a. The increase in standard deduction, which is effective for the whole year 1977, is assumed to go into effect for purposes of withholding on June 1, 1977. The overwithholding during the first months of the year will be credited against tax liability or refunded after the final 1977 tax returns are filed early in 1978.

eral debt held by the public by 22 percent. In these circumstances, it is legitimate to inquire whether the budget is getting out of hand.

As indicated earlier, budget outlays are inflated, and receipts are depressed, by the automatic stabilizers in a period of high unemployment. The longer-run condition of the budget can be discerned more clearly if the effects of the stabilizers are removed and the budget figures are adjusted to a full-employment basis.

The effect of a recalculation of the budget for fiscal years 1977 and 1978 at full employment (assuming an unemployment rate of 4.9 percent) is shown in table 2-8. The ratios of outlays to the gross national product are reduced from 22.3 percent to 20.3 percent in 1977 and from 22.6 percent to 21.0 percent in 1978 (see table 2-9). The deficits are reduced from $48.7 billion to $6.3 billion in 1977 and

Table 2-9. Relation of Federal Unified Budget Outlays and Deficit to the Gross National Product and to Full-Employment Gross National Product, Fiscal Years 1977 and 1978

Fiscal year	Percent of actual GNP	Percent of full-employment GNP[a]	
		Unadjusted	Adjusted for temporary factors[b]
Budget outlays			
1977	22.3	20.3	20.1
1978	22.6	21.0	20.5
Deficit			
1977	−2.7	−0.3	−0.1
1978	−2.8	−0.9	−0.3

Sources: Actual figures are from *Fiscal Year 1978 Budget Revisions, February 1977*, pp. 99, 101. Full-employment figures are author's estimates (see appendix A, series B).

a. Outlays as well as GNP are on full-employment basis, assuming an unemployment rate of 4.9 percent.
b. For temporary factors, see table 2-8.

from \$57.9 billion to \$20.1 billion in 1978. These are large reductions, but the spending ratios are uncomfortably close to the 21 percent goal emphasized by President Carter, and the remaining deficits are also large.

Part of the explanation for the relatively high spending ratios and large deficits is that the fiscal stimulus proposed by the Carter administration will not increase outlays and reduce receipts permanently by the amounts projected for fiscal years 1977 and 1978. The strategy was to concentrate the stimulus on expenditure increases that would disappear when the economy reached more satisfactory levels of unemployment. Thus, the public works and public service employment programs are conceived to be temporary, and countercyclical revenue sharing automatically phases out when the national unemployment rate goes below 6 percent. However, since the full-employment adjustments reflect only the effect of the automatic stabilizers, such discretionary fiscal actions reduce full-employment budget receipts and raise full-employment budget expenditures, even though they are scheduled to terminate.

The effects of such temporary factors on the full-employment budgets for fiscal years 1977 and 1978 are also shown in tables 2-8 and 2-9. These adjustments reduce budget outlays to 20.1 percent of full-employment gross national product in 1977 and 20.5 percent in 1978. They also reduce the 1977 full-employment deficit of \$6.3 billion to \$1.3 billion, and the 1978 full-employment deficit of \$20.1 billion to \$7.3 billion.

These adjustments do not fully account for the outlays that are likely to be temporary. Consequently, the adjusted spending ratios, and thus the deficits, may be overstated. Nevertheless, it is clear that 1978 budget outlays are high relative to the full-employment gross national product and to budget receipts at that level. The difference of 0.5 percent between the adjusted federal spending ratio at full employment in 1978 and President Carter's goal of 21 percent for 1981 amounts to $11 billion in 1978 and $14 billion in 1981. An additional margin will be provided by the growth in tax receipts as the economy continues to grow. How much the 1981 margin will be, and whether it will be sufficient to finance new expenditure programs and leave a surplus to make room for the higher private investment needs that may be expected at that time, is discussed in chapter 11.

Note: The Expenditure Shortfall

In recent years, successive estimates of budget outlays by the Office of Management and Budget have exceeded actual outlays by significant amounts. In his January 1976 budget, President Ford estimated budget outlays for fiscal year 1976 at $373.5 billion. Revised estimates on March 25, 1976, by the OMB raised the total by almost $1 billion, to $374.4 billion. In the midyear budget review, issued on July 16, 1976, the outlay estimate for fiscal year 1976 was still $369.1 billion. Estimates by the staffs of the congressional budget committees and of the Congressional Budget Office were of the same order of magnitude. As it turned out, fiscal year 1976 outlays totaled only $366.5 billion—$7.9 billion below the OMB estimate made three-quarters through the fiscal year and $2.6 billion below the estimate made two weeks after the end of the fiscal year.

This experience was repeated for the transition quarter lasting from July 1 to September 30, 1976. The budget estimate made in January 1976 was $98.0 billion. This was revised in March to $98.5 billion and in July to $102.1 billion. The latter adjustment was made in the expectation that part of the previous fiscal year's shortfall would be made up in the transition quarter. The final figure turned out to be $94.7 billion, $7.4 billion below the last estimate and $3.3 billion lower than any of the previous estimates.

What is curious about the shortfall is that it cannot be attributed to any one or a few categories of budget outlays. The shortfall has been evident both in defense and nondefense expenditures and has affected most budget categories.

The existence of the shortfall began to be noticed during the fall of 1976. Many economists believe that the lower rate of federal spending contributed to the reduced rate of growth of the economy during the latter half of 1976. Although part of the shortfall can be accounted for by financial transactions and other asset transfers that reduce budget outlays but do not affect current economic activity,[22] other spending categories were underestimated as well. The shortfall continues to puzzle the experts, and no satisfactory explanation has as yet been provided either by the OMB or by the congressional staffs. It is particularly mystifying that numerous government agencies underspent their targets at roughly the same time and over such an extended period. Some budget analysts have conjectured that, in an atmosphere in which the White House, the OMB, and the CBO were expected to be critical of overspending, the agencies estimated outlays on the higher end of a plausible range to give themselves a margin of safety.

The April 1977 budget estimates assumed a shortfall of $7.5 billion during fiscal year 1977, but made no change in the 1978 estimates on this account. If the shortfall continues, fiscal year 1978 outlays will again be lower than the official estimates.

22. For the transition quarter, asset transactions accounted for 25 percent of the shortfall below the July 1976 estimate.

CHAPTER THREE

Fiscal Policy

JOSEPH J. MINARIK

THE BUDGETS proposed by Presidents Ford and Carter for 1977 and 1978 had in common the explicit purpose of using fiscal policy to stimulate the economy. This chapter assesses the economic conditions that gave rise to this budgetary strategy, the prospects for more rapid growth, the fiscal policy tools chosen in both budgets, and the monetary policies the budgets require. It also considers President Carter's later changes in his fiscal policy and their implications for economic recovery.

The State of the Economy, 1977

When the Carter administration took office in January 1977, the performance of the economy was clearly unsatisfactory. The unemployment rate had been too high for at least two years; the inflation rate, while far better than in 1974–75, was still unacceptably high; and the gross national product was growing too slowly to reduce unemployment. This picture of the economy does not tell the whole story, however; it is also important to see where the economy has been before evaluating where it is and where it is going.

The author is grateful to Barry Bosworth, Robert W. Hartman, Bruce K. Mac-Laury, Arthur M. Okun, and John L. Palmer for commenting on earlier drafts of this chapter; to Robert Gough and Richard M. Young, who provided economic forecasts; and to Robin Mary Donaldson, who programmed the tax simulations, which were supported by a grant from the RANN program of the National Science Foundation.

55

Table 3-1. Gross National Product Growth Rate, Unemployment Rate, and Inflation
Rate, 1972–77
Percent

Year and quarter	Real GNP growth rate	Unemployment rate[a]	Inflation rate[b]
1972:1	7.6	5.9	5.8
2	7.9	5.7	2.8
3	5.3	5.6	3.4
4	8.5	5.3	4.7
1973:1	9.5	5.0	5.8
2	0.4	4.9	7.0
3	1.7	4.7	7.5
4	2.1	4.7	9.6
1974:1	−3.9	5.0	9.5
2	−3.1	5.1	11.5
3	−2.6	5.6	12.4
4	−6.8	6.7	12.7
1975:1	−9.9	8.4	10.1
2	5.6	8.9	4.5
3	11.4	8.6	7.0
4	3.3	8.5	7.1
1976:1	9.2	7.6	3.2
2	4.5	7.5	5.2
3	3.9	7.8	4.4
4	2.6	7.9	5.8
1977:1	6.4	7.4	5.5

Source: U.S. Bureau of Economic Analysis.
a. Mean of monthly unemployment rates within each quarter.
b. As measured by gross national product deflator.

From the quarterly output, employment, and inflation data presented in table 3-1, it is clear that the economy was moving in the
right direction in 1972. The inflation of the late 1960s was slowly
diminishing, helped by the imposition of price and wage controls.
Unemployment was unacceptably high, but it fell steadily throughout
the year. Although the economy seemed to be on course, it was
hardly two years away from simultaneous double-digit inflation and
near–double-digit unemployment; the difficulties of that time are at
the root of the problems today.

Inflation hit the economy from four sides. First and foremost, the
Organization of Petroleum Exporting Countries raised the world oil
price by 300 percent, causing rapid price increases in petroleum
products and in virtually all other goods and services through the in-

creased cost of transportation and power. Second, and nearly as spectacular, two consecutive bad harvests over much of the world lowered the supply of grain, raising grain prices and also those of domestic meats through the cost of feed. Third, two devaluations of the dollar raised the prices of imports. Finally, the 1972 recovery became too rapid (as it did in other industrialized countries as well) and caused some inflationary pressure, accelerated by the removal of price and wage controls in early 1973.

The Nixon administration responded to the excess demand inflation by slowing the economy; the added inflation caused by the subsequent oil, grain, and devaluation "shocks" only reinforced this policy. Consumer confidence was shaken by the inflation, however, and personal consumption fell more rapidly than expected. The drain of purchasing power caused by higher payments to the OPEC countries[1] intensified this economic depressant, and the result was not a gradual slowdown but a tailspin—the worst economic downturn since the Great Depression, with the unemployment rate reaching a peak of 9 percent.

When the seriousness of the recession became clear, budget policy swung back toward stimulus. The Tax Reduction Act of 1975 provided a quick economic stimulant through tax rebates and continuing cuts. This action, plus additional expenditures on job creation programs, increased consumer buying. Businesses had been laying off workers and attempting to sell off unwanted goods, but in 1975 consumers cleared the shelves, making room for a sharp increase in inventory investment in early 1976. Businesses were rehiring and increasing production, and unemployment declined.

The economy then experienced a pause in recovery in mid- and late 1976, with reduced real growth and rising unemployment. Once inventory investment had completed its sharp turnaround early in the year, some other element of final demand was needed to take over the lead, but no new leader was forthcoming, as is evident from table 3-2.

By the beginning of 1976, real gross national product exceeded the prerecession peak of the fourth quarter of 1973. Personal con-

1. When the increased amounts paid by the United States for imported oil moved into foreign hands, they returned in the form of OPEC purchases or investments only with a lag. Because these funds were not being spent in the United States for extended periods, sales of domestically produced goods and services declined.

Table 3-2. Real Gross National Product and Other Selected Economic Indicators, 1972–77
Billions of 1972 dollars at seasonally adjusted annual rates

Year and quarter	Gross national product	Personal consumption expenditures	Investment Business fixed	Residential	Inventory
1972:1	1,141.2	713.7	113.3	60.9	4.8
2	1,163.0	728.1	114.6	61.6	10.1
3	1,178.0	737.5	116.5	61.7	12.1
4	1,202.2	752.8	122.9	63.8	10.8
1973:1	1,229.8	767.7	128.5	64.4	11.7
3	1,231.1	766.8	130.7	62.0	14.8
3	1,236.3	770.4	132.5	58.3	14.1
4	1,242.6	765.9	132.4	54.0	25.4
1974:1	1,230.4	761.8	133.5	49.9	11.4
2	1,220.8	761.9	131.6	47.0	9.4
3	1,212.9	764.7	127.3	43.9	5.1
4	1,191.7	748.1	121.8	39.3	8.0
1975:1	1,161.1	754.6	114.4	35.4	−20.5
2	1,177.1	767.5	110.6	36.8	−21.2
3	1,209.3	775.3	110.1	39.6	−1.0
4	1,219.2	783.9	110.5	41.9	−5.5
1976:1	1,246.3	800.7	112.6	44.1	10.4
2	1,260.0	808.6	114.9	45.7	11.1
3	1,272.2	815.7	117.5	47.4	10.2
4	1,280.4	829.7	117.9	51.1	0.9
1977:1	1,300.3	843.8	122.3	51.6	9.2

Source: U.S. Bureau of Economic Analysis.

sumption reached its old peak by the third quarter of 1975, but the other major sectors lagged well behind. Business fixed investment, which is normally the prime mover in later stages of recovery, has increased only moderately and still remains far below its old peak. Residential investment has recovered strongly, but it had fallen so low that it, too, remains below where it was in 1973. Government purchases have done little to take up the slack. Unless the investment sectors of the economy can be revived, the recovery seems likely to remain sluggish.

While the incoming Carter administration was formulating a response to the late 1976 slowdown, another shock—the extraordinarily cold weather in the East and Midwest in January 1977—hit the economy. It appears that the effect of this interlude was temporary. Food and fuel prices did jump in the early months of 1977, but the moderate temperatures of February and March forestalled any significant impact on consumer demand or further shutdowns due to fuel shortages.

Prospects for a Revitalized Recovery

There is little question that the present recovery leaves much to be desired, and that faster growth and a reduction in unemployment would be most welcome. It does not necessarily follow, however, that government should stimulate the economy, because too rapid growth could cause an inflation that would stifle the economy later. The big issue, therefore, is the trade-off between inflation and unemployment. Would stimulus set off an accelerating inflation, or would it add only moderately to price increases?

Both the Ford and Carter administrations, in their formal budget proposals, made the case for cautious stimulation of the economy. Both anticipated that their programs would reduce the unemployment rate and foresaw no inflationary explosion in the process. Yet both showed real concern for avoiding rekindling inflation. The reasons for this agreement across party lines can be seen in the character of the present inflation.

Today's upward pressure on prices is largely the legacy of the inflationary burst of 1974–75 in oil and grain prices. As these increases entered into other products as costs, the inflation became more general. Workers and their employers agreed to higher wages to try to maintain standards of living, but prices increased faster and real wages fell on average until well into 1976. Now wages are increasing to catch up with past inflation, and these increases are passed on in higher prices.

Other pressures on prices and costs will most likely maintain the upward momentum. Domestic petroleum prices will gradually increase to the world market level (more rapidly under President Carter's energy program), feeding additional inflationary pressure into the system. Natural gas prices can be expected to increase as well.[2] The bad weather of the winter of 1976–77 may add further impetus through increased food prices. Thus, since the present inflation was clearly not caused by excess aggregate demand, it is unlikely

2. See chapter 10.

that modest increases in demand will noticeably increase the inflation rate.

It would be incorrect to assume that the economy could expand at any pace or to any level without aggravating the inflation problem, however. In fact, overexpansion would probably add to the already considerable momentum of inflation and even more seriously hinder economic progress. All this suggests that caution is needed to avoid additional inflationary pressure through excess aggregate demand. Excess demand could add to inflation in one of two ways: first, by pushing the economy to too high a level of output (at more than "full employment," with excess demand in many sectors) or second, by letting the economy grow at too fast a rate (the "speed limit" problem). Both of these concepts and the issues surrounding them are controversial, and need some discussion.

What Is Full Employment?

There is considerable controversy at present over the concept of full employment. Previous measures of the level and rate of potential output have been revised downward, and the full-employment unemployment rate revised upward, by President Ford's Council of Economic Advisers.[3] As indicated in appendix A, the rate of growth of potential output will have considerable effect on the long-run balance between federal receipts and outlays.

For the short run, however, the economy is so far below the most pessimistic estimates of potential output that the debate over full employment is largely irrelevant. Even under the most favorable conditions, it is unlikely that the economy will encounter general excess demand for at least two years. Therefore, there will be time to adjust output targets up or down as the economy approaches full employment, given timely action by the executive branch and Congress. More informed choices can be made when the economy is closer to full employment than its present underutilized state.

What Is the Speed Limit?

Once the tentative output target is chosen, the speed of approach to that target (normally expressed in terms of the annual growth rate

---

3. *Economic Report of the President, January 1977*, pp. 45–57. See also "New Estimates of Capacity Utilization: Manufacturing and Materials," *Federal Reserve Bulletin*, vol. 62 (November 1976), pp. 892–905.

of the gross national product) must be chosen as well. The desired growth rate determines the amount of stimulus to be applied, although many different combinations of programs could supply that stimulus. Given the distance of the economy from full employment, the speed limit is now the major fiscal policy issue.

The most basic constraint on speed comes from the target itself. The economy can grow at 3.5 to 4.0 percent per year (through growth in the size of the labor force and in productivity) at full employment. But to reach full employment from a state of underutilization, the economy must grow at a faster rate than its long-run potential. If the economy were to arrive at full employment growing substantially faster than potential, it would overshoot the target and (if the target were accurately chosen) set off an unacceptable inflation. This would require that growth be stopped and reversed, which would have adverse effects. Therefore, it is necessary that the economy be slowed down as it reaches its target (always leaving maneuvering room for the uncertainty of forecasting, the lags in execution of policy, possible shocks, and so on).

Other factors limit the choice of a growth rate even before the economy reaches its target. As the economy begins to grow faster than its long-run potential, some sectors will act as bottlenecks to growth when they cannot increase production without some delay. Prices of products in short supply because of bottlenecks tend to rise, but prices of other goods in excess supply often fail to fall, resulting in net inflationary pressure. The faster the growth rate, the greater the number of sectors that will be unable to keep pace, and the greater the risk of inflation. The recent recession saw a deep drop in real investment in plant and equipment, so while excess capacity is prevalent now, it is possible that too rapid growth would outrun the ability of some sectors to grow, thereby creating bottlenecks. One estimate suggests that an average growth rate of about 6 percent over the four years 1977–80 would be enough to push the economy into bottlenecks at the end of the period.[4]

The Ford and Carter budgets accepted the argument of potential bottlenecks and the associated constraint on growth in the near term. The Carter budget aimed for about 5.5 percent growth in 1977 and 1978, bringing the unemployment rate to approximately 6 percent;

4. Otto Eckstein, "Inflation and the Future of the Financial System," *Data Resources Review*, vol. 6 (March 1977), p. 1.13.

Ford projected a growth rate just over 5 percent. At that pace both foresaw time for policy adjustments before the onset of bottleneck problems.

In early April, President Carter withdrew the first part of his stimulus package, the rebate of 1976 personal income taxes and the business tax cuts. A combination of political and economic factors contributed to this decision. The purpose of the rebate was to stimulate the economy in early 1977, until the spending programs in the stimulus package could begin on a meaningful scale. The business community saw this short-term plan as evidence of a fine-tuning attitude toward policymaking, a tendency to boost the economy and risk inflation at any trace of bad news. Some members of Congress thought the equal rebate payment to every citizen capricious, and some would have preferred using the funds to create jobs directly. Facing political battles on energy and water projects, President Carter may have found that a fight over the rebate would have been too costly. Furthermore, new economic news caused doubt as to the need for the rebate. Gross national product figures for the first quarter of 1977 showed that personal consumption, especially durable commodities, had risen strongly despite the cold weather of January. Inflation also increased. In light of the political costs and with some feeling that the economic case had been weakened, President Carter withdrew the rebate and business tax proposals.

The argument that could be made against this decision is that the upbeat economic news for the first quarter could easily be temporary. Personal saving was extraordinarily low and inventory investment increased, so the growth of consumption might well slow down later in the year. The danger that the rebate might generate additional inflation was not specified as a motive for withdrawing the proposal, but virtually all observers felt it would add 0.1 percent or less to the inflation rate. Thus, the evidence that the rebate was unnecessary was inconclusive, and its cost in terms of added inflation would have been small. On the other hand, if the economy proves to need stimulation, the withdrawal could be costly.

Inflation

Inflation is perceived by many people as the nation's most serious economic problem. It discourages consumers, inhibits long-term planning, and distorts economic activity. Inflation also alters the distribution of income, with particularly detrimental effects for the aged and others living on fixed incomes. In theory, the economy could grow in real terms even during rapid inflation; in practice, public resistance forces contractionary policies when inflation reaches abnormally high rates.

Based on past experience, the deep recession and moderate recovery of 1974–76 should have stopped inflation. Today's inflation is clearly out of the ordinary, however. Although the economy was somewhat overheated in 1973, the extreme inflation of the following years really arose from the oil and agriculture shocks. These events directly injected higher costs into the economic system, and their effects have proved extremely difficult to shake off; in fact, they have become a built-in force in the economy. As wages pursue past price increases and prices pursue wages, inflationary momentum continues; it must be broken before the rate of price increases can be slowed. Over the last two years, the rate of inflation for consumer products other than food and petroleum has been about 5 to 6 percent, showing no tendency to slow down (or accelerate, for that matter).[5] In 1976 food and fuel prices increased more slowly than other prices, making the overall index look better than the actual inflationary situation. Wages have increased at about 8 percent a year, in keeping with the longstanding relationship that, because of productivity increases, wages rise about 2 percent more than prices.

The federal government has at times become directly involved in price and wage setting to slow inflation. A system of controls similar to that imposed under the Nixon administration could arrest the inflation momentum and progressively reduce the pressure passed through from prices to wages. Unfortunately, controls have undesirable effects as well. A freeze on prices and wages stops all price increases, justified or not. To avoid the resulting economic distortions, provision must be made for review and adjudication of exceptions—literally millions of them. The result is a herculean problem of administration and enforcement, public perception of injustice, and a clearly visible and often lucrative payoff for cheating. On top of all these problems,

5. Excluding food and fuel is not meant to indicate that they do not count, but rather that they have changed more in response to the vagaries of the weather and international politics than to economic forces; therefore, measures of ongoing inflationary forces are best made without them. Of course, a sharp increase in food or fuel prices today would have implications for ongoing inflationary forces tomorrow.

the prospect of controls can generate inflation as sellers try to increase prices before controls cut them off. In light of these considerations, almost all observers feel that formal controls should be reserved for wartime or other periods of real emergency.

A more limited government intervention involves guideposts of the type used in the Kennedy and Johnson administrations. Guideposts set nonbinding target rates of increase for wages. They further specify that firms whose unit labor costs fall as a result of the wage restraint should lower their prices, and those whose unit labor costs rise could increase their prices, leading to price stability on average without requiring that every price be stable. If the rate of inflation were zero, the target wage increase would be the average rate of labor productivity growth; but in an inflationary situation, the target could be set higher and gradually reduced to slow prices over time.

One of the problems with such voluntary guideposts is that the only power to reverse a business or union decision lies with public opinion, so that only conspicuous violations are reversible. Large labor unions are particularly concerned that their wage contracts will be policed while other wage deals and most prices will not. Violations felt to be worthy of action require a virtual duel between one union or corporate official and the President of the United States, who has no legal enforcement powers. During the Vietnam War inflation in the Johnson administration, business and labor officials began to defy the guideposts, and they had to be dismantled to avoid serious governmental embarrassment. Again, many believe that the cure may be worse than the disease; others believe that a carefully designed guidepost system may help to contain inflation in an economy where excess demand is not a problem.

A still more limited form of government intervention is "jawboning," or public lobbying in wage and price deliberations and criticism of past decisions. Here reliance is placed on the fear or the fact of presidential displeasure to persuade unions to moderate their negotiating positions, to stiffen management's back at the negotiating table, and to translate the resultant lower wage pressure into lower prices. The jawboning strategy is most effective before decisions are made; such a strategy was apparently behind President Carter's informal request for prenotification of wage and price increases as a gesture of cooperation. Union officials quickly rebuffed that request, clearly feeling that they would be singled out because of their size to be the shock troops in the war against inflation. While that possibility was repugnant to the unions, the government's strategy could also have been to act only where union demands were clearly out of bounds. Given that the President would have no enforcement powers in any event, it seems unfortunate that labor would not cooperate, if only because it weakens the President's hand when he attempts to influence management on price increases.

President Carter ruled out controls and guideposts as anti-inflation weapons quite early in his administration, and his first steps toward jawboning policy were unsuccessful. On April 15, 1977, however, he released a multifaceted anti-inflation program. The program is both less comprehensive and less powerful than any of the activist programs described earlier. It aims mostly at particular sectors of the economy rather than the whole, and it involves little direct intervention, so its potential for reducing inflation remains to be seen.

Under the President's program, the Council on Wage and Price Stability will monitor wage and price developments in various sectors of the economy and will attempt to identify material and capacity shortages. Monitoring could conceivably have some influence through publicizing excessive wage settlements or price increases, but there is little doubt that this tool would have been more effective with pre-notification. The council's research on capacity problems could encourage producers to head off bottlenecks, although the government may not have anything to add to the information producers accumulate in their day-to-day operations.

The program also calls for government stockpiling to smooth out fluctuations in commodity prices. This would reduce the frequency of commodity shocks, which help maintain the inflationary momentum. Negotiations would be undertaken to moderate price fluctuations in international trade, and free trade will be encouraged to promote efficiency and lower prices.

Simplification of government regulation is also included. Government rate-setting practices are to seek greater efficiency and lower cost, and environmental, safety, and health regulations are to minimize added cost and red tape. The Council on Wage and Price Stability is to monitor the price and cost implications of regulations. Because the distinction between necessary and unnecessary regulations (and therefore worthwhile and wasteful regulatory costs) is controversial, any judgment on the effectiveness of these programs must await their execution.

Vigorous enforcement of antitrust laws is another part of the program. There are clear benefits to competitive markets, and antitrust enforcement is desirable on these grounds alone; but it is not clear that such enforcement will reduce the rate of increase of prices. Firms with market power will charge *higher* prices than they would under competition, but it does not follow that those prices will then *increase* at a rate faster than average. In general, such firms could add to inflation only if their degree of market power were to increase, or if they had not been fully exercising their power previously. Therefore, antitrust action may lower the price of a product to begin with, but there is no basis for predicting how the price would change after the initial adjustment.

In addition to the policies mentioned above, other standard items are found on President Carter's list. The federal government pledges fiscal responsibility and an upcoming balanced budget; future tax reform proposals will include investment incentives to promote greater capacity and prevent bottlenecks; and government labor market policies will fight discrimination and speed the matching of workers and jobs, in an attempt fully to utilize human resources. The only direct government intervention proposed was in medical care, where the federal government will put a ceiling on hospital care cost increases and is considering control on the incomes of private physicians as well.

While President Carter's policies may reduce inflation somewhat in various individual sectors, there is little really new in his program, which suggests that progress in the future may be no greater than it has been in the past. Neither the scope of the individual policies nor the magnitude of their expected benefits offers a great deal of encouragement.

Moreover, several elements of President Carter's energy program, most notably the increase in the domestic price of oil to the world market price and the proposed gasoline taxes, will have inflationary effects. The higher energy prices will raise the consumer price index and will increase wages directly through the many escalator clauses based on inflation. The program calls for refunding the tax proceeds to the public to offset part of the increased cost of living, but the method chosen also has implications for inflation. If the tax receipts had been used to reduce state sales taxes, which are added directly to prices (or perhaps to reduce employer payroll taxes, which may be passed on to consumers through prices), the higher prices for energy-related products would have been offset by lower gross-of-tax prices for all other products; therefore the net effect on the price level would be close to zero. However, the Carter administration judged that practical difficulties with the sales tax reduction (including how to treat states that do not have sales taxes) precluded that approach, and decided to refund the proceeds through the income tax or to use them for other programs. Thus, faster general inflation may be a consequence of the energy program, whatever its other merits.

Fiscal Policy Tools for the Recovery

There is little difference between the Ford and the original Carter budgets in their strategy for economic recovery. Both budgets plan for a moderately paced growth over about four years, with flexibility to alter the pace of the recovery or the ultimate target. In terms of the tactics of the recovery, however—the choices of policy instruments to reach the targets—the Ford and Carter proposals are far apart. This difference is increased by President Carter's revised proposals, which dropped most of the tax cuts. In essence, Ford relied on tax reductions, Carter on higher spending.

Stimulating the Economy through Government Spending

Government spending should be used to stimulate the economy only if it meets two basic requirements. First, the programs must be able to start up and spend money quickly; it does no good for funds to sit in the pipeline while the economy stagnates. Second, the programs must be easy to terminate promptly; spending can be harmful if it continues after a recovery turns into a boom. Some ongoing government programs (transfer payments particularly) are capable of generating additional spending quickly, but they are usually difficult to terminate. Other programs (public works, for example) invariably start slowly and are subject to some termination problems as well.

The Ford budget rejected government spending as a fiscal stimulus; it proposed $7 billion in program increases for fiscal 1978 (largely concentrated in national security, international affairs, and natural resources, environment, and energy programs), but $12 billion in decreases (mostly in education, training, employment and social services, health, and income security areas). President Ford believed that government spending is less desirable than private spending at the margin, and feared that temporary government expenditures have a way of becoming permanent. The Carter budget restored most of the major Ford cuts but avoided large new initiatives. Additional spending was concentrated in programs that were designed to be self-terminating—employment and training programs and countercyclical revenue sharing—to avoid preempting funds that will be needed later.

The major difference in spending priorities between the Ford and Carter proposals is that the former eliminates and the latter emphasizes specific job creation programs. These programs are based on the Comprehensive Employment and Training Act of 1973 (CETA) and the Public Works Employment Act of 1976 (accelerated public works). Under CETA, the federal government pays part of the costs to state and local governments of hiring unemployed workers to perform community service activities. Under the public works program, the federal government pays the entire cost of small-scale construction projects proposed by localities.

CETA attempts to go into action quickly while keeping the choice of services to be provided flexible. The administrative costs of CETA are met by states and localities, which have the necessary infrastructure, so actual hiring of workers can occur relatively quickly. The choice of actual projects is up to the participating state or locality, provided that CETA workers do not replace regular public employees. Because jobs are designed to be temporary, proponents maintain that expenditures can be cut off when required.

The accelerated public works began with applications from localities for federally funded construction projects of a small enough scale and with sufficient prior planning that construction could begin within ninety days of funding. Advocates of accelerated public works claim that such programs provide localities with needed capital improvements while spending appropriated funds quickly and terminating promptly.

Proponents of these programs emphasize their creation of new jobs at the very first stage of the process, without waiting for new hiring to be induced by increased consumption or investment spurred by, for example, a tax cut. Several studies have concluded that such programs can be more "efficient" in creating new jobs than tax cuts (in the sense that they have less direct budgetary cost and act some-what faster), although the variation in the estimates is large.[6] Further, if job programs can be directed at the long-term unemployed and disadvantaged, perhaps including some training, they could prevent further unemployment and dependency.

Opposition to job creation programs centers on the fact that the fiscal policy values—fast starting and termination—are in competition with the other objectives—benefits to employees and output from the public sector. If the trade-off among these values is not correctly managed, the benefit of the programs may be lost, to the long-run detriment of other considerations.

The major drawback of accelerated public works programs is that they could have great difficulty in moving fast enough for fiscal policy purposes. Construction projects in general are notorious for delays for legal reasons, shortages of materials, unfavorable weather, and many other factors, and previous experience with accelerated public works programs is discouraging.[7] The result could be long delays before the appropriated funds ever reach the economy, with the danger that the funds might be spent when restraint rather than stimulus is in order. Another risk is that localities not initially given grants will protest the selection process so vigorously that more projects will be added as recovery proceeds, giving everyone a piece of the pie at the expense of sound fiscal policy.

CETA is also subject to objections. Hiring the long-term unemployed, youths, and the disadvantaged takes more time than hiring without restrictions, and so a targeted CETA program will move more slowly than it could otherwise.[8] If the program is to be any more beneficial to the workers than simple income support, it must provide training and real work experience; planning such programs takes time and may eliminate their fiscal policy benefit. Additional CETA funding could induce localities to reduce their own spending and hiring from what it would otherwise have been, thus canceling part of the fiscal policy benefits. CETA would have termination problems as well, because the workers who would lose their jobs and the groups receiving the services of the program would lobby for its continuation.

In short, the job creation programs, especially accelerated public

6. See chapter 5.
7. Nancy H. Teeters, "The 1972 Budget: Where It Stands and Where It Might Go," *Brookings Papers on Economic Activity, 1:1971*, pp. 232–33.
8. Michael Wiseman, "Public Employment as Fiscal Policy," *Brookings Papers on Economic Activity, 1:1976*, p. 77.

works, may not be able to provide valuable public sector output and long-term benefits to carefully selected workers while still maintaining their quick-starting, quick-stopping attributes. The greatest danger is that spending will be delayed by programmatic concerns, forcing the economy to wait for the initial stimulus and then overstimulating it after the recovery.

Stimulating the Economy through Tax Cuts

The federal government levies taxes on individuals and businesses; reductions in each of these areas were recommended by Presidents Ford and Carter.

PERSONAL TAXES. Personal tax changes have in the past been the most prominent fiscal tool. When the government reduces its tax collections, individuals spend part of their additional disposable income (usually most of it, according to proponents of this strategy), and the recipients of that expenditure do the same. The money thus passes through the economy (the "multiplier" effect), increasing incomes and employment. The tax cuts are financed by increased government borrowing, and the holders of additional debt are assumed not to alter their demand behavior significantly and therefore not to impede the multiplier process. Tax increases to slow the economy generate the same process in reverse.

The personal tax most commonly used for fiscal policy purposes is the individual income tax. Tax cuts in the past have been reductions in marginal tax rates, increases in the personal exemption and standard deduction, introduction and enlargement of personal credits, and a rebate of part of taxes on prior-year income. The only tax increases since World War II were surcharges imposed during the Korean and Vietnam Wars. Any of these changes can be permanent or temporary.

Advocates of tax cuts as a stimulative fiscal tool claim that they are the fastest acting and the most easily reversible measures. A tax cut takes effect within a few months as the withholding tables are changed (for tax cuts on current-year income) or checks are mailed (for tax rebates on prior-year income). The decision between permanent and temporary tax cuts depends on preferences for the future size of the public sector, with temporary reductions leaving future revenues intact.

The consumption resulting from the tax cut is of high value to the recipients, because they have an unconstrained choice of uses for the money. If the tax cut is directed at the low-income population through a credit payable to those with no tax liability, it helps those whose needs are greatest. The additional jobs resulting from the tax cut can be expected to continue as the economy recovers and grows.

Opponents of tax cuts argue that they are not effective in stimulating the economy. When tax cuts are temporary, they argue, recipients regard the extra income as a windfall rather than a change in their permanent income, and save the money rather than changing their spending plans; when tax cuts are permanent, small amounts of extra disposable income affect spending decisions only with a lag. Furthermore, tax cuts reduce future government revenues and thereby preempt the necessary funds for new programs. This may be true even of temporary tax cuts, because Congress tends to extend them for years and they are ultimately absorbed into the permanent tax system.

Both the Ford and Carter administrations decided to use tax cuts, but in different ways and for different reasons. The Ford budget relied entirely on tax cuts for fiscal stimulus and to offset increased effective tax rates due to inflation, using permanent rate reductions and increases in the personal exemption and minimum standard deduction. This method answers some of the objections to tax cuts in that it permanently increases disposable income and thereby encourages households to increase their planned consumption. It also reduces future revenues and thus limits the growth of federal spending. The rationale for this policy is that taxpayers are better judges of how to spend their money than government, so government spending should be cut back; the best way to do so is to cut taxes so that less revenue is available. The Ford budget proposed additional tax reductions to hold effective personal tax rates at their 1979 level. President Ford's tax proposals, therefore, would have effects beyond macroeconomic policy and cannot be judged on those grounds alone.

The original Carter budget also put most emphasis on tax cuts, but it used different methods. The original proposals showed a great concern for maintaining future tax revenues to finance new programs. More than half of the proposed personal tax reduction was a rebate on 1976 income, the one type of tax cut that has proven temporary. This method had a good chance of maintaining budget revenues, but it was subject to the criticism (as yet unproven) that one-shot tax cuts are saved rather than spent. In partial answer to this argument, the

Table 3-3. Personal Income Tax Liability before and after Proposed $50
per Person Rebate, 1976

Adjusted gross income class (thousands of dollars)	Amount of tax liability (billions of dollars)		Average reduction per return	
	1976 law	After rebate[a]	Amount (dollars)	Percent
0–2.5	−0.1	−0.3	197	...
2.5–5	0.4	−0.3	73	176.3[b]
5–7.5	3.3	2.3	98	30.4
7.5–10	6.7	5.5	120	17.5
10–15	19.8	17.2	155	13.2
15–20	23.6	21.6	168	8.6
20–25	18.6	17.5	176	6.0
25–30	12.1	11.8	98	2.4
30–50	18.7	18.7	0	0
50–100	16.0	16.0	0	0
100–200	8.0	8.0	0	0
200–500	3.8	3.8	0	0
500–1,000	1.1	1.1	0	0
1,000 and over	1.3	1.3	0	0
All classes[c]	133.5	124.5	126	6.8

Source: Brookings 1972 Tax File, projected to 1976.
a. Excluding the proposed $50 per person payment to social security and other transfer payment recipients.
b. Tax reductions of greater than 100 percent result from negative taxes to households with children and earned income.
c. Includes returns with negative adjusted gross income, not shown separately.

remaining personal tax cuts in the Carter program were permanent,
in the form of increases in the standard deduction. Unlike other vehicles for permanent tax reduction, however, increases in the standard
deduction cause approximately constant rather than growing revenue
losses over time, because taxpayers tend to shift from the standard to
itemized deductions as their incomes increase. With elimination of
the rebate, the only personal tax reduction remaining in the package
is the higher standard deduction. This will reduce revenues by more
than $4 billion in a full year.[9]

Only the original Carter proposal would affect calendar 1976 personal income taxes. Table 3-3 shows that the $50 per capita rebate
leads to a falling percentage reduction of taxes up to the $25,000
income level, the point at which a phaseout provision was inserted

9. President Carter recommended a flat standard deduction of $2,200 for single
persons and $3,000 for married couples. Congress accepted the $2,200 limit for single
persons and raised the deduction for married couples to $3,200.

by the House Ways and Means Committee.[10] That structure would have made the rebate highly progressive.

President Ford proposed substantially larger tax reductions for calendar 1977 than President Carter, but the Carter proposal allocates its reductions much more heavily to the low end of the income scale, as is shown in table 3-4. The Ford budget would remove the earned income credit that provides negative taxes for the working poor and would substitute an increase in the personal exemption for the $35 per capita credit, which would benefit high-income taxpayers more in dollar terms. The Carter budget restricts the permanent tax cut to an increase in the standard deduction; this benefits only taxpayers who do not itemize their deductions, mostly those with lower incomes. The Ford budget proposed an increase in the low-income allowance, or minimum standard deduction, but not in the percentage standard deduction.

BUSINESS TAXES. The purpose of business tax cuts is to stimulate investment and employment. President Ford proposed two measures to encourage investment. One is a gradual "integration" of the corporate and personal income taxes by providing a deduction at the corporate level for dividends paid out and a credit at the individual level for corporate taxes paid on dividends. This proposal was designed to eliminate the incentive in the present law to finance corporate investment through debt rather than through equity capital. It is not a direct incentive for corporations to invest, however. Reduced taxes on dividends will encourage firms to pay out more at the expense of retained earnings; any net incentive to investment must work through increased sales of common stock by firms in a presumably more buoyant stock market. The second proposal is a reduction in the top corporate tax rate from 48 to 46 percent. This provision would raise the return on investment slightly and put more funds in the hands of corporate managers for all uses—including but not limited to investment in plant and equipment.

To encourage investment, the Carter budget proposed an increase in the investment tax credit from 10 to 12 percent. The credit reduces business taxes by a percentage of the amount spent on machinery, thereby reducing the net-of-tax cost of investment. The present 10

10. Taxpayers with adjusted gross income of up to $25,000 would have received the full $50 rebate; at $26,000 the rebate was to be $40; at $27,000, $30; and so on until the rebate reached zero at $30,000.

Table 3-4. Personal Income Tax Liability before and after Proposed Ford and Carter Tax Reductions, 1977

Adjusted gross income class (thousands of dollars)	Tax under 1976 law (billions of dollars)	Ford proposal[a]			Carter proposal[b]		
		Tax (billions of dollars)	Average reduction per return		Tax (billions of dollars)	Average reduction per return	
			Amount (dollars)	Percent		Amount (dollars)	Percent
0–2.5	−0.1	0.0	−156	...	−0.1	...	...
2.5–5	0.4	0.8	−39	−75.1	−0.1	66	126.5
5–7.5	3.2	3.0	29	8.8	2.3	98	29.4
7.5–10	6.8	5.8	99	13.8	5.7	116	16.1
10–15	18.9	16.7	139	11.6	17.8	69	5.8
15–20	25.8	23.5	176	8.9	25.4	28	1.4
20–25	23.0	21.4	215	7.2	22.9	15	0.5
25–30	16.6	15.7	222	5.4	16.6	12	0.3
30–50	27.0	26.1	231	3.5	27.0	8	0.1
50–100	19.8	19.4	356	2.0	19.8	5	*
100–200	10.4	10.3	436	0.9	10.4	2	*
200–500	4.7	4.7	455	0.4	4.7	1	*
500–1,000	1.3	1.3	444	0.1	1.4	1	*
1,000 and over	1.6	1.6	431	*	1.6	†	*
All classes[c]	159.5	150.2	125	5.8	155.2	57	2.7

Source: Brookings 1972 Tax File, projected to 1977.
* 0.05 percent or less.
† $0.50 or less.
a. Includes repeal of the earned income credit and the $35 per capita on optional taxable income credit; an increase in the personal exemption from $750 to $1,000; a reduction in tax rates in lower and middle income brackets; and an increase in the low-income allowance from $2,100 to $2,500 for joint returns and from $1,200 to $1,800 for single persons.
b. Includes conversion of the low-income allowance and percentage standard deduction to a flat standard deduction of $3,200 for married couples and $2,200 for single persons.
c. Includes returns with negative adjusted gross income, not shown separately.

percent credit expires at the end of 1980; the Carter proposal was left open-ended. Critics of the credit have claimed that it reduces taxes for investment that business would make anyway. The increase, without a termination date, was vulnerable to this charge because it gave no incentive to invest in 1977 rather than later. When he withdrew the rebate, President Carter asked that the increase in the investment credit also be dropped, and Congress agreed.

The difference in philosophy between these two proposals is significant. President Carter's business tax cuts were about half the size of the Ford cuts in terms of lost revenue; the objective appears to be a strong recovery of final sales, together with a subsidy tied to actual investment. The Ford approach is more narrowly focused on corporate tax cuts, with the tax reductions unrelated to actual investment. The Carter budget therefore assumed that business is primarily concerned about future sales, and will invest more once assured of a business upturn, with only a small boost in the investment credit. The Ford budget, on the other hand, seemed to assume that business primarily lacked only the funds to invest. With the removal of the rebate and the investment credit, the Carter tax package now relies on the economy's own momentum to boost investment.

To restrain inflation, encourage employment, and provide a tax cut for labor-intensive businesses, the Carter budget provided an alternative to the increase in the investment tax credit: a refundable credit of 4 percent of social security payroll taxes paid by employers against corporate or noncorporate income taxes. This credit would lower labor costs per unit of output and thus lower prices in competitive markets (by perhaps 0.5 percentage point) and possibly encourage additional employment. Congressional critics of this proposal argued that a credit with a higher rate and a lower wage base restricted to additional employees would be more effective in encouraging new employment. They believed that such a credit would put the unemployed and the disadvantaged back to work. The Carter administration's reply was that measuring additional employment is extremely difficult (particularly for new firms and firms that use seasonal and transient labor), and that restricting a credit to additional employment would deny a subsidy to declining firms that might lay off fewer workers with the credit. They also feared that large tax credits on a small wage base would unduly encourage the use of part-year and part-time work, thus hindering the chances for reemployment of unemployed workers who are the main support of their families.

This proposal was also abandoned by the administration, but Congress insisted on an employment tax credit of up to $2,100 for additional employees hired, after allowing for a normal growth in the work force of 2 percent a year, with a maximum credit of $100,000 a firm. Whether this provision will in fact combat inflation and increase employment remains to be seen.

Monetary Policy

The performance of the economy is influenced by monetary policy as well as fiscal policy. Monetary policy operates by controlling the growth of bank reserves, thereby affecting the money supply, interest rates, and ultimately the borrowing and spending decisions of households and firms. When interest rates are low, the cost of borrowing money is low, and borrowing to purchase homes, automobiles, and productive plant and machinery is encouraged; when rates are high, such borrowing is discouraged.

The role of monetary policy in the current recovery will be important, and possibly controversial. Investment has been the missing factor in the recovery thus far and was a major objective of the stimulus packages; investment is also sensitive to changes in interest rates. The large sums needed to buy factories and machinery are often raised through borrowing. High interest rates could thus discourage investment and stall the recovery.

Interest rates declined in 1976 and there was no shortage of credit, so the low level of investment must be ascribed to other factors. 1977, however, should prove more difficult for monetary policy. A revitalization of investment demand, in addition to the borrowing activities of the federal government, may increase pressure on credit markets.

In this situation, the task of the Federal Reserve, which controls monetary policy, is to help keep the recovery going without generating additional inflationary pressures. The decline in interest rates in 1976 was due at least in part to the weak demand for funds on the part of businesses. This trend may not continue in 1977 and indeed may reverse, given an expected 12 percent growth in nominal gross national product. Based on the experience of 1976 and assuming increased investment demand, the money stock might need to grow

Table 3-5. Budget Outlays, Receipts, and Deficits, Ford and Carter Budgets, Fiscal
Years 1977 and 1978
Billions of dollars

Item	1977	1978
Ford budget[a]		
Outlays	404.9	446.2
Receipts	355.0	394.2
Deficit	49.9	52.0
Original Carter budget[a]		
Outlays	411.4	462.8
Receipts	350.4	402.4
Deficit	61.0	60.4
Revised Carter budget[a,b]		
Outlays	408.2	462.6
Receipts	359.5	404.7
Deficit	48.7	57.9

Sources: *The Budget of the United States Government, Fiscal Year 1978;* Office of Management and Budget, *Fiscal Year 1978 Budget Revisions, February 1977;* OMB, "Current Budget Estimates, April 1977" (processed); and table 2-12, this volume.

a. Outlays and receipts have been revised to accord with the April reestimates by OMB.

b. Assumes no business tax reductions in 1977. In the end, Congress added an employment tax credit to the Tax Reduction and Simplification Act of 1977.

at or slightly above the upper end of the Fed's publicly stated target ranges to keep interest rates from choking off business spending.[11]

Fiscal Policy in the Ford and Carter Budgets

Fiscal policy has changed sharply and often in 1977. The year began with President Ford's expansionary revisions to the fiscal year 1977 budget and proposals for 1978. President Carter then offered still more stimulative 1977 revisions and a 1978 budget to continue the stimulation. Finally, President Carter drastically altered his own 1977 plans. This section discusses the three stages of development of the budget and examines each as an alternative fiscal policy program.

Table 3-5 summarizes the three budget packages for fiscal years 1977 and 1978. A comparison of President Ford's and President Carter's original budgets bears out several of the observations in the preceding sections. The original Carter proposal was more stimulative, with larger deficits for both fiscal years and with a greater con-

11. Larger than expected increases in the velocity of M_1, the sum of currency and demand deposits, have arisen from changes in bank regulations and public attitudes; these velocity increases have allowed the economy to grow at a faster rate than would have been expected on the basis of M_1 growth alone. The plans of the Federal

centration of stimulus in fiscal 1977.[12] The Ford budget relies entirely on tax cuts for stimulus; the Carter budget depends mainly on expenditure increases, but also includes a tax cut.

The new Carter budget, omitting the rebate, shows a different pattern. The budget deficit will increase by approximately $9 billion from fiscal year 1977 to 1978, a most unusual strategy for recovery. Thus, the federal government will provide more stimulus in 1978, when a healthy recovery might be underway, than in 1977, when the vigor of the economy is in at least some doubt. The difference may be reduced by slower than anticipated spending in the CETA and accelerated public works programs, which now constitute a major part of the Carter stimulus package, but this would increase expenditures in fiscal year 1979, when there may be even less need for stimulus.

The stimulative effect of the revised Carter budget is reduced in both 1977 and 1978, but with nearly all the reduction falling in the earlier year. For 1977, the Carter deficit is somewhat smaller than the deficit proposed by President Ford, which may be surprising in light of President Carter's campaign promise to reduce unemployment faster. For 1978, however, the Carter proposal is more stimulative than the Ford budget.

The Carter administration estimates that real output will grow at a 4.9 percent annual rate over calendar 1977 without the rebate. At that rate, unemployment would be between 6.5 and 7.0 percent by the end of the year. Growth under the Carter budget should be similar to what might have been expected under the Ford budget; some observers would hold that a 4.9 percent growth rate is somewhat optimistic for both budgets. The rebate would have added approximately one-half percent to the growth rate.

The key element in the rebate decision is the range of possible growth rates for the next two years, together with the likely effect of

---

Reserve call for an increase in M_1 of 4½ to 6½ percent and assume an increase in velocity that may or may not be forthcoming. The relation between output and M_2, the sum of M_1 and time deposits in commercial banks, has been more predictable. The Federal Reserve plans for M_2 to grow at 7 to 9½ percent, slower than the 10.9 percent rate of 1976; it is possible that 10 percent or even slightly faster growth will be needed for the recovery to proceed. The faster growth is required by the expected faster growth of consumer and business borrowing; some of this pressure should be alleviated by allowing interest rates to rise slightly over the year.

12. The original versions of both budgets put relatively more stimulus in fiscal 1977. An outlay shortfall has since appeared for fiscal 1977, and fiscal 1978 expenditures have been reestimated upward, raising the deficit for 1978 and lowering it for 1977. For a discussion of the shortfall, see chapter 2, pp. 53–54.

the rebate on business activity. It is entirely possible that without the rebate the economy will grow slowly over much of 1977 and 1978, at an average rate under 5 percent; if so, the added stimulus would be in order. On the other hand, investment has been extremely slow for the past three years, leaving the economy with a small capital stock relative to today's potential output, given the size of the labor force. It is therefore possible that a vigorous investment recovery could begin if business were to choose to make up for lost time. President Carter clearly had this in mind in deciding to withdraw the rebate. The additional impetus of the rebate would have made such a recovery somewhat more likely with a limited risk of increased inflation, however, particularly in light of the enormous underutilization in the economy today and the speed of the action of the rebate.

Expectations of conditions under President Carter's economic policy could be summarized as follows. For the balance of calendar 1977, fiscal policy will be no more expansionary than was expected under the Ford budget. In all likelihood real growth will be between 4 and 5 percent. Late in 1977 a large increase in spending on job creation programs is scheduled to begin; whether this spending is on time or late is one of the big question marks in the economic outlook. Without this spending in late 1977, economic growth may be slow in 1978, with only marginal progress against unemployment. An alternative scenario for these two years is a more rapid recovery sparked by consumer spending early in 1977 and sharply higher investment spending late in the year.

CHAPTER FOUR

The Defense Budget

BARRY M. BLECHMAN *and* OTHERS

IN FISCAL YEAR 1978 the U.S. defense budget will again increase
substantially, the result of planning decisions taken three years ago.
At that time, the Ford administration argued that the decline in
defense spending and military force levels since 1968 had gone about
as far as it could without endangering the nation's security. Consequently, larger defense appropriations were requested to increase the
number of Army divisions, Navy ships, and Air Force tactical aircraft wings, accelerate the modernization of both strategic and conventional weapon systems, and improve the readiness of military units
for combat. In the face of a growing Soviet military threat, administration spokesmen stated, a sustained defense buildup was necessary
to assure U.S. security "over the long-haul." Even on the assumption
that substantial savings would be realized by more efficient management of defense resources, this meant a steady rise in spending in real
terms (i.e., after allowing for inflation) well into the future. Although
Congress refused to authorize real growth in defense obligations in
fiscal 1975, it did approve the principal elements of the Ford program, making future increases inevitable. The defense budget has
risen each year since.

The importance of fiscal 1975 as a turning point in U.S. defense

The authors are grateful to Edward R. Fried for his advice and comments, to
Penelope Harpold, Christine Lipsey, and John Baker for ensuring accuracy, and to
Georgina S. Hernandez for typing the manuscript.
See individual sections for their authors.

Table 4-1. Trend of the Defense Budget, Current and Constant Fiscal 1978 Dollars, Selected Fiscal Years, 1964–82

Component	1964	1968	1975	1977	1978[a]	1982[b]
Total obligational authority						
(billions of current dollars)	50.6	75.6	87.8	110.2	120.4	166.8
Baseline forces	48.4	53.6	79.2	100.9	110.3	153.7
Retired pay	1.2	2.1	6.2	8.2	9.1	12.1
Military assistance	1.0	.6	1.6	1.1	1.0	1.0
Cost of Vietnam War	...	19.3	.9	...	...	...
Total outlays (billions of						
current dollars)	50.8	78.0	86.0	98.3	110.1	156.4
Total obligational authority						
(billions of 1978 dollars)	124.7	154.7	106.6	116.9	120.4	138.6
Baseline forces	119.5	113.3	95.7	107.1	110.3	128.0
Retired pay	3.1	4.6	7.8	8.7	9.1	9.8
Military assistance	2.1	1.1	1.9	1.1	1.0	.8
Cost of Vietnam War	...	37.7	1.2	...	...	...
Total outlays (billions of 1978						
dollars)	123.2	158.3	105.0	104.6	109.7	129.2
Total defense outlays as a percentage of						
GNP	8.2	9.4	5.9	5.5	5.6	5.4
Federal budget outlays	42.9	43.6	26.4	23.9	25.0	28.0

Sources: 1964–77, from data provided by the Department of Defense, 1977; 1978 budget from Department of Defense, "Annual Defense Department Report, FY 1978" (January 17, 1977; processed), and "FY 1978 Amended Department of Defense Budget," news release 72-77 (February 22, 1977); 1982 projections from Department of Defense, "FY 1978 Department of Defense Budget," news release 17-77 (January 17, 1977). Figures are rounded.
a. As proposed by the Ford administration and amended by President Carter.
b. As projected by the Ford administration.

policy is reflected in the budgetary data shown in table 4-1. By then, as measured in constant dollars, defense expenditures had declined by one-third from the Vietnam War peak. This decline proved to be an important source for financing both domestic programs and tax reductions. Actually, the reduction in defense spending amounted to more than a dismantling of the additional forces that had been created to fight the war. If the effects of inflation are discounted, the fiscal 1975 cost of baseline forces (excluding retired pay, military assistance, and residual Vietnam War expenses) was about one-fifth lower than in fiscal 1964, the last pre-Vietnam peacetime budget. From 1964 levels, military manpower in 1975 was down by one-fifth, the number of Navy ships by close to one-half, and the number of strategic defensive forces by more than two-thirds.

The defense buildup that began three years ago is reversing these

Table 4-2. Changes in Total Obligational Authority for Baseline Forces between Fiscal Years 1975 and 1978
Billions of fiscal 1978 dollars

Component	Change
Procurement	13.8
Purchases for operations and maintenance	3.3
Research and development	1.7
Pay and related items	−1.7
Military construction	−0.6
Total	16.5

Source: Authors' estimates derived from data provided by the Office of the Assistant Secretary of Defense, (Comptroller), March 1977.

trends. For fiscal 1978 President Ford requested authority to obligate $123 billion for national defense; $13 billion more than the previous year, or an increase of $7 billion (6 percent) allowing for inflation. Further annual real increases of 3 percent were projected for fiscal 1979 through 1982. The Ford 1978 defense budget would have shown real growth of $16.5 billion, or 16 percent, from fiscal 1975, most of which would have been earmarked for investment—to procure new military hardware and to expand research and development. The cost of defense manpower, a rising expense in the first half of the 1970s, has actually declined slightly during the past three years (table 4-2). As shown in table 4-3, the five categories of combat forces have shared this increase in procurement funds in rough proportion to their share of the total budget, except for a relative increase in the amount allocated to tactical air forces at the expense of ground combat forces.

President Carter's amendments to the 1978 budget would not change this picture much. His proposals would reduce total obligational authority for defense by $2.8 billion and outlays by $400 million. Some weapon programs would be terminated (e.g., the nuclear strike cruiser, the A-7 aircraft, and the nonnuclear version of the LANCE missile); for others, the number to be purchased in fiscal 1978 would be cut back (e.g., the B-1 bomber and the F-15 fighter); and the decision to go ahead with some programs would be deferred (e.g., procurement of a new tanker-cargo aircraft and full-scale development of the M-X missile). Although these changes may signal important future shifts in defense priorities, in themselves they neither constitute a clear departure in force planning nor necessarily presage

Table 4-3. Distribution of the Increase in Procurement Authorizations
between Fiscal Years 1975 and 1978
Amounts in billions of fiscal 1978 dollars

Type of force	Increase in procurement funds, 1975–78		Type of force as a percentage of baseline budget, 1975
	Amount	Percentage of total	
Tactical air[a]	4.4	32	25
Ground combat[b]	3.6	26	31
Strategic[c]	2.8	20	21
Naval[d]	2.7	20	20
Mobility	0.3	2	3
Total	13.8	100	100

Sources: Authors' estimates derived from data appearing in *The Budget of the United States Government—Appendix*, fiscal years 1975–78; Department of Defense, "Program Acquisition Costs by Weapon System, Department of Defense Budget for Fiscal Year 1975," and for fiscal years 1976, 1977, and 1978. Each type of combat force's share of the total baseline budget is calculated by the methodology used in previous editions of *Setting National Priorities*, in which all support costs, direct and indirect, are allocated ot combat forces.

a. One-half of the increase would be used for procurement of Air Force fighter-attack aircraft; the remainder for support equipment, ordnance, and electronic warfare. Navy aircraft procurement remained roughly constant in real terms.

b. The proposed increase would be spread among hundreds of items. Total tank acquisition (M-48, M-60, and XM-1) would show net real growth of about $0.4 billion; Marine Corps equipment purchases would rise by $0.2 billion.

c. Increase accounted for by strategic submarine and missile programs and manned bombers and their armament. These rises would be offset somewhat by decreased spending for land-based missiles.

d. Spending for nuclear-powered submarines and surface ships would remain roughly constant; the increase would be used mainly for conventionally powered escorts.

future reductions in military spending. In effect, the new administration has not yet articulated the direction of its defense planning.[1]

For present purposes, therefore, it can be assumed that, as outlined in President Ford's budget, defense expenditures are likely to (1) rise at about the same rate as the gross national product, declining only slightly to 5.4 percent of the nation's resources; and (2) absorb a moderately rising proportion of the total federal budget, growing from the present 25 percent to about 28 percent over the next five years. In relative terms, this budgetary prospect is by no means alarming; the proportionate burden of defense will remain substantially lower than it was ten or fifteen years ago. Nonetheless, budgetary resources will continue to be scarce in the years ahead. Hence, the fact that the level of defense expenditures is already large in absolute

1. In general, compared to the Ford defense program, the Carter budget amendments indicate less emphasis on strategic nuclear forces, a more stringent review of the need for high-cost weapon systems, greater emphasis on strengthening U.S. military capabilities in Europe, and a shift away from nuclear-powered surface warships. The significance of these changes for future defense costs cannot be determined, however, until next year's budget, which the Carter administration alone will shape.

terms and will rise further in the future poses difficult questions about how the requirements of national security should be met and about how those requirements compare with competing national priorities.

In seeking reasons for the continuing buildup of U.S. military capabilities, we should look to the political scene abroad, which has in some respects improved recently but still remains dangerous.

Both the Syrian and the Egyptian governments appear to have adopted a more moderate approach to the issues concerning Israel and the Palestinians. There seems at least a chance that negotiations between Israel and its neighbors will begin this year. Moreover, the Soviet position in the Middle East has continued to erode both politically and militarily. Consequently, for the next year or so, the likelihood of a new Arab-Israeli conflict with its attendant risk of U.S. military involvement seems low.

In China, the uncertainty about who would succeed Mao has been resolved, and a pragmatic leadership seemingly committed to continuing rapprochement with the United States has come to power. Elsewhere in East Asia, fears that the U.S. defeat in Indochina would result in new fighting in Southeast Asia or in a more aggressive stance by the North Koreans appear to have been ill founded. For the present, at least, political relations in East Asia are relatively calm.

On the other hand, Soviet policy has not changed. The USSR clearly is willing to use force, or to support the use of force by others, to exploit opportunities for expanding its influence in the third world. The tough stance adopted by communist officials against dissidents in the USSR, East Germany, and Czechoslovakia and renewed pressure on Yugoslavia show that Soviet leaders are determined to maintain their control of Eastern Europe. And the buildup of Soviet armed forces continues without apparent letup.

A sober judgment thus would be that the risk of U.S.-Soviet armed confrontation remains what it has been for many years: low though not negligible. Although it has been possible to reach some arms control agreements with the Russians and the East-West political situation in Europe has been stabilized, U.S.-Soviet relations are still the uneasy mixture of cooperation and competition that has marked them throughout the postwar period. In judging the risk of conflict, however, one must concentrate on the conflicts within specific countries or regions that could bring the superpowers into collision.

Although there has been some improvement in the Middle East, the gap between the Arab and Israeli terms for peace remains wide. If progress toward resolution of these differences remains elusive, the dynamics of Arab politics will make it difficult to avoid hostilities once Egyptian and Syrian military capabilities have been strengthened sufficiently. In the event of a new war, the possibility of Soviet intervention could not be precluded. If that occurred, only U.S. counteraction could restore the balance.

The results of continuing tension between Eastern European nationalism and Soviet domination are hard to predict. There are special risks in Yugoslavia, where post-Tito internal conflict could lead to Soviet intervention, which, if it did not succeed quickly, could lead to wider conflict.

In Korea, two hostile and seemingly unpredictable regimes confront each other. Conflict is deterred by the existence of a rough balance of military power on the peninsula and the restraints imposed by the major powers. If that balance should change—through expansion on one side and decline on the other or through internal disruption in one of the Korean states—conflict could ensue. Neither the United States nor the USSR could in such a circumstance readily countenance the destruction of its ally.

Admittedly the risks of such confrontations are small. A succession of Arab-Israeli wars has failed to involve U.S. and Soviet military forces in armed conflict. The likelihood of Soviet intervention and Western counterintervention in Yugoslavia is low. The likelihood of large-scale aggression in Korea is slight. Still, the risks are there and, taken together, they are not trivial. And even where there now appears to be virtually no risk of conflict—notably in Central Europe—most observers agree that the maintenance of a stable and visible balance of military power is essential to prevent adverse political developments.

None of this is new. But one factor has changed: the quality and quantity of military power that the Soviet Union can bring to bear in support of its political objectives around the world. It is this worrisome evolution of Soviet military capabilities that has provided the main impetus for a rising U.S. defense budget and the receptive attitude toward higher defense appropriations of Congress and the public.

Developments in Soviet Military Capabilities*

In dollar terms, Soviet defense outlays for 1976 are estimated to have been $120 billion, about one-third more than those of the United States.[2] This estimate is derived by assessing the size of the Soviet defense effort in some detail, and costing each operational unit, procurement program, and so forth, at U.S. prices. This methodology has its drawbacks. For instance, measuring the Soviet defense budget in U.S. defense prices means that the high pay scales of a volunteer army are applied to the large conscripted force of the Soviet Union. This is illogical because if the USSR had to pay American wages to its military personnel it probably would not maintain so large a standing force. The CIA also measures the Soviet defense budget in rubles, but this too causes problems—principally because the ruble price of many items of military hardware can only be approximated very roughly. Still, so long as common assumptions are applied, comparisons of annual data on Soviet defense spending, expressed in either rubles or dollars, can indicate important trends.

Since the mid-1960s, these data reveal steady growth in the Soviet defense budget, averaging about 3 percent annually when expressed in constant U.S. prices, and around 5 percent annually when expressed in rubles. This suggests a cumulative increase over the period of between 40 and 70 percent. These aggregate figures, however, cloak important distinctions in the relative emphasis placed on different types of forces; they are best examined individually.

Strategic Nuclear Forces

Soviet leaders accord high priority to the strategic rocket forces. Since 1964 Soviet aggregate strategic nuclear capabilities have increased roughly fivefold (see table 4-4). Improvements have been made steadily and continue to be made.

At present, three new types of intercontinental ballistic missiles (ICBMs) are being deployed, deployment of a fourth is expected shortly, and two new types of submarine-launched ballistic missiles (SLBMs) have been flight-tested. Four of the six can be equipped with multiple independently targetable reentry vehicles (MIRVs);

* This section was prepared by Robert P. Berman.
2. U.S. Central Intelligence Agency, "A Dollar Cost Comparison of Soviet and U.S. Defense Activities, 1966–1976," SR 77-10001U (January 1977; processed).

Table 4-4. Soviet Strategic Forces, 1964, 1970, and 1976

Description	1964ᵃ	1970	1976
Force levels (launchers)	473	1,685	2,498
ICBMs	190	1,287	1,567
SLBMs	108	254	791
Heavy bombers (long range)	175	145	140
Throw-weight (millions of pounds)ᵇ	2.2	6.6	9.6
Missiles only	.8	5.5	8.6
Targetable warheads (missile reentry vehicles and bombs)ᶜ	649	1,832	3,228
Missiles only	298	1,541	2,948
Equivalent megatonnageᵈ	1,102	3,396	4,861
Missiles only	534	2,923	4,406

Sources: Authors' estimates derived from International Institute for Strategic Studies, *The Military Balance, 1976–1977* (London: IISS, 1976), pp. 8, 73–75; Stockholm International Peace Research Institute, *World Armaments and Disarmament: SIPRI Yearbook 1976* (M.I.T. Press, 1976), pp. 24–27; "Annual Defense Department Report, FY 1978," p. 58; and declassified posture statements of the Secretaries of Defense to the U.S. Congress, Fiscal Years 1963–73 (processed).

    a. Figures for 1964 include *Golf*-class and *Zulu*-class ballistic missile submarines.

    b. The weight-carrying capacity of missiles and bombers is not directly comparable. This index includes the payload of each system that could be used to carry nuclear weapons, its protective structure, and associated guidance system.

    c. Targetable warheads include only weapons associated with on-line forces.

    d. Equivalent megatonnage is a measure of the area destruction capacity of a nuclear arsenal based on the number and explosive yields of its various component weapons and the fact that the extent of the ground area that would be destroyed by a nuclear explosion does not increase one-to-one with increases in the yield of the nuclear warhead.

all incorporate significant improvements in accuracy. Six additional intercontinental missile systems are said to be in earlier stages of development and may be operational in the 1980s.

Soviet strategic air defenses also are being modernized, despite declining budgetary emphasis on this function. Although the number of interceptor aircraft in PVO Strany, the USSR's air defense command, has dropped by about one-third since 1964, the force's total capabilities are probably greater now because of the introduction of advanced surface-to-air missiles, aircraft, and radars.

Other developments in Soviet military capabilities have also raised concern among some American observers because of their possible implications for the outcome of strategic nuclear conflicts.

• A new medium-range bomber, Backfire, and a new intermediate-range ballistic missile, SS-20, are being deployed. Although both systems appear to be primarily designed for use in Europe or against China, they could be used against the United States. The Backfire could reach targets in the continental United States if refueled during flight, staged through Arctic bases, or recovered in third nations (e.g.,

Cuba). The SS-20 apparently uses the same transporter and the first two stages of a new Soviet ICBM. Some American analysts believe that as a consequence deployed SS-20s could be converted rapidly for intercontinental use.

• Since 1971, Soviet civil defense efforts seem to have intensified. These include the construction of hardened command-and-control centers and storage sites for various critical items, the preparation of city evacuation plans, and possibly measures to protect essential industrial plants from nuclear attack.

• Finally, the Soviet Union has been experimenting with techniques to destroy satellites. An attack on U.S. early warning and other intelligence and communications satellites would probably be the first step in any sizable nuclear exchange.

Although the individual significance of each of these measures is a matter of some controversy, the sheer scope and momentum of the Soviet strategic program is not, and has caused widespread concern in the United States.

Ground Forces

The ground forces dominate the Soviet defense establishment. From 1964 to 1976 Soviet ground forces expanded from 140 divisions to 170, an increase of 21 percent, and were extensively redeployed. The largest increase took place in the Far East, where more than 26 divisions have been sent since 1964. The number of Soviet divisions deployed in Eastern Europe was increased from 26 to 31 when one of the army groups that occupied Czechoslovakia in 1968 remained there. In the western Soviet Union, where the immediate strategic reserve for war in Europe is located, the number of divisions increased from 60 to 66.

Changes in the structure of Soviet ground forces are summarized in table 4-5. Although the greatest growth in divisions occurred in the Far East, one-half of the Soviet Army is clearly positioned for war in Europe. There are other indications of this priority. New types of equipment for the ground forces, for example, are usually deployed first to Soviet forces in Eastern Europe, particularly to the Group of Soviet Forces Germany. Indeed, the size of each of the 20 divisions that now make up the GSFG has been increased, with a better than 20 percent rise in the manpower assigned to each, a 40 percent increase in the number of tanks in each of the 10 motorized rifle divi-

Table 4-5. Changes in Soviet Ground Forces, by Type and Location, 1964 and 1976
Number of divisions

Type	Eastern Europe		Western USSR		Far East		Central and southern USSR	
	1964	1976	1964	1976	1964	1976	1964	1976
Armored	13	16	20	23	3	7	14	4
Motorized	13	15	34	37	13	35	23	26
Airborne	0	0	6	6	1	1	0	0
Total[a]	26	31	60	66	17	43	37	30

Sources: Authors' estimates derived from data appearing in IISS, *The Military Balance, 1964–1965* (London: IISS, 1964); IISS, *The Military Balance, 1976–1977;* and *Fiscal Year 1978 Authorization for Military Procurement, Research and Development, and Active Duty, Selected Reserve, and Civilian Personnel Strengths,* Hearings before the Senate Armed Services Committee, 95:1 (GPO, 1977), pt. 2, p. 1155.

a. There are also twenty mobilization divisions (including at least one airborne unit) that are under strength but assigned full division equipment sets.

sions, and a doubling of the artillery assets in both motorized rifle units and armored divisions. The net effect has been to further increase the shock power of the GSFG, which remains the preeminent combat force in Europe.

Qualitative improvements in equipment for Soviet ground forces have also been impressive. New tanks and armored personnel carriers, clearly superior in design to their predecessors, have been deployed. Soviet armored personnel carriers now mount cannons and antitank weapons, the first in any army to do so. The mobility of Soviet forces is improved because towed artillery has been augmented with self-propelled units and because mobile gun and missile air defense systems have been introduced. These new weapons finally provide the mobility and firepower needed to generate the shock power and achieve the rapid advance long emphasized in Soviet military doctrine.

Naval Forces

Since 1964 the Soviet Navy has accounted for a relatively steady and relatively small (less than 20 percent) share of the Soviet defense budget. As a result, from 1964 to 1976 the number of major surface combatants dropped by about 5 percent, the number of minor surface combatants by nearly 35 percent, and the number of submarines by 35 percent. Still, despite its smaller size, the Soviet Navy is a more capable force today than it was in 1964. Aggregate tonnage, a crude measure of capabilities, increased considerably, and there were sharp jumps in the number of surface-to-surface and surface-to-air missile systems deployed on Soviet warships. Conventional submarines were

Table 4-6. Soviet Naval General Purpose Forces and Capabilities, 1964 and 1976

Description	1964	1976
Aircraft carriers	0	1
Helicopter cruisers	0	2
Cruisers	20	31
Destroyers	114	87
Frigates	102	107
Minor combatants carrying missiles	110	137
Minor combatants	700	391
Conventional submarines	371	176
Nuclear submarines	22	78
Amphibious ships	12	82
Minesweepers	450	365
Other[a]	250	255
Total displacement (millions of tons)	2.2	2.6
Surface-to-surface missile launchers	456	1,270
Surface-to-air missile rails	20	302
Area (long-range) antisubmarine weapons	0	184

Sources: Authors' estimates derived from IISS, *The Military Balance, 1964–1965*, pp. 5–6; *Jane's Fighting Ships, 1965–1966* (McGraw-Hill, 1965), pp. 425–46; IISS, *The Military Balance, 1976–1977*, pp. 8–9; *Jane's Fighting Ships, 1976–1977* (McGraw-Hill, 1976), pp. 688–753; and *Fiscal Year 1978 Authorization for Military Procurement*, Hearings, pt. 2, p. 945.

a. Includes a variety of support ships, such as intelligence collection vessels, oilers, repair ships, and depot ships.

replaced with nuclear-powered submarines. Moreover, a new type of weapon system—area (long-range) antisubmarine torpedo and rocket launchers—first appeared on Soviet warships during the period and have been deployed extensively since. These changes are summarized in table 4-6.

The primary mission of the Soviet Navy continues to be defensive: to protect the Soviet Union from Western sea-based strike forces and to deter the latter from intervening in regions, like the Middle East, close to Soviet shores. In the first instance, Soviet naval forces are directed against Western aircraft carrier task groups deployed in waters such as the Mediterranean, where their aircraft are capable of striking Soviet territory. As the range of these carrier-based aircraft has grown, Soviet naval forces have had to be deployed further and further from Soviet territory to carry out this mission.

Increasingly in recent years, however, the threat to the USSR from the seas has originated not from the aircraft carrier but from the strategic submarine. The Soviet Union also has deployed a considerable portion of its strategic capabilities at sea in submarines. Accordingly, emphasis in Soviet naval construction and operations has turned more and more to antisubmarine warfare—both to protect

Soviet strategic submarines and to be able to destroy Western strategic submarines should a nuclear exchange appear imminent.

By virtually all accounts, the Soviet Navy poses little threat to Western submarines. However, the recent deployment of the first *Kuril*-class aircraft carrier (at least two more are under construction) could help Soviet strategic submarines penetrate the barriers that Western navies would establish in attempts to prevent the submarines from reaching their operating areas in times of crisis or war.

Of course, the Soviet Navy could be used for many other missions. In the event of war in Europe, its attack submarines could attempt to isolate the continent, preventing U.S. reinforcements and supplies from arriving in time. In peacetime, the Soviet Navy promotes Soviet interests abroad, supports Soviet foreign policy, and counters Western efforts at "gunboat diplomacy." On the other hand, there are some things that the Soviet Navy cannot do because it continues to lack capabilities essential to projecting Soviet power into distant regions against opposition: significant sea-based air power, amphibious assault capabilities, underway replenishment and at-sea repair capabilities, an extensive network of overseas bases, and greater endurance in its warships.

Air Forces

The Soviet Union maintains five separate air components, each with a special mission. As shown in table 4-7, the relative emphasis given to each changed markedly between 1964 and 1976.

As noted, the air defense forces have been de-emphasized, suffering a one-third cut in strength. The main beneficiary of this reallocation of resources was Frontal Aviation—the tactical air arm, whose missions are to support Soviet ground forces by attacking maneuvering NATO forces and to stage independent air strikes against targets such as enemy airfields. Frontal Aviation's fixed-wing assets were increased by about one-third; its load-carrying capacity was more than doubled. Like the ground forces they support, about one-half of Frontal Aviation's aircraft are deployed for European operations and one-fourth for the Far East; the remainder are held in reserve.

These changes in the size and capability of Frontal Aviation reflect significant changes in Soviet military doctrine. In the past, Soviet tactical aviation was controlled directly by the ground forces or used for defensive operations behind the battle lines. Now, Soviet ground

Table 4-7. Soviet Air Forces and Their Composition, 1964 and 1976

	1964		1976	
Description	Fixed wing	Helicopters	Fixed wing	Helicopters
Air Defense Command				
Number of aircraft	4,040	...	2,590	...
Total weight (millions of pounds)ᵃ	65.6	...	86.4	...
Naval Aviation				
Number of aircraft	800	200	950	250
Long-Range Aviation				
Number of aircraft	1,100	...	849	...
Frontal Aviation				
Number of aircraft	3,360	n.a.	4,600	2,950
Offensive load-carrying capacity (millions of ton-miles)ᵇ	1.2	...	3.2	...
Military Transport Aviation				
Number of aircraft	1,700	790	1,550	320
Total lift (millions of ton-miles)ᶜ	9.5	n.a.	25.8	n.a.

Sources: Authors' estimates derived from James D. Hessman, "The Soviet Union Moves Ahead: On Land, On the Sea, and In the Air," *Armed Forces Journal* (August 17, 1970), p. 34; IISS, *The Military Balance, 1976–77*, p. 10; *Allocation of Resources in the Soviet Union and China—1975*, Hearings before the Subcommittee on Priorities and Economy in Government of the Joint Economic Committee, 94:1 (GPO, 1975), pt. 1, p. 148; and William Green and Gordon Swanborough, *The Observer's Soviet Aircraft Directory* (Frederic Warne, 1975).

n.a. Not available.

a. A rough measure of aggregate capability; heavier aircraft often have greater range and carry more avionics and air-to-air missiles. The relation between weight and capability is influenced by numerous factors, however, including the materials used to construct the aircraft, engine efficiency, and the aircraft's design.

b. The product of combat radius and payload, summed over all Frontal Aviation aircraft.

c. The product of combat range and lift capacity per day, summed over all airlift aircraft assigned to Military Transport Aviation.

forces themselves are responsible for gaining air superiority over the battlefield and providing fire support to front-line troops through the use of mobile gun and missile air defense systems, artillery, and rockets. Freed of its past defensive responsibilities, Frontal Aviation is being equipped with aircraft with lesser dog-fighting capabilities but longer ranges and larger payloads. By the early 1980s, it will be able to launch conventional strikes at primary NATO airbases, nuclear storage sites, and command-and-control facilities at the onset of a European war. Such an attack could severely cripple NATO.[3]

Increases in the strength of Soviet military units and improvements in Soviet weapon systems are not sufficient reason to spend more

3. Changes in Soviet air forces are described in detail in Robert P. Berman, *Soviet Air Power in Transition* (Brookings Institution, 1977).

money on U.S. military forces. For one thing, gains in Soviet military capabilities must be judged in light of past and prospective changes in U.S. and allied military capabilities; they are constantly improving, too. Needed are net assessments of relative capabilities—judgments about the changes likely to occur in the military balance should present trends continue—and of the consequences of the changes that seem likely. Obviously, when Soviet military capabilities do not directly threaten U.S. interests—for instance, forces on the Chinese border—a Soviet gain may not require a U.S. response. Judgments like these are discussed in the two sections that follow; first for strategic nuclear forces and then for general purpose (conventional) forces.

The Strategic Balance

Since 1960 U.S. strategic offensive forces have had three components. Land-based ICBMs now consist of 1,000 Minuteman missiles and 54 older Titan missiles. Five hundred and fifty of the Minuteman missiles are equipped with MIRVs, usually three reentry vehicles per missile. These systems permit each missile to deliver nuclear warheads to a number of targets spaced quite far apart. Sea-based strategic forces consist of thirty-one Poseidon and ten Polaris nuclear-powered submarines, each carrying sixteen intermediate-range SLBMs. The missiles on the Poseidon submarines also carry MIRVs. Strategic bomber forces consist of twenty squadrons of B-52 long-range heavy bombers armed with air-to-surface missiles and gravity bombs, plus four squadrons of intermediate-range FB-111 bombers similarly armed.

Together, the three offensive components form what is known as the triad. Because each system depends on different techniques to assure its survivability against a Soviet first strike or its ability to penetrate Soviet defenses, each is believed to be capable of carrying out a retaliatory mission independently. The maintenance of these relatively independent capabilities in three separate components is a hedge against the sudden appearance of countermeasures that would negate the effectiveness of any two of the components.

Each of these strategic components is now being modernized at substantial cost. Between fiscal 1975 and 1978 spending for the procurement of strategic weapon systems increased by $2.8 billion in constant 1978 dollars. By the early 1980s annual real expenditures for strategic forces could rise by another $4 billion to $5 billion.

Specifics of the modernization program are outlined below.

ICBMs. A higher-yield warhead known as the Mark 12A has been designed for Minuteman missiles, and the missile's guidance system is being improved to increase its accuracy. These measures will greatly improve the capability of the Minuteman force to destroy hardened targets. Minuteman silos also have been upgraded to improve their hardness and survivability.

At the same time, a new ICBM—the M-X—is being developed to replace Minuteman. Under present plans, the M-X would be mobile, designed to move along hardened and covered trenches. Because the precise location of any one M-X would not be known, many warheads would have to be fired at each trench to be sure of destroying the missile inside. Thus, deployment of this weapon system could offset any gain in the USSR's ability to destroy hardened targets. The M-X would also provide the United States with much greater capability for destroying hardened targets because it could carry more and larger warheads than Minuteman. Under the Ford 1978 budget, the M-X missile would attain an initial operational capability in December of 1983, one year earlier than was envisioned in the fiscal 1977 program. The Carter budget restored the program to its former schedule.

The decision whether to acquire the M-X missile, and if so, what specific characteristics it should have, will be the single most important weapon system decision faced by the Carter administration. The program will be extremely expensive, primarily because of the cost of constructing the trenches. Preliminary estimates indicate that it would cost around $34 billion to deploy a force of 300 missiles; 40 percent of this amount would be used for construction. More important, the design of the missile is at the heart of the dispute over U.S. strategic planning and force posture. Because mobile missiles greatly complicate the verification of arms control agreements, the United States has resisted building such weapons for many years, making a unilateral statement in connection with the 1972 strategic arms limitation talks (SALT) agreements that it would consider the deployment of land-mobile missiles as violating the spirit of these accords. This philosophy obviously has changed in recent years, mainly because of concern about the survivability of fixed-site ICBMs like Minuteman.

SLBMs. The present U.S. force of strategic submarines was constructed between 1959 and 1967. Because submarines generally require about five years to build and last about twenty to twenty-five years, new submarines must be authorized now if the SLBM force is to remain at its present size. Such a program has been pursued for several years. Eleven new *Ohio*-class submarines have been authorized already; two more were requested for fiscal 1978 in both the Ford and the Carter budgets. The *Ohio* class is much larger than existing Poseidon submarines and carries 50 percent more missiles. It will also be faster, quieter, and capable of operating at greater depths than present strategic submarines.

A new missile is also being built—the Trident I. This missile would be deployed on *Ohio*-class submarines and also retrofitted into ten existing Poseidon submarines. Trident I missiles, which would carry MIRVs, would have a range of about 4,000 nautical miles; the Poseidon's range is 3,000 miles or so. A second generation Trident missile—Trident II—is in a much earlier research stage. This missile would have a 6,000-mile range and potentially could be much more accurate than Trident I if fitted, as has been suggested, with maneuvering reentry vehicles.[4]

Bombers. The Air Force plans to replace existing strategic bombers with the B-1, a high performance aircraft designed to penetrate the dense and technologically sophisticated Soviet air defenses that are expected to exist toward the end of the century. The Ford program envisioned buying 244 B-1 bombers; the first eight production models were included in the fiscal 1978 budget. The Carter budget reduced the fiscal 1978 request to five aircraft, and withheld judgment on the full program.

The primary armaments for the B-1 would be SRAMs (short-range attack missiles) and gravity bombs. B-1s, as well as existing B-52s, also would be armed with long-range air-launched cruise missiles. Cruise missiles would be used to saturate Soviet area defenses; SRAMs, which have much greater speeds but more limited range,

4. Maneuvering reentry vehicles would be powered and guided during the final stages of their flight, rather than falling freely on a ballistic trajectory as do existing reentry vehicles.

would be used to attack targets that are heavily defended by surface-to-air missiles.

Cruise missiles. These new weapons have more far-reaching implications. Two cruise missiles are now under development. The Air Force program would produce an air-launched missile to be carried in bombers. The missile emerging from the Navy program, Tomahawk, could be deployed on aircraft, on surface ships, on submarines (from which it could be fired through the torpedo tubes), or on mobile ground launchers. If this missile were deployed on a ship or ground launcher, it in effect would add a fourth offensive component to the U.S. strategic force posture. The Ford and Carter budgets maintain both cruise missile programs virtually intact.

U.S. strategic air defenses. These also are being modernized. Both force levels and a planned modernization program for air defenses were cut back sharply following the 1972 SALT agreements. All surface-to-air missiles previously assigned to the Continental Air Defense Command have been phased out of the force structure; the number of interceptor aircraft has also been reduced. At present, U.S. strategic defensive forces include only six interceptor aircraft squadrons on active duty and eleven squadrons assigned to the Air National Guard, and several early warning systems. There are other aircraft and some surface-to-air missiles located in the United States that would provide air defense in the event of an attack, but for one reason or another these forces are not counted in the strategic category.

The continuing momentum in the Soviet strategic program and particularly the development of the Backfire bomber have led to new pressure to rebuild U.S. continental air defenses. The first explicit result of this pressure was included in President Ford's 1978 budget: $30 million to initiate the procurement of F-15 aircraft configured as interceptors to replace the F-106 aircraft now in the force. President Carter's budget proposal deferred this request pending reevaluation of air defense requirements. But two other elements of what had been planned for strategic air defense modernization have continued in development, despite the cutback in strategic air defense, because both also have roles in the general purpose forces; their strategic mission is again coming to the fore. The first is the Airborne Warning and Control System (AWACS), which is viewed as a survivable way both to detect low-flying aircraft and to ensure command and control

Table 4-8. Indexes of U.S. Strategic Capabilities in 1977, and upon Completion of the B-1, M-X, and Trident Programs

Description	1977	Modernized[a]
Force levels (launchers)	2,127	1,964
Missiles only	1,710	1,720
Throw-weight (millions of pounds)[b]	9.26	11.78
Missiles only	5.06	6.90
Independently targetable warheads		
(missile reentry vehicles and bombs)	8,557	13,864
Missiles only	6,823	9,960
Equivalent megatonnage[c]	2,847	6,464
Missiles only	1,905	3,737

Sources: Authors' estimates derived from IISS, *The Military Balance, 1976–1977*, pp. 5, 106–08; "Annual Defense Department Report for FY 1978," pp. 58–79; *Full Committee Consideration of Overall National Security Programs and Related Budget Requirements*, Hearings before the House Committee on the Armed Services, 94:1 (GPO, 1975), pp. 228, 247; Donald E. Fink, "Minuteman Experience Aiding MX," *Aviation Week and Space Technology*, vol. 105 (July 19, 1976), pp. 113–20; and Clarence A. Robinson, Jr., "New Propellant Evaluated for Trident Second Stage," *Aviation Week and Space Technology*, vol. 103 (October 13, 1975), pp. 15–19.

a. The "modernized force" is assumed to be consistent with the constraints imposed by the 1974 Vladivostok accord. It consists of 300 M-X ICBMs, 300 Minuteman III ICBMs, and 720 Trident SLBMs, for a total of 1,320 MIRV-carrying missiles; plus 400 Minuteman II ICBMs and 244 B-1s. The B-52s are assumed to have been phased out by the time all these new systems have been acquired. If Trident II were introduced, there would be a 33 percent increase in missile throw-weight and a 20 percent increase in total throw-weight; a 43 percent increase in missile warheads and a 31 percent increase in total warheads; and a 43 percent increase in missile equivalent megatonnage and a 25 percent increase in total equivalent megatonnage.

b. The weight-carrying capacity of missiles and bombers is not directly comparable. This index includes the payload of each system that could be used to carry nuclear weapons, its protective structure, and associated guidance system.

c. Equivalent megatonnage is a measure of the area destruction capacity of a nuclear arsenal based on the number and explosive yields of its various component weapons and the fact that the extent of the ground area that would be destroyed by a nuclear explosion does not increase one-to-one with increases in the yield of the nuclear warhead.

of the air defense battle. The purchase of nineteen of these aircraft has already been authorized, ostensibly to be used in Europe. But Air Force spokesmen state that of the twenty-eight AWACS aircraft the United States plans to buy, only seven would be earmarked for NATO. Four more would be used for air defense over the North Atlantic, and the remainder would be designated for the defense of North America—strategic air defense. NATO requirements are to be filled by additional AWACS aircraft purchased by European nations. Second, a new and very capable surface-to-air missile system, known as Patriot, also is continuing in development. This system is being developed primarily for use on NATO battlefields, but it could also be used for continental air defense should a decision be taken to rebuild the U.S. system.

Together, these programs would substantially increase U.S. strategic capabilities. Although the total number of strategic launchers (missiles and bombers) would decline somewhat, completion of the B-1 and M-X programs and complete replacement of the Polaris/ Poseidon force with Tridents would significantly increase the throw-weight, number of warheads, and equivalent megatonnage of U.S. strategic forces. This is shown in table 4-8. The deployment of cruise missiles would add to these totals.

The cost would run high. Completing the B-1 program would cost $18 billion; the M-X program would require at least $34 billion; and to build up to a force of thirty Trident submarines would mean expenditures of roughly another $25 billion. Cruise missiles and air defenses would add more. Obviously, many other uses could be found for this money, in both the defense and the domestic sectors. Thus, it is well to ask what eventualities these programs are designed to meet and whether they are likely to accomplish their purposes.

In recent years, Soviet strategic deployments have given rise to two kinds of concern in the United States.

The most specific pertains to an expected Soviet advantage in the two nations' relative ability to destroy hardened targets. Aside from the greater number of missiles in its inventory, the Soviet Union has the advantage in that its missiles are larger than those of the United States (have greater "throw-weight"). This means that Soviet missiles, when equipped with MIRVs, could carry more warheads than U.S. missiles or that each Soviet warhead could have a greater yield, or both. The generation of Soviet missiles now being deployed has accentuated this superior throw-weight. Assuming that eventually the Soviet Union masters the various techniques necessary to achieve the high accuracies that characterize U.S. missiles, sometime in the next decade, unless changes are made in the U.S. force posture, the USSR would have a decided advantage in relative capability for destroying hardened targets, notably missile silos. In extreme crises, it is argued, this superiority would give the USSR more options than would be available to the United States. It could, for example, use a portion of its ICBM force in a first strike against U.S. ICBMs, deterring a U.S. response against Soviet cities or military facilities by dint of the large number of missiles that would remain available to answer any U.S. retaliation. Moreover, the argument goes, such exchanges need not actually occur to have an effect on the course of world affairs. Such Soviet superiority in "hard-target kill capabilities" supposedly could make the United States timid and the Soviet Union bold when confrontations occurred, leading to outcomes unfavorable to the United States.

Although improvements to the Minuteman force will help, the M-X program is the primary way in which the Department of Defense plans to offset this projected Soviet advantage. According to the department, deployment of the M-X would enable the United States to nearly match Soviet "hard-target kill capabilities" throughout the 1980s. Even without the M-X, U.S. hard-target kill capabilities are expected to remain greater than those of the Soviet Union until 1983, the result primarily of deployment of the Minuteman Mark 12A reentry vehicle and improvements in the Minuteman guidance system. Beyond 1983, however, the USSR is expected to outpace the United States in this aspect of the strategic competition unless M-X is deployed. That Soviet capabilities are not expected to rise sharply until 1983 indicates that the ICBMs now being deployed by the USSR are not sufficiently accurate to destroy hardened targets effectively.

Recent changes in the strategic balance have also evoked a less specific, less tangible sort of concern in some Americans—that the sheer pace and range of Soviet strategic developments will soon result in a worldwide image of Soviet power in the ascendant. Although specialists are aware that U.S. strategic capabilities have improved significantly since 1964, these changes have been far less dramatic than the regular unveiling of new Soviet missiles, and it may appear that the United States is being overwhelmed. Such impressions, superficial though they may be, presumably could have political consequences if they became widespread.

At the extreme, such concern is transformed into a fear that the USSR is seeking a capability to fight and survive a nuclear war. Hard-target kill capabilities are an important element in these calculations. Other elements include the enormous resources that the Soviet Union devotes to strategic air defenses, the Soviet civil defense program, and various other programs such as experiments with techniques for destroying early warning satellites. Typically, the war is envisioned as opening with a preemptive Soviet missile attack on U.S. ICBMs, strategic submarine bases, bomber bases, and command-and-control facilities. At the end of this initial salvo, the supposition goes, all that would be left of U.S. strategic forces would be the 30 percent of the

bomber force that is maintained on alert, and the twenty or so strategic submarines that are usually at sea. The former, it is argued,
would suffer such heavy losses from Soviet air defenses that they
would be unable to carry out more than a small part of their retaliatory mission. The latter—though likely to survive any attempt to find
and destroy them—carry missiles with warheads that are too small to
do much damage against a Soviet society protected by extensive civil
defenses. Again, as in worries about Soviet superiority in hard-target
kill capabilities, the concern is not so much that such a war will actually come about but rather that if such a situation became plausible
U.S. political influence would be severely weakened.

Implications of the U.S. strategic modernization program for these
broad political concerns are difficult to assess. Introduction of the
B-1 would certainly enhance the bomber force's ability to penetrate
advanced Soviet air defenses, should they be developed. The greater
throw-weight of Trident II would permit the deployment of higher-
yield warheads on U.S. SLBMs, so that submarines surviving a Soviet
first strike could inflict greater damage on Soviet society, regardless
of civil defense preparations. U.S. air defense modernization would
provide some shield against the marginal threat posed by the Backfire.
In short, each of the measures would reduce whatever limited ability
the Soviet Union developed to wage a nuclear war and survive. Taken
together, the U.S. programs should help to erase the image of Soviet
strategic momentum, with all that might portend for international
behavior during crises and at more peaceful times. Still, questions
remain: whether the worries just described are realistic or more in
the nature of phantoms created by U.S. decisionmakers to which they
are now reacting; and if these worries are well founded, are there less
costly ways to respond?

Are the Worries Realistic?

There seems little doubt that one fear—a growing image of Soviet
momentum and ascendancy in the strategic field—is well founded.
Increasingly, statements by public officials in this country and abroad
and opinion polls of the general population indicate awareness of and
concern about the scope and pace of the Soviet strategic buildup. It is
not clear to what extent the Soviet Union itself shares the view that
it is gaining the upper hand in the strategic balance, but it cannot have
failed to note the apprehension in the West, and that in itself might

lead it to behave rashly under certain circumstances. Although the links between perceptions of relative strategic capabilities and foreign policy behavior are not well understood, the fact that many decision-makers around the world believe such links exist is sufficient reason for prudent defense planners not to discount the phenomenon.

Concern about Soviet hard-target kill capabilities is less easily substantiated. The size and number of its ICBMs certainly provide the Soviet Union with a theoretical ability to destroy most of the United States' ICBMs in a first strike, once it masters the techniques necessary to improve the accuracy of its missiles. But carrying out a pre-emptive first strike is likely to prove far more difficult in practice than in theory. Such a military operation would require split-second timing and coordination, and its effectiveness would be influenced by factors of which we know very little—such as the effects of the first nuclear explosions on warheads arriving later, the reliability of missiles, and so forth.

Moreover, an examination of official statements on relative hard-target kill capabilities over the past few years indicates a proclivity on the part of the United States to emphasize potential Soviet capabilities and to underestimate its own. For example, U.S. officials do not now expect Soviet hard-target kill capabilities to increase significantly until 1982 whereas improvements to Minuteman will soon augment U.S. capabilities; however, statements of U.S. defense officials over the past five to ten years left a more alarming impression.

The most extreme fear—the potential Soviet capacity to fight and survive a nuclear war—is clearly farfetched. The assumptions underlying it present a most optimistic picture from the Soviet perspective and a most pessimistic one for the United States. It is assumed, among other things, that the difficulties of mounting a coordinated, massive attack on U.S. nuclear forces are overcome, that the large number of Soviet weapons that would be involved work reasonably well, that the United States does not launch its own ICBMs upon warning of an attack, that the Soviet Union overcomes the so far impossible task of reliably detecting and intercepting bombers penetrating at low altitudes, and—most incredibly—that civil defenses, such as evacuating cities, are sufficient to protect most of the Soviet population from the nearly 3,000 warheads expected to be launched from U.S. submarines operating at sea and thus surviving the attack, and that these civil defense measures do not, while in preparation, alert the United States that something is afoot.

Moreover, even though those who cling to this worry state that they fear not so much the eventuality of such a war as what forecasts of such capabilities might mean for U.S. political influence, the premise remains the same—that Soviet leaders would gauge the risks associated with this remote combination of assumptions as low enough to make them willing to push hard during serious political confrontations, believing that, should matters by some extreme chance go against them, the Soviet Union could fight a nuclear war and survive relatively well. It is difficult to conceive of a Soviet leader reaching such a conclusion—to rest the fate of his nation and to risk 50 million or 100 million fatalities—on the basis of computer simulations and elaborate assumptions about the course of nuclear war. Certainly no sane person would make such a decision.

How Should the United States Respond?

In view of this assessment, how should the United States respond to the Soviet strategic buildup? Although it is not possible to evaluate each aspect of the U.S. strategic program in this chapter, a few general guidelines may be suggested.

1. Proposed strategic programs would do little to specifically counter the additional threats to the United States posed by new Soviet strategic capabilities. At worst, there is even a slight risk that some aspects of the U.S. program might actually increase the risk of nuclear war by making the Soviet Union fear for the survivability of its own ICBMs, thus giving it additional incentive to strike first in a crisis. At best, programs to modernize U.S. strategic forces can only offset the feared political effects of Soviet strategic advantages. There is only one way to actually reduce the nuclear threat to this nation, and that is to negotiate agreements in which the United States and the Soviet Union mutually reduce strategic force levels and eliminate weapons like fixed-site ICBMs that, because of their potential vulnerability, invite instability in the strategic balance. Thus first priority should be given to the SALT negotiations, which should attempt to achieve significant reductions in strategic force levels and restraints in weapon modernization programs.

2. In evaluating proposed weapon programs, careful considera-

tion must therefore be given to their possible effects on the negotiations. This cuts two ways. Some programs may complicate the negotiations or make it difficult for the USSR to accept a freeze on current capabilities; this may have been the case with the U.S. deployment of MIRVs before the 1972 agreement, for example. At the same time, it seems clear that there must be sufficient momentum in the U.S. strategic program to make the Soviet Union perceive advantages in limiting its own forces.

3. If there is one dimension of the strategic arms competition in which the United States has always maintained an advantage, it is in technology. Soviet missiles may be larger and more numerous, but U.S. missiles are more accurate, more combat-ready, and more efficient.[5] Moreover, the United States has generally been the first to introduce new types of systems—from the atomic bomb itself to MIRVs. Thus, to some extent, the United States may retain a decided advantage over the USSR, which probably has some political impact, in that it is widely believed to be the leader in weapons technology.

Today, that advantage seems to have crystallized in the cruise missile. Just as the USSR is deploying a new generation of SLBMs and ICBMs that are roughly comparable to their U.S. counterparts, this nation has come up with a new type of system which, as the USSR is well aware, promises to enable it to deploy—at relatively low cost—a large number of additional strategic weapons. Thus, the cruise missile programs could provide a potent lever for the United States in the negotiations, one that could be used to wrest serious Soviet concessions in areas that concern the United States, such as missile throw-weight.

4. Because of the time remaining before the USSR deploys forces with significant hard-target kill capabilities, even according to what are probably conservative Defense Department estimates, it is not necessary to move immediately to augment U.S. capabilities in this area. The new Minuteman reentry vehicle and guidance improvements are probably sensible, but development of the M-X need not be accelerated as was envisioned in the Ford 1978 budget. Rather, the United States can afford to develop the M-X at a more leisurely (and more efficient) pace, looking to the SALT negotiations to elimi-

5. Efficiency is not just a matter of pride. More efficient rocket engines, guidance and control software, and warhead designs may mean that smaller missiles could carry greater destructive power.

. nate the problem before it becomes a reality. Similarly, there seems to be no need at present to develop the Trident II missile and its proposed maneuvering reentry vehicle beyond preliminary conceptual studies.

5. Finally, the need to augment U.S. strategic offensive and defensive capabilities on the basis of broad and undifferentiated worries about Soviet war-fighting capabilities is not a compelling one. There are risks in the future strategic balance, but none so serious as to warrant a crash program to build up U.S. capabilities. Proposals to modernize the U.S. forces—like the B-1 and Trident—can be examined carefully and compared with alternative ways of replacing the forces that, because of age or technological obsolescence, will have to be taken out of service.

The Balance of Conventional Forces

Unlike strategic forces, U.S. and Soviet conventional (or general purpose) forces do not threaten each other's territory directly. Instead, these forces are arrayed against each other in third areas, where trends in the balance of U.S. and Soviet conventional military capabilities are believed to have a significant impact on the course of world events. Three such areas are most important: Europe, the Middle East, and East Asia.

The Military Balance in Europe*

The importance of Europe to the security and economic and political well-being of the United States has been discussed at length in earlier volumes of *Setting National Priorities*. U.S. armed forces play three roles in protecting these interests.

By balancing Soviet power and deterring Soviet adventures, U.S. forces in Europe have permitted political rapprochement between East and West to develop and continue.

By making credible U.S. guarantees for the security of Western Europe, U.S. forces have helped avoid West German perception of a need to develop nuclear weapons, thus also facilitating East-West rapprochement and greater cooperation among the nations of Western Europe.

Finally, the presence of sizable U.S. forces in Europe has strength-

* This section was prepared by Frederick W. Young.

Table 4-9. The Balance of Forces in Northern and Central Europe, 1970 and 1976

	NATO			Warsaw Pact		
Component	1970	1976	Change (percent)	1970	1976	Change (percent)
Combat and direct support troops (thousands)	580	635	9	900	910	1
Tanks (number deployed with units)	5,500	7,000	27	14,000	19,000	35
Tactical aircraft	2,200	2,100	−5	3,940	4,200	6
Tactical nuclear warheads[a]	7,000	7,000	0	3,500	3,500	0

Source: IISS, *The Military Balance, 1970–1971* and *1976–1977.*
a. Warsaw Pact figures have not been verified in official sources.

ened the close economic and political cooperation that now characterizes relations between the United States and Western Europe.

TRENDS IN THE EUROPEAN BALANCE. Most public comment on the military situation in Europe emphasizes a decade-long buildup in Warsaw Pact forces. Yet focusing solely on Pact capabilities ignores the substantial efforts of NATO nations to improve their own military capabilities. NATO's military position vis-à-vis the Warsaw Pact clearly weakened during the late 1960s when the Soviet Union substantially increased its conventional forces in Eastern Europe. But since about 1970 both sides have been expanding and modernizing their forces at comparable rates. As a result, gross comparisons of force levels, like the one in table 4-9, show no significant change in the balance of forces so far in the 1970s.

Changes in the balance of forces resulting from the modernization of weapon systems are more difficult to assess, yet in side-by-side comparisons of similar weapons' technology, NATO appears to have done rather well.

First, the modernization of Warsaw Pact air forces has been substantially matched by NATO. While the Warsaw Pact has acquired more new combat aircraft in the last few years, the aircraft acquired by NATO can carry a larger total payload. Other improvements, such as those in avionics and precision-guided ordnance, also have favored NATO.

Second, both sides have been modernizing their armored forces. The Soviet Union has produced about 17,000 tanks since 1970, including 2,000 of the new T-72 design. NATO has acquired about 4,000 new tanks during this period—mostly the U.S. M-60 and the

West German Leopard I, both of which appear to be as capable as the T-72. The Warsaw Pact, which traditionally has emphasized armor, continues to have about three times the tank inventory of NATO, but NATO has made impressive strides in closing the gap in tank production rates—the ratio by which NATO is outproduced having been cut from about 4:1 to about 2:1.

Third, increases in antitank capabilities seem roughly balanced. NATO's antitank guided missiles are considerably easier to operate and have shorter flight times than those deployed by the Warsaw Pact. Shorter flight times are a significant advantage because they increase the probability that the antitank gunner will be able to guide the missile to its target before the target disappears from his view and because they reduce the amount of time the gunner must remain exposed to enemy observation and fire. On the other hand, Pact antitank gunners enjoy greater protection from artillery and small arms fire because their weapons are more often designed to be operated from inside armored vehicles.

Fourth, improvements in air defense capabilities also appear roughly balanced. Since 1970 the Soviet Union has introduced four mobile air defense missile systems, which, along with continued procurement of previously introduced items such as the ZSU-23-4 air defense gun, have greatly increased the protection offered by Pact air defenses to combat units on the front lines. This specific effort has not been matched by NATO. However, with NATO's deployment of very capable fighter aircraft such as the F-15, its air combat capabilities have increased more than those of the Warsaw Pact.

Fifth, both sides have deployed roughly comparable tank-destroying helicopters.

Sixth, the Soviet Union has doubled the number of artillery tubes with its forces; NATO has increased its artillery capabilities by developing substantially more effective artillery munitions.

The list could go on, but it seems evident—within the limits of uncertainties surrounding any such assessments—that the modernization of Warsaw Pact forces has been effectively matched by NATO improvements. Even if one accepts this conclusion, however, a question remains: have the characteristics of these new weapons changed the nature of warfare in a way that would favor one side or the other? Two hypotheses seem to have gained wide acceptance: (1) new weapons have increased the rates at which matériel would be destroyed and consumed in battle; and (2) the expected ratio of combat losses has shifted in favor of defensive ground forces at the expense of attacking ground and air forces.[6]

In Europe, the second hypothesis favors NATO, which, despite the necessity for counterattacks, is likely to be on the defensive more than the Warsaw Pact. The first hypothesis, however, favors Warsaw Pact efforts to achieve a quick victory before NATO reinforcements could be mobilized. Combined with long-standing concern about a mismatch between the Soviet emphasis on short wars and NATO preparations for more protracted conflicts, this presumption that battle in Europe would result in heavy losses and the rapid consumption of matériel has contributed to current misgivings about the adequacy of NATO's defenses should it fall victim to a surprise attack.

In effect, the current balance of forces is such that neither side could be guaranteed a favorable outcome should war break out in Europe. Assuming that the Warsaw Pact would begin to mobilize for war before NATO did, its greatest military advantage would exist in the first few days of a crisis. Thereafter, if an uninterrupted buildup of forces were to continue on both sides, the ratio of opposing combat forces available in Europe would continue to shift in NATO's favor unless the Soviet Union were willing to move large numbers of troops from its Central, Southern, and Far Eastern military districts—an unlikely development in view of the threat from China. In the very long term, the ratio would probably continue to shift in NATO's favor because of its far larger population and economic base and consequently greater potential for raising and supporting military forces.

Because of these disadvantages, the most attractive strategy for the Warsaw Pact would be an attempt to achieve victory in the shortest possible time—not surprisingly, the very strategy advocated by Soviet military doctrine. The chances of success in such an effort would ob-

6. For the most part, these hypotheses are based on the demonstrated effectiveness of antitank guided missiles, surface-to-air missiles, and air defense guns in the 1973 Arab-Israeli war. Three factors, though, should make one wary of drawing too sharp a comparison between October 1973 and a future war in Europe. First, changes in tactics made during the 1973 war reduced then, and others proposed since would reduce still further, the effectiveness of these new weapons. Second, weather and terrain in the Middle East provide far better visibility for the location and identification of targets than would be the case in Europe. Finally, weapons employed in the 1973 war were generally less capable than similar but more modern weapons now being deployed in Europe by both the Warsaw Pact and NATO.

viously be greatly enhanced if the Warsaw Pact were able to achieve strategic and tactical surprise.

THE RISK OF SURPRISE ATTACK. The Warsaw Pact could initiate a surprise attack on Western Europe with either nuclear or conventional weapons. If the USSR were willing to use nuclear weapons, its forces clearly would have the capability of destroying most of NATO's military resources in nearly simultaneous attacks. Warsaw Pact ground forces would then be able to occupy what was left of Western Europe without facing major opposition. However, since the uncertainties involved in any nuclear war—particularly the risk that the West's response would be to destroy Soviet cities—are great, a surprise nuclear attack would seem to be an attractive military option for the Soviet Union only if it should believe that war was necessary and that a conventional attack would inevitably escalate to large-scale nuclear warfare.

A more likely possibility would be a surprise attack with conventional forces. If all Pact forces in Eastern Europe were to attack at full strength without warning, existing NATO forces would doubtless be faced with the unfortunate choice of yielding substantial territory or using nuclear weapons. Moreover, the cost of providing conventional capabilities sufficient to stop such an attack would be considerably more than NATO is now willing to spend. But such fears rest on pessimistic assumptions. In reality, the Soviet Union would face severe problems in orchestrating a surprise attack—problems of sufficient magnitude to place an effective conventional defense well within NATO's reach.

It is unrealistic to assume that the ground forces of the Warsaw Pact could launch a major attack without any warning. For one thing, Eastern European army units are manned in peacetime at less than 75 percent full strength. For another, the normal peacetime activities of Soviet ground forces in Eastern Europe, which are believed to be almost fully manned, include training and maintenance activities that at most times would inhibit their immediate availability. Finally, supplies that would be consumed relatively quickly in combat, particularly ammunition and fuel, would have to be distributed to combat units before an attack. In short, Soviet preparations for an attack would probably take at least a few days and Eastern European preparations somewhat longer. These efforts would be noticed by the West almost immediately.

The frequently cited danger that NATO would receive this strategic warning but be unable to react because of political indecision seems exaggerated. There is no doubt that a political decision for NATO to mobilize could take some time—perhaps days. But military commanders of active units have the authority to cancel training and begin preparation for war before that. For example, such steps as loading vehicles, conducting last-minute maintenance, and updating and reviewing operational plans should allow NATO ground forces to begin to move almost immediately after a political decision is reached. Since armored or mechanized forces can travel more than 200 kilometers a day if unopposed, well-prepared forces located as far away as the Benelux countries would have a good chance of reaching defensive positions near the East German border within forty-eight hours of a political decision to mobilize.

The danger of a surprise attack by Warsaw Pact air forces also seems exaggerated. To be sure, aircraft based in Eastern Europe could reach targets in Western Europe after flights of only fifteen to twenty minutes. However, a large-scale air attack could not be conducted without preparations, and would not be conducted before the initiation of preparations for the ground attack. Thus, again without need for a political decision to mobilize, NATO military commanders should have time to shelter aircraft, and possibly to disperse some to auxiliary airfields, as well as to place air defenses on alert.

Another possible indicator of an impending Soviet attack would be the activity of Soviet naval forces. Most of the time, a preponderant fraction of the Soviet Navy is located in the Barents, Baltic, and Black seas, where ships would be of little use for a conflict in Western Europe and where they would be fairly vulnerable to NATO operations to restrict their movements. Accordingly, the Soviet Union would be taking a sizable risk by initiating an attack in Central Europe without first moving much of its Navy into the Mediterranean and the Atlantic. Such a step would require several days to accomplish and would provide NATO with another warning signal.

There would be dangers to NATO even if strategic warning were available. The Soviet Union might decide to build up its forces in Eastern Europe for weeks or even months before initiating an attack. Soviet leaders might decide that stocks pre-positioned near the front lines were too small, that Eastern European forces were too unreliable, or that lines of communication were too vulnerable to guarantee an adequate supply of forces and matériel after the initiation of hostilities. Indeed, despite the military advantages of surprise, the USSR might decide that an overt mobilization effort could provide a show of force sufficient to bring about the favorable settlement of a crisis without war. Even with warning, the longer NATO waited to mobilize, the worse its military situation would become. And the fact that NATO's military position would begin to improve as soon as it took steps to mobilize could in itself provide an incentive for the Warsaw Pact to attack as soon after NATO mobilized as possible. Ironically, this realization might make it difficult for NATO political leaders, hopeful of a peaceful settlement, to decide to mobilize for war.

In summary, the Soviet Union and its allies in the Warsaw Pact could threaten NATO militarily in a number of ways, all of which are unlikely but none of which can be ignored. Present NATO conventional forces would have a good chance of conducting a forward conventional defense if an attack occurred after some period of tension and mobilization on both sides or if the Soviet Union received less than full cooperation from its Eastern European allies. There is room for worry, however, about NATO's capability if all Warsaw Pact forces were committed on short warning or if NATO were slow to mobilize. In these cases, the Warsaw Pact would have a fair, though far from certain, chance of forcing NATO to choose between the first use of nuclear weapons and a large loss of territory. For these reasons, NATO's first priority should be to increase the conventional capabilities of immediately available and readily mobilizable forces.

u.s. proposals. Five of the proposals in the 1978 budget for strengthening U.S. military forces for Europe are discussed below.

1. *Redeployment of an Army brigade from Southern Germany to the North German Plain.* The best route of advance for a Warsaw Pact armored thrust into Western Germany is through the northern plain. The more mountainous terrain to the south inhibits the mobility of attacking armor and provides better defensive positions for NATO forces. Moreover, NATO forces in southern Germany, which include all U.S. forces, all French forces, and two of four German corps, are stronger and better equipped than those in the north. Thus shifting a U.S. brigade to the north seems a step in the right direc-

tion in that it strengthens the weakest link in NATO's capability to conduct a forward conventional defense on the ground.

2. *Conversion of two active Army infantry divisions and one reserve brigade to mechanized forces.* Present Department of Defense plans to convert infantry forces stationed in the United States to mechanized units are also sound. Although mechanized divisions are more expensive than infantry, their greater capability in the European military environment more than justifies the additional cost. Even the USSR, which by U.S. standards pays a pittance for manpower and a premium for equipment, has chosen to field armored and mechanized forces to the virtual exclusion of infantry.

3. *Increase in stocks of pre-positioned equipment.* A mechanized division can be moved to Europe just as quickly as an infantry division only if its equipment is pre-positioned on the continent. Thus providing equipment stocks in Europe for additional mechanized divisions is an essential element of plans to strengthen NATO's combat capability in the critical initial stages of conflict. This does not require the procurement of additional sets of equipment. For many items, the U.S. Army already plans to buy enough war reserve stocks to provide additional equipment sets for several more divisions.[7] Units based in the United States could train with these war reserve stocks while their own equipment was stored in Europe. Another way to increase pre-positioned stocks without increasing procurement would be to have reserve units share equipment for training.

4. *Increase in strategic airlift capabilities.* The airlift enhancement program proposed by the Department of Defense would increase U.S. ability to reinforce forces in Europe in the critical first few weeks following mobilization (table 4-10). Sealift, though capable of providing many times the capacity of even the improved airlift after three or four weeks of mobilization, simply could not respond during the critical initial period. Pre-positioning equipment in Europe would be another, and in some respects still better, way of accomplishing the same purpose.

The airlift enhancement program would increase the amount of matériel that could be shipped from the United States to Europe by air in the first thirty days from about 180,000 tons to about 320,000 tons, for a ten-year cost in excess of $2 billion. The 143,000-ton in-

7. War reserves are stocks of equipment that would be used to replace initial equipment sets lost to enemy action or consumed in battle.

Table 4-10. Cost of Proposals for Airlift Enhancement

Proposal	Ten-year cost (millions of 1976 dollars)	Increase in 30-day capability (thousands of tons)	Cost per ton of increased capability (dollars)
Increased utilization rates of C-5A and C-141 aircraft	1,057	32.5	32,000
Modification of C-141 aircraft	550	19.6	28,000
Modification of commercial aircraft	550	91.0	6,000
Total or average	2,157	143.1	15,000ᵃ

Source: Comptroller General of the United States, "Information on the Requirement for Strategic Airlift," GAO Report B-162578 (June 8, 1976; processed), p. 7.

a. Average.

crease in capability is roughly equivalent to the weight of the unit equipment of three mechanized infantry divisions. The cost of the program is just about what it would cost to buy the same equipment and store and maintain it in Europe for ten years. Thus, if equipment for mechanized forces is representative cargo and if the amount of matériel available in Europe thirty days after mobilization is the proper measure of merit, buying and storing additional matériel in Europe is about as attractive as the airlift enhancement program. Pre-positioning would clearly be the better alternative if it could be accomplished without buying additional equipment, but improved airlift might be necessary to protect U.S. interests in other regions, such as the Middle East. The proposed program should therefore not be judged strictly on the basis of needs for war in Europe.

In any case, certain portions of the airlift program are decidedly worse than others. As shown in table 4-10, the proposals to increase the utilization rates of C-5A and C-141 military transports and to modify C-141s are about five times as expensive per ton of increased capability as the proposal to modify commercial aircraft. About 60 percent of the proposed increased capability could be obtained for about 25 percent of the total cost if the modification of commercial aircraft were retained and the other proposals were dropped.

5. *Hardening of airbase facilities in Europe.* The most significant element of the proposal to harden airbase facilities in Europe is a plan to construct about 250 aircraft shelters from fiscal 1978 to 1983. The proposed program would increase the number of U.S. shelters in Europe to about 950, enough to accommodate about half the

number of aircraft the United States might reasonably expect to operate in the European theater at any one time. Shelters greatly reduce the vulnerability of aircraft on the ground to air attack and also provide relatively safe places to perform aircraft maintenance. Each shelter normally holds one aircraft, which may have cost as much as $12 million. The estimated cost of each shelter, on the other hand, is about $0.8 million. Thus, until there are sufficient shelters for all expensive combat aircraft, building new shelters would appear to be well worth their cost. This would change if the Soviet Union developed and deployed weapon systems capable of finding and destroying shelters efficiently; that, however, appears unlikely.

The Balance of Forces in the Middle East*

U.S. armed forces serve important purposes in the Mediterranean, the Middle East, and the Indian Ocean. They embody U.S. commitments to the states on the southern flank of NATO. They provide the ultimate guarantee of the survival of Israel. Their acknowledged strength has made it possible for the United States to assume an important role in coaxing both Israelis and Arabs away from violence and toward negotiations. And they stand ready to protect the flow of oil to the United States, its allies, and its friends.

The extent to which the United States honors its commitments in the Middle East and its confidence in its ability to support them militarily have been tested on several occasions, most recently during the October 1973 Arab-Israeli war. There are bound to be future tests of similar importance and danger. In such crises and even in less serious situations, one of the principal elements in the United States' ability to exert its influence effectively has been the perception of local actors and Soviet leaders alike that the United States is both willing and able to prevent the Soviet Union from intervening unilaterally in the region with combat forces.

Neither the United States nor the Soviet Union currently stations combat forces in the Middle East itself, but each maintains a large and powerful naval force in the Mediterranean.[8] These fleets are approximately the same size, although their capabilities differ significantly.

* This section was prepared by Robert G. Weinland.
8. Each nation also maintains a smaller naval force in the Indian Ocean. These have little military significance and are not discussed here.

Although its strength can vary widely—especially during international crises—the core of the Soviet Mediterranean Squadron consists of some fifty to fifty-five ships. Roughly half are combatants; of these, about half are submarines and half are various types of surface ships. The remaining twenty-five or so units are auxiliaries. The submarine contingent, which includes both torpedo- and cruise-missile-launching units, provides the Squadron's most effective firepower. Until five years ago the Squadron was supported by reconnaissance, antisubmarine warfare, and missile-launching aircraft operating from bases in Egypt. Since the expulsion of Soviet forces from Egypt in 1972, the Squadron has operated largely without direct air support.

Most of the Squadron's firepower is designed for use primarily against surface ships, principally as a counter to U.S. aircraft carriers—and it poses a serious threat to them. The Squadron also has some capability for antisubmarine warfare, although not enough to significantly threaten U.S. strategic submarines operating in the Mediterranean. If the Soviet Union succeeded in reintroducing land-based naval aircraft in the Mediterranean, their already formidable ability to attack the carriers would receive still another boost, but their antisubmarine capability would not change appreciably.

As matters now stand, the USSR would not find attacking the Sixth Fleet an easy task. Aside from the defensive potential of the carriers' own aircraft, the Sixth Fleet would receive significant additional protection from U.S. Air Force fighter aircraft operating from NATO bases in Italy and Turkey. (More accurately, it could receive such protection if fleet air defense was a priority mission of those aircraft and they had permission of the host nations to carry it out.) At the moment, the nearest Soviet missile-carrying aircraft are based along the northern coast of the Black Sea; to reach and attack targets located in the Mediterranean, they would have to cross NATO-controlled airspace. Even in a non-NATO contingency, once detected attempting to penetrate NATO airspace, they probably would have to fight. Allied air defense capabilities are not insignificant, and Soviet aircraft would probably suffer considerable losses on their way to the Mediterranean.

The size and composition of the Sixth Fleet do not change often. When they do vary, it is not by much. The Sixth Fleet is normally composed of some forty to forty-five units. Three-fourths are combatants, organized into two aircraft carrier task groups and one amphibious landing force; roughly 2,000 Marines are embarked on the latter. A network of underway replenishment and afloat maintenance and repair forces supports all three groups.

In contrast to its Soviet counterpart, the Sixth Fleet's most effective firepower is concentrated in its air component—about 200 aircraft, most of which are carrier-based. Some reconnaissance and maritime-patrol–antisubmarine aircraft are based ashore, operating from airfields in Spain, Italy, and Greece. The Sixth Fleet's submarine component, much smaller than that of the Soviet Mediterranean Squadron, is employed primarily for antisubmarine warfare.

A NET ASSESSMENT. If military resources were employed with equal skill, the eventual result of combat between U.S. and Soviet forces in and near the Mediterranean would almost certainly be Soviet defeat. Achieving that outcome would cost the United States a great deal. Its losses of ships and aircraft would be high, although such losses could be reduced substantially if the United States were joined in combat by its NATO allies. Still, the fact remains that the USSR has gone to great lengths to establish a position from which it can make the United States pay a price for undertaking military action in and around the Middle East; the United States could not dislodge the USSR from that position without paying the price.

Given this assessment, two questions remain. First, when crises and local conflicts erupt in the region, could the United States continue to provide a reasonable degree of direct support to its allies and friends without first having to fight the USSR? Second, if the USSR must in the process be fought, how long would it take and what forces would be required for the United States (or NATO) to establish the degree of control over the area that the situation called for? In view of the predominant position of the aircraft carrier in the current U.S. military posture in the Mediterranean and of the steps the Soviet Union has taken to prevent the carriers from carrying out their missions, the answers to these two questions depend in large part on assessments of carrier survivability and effectiveness. Could the carriers survive the attacks that the USSR would be likely to launch against them? Could they not only survive but also conduct effective operations?[9]

An honest answer to the question of survivability must be that it

9. Nuclear weapons play no role in this discussion; if they were used, few, if any, warships in the region could be expected to survive.

would depend on a number of factors, many of which are not really knowable in advance: whether the carriers were alerted and prepared for an attack, the strength and tactical character of the attack, the actual performance of offensive and defensive systems, and so forth. How effective the carriers would be if they did survive the attack, however, largely depends on something that is knowable in advance: the numerical strength of the carrier force. Adding carriers to a task force multiplies its overall defensive capability, reduces the impact of losses, and frees a larger proportion of each carrier's air wing for tasks other than the immediate defense of the force. In short, the classic military principle of concentration of forces continues to be valid in conventional naval warfare. Beyond that, little can be said about the effectiveness of the carrier force that is not intimately interwoven with questions of the design capabilities and actual combat performance of sensors, command-control-and-communications systems, and weapons.

Answers to these capability and performance questions can only be estimated, but in the end these estimates will largely determine the answer to the first question: will the United States have to fight in a crisis in the Mediterranean? If the USSR believes itself unable to extract a significant price from the United States in the event of war in the Mediterranean, it is unlikely to press whatever issues might be at stake. But if the price it can force the United States to pay is estimated by Soviet leaders to be high, deterring Soviet intervention in the Middle East is likely to be more difficult.

MAINTAINING A CREDIBLE U.S. MILITARY POSTURE. Perceptions of relative military capabilities are affected by the statements and styles of political leaders, by national moods engendered by economic trends, by extraneous events such as satellite launches and moon walks, by memories of past wars won or lost, and by countless other factors. This is not to gainsay the importance of the actual physical capacities of the military units—quite the contrary. Perceptions of relative military capabilities may vary within a broad range, but the boundaries of that range are determined—through ill-understood processes—by how, in fact, those relative capabilities would be assessed by an "objective observer." Thus though much can be done to improve (or to damage) perceptions of the U.S. military posture in the Mediterranean through nonmilitary means, in the end it is the actual capabilities of the forces deployed there that count.

Nothing in the Ford administration's defense program, or in the changes made in it by the Carter administration, would have a significant short-term impact on the U.S.-Soviet balance in the Middle East, although options are available that could have immediate and beneficial effects. Some of the steps that are proposed in the 1978 budget should improve the situation, but since all involve the acquisition of new hardware, they would have little bearing until the mid-1980s.

Chief among these long-term improvements is the initiation of programs to acquire, first, aircraft carriers that are sufficiently smaller, and hence cheaper, to be obtainable in larger numbers than would be the case for the present *Nimitz*-class, and second, high-performance combat aircraft that can operate from other than large-deck carriers—i.e., interceptor, attack, and other types of vertical or short takeoff and landing aircraft that can be deployed aboard carriers of any size or on other warships. In addition, acquisition of the AEGIS air defense system should help escort ships protect the carriers from attack. The Carter administration's decision to deploy AEGIS aboard conventional rather than nuclear-powered ships means that more of these systems can be bought and that they should reach operational status sooner. In the same vein, accelerating the installation of towed sonar arrays in both surface combatants and submarines—a step not proposed for fiscal 1978—would increase the Sixth Fleet's ability to detect submarines at very long ranges, in the process providing the carriers with even better protection against surprise.

In the short term, a number of steps are available that would immediately improve the balance in the Middle East. These include modifications in the way existing U.S. forces are used, as well as diplomatic efforts to improve the political-military environment in which U.S. forces deployed in the Middle East must operate.

First, carrier operating patterns could be modified to increase the Navy's capability to surge a truly large force into the Mediterranean or the Indian Ocean *when the situation warrants such a presence there*. This could be accomplished by improving maintenance, manning, and training procedures so as to decrease the "turn-around time" between cruises; modifying the current, essentially rigid pattern of forward deployments, which results in a large fraction of the available force being present in the Mediterranean whether the situation requires its presence there or not, using up whatever slack might otherwise be available for crisis deployments; and shifting from the equally rigid 50-50 split between Atlantic and Pacific that has for decades characterized the disposition of Navy general purpose forces to a more flexible posture so as to increase the number of ships operating in the Atlantic and thus available for deployment to the Mediterranean (and should the situation in the Pacific take an unexpected turn, to augment the forces remaining there).

Second, the activity levels of deployed naval forces—the time ships and aircraft actually spend at sea and in the air—could be increased substantially. At present, the resources allocated to operations provide only "the minimum operational time they need to perform the absolutely necessary combat training."[10] This, however, does not provide the steaming days and flight hours necessary to maintain optimal proficiency. As the gap between U.S. and Soviet naval capabilities continues to narrow, the importance of operational proficiency increases. Furthermore, constraints on operating time often have debilitating collateral effects. Given both the fiscal constraints on operations and the present political situation in the eastern Mediterranean, which has restricted the Sixth Fleet's access to Greek and Turkish ports, not only has the fleet become less active, but it has become something of a fixture at bases in the western Mediterranean. This imposes rather heavily on the hospitality of Spain and Italy, and possibly gives misleading signals to both friends and opponents.

Third, and closely connected with the problem outlined above, is the question what the United States might do to regain access to the military facilities previously provided by Greece and Turkey. The present situation, in which access to local facilities has been curtailed in both nations, is—from a military standpoint, at least—the worst of all possible worlds. If friendly relations with both Greece and Turkey cannot be restored, the United States could decide, in effect, to choose one side or the other. Potential gains must of course be weighed against the costs of further alienating one side in the controversy. Presumably, however, neither would align itself with the Warsaw Pact, and such a decision would permit the return of U.S. forces to bases in the nation that was selected, increasing the freedom of movement of the Sixth Fleet and permitting the U.S. Air Force to deploy a larger number of tactical air squadrons to the eastern Medi-

10. "Annual Defense Department Report, FY 1978," p. 189.

terranean. Ultimately, the benefit would be the reestablishment of a more favorable balance in the eastern Mediterranean, improving the ability of the United States to defend its NATO allies (including Greece and Turkey) and strengthening its influence on the course of events in the Middle East.

The Military Balance in East Asia*

In East Asia, the possibility of direct confrontation with the Soviet Union is more remote than in Europe or the Middle East. The Soviet Union maintains approximately one-fourth of its ground and tactical air forces in the Far East, but they are arrayed primarily against Chinese forces across the border in Manchuria. They do not threaten U.S. interests directly and the likelihood of U.S. forces being drawn into conflict with them is minute. Despite concern about what might happen following Mao's death, there is little, if any, indication of an improvement in Sino-Soviet relations sufficient to free these Soviet military forces for use against NATO.

Direct U.S. military involvement with China is also a remote possibility. China, though its armed forces are immense, has little ability to project military power beyond its borders. Its small nuclear weapons inventory is a threat primarily to the USSR. Since the early 1960s, when China's direct access to Soviet military technology was severed, its forces have been operating with increasingly obsolescent equipment. While the China-Taiwan question remains a possible source of friction for the United States, the adjustment of U.S. relations with those nations is proceeding diplomatically.

The reason for the U.S. military presence in East Asia is not that U.S. interests are directly threatened, but that trends in the Asian military balance might influence the policies of the principal U.S. ally in the region, Japan. That Japan has eschewed the buildup of a strong armed force despite its obvious economic capacity to do so is in part the result of a continuing faith in the U.S. defense commitment, as embodied in the U.S.-Japan Mutual Security Treaty. Japan's policy of maintaining a low military profile, a policy strongly supported by the United States, was reaffirmed in 1976 when Japan ratified the Treaty on the Non-Proliferation of Nuclear Weapons. There are other obstacles to Japan's development of nuclear weapons, not the least of which is adverse domestic opinion. Nevertheless, a nuclear-

* This section was prepared by Stuart E. Johnson.

armed Japan is not an inconceivable future development; if it happened, the effects would be unsettling throughout Asia. Since Japan is unlikely to decide to develop nuclear weapons unless it is suddenly imbued with an overriding sense of national insecurity, the U.S. forces that provide visible confirmation of American defense commitments in Northeast Asia have assumed major political significance.

While watching with interest the relative strength of all U.S. armed forces, Japanese leaders take special note of the naval balance in the western Pacific and prospects for stability on the Korean peninsula. An island with meager natural resources, Japan has developed an economy critically dependent on generous imports of raw materials and access to world markets for exports. The flow of petroleum from the Persian Gulf is the most obviously vital sea lane, but the trans-Pacific trade route is also important. Japanese leaders also are concerned about the possibility of violent conflict in nearby Korea. When threats to the security of South Korea are accentuated, as after the fall of the U.S.-backed regime in Vietnam, Japanese officials express greater concern about their own security.

THE THREAT OF A BLOCKADE OF JAPAN. Compared to Soviet naval capabilities elsewhere, the maritime threat in the Pacific is a relatively small one. There has been a relative increase in the Pacific Fleet's strength since 1968, but this reflects the initiation and growth of Soviet naval operations in the Indian Ocean. These deployments are supported by the Pacific Fleet, which has received additional resources to carry out this task. Even so, the Soviet Pacific Fleet remains the weak sister of the four fleets that make up the Soviet Navy.

Arrayed against the Soviet Pacific Fleet are the small but relatively modern Japanese Navy and the more powerful U.S. Seventh Fleet. The latter includes two aircraft carrier task groups, one of which is home-ported at Yokosuka, Japan. The United States also maintains the Third Fleet—including four more carrier task groups—in the eastern Pacific. Many of these ships could move westward fairly rapidly to reinforce the Seventh Fleet if needed. Finally, the United States maintains some land-based antisubmarine and fighter aircraft in the western Pacific, which would be useful in any naval battle that took place there.

The prospects of a blockade of Japan succeeding are related to how long both the Soviet Union and Japan think it could be maintained, and how long the Japanese economy could survive without the normal flow of imports. Petroleum reserves illustrate the magnitude of this question. In the wake of the 1973 oil embargo, Japan set a goal of stockpiling ninety days' supply of petroleum. The stockpiles now contain more than sixty days' worth and are scheduled to reach the objective by 1979. This reserve, coupled with rationing measures, would make a successful blockade of Japan's petroleum shipments a tenuous proposition so long as the Japanese were prepared to resist the coercion. This, in turn, would hinge on Japanese leaders being convinced that they have the support of the United States and that the U.S. and Japanese navies are adequate to defeat the Soviet Navy in the Pacific.

On balance, this task does not seem too difficult. Most of the Soviet Pacific Fleet's operations originate in Vladivostok; ships from this naval complex must pass through one of several straits bounded by Japanese territory before reaching open waters. The straits are choke points that can be mined or blockaded, bottling up Soviet submarines and warships caught inside the Sea of Japan and isolating those already deployed. Without free access to their home port, Soviet combatants previously deployed would not be effective for long. Soviet naval facilities elsewhere, such as those in Somalia, could provide only limited assistance. To circumvent the restricted access from Vladivostok to the open ocean, the USSR has expanded operations at Petropavlovsk on the Kamchatka peninsula, but this has not solved the problem. Petropavlovsk does not have adequate road or rail links with the mainland and must be supplied by ship, a vulnerable link. Without this resupply, it is not clear how long operations from Petropavlovsk could continue.

Thus fewer forces are needed to counter the Soviet Navy in the Pacific than elsewhere; the Soviet Pacific Fleet is less capable and the geography of the region places the Soviet Navy at a distinct disadvantage. In all likelihood, the forces the United States now maintains in the region are larger than required by a realistic assessment of needs. Hence, in military terms, shifting some U.S. naval forces from the Pacific to the Atlantic to help counter the threat to U.S. interests in the Middle East seems sensible. The difficulty would be to do so without implying a lessening of the U.S. commitment to the defense of Japan, particularly in view of the changes being made in U.S. forces in Korea—the second Japanese concern.

THE THREAT IN KOREA. More than two decades after the signing of the armistice in 1953, North Korea and South Korea remain implacable enemies and maintain large, heavily armed forces arrayed against one another. Although all Chinese troops have long since left North Korea, 40,000 American military personnel remain in the South.

In 1971 the U.S. Army's Seventh Infantry Division was removed from Korea, leaving the Second Infantry Division as the last U.S. ground combat force on the peninsula. This withdrawal reflected the general satisfaction of the U.S. and South Korean governments with the military balance. Still, in that same year, the Republic of Korea (ROK), with $1.5 billion assistance from the United States, embarked on a five-year program to upgrade the quality of its armed forces. Today, ROK active ground forces are well armed and total about 560,000 men; they face a North Korean army of 430,000 men. ROK forces have developed significant capabilities against armor— the essence of the threat against them. In addition, the mountainous terrain in Korea means that tank forces would be generally restricted to corridors. Consequently, the amount of armor that the North could usefully employ in battle would be limited and its massed road-bound armor would be vulnerable to attack by air or ground forces. In short, the balance of ground combat forces appears to be adequate; from a strictly military standpoint, the U.S. Second Division contributes only marginally to the South's combat potential. In March 1977 President Carter announced his intention of removing all U.S. ground forces from the peninsula by 1982.

The ROK Air Force, on the other hand, is not adequate for South Korea's needs. The North has about three times as many aircraft as the South. Although ROK aircraft are generally more modern and its pilots are believed to be well trained, South Korea could not rely on its air power surviving against the North. However, the United States maintains a full air wing of F-4D/E tactical fighter aircraft in Korea, sixty-six in all.[11] These units train with ROK units and are prepared to operate jointly with them. Although adding in the U.S. aircraft does not wholly eliminate the North's advantage in numbers, the combined ROK and U.S. air resources represent an overall capability at least comparable to that of North Korea. Moreover, U.S. Air Force and Marine Corps aircraft based in Japan would be available for

11. There are actually two wing headquarters in Korea, but together they include only three combat squadrons—the usual complement of one wing.

rapid reinforcement, as would U.S. Navy aircraft based on carriers. To hedge against a situation in which the *Midway*—the carrier based at Yokosuka—was in port for repairs and thus not available, a support kit enabling the carrier aircraft to operate routinely from land bases would enhance their operational flexibility at modest cost. There is no plan to reduce the U.S. Air Force presence in Korea.

Aircraft alone cannot defend South Korea against air attacks. Since flight times from North Korean air bases near the demilitarized zone are short, interceptor aircraft would have difficulty reacting effectively. Thus additional air defense has been provided by stationing U.S. Nike-Hercules and Hawk surface-to-air missiles in South Korea. The Nike-Hercules missile sites were recently transferred from U.S. to ROK control, but the Hawk missiles are still operated by the U.S. Army. Many are situated to defend communications and surveillance installations and air defense radar sites, which are generally located on high ground and therefore vulnerable to strikes from the air. Plans to train ROK operators of the Hawk have been formulated; the transfer of responsibility for the system is scheduled for 1982.

Another U.S. Army unit in Korea is the Missile Command, which controls nuclear warheads for surface-to-surface missiles. The Army chief of staff, General Bernard Rogers, recently announced that some of these weapons were being withdrawn. The U.S. Air Force also maintains nuclear weapons on the peninsula.

The balance in Korea is likely to continue to favor the South. The ROK government's new five-year Force Improvement Plan will result in the modernization and modest expansion of the ROK Air Force. The North's air force is likely to remain numerically superior, but the ROK Air Force should, upon completion of the plan, be able to put up stiff resistance to air attack and, combined with the USAF air wing, should be sufficient to provide a sure air defense and ground attack capability.

TAILORING U.S. FORCES TO THESE THREATS. Now that the ROK has succeeded in building up a strong conventional defense, it would seem appropriate for the U.S. nuclear weapons remaining in Korea to be removed. Maintaining the weapons in Korea—symbolic of U.S. reliance on nuclear threats—contradicts the emphasis in U.S. policy on curbing the proliferation of nuclear weapons, as well as incurring some risk of seizure or accident. The Carter administration has moved at least partway toward the adoption of such a course by withdrawing some nuclear-capable surface-to-surface missiles; removing the remaining Army and Air Force weapons would also make sense. If a threat from the North seemed imminent and a strong deterrent signal seemed advisable, nuclear weapons could be returned to Korea in short order.

Since the U.S. Second Division contributes only marginally to ROK defenses, the administration's decision to withdraw it and turn over full responsibility for ground combat to South Korea makes sense militarily. U.S. Air Force units will remain in Korea, training and exercising with the ROK Air Force and providing evidence of the U.S. commitment to South Korea's defense. Army air defense units will remain while ROK personnel are trained to operate the Hawk installations, and U.S. personnel that operate sophisticated communications and surveillance systems would remain as well. All told, there might be 12,000 U.S. military personnel in Korea following withdrawal of the division and supporting logistics units.

The favorable ground balance on the Korean peninsula also raises the question whether it is necessary to maintain the Third U.S. Marine Division on Okinawa. The presence of the division causes some difficulties with the local population and, because Marines on this tour of duty are unaccompanied by their families, aggravates recruitment and retention problems for the Corps. The Japanese pay little attention to the Marines as evidence of U.S. commitments. A modest Marine presence in the western Pacific remains desirable for various minor contingencies, but these purposes could be fulfilled by maintaining one or two battalions afloat on amphibious ships in the region and supporting them, in turn, from Hawaii or by a smaller Marine force on Okinawa.

Thus on military grounds alone sizable reductions could be made in the U.S. military presence in East Asia: the ground forces and nuclear weapons could be withdrawn from Korea, many of the Marines could leave Okinawa, and part of the Navy now in the Pacific could be redeployed. Clearly, changes like these—or even more modest ones—should be carried out gradually, leaving ample time for the South Korean and Japanese governments to adjust their own military plannning to the new situation.

Moreover, other steps would have to be taken to ameliorate the political consequences of the withdrawals; to avoid giving the false impression that these reductions implied lessened U.S. commitments in Northeast Asia. Consultations with concerned governments, strong public reaffirmation of commitments, accelerated arms transfers to

South Korea and Japan, and military exercises designed to show the U.S. ability to return to the peninsula in force, should that become necessary, would all be helpful.

In essence, what has happened in East Asia is that a military force posture built for a different time and different political circumstances has acquired a symbolism far beyond its present military relevance, making it difficult to adjust the U.S. military presence in the region to new political realities. But symbols can be changed without adverse consequences if done slowly and carefully. To leave U.S. forces in Asia unchanged would be to foolishly squander substantial resources at a time when the Soviet military buildup makes their potential contribution to the defense of U.S. interests in other regions all the more valuable.

Easing the Burden of Defense*

The degree to which efforts to match, or offset, improvements in Soviet military capabilities increase the financial burden of defense will largely depend on how efficiently U.S. defense resources are managed. Quite apart from changes in force levels, accelerations or slow-downs in weapon modernization programs, and increases or decreases in the operational readiness of military units, the future trend in de-fense spending will rest on the success or failure of measures to raise the amount of relevant combat potential received for each dollar allocated to defense. In turn, over the past decade, the question of efficiency has been dominated by changes in the cost of manpower.[12]

From 1968 to 1975 manpower costs increased by about 42 percent while the remainder of the defense budget decreased by 7 percent. In effect, spiraling manpower costs required retrenchment in weapon acquisition programs and operations. Since fiscal 1975, how-ever, manpower costs have grown by only 20 percent while the rest of the budget increased by 61 percent. In other words, more effective control of manpower costs made it easier to accelerate the acquisition of weapons, raise the level of operational readiness, and even expand force levels. These contrasting situations are illustrated in table 4-11.

Three factors caused the sharp increase in manpower costs during

* This section was prepared by Martin Binkin.
12. As used here, manpower costs include the direct cost of military and defense civilian employees, payments to retired military personnel, the costs associated with individual training, medical support, recruitment, and education of overseas dependents, and a portion of base operating costs.

Table 4-11. Manpower and Other Defense Costs, Fiscal Years 1968, 1975, and 1978
Total obligational authority in billions of dollars

Cost	1968	1975	1978	Percentage increase 1968–75	1975–78
Total	75.6	87.8	120.4	16	37
Manpower	36.1	51.2	61.3	42	20
Other	39.5	36.8	59.1	−7	61
Manpower as a percentage of total	48	58	51	...	...

Source: Office of the Assistant Secretary of Defense (Manpower and Reserve Affairs), "Manpower Requirements Report for FY 1978" (March 1977; processed), p. XV-13.

the earlier period. First, the price of manpower rose because of both a jump in federal pay and an upward creep in the average grade of military and civilian employees; second, the cost of military retirement steadily escalated as the number of retirees and the size of their pensions increased; and third, the ratio of support to combat forces rose as the drop in the size of the defense work force did not keep pace with the drop in combat force levels.

In the past several years, steps have been taken to reverse these trends. Growth in the price of defense manpower has been markedly curtailed, the rise in the cost of military retired pay has been partly checked, and there are signs that the armed services are moving toward a more efficient use of defense manpower.

The price of defense manpower has been restrained largely by changes in the methods by which annual pay increases are calculated.[13] First, an anomaly in the formula used to compute annual military pay raises, which had the effect of increasing military pay by more than was necessary to maintain comparability with the private sector—the legal criterion—was corrected in 1974. Second, the proportion of military pay raises allocated to the allowance for quarters, or housing, was increased, thus raising the "rent" paid by military personnel occupying government housing—actually, the amount withheld from their checks for quarters—and thereby reducing the military payroll. Third, the process by which "white-collar" pay was set was adjusted in 1976 by broadening the occupational base of the

13. In addition, to offset inflationary pressures in 1975, the administration imposed a 5 percent limitation on the cost-of-living raise in federal salaries (military and civilian). The purpose of this "pay cap" was said to be to "set an example for the rest of the economy." See The Budget of the United States Government, Fiscal Year 1976, pp. 7–8. Perhaps incidentally, this pay cap also compensated for previous cost-of-living raises that seemed to exceed the rate of inflation.

Table 4-12. Average Annual Percentage Increases in Pay of Defense Employees
and in the Consumer Price Index, Fiscal Years 1968-75 and 1975-78

Description	1968–75	1975–78
Composite defense payroll	9.0	6.4
Military pay	10.5	5.8
Civilian pay	8.1	7.7
Classified (white-collar)	6.9	6.0
Wage board (blue-collar)	8.2	9.7
Military retirement pay	8.5	7.7
Consumer price index	6.2	6.3

Source: Author's estimates derived from data appearing in Office of the Assistant Secretary of Defense (Comptroller), "National Defense Budget Estimates for FY 1978" (1977; processed), p. 123.

annual comparability survey and adopting more statistically sound methods of applying the survey data. Finally, the "1 percent kicker," the 1 percent added to cost-of-living increases which overcompensated for the delay between a rise in prices and the retiree's receipt of a larger annuity, was eliminated from retired pay adjustments. Though each change was seemingly minor, the financial implications have been marked. Because of these changes, fiscal 1978 manpower costs are at least $4 billion, about 6 percent, below what they otherwise would have been. Over time, the savings will grow larger.

As a result, the average annual rate of increase in the defense payroll slowed from 9.0 percent during the fiscal 1968–75 period to 6.4 percent during the past three years (table 4-12). The sharpest reduction occurred in military pay; indeed, since 1975 military pay increases have not kept pace with the cost of living. White-collar civilian employees fared slightly better, but their pay also failed to match increases in the consumer price index. On the other hand, although the average annual rate of increase in military retired pay declined, it remained higher than the rate of inflation. Blue-collar defense workers did even better. Since 1975 their annual pay raises, calculated by a unique method, have increased at an even faster rate than in the earlier period. Legislation to reform the federal wage system for blue-collar employees, proposed in 1976 but not passed by Congress, has been resubmitted.[14]

14. As matters now stand, many blue-collar defense employees are better paid than their counterparts in private industry. Three changes have been proposed to correct this situation. The first would match the average federal wage to the average local prevailing wage, instead of using the present system in which step 2 of the federal wage scale is matched to the local wage. Since most federal workers are paid

Table 4-13. Average Annual Percentage Changes in Per Capita Pay Attributable to Changes in Grade Structure, Fiscal Years 1968–75 and 1975–78[a]

Classification	1968–75	1975–78
Military personnel	1.14	−1.00
Civilian personnel		
Classified (white-collar)	.63	1.11
Wage board (blue-collar)	.19	.28

Source: Author's estimates derived from unpublished data provided by the Office of the Assistant Secretary of Defense (Comptroller), March 1977.

a. Strictly speaking, some of the variation in per capita pay can be attributed to factors other than changes in the grade structure, such as differences in the amount of civilian overtime pay. Because the overall effect of these other factors is relatively small, it has been ignored.

Changes in grade distribution also affected the average pay of military and civilian employees. On the military side, the upward creep in the grade structure, characteristic of the 1968–75 period, has been reversed in the past three years, bringing significant savings. On the civilian side, the upward pressure on the white-collar grade structure, which was most evident in the 1968–72 period, has accelerated once again after stabilizing between fiscal years 1973 and 1975. These changes are summarized in table 4-13. To illustrate the financial implications, consider that if the grade distribution that existed in fiscal 1975 prevailed in fiscal 1978, the 1978 military pay bill would be close to $600 million greater, the white-collar payroll would be about $350 million lower, and the blue-collar payroll some $50 million lower.

Steps also have been taken to improve the efficiency with which defense manpower is used, but results are difficult to measure. One way to quantify the gains is to estimate manpower costs (in constant dollars) associated with each unit of output of the armed forces and compare the results for different years. This highly aggregated measure is shown in table 4-14.

Conclusions about the gains traceable to greater manpower efficiency depend largely on the measure of output used. This is most apparent for the Navy, which now spends close to 65 percent more for manpower per ship than it did in fiscal 1964. When adjustments are made to account for increases in technology, complexity, and capabil-

at steps 4 or 5, they often receive up to 12 percent more than the local average. Second, the Monroney Amendment, which bases wage rates in some small communities on higher rates "imported" from large urban areas, would be repealed. Finally, the uniform night shift differential pay rate would be replaced by locally established differentials.

Table 4-14. Changes in Manpower Costs and in Various Measures of Military
Output, Fiscal Years 1964 and 1978

Description	1964	1978	Percentage change, 1964–78
Army			
Manpower costs (billions of 1978 dollars)[a]	20.5	18.4	−10
Active and reserve maneuver battalions	368	373	1
Active and reserve armored division			
equivalents[b]	21.3	26.9	26
Navy[c]			
Manpower costs (billions of 1978 dollars)[a]	15.7	13.1	−17
Ships (number)	917	464	−49
Standard displacement (millions of tons)	7.6	5.3	−30
Shaft horsepower (millions)	26.6	18.2	−32
Electrical generating capacity (megawatts)	1.9	2.0	5
Air Force			
Manpower costs (billions of 1978 dollars)[a]	20.4	13.9	−32
Strategic forces			
Total number of aircraft and missiles[d]	2,782	1,955	−30
Missile throw-weight (millions of pounds)[e]	2.1	2.2	5
Bomber payload (millions of pounds)[f]	49.8	23.8	−52
Air defense forces			
Number of aircraft	1,543	321	−79
Total aircraft weight (millions of tons)	44.1	11.9	−73
Tactical air forces			
Number of aircraft	2,624	2,400	−9
Offensive load-carrying capacity (millions			
of ton-miles)[g]	5.8	13.3	129
Airlift forces			
Number of aircraft	2,243	1,078	−52
Total lift (millions of ton-miles)[h]	18.5	42.3	129

Sources: Army output measures based on data appearing in Department of Defense, "A Report
to Congress on U.S. Conventional Reinforcements for NATO" (June 1976; processed). Navy measures
based on unpublished data provided by the Department of the Navy, March 1977. Air Force figures derived
from data appearing in IISS, *The Military Balance, 1964–1965* and *1976–77;* Strategic Air Command, "The
Development of the Strategic Air Command, 1946–1976" (March 21, 1976; processed), pp. 113–18; *Department of Defense Appropriations for Fiscal Year 1978*, Hearings before the House Appropriations Committee, 95:1, pt. 1 (GPO, 1977), pp. 474–569; Department of Defense, "Department of Defense Manpower,
FY 64–FY 77: The Components of Change" (April 1975; processed), pp. 19, 24, 25. Manpower costs
based on data provided by the Office of the Assistant Secretary of Defense (Comptroller), March 1977.

a. Constant-dollar figures tell us how much the personnel on duty in 1964 would have cost if 1978
pay rates had then obtained, providing a realistic comparison of the level of resources devoted to defense
manpower. In these terms, the Army will spend about 10 percent less on manpower in fiscal 1978 than
it spent in fiscal 1964.

b. An armored division equivalent is a measure of overall combat capability that takes into account
both the quality and quantity of weapons composing a land force. It is based on the on-hand capabilities
of a U.S. armored division operating on terrain such as would be encountered in Europe. It does not take
into account sustaining capabilities, such as ammunition and fuel stocks.

c. Excludes strategic submarines.

d. Includes strategic bombers, tanker aircraft, and ICBMs.

e. Ballistic missile throw-weight is the maximum useful weight that has been tested on the boost
stages of the missile. It includes the weight of the reentry vehicles, penetration aids, dispensing and release

ity, however, a different picture emerges. For example, if the size of ships or their engines' power is taken into account and manpower costs are counted per displacement ton or shaft horsepower, the loss of manpower efficiency is less marked. If electrical generating capacity—a proxy for technological sophistication—is used as an output measure, the Navy is using manpower less intensively (more efficiently) than it did in 1964.

Similar conclusions apply to the use of Air Force manpower. Manpower cost per major weapon platform (aircraft or missiles) has gone up substantially since 1964. When adjustments are made to account for improvements in capability, however, different results are obtained. Most notable have been improvements in the tactical and airlift forces, where manpower costs per unit of capability have been cut dramatically.

Reductions in Army manpower costs are evident by almost any measure. Manpower cost per maneuver battalion is about 12 percent lower than in 1964; after adjusting for improvements in capability, manpower cost per unit (armored division equivalent) is about 30 percent lower than in 1964.

Caution must be exercised in interpreting these results, since the data do not include the cost of contracted services. While there are signs that the services are relying on contract support to an increasing extent, the magnitude of the shift is unknown. To the extent that this is true, actual manpower costs per unit of output would be greater than those shown in table 4-14.

In any case, much greater manpower savings are possible. The savings that would be realized from the legislation to rectify the upward bias in present methods for calculating raises in the pay of blue-collar employees would amount to $200 million in fiscal 1978 and grow to $700 million a year within five years. Also, early attention to controlling the continuing growth in the average grade of white-collar civilians could produce large savings; as noted, merely returning to the grade distribution that prevailed in fiscal 1974 would save $350 million at fiscal 1978 prices. Defense manpower could also be used more efficiently if measures discussed in previous editions of

---

mechanisms, reentry shrouds, covers, buses, and propulsion devices with their propellants, all of which are still present at the end of the boost phase.

f. Bomber payload is the maximum weight of ordnance that an aircraft can carry.

g. The product of combat radius and payload, summed over all tactical aircraft in the inventory.

h. The product of combat radius and lift capacity per day, summed over all airlift aircraft.

Setting National Priorities were put into effect: the length of military training courses could be shortened, more people could be trained on the job instead of in classrooms, tours of duty could be lengthened, and the reserve structure could be streamlined.

High on the list of possible reforms are changes in the military retirement system. The Carter administration has announced that it plans to establish a blue-ribbon panel to examine the military compensation system, including its retirement provisions. If these provisions were simply aligned with those governing federal civilian retirement, savings would be substantial over the long term.

Emerging problems surrounding the all-volunteer forces may make the quest for manpower savings more difficult. Two disquieting factors on the horizon are the imminent decline in the number of young men in the population as the postwar baby boom runs its course and the diminishing proportion likely to volunteer as the economy improves. Both factors will make military recruitment more difficult.

A few years from now, as the effects of dwindling birthrates in the 1960s begin to be felt, the number of young men reaching the age of eighteen each year will decline sharply from present levels, dropping 15 percent by 1985 and over 25 percent by 1992. If the armed forces remain at their present size, recruiting will be more difficult; instead of having to attract one of every six males, as is now the case, the military services eventually will have to attract one of every four. Moreover, assuming that the economy continues to recover, the number of male high school graduates attracted to military service could become disturbingly small and require an increase in military pay relative to civilian pay in order to meet recruitment needs. If this is not done, if military pay raises only match civilian pay raises, by 1981 the services will be fortunate to attract 80 percent of their stated needs for high school graduates; by 1985 that figure is likely to decrease to 63 percent. The greater the economic recovery, of course, the greater the shortfall.

As it becomes harder for the military services to meet their quantitative or qualitative goals, pressure will mount to solve these problems by returning to conscription, by reducing military strength levels, or by further increasing military pay. But there are other ways to overcome these difficulties, should they develop, or better still to avert them altogether.

For example, the armed forces could effectively use more women and civilians, thereby reducing the demand for male volunteers and alleviating the recruiting problem.[15] Moreover, partly because of excessively liberal discharge policies, volunteers are leaving the services before they complete their first enlistment at almost twice the rate that prevailed before the draft was abolished. Through tighter management and more careful recruitment, the average length of enlistment could be increased, personnel turnover would decrease, and fewer recruits would be needed each year.

It may also be the case that current educational, aptitude, and physical standards are higher than necessary, or simply inappropriate for the satisfactory performance of many military duties. Relatively minor adjustments in these standards could yield substantial increases in the supply of qualified males. For example, simply extending maximum and minimum weight limits by 10 percent would increase the supply of eligible recruits by 5 percent. Returning to the more lenient educational and aptitude standards of 1974 would reduce the need for highly qualified males by close to 15 percent.[16]

Finally, this situation makes it all the more important to ensure that military personnel are fully aware of the value of their compensation. The compensation system used today, which is geared to meet the needs of the military establishment of an earlier era, is out of date. Those already in the armed services, prospective volunteers, and lawmakers are often unaware of the full value of military compensation simply because some of its elements are received in kind or as part of a confusing system of special allowances and tax benefits. Moreover, because its underlying rationale calls for paying people on the basis of their "needs" rather than strictly for their contribution to national security, the compensation system in some instances attracts those who are costly in relation to their skills. As a result, the United States is paying more than is necessary to field its present military forces. Many of these problems could be resolved by paying the military in much the same fashion as civilians are paid. The present hodgepodge of military pay, allowances, and tax benefits would give way to the payment of a single "salary." Earnings would become

15. See Martin Binkin and Shirley J. Bach, *Women and the Military* (Brookings Institution, 1977).
16. Congressional Budget Office, *The Costs of Defense Manpower: Issues for 1977* (GPO, 1977), pp. 52–53.

more apparent, more understandable, and hence easier for everyone to evaluate.

Because such proposals call for changes in defense manpower management, they are unpopular among military traditionalists. Yet the risks of adopting these options to make the all-volunteer system work would be small compared to the social and political costs of renewing conscription, the financial cost of increasing incentives, or the military cost of reducing strength levels.

Reversing the Trend in Defense Spending

With each passing year it has become more difficult to explain the continuing momentum in the Soviet defense buildup.

At first it seemed likely that the buildup was a reaction of the new Soviet leadership to Nikita Khrushchev's foreign policy reverses from about 1957 through 1962. At the time Soviet armed forces were being cut back drastically, Khrushchev pursued an aggressive foreign policy, more aggressive than could be supported with the military power then available to the USSR. Partly as a result, the Soviet Union suffered a string of political setbacks: in Central Europe, in the Congo, in Cuba, and elsewhere. Moreover, fears stemming from this aggressive stance plus coincident Soviet technological breakthroughs spurred a major rebuilding of U.S. military capabilities during the Kennedy years. This disastrous Soviet foreign policy was no doubt a major factor leading to Khrushchev's overthrow in 1964. And determined to avoid a similar fate, his successors accelerated Soviet defense programs to catch up with the United States.

By the end of the 1960s, however, and certainly by 1972, when a special Soviet position in Eastern Europe and parity in strategic arms had been ratified in formal agreements, it seemed logical that this military buildup would slow down. The Soviet economy (and Soviet consumers) would certainly have benefited from a reduction in the 12 to 15 percent share of Soviet resources consumed by its defense establishment. But there is no evidence of such a reallocation.

Explanations come readily to mind, ranging from the difficulty of turning off bureaucracies once they have been turned on, to speculations that the Soviet military received a promise of continuing high budgetary allocations in exchange for their cooperation on a policy of political rapprochement with the West, to ruminations on the nature of the Russian character as shaped by the searing experience of World War II, to fears that the USSR is indeed seeking military superiority to enable it to coerce, and eventually to dominate, the West. Each of these reasons could have something to do with the continuing buildup. In any case, it seems clear that, as in the late 1950s, the Soviet Union has again underestimated the West, failing to foresee the degree to which its apparent gains would cause the West to become apprehensive and step up its own military preparations. But this is exactly what has happened in the United States since 1975.

The assessments in earlier sections of this chapter demonstrate the value of detailed analyses of the Soviet military buildup. An across-the-board U.S. response stemming from a diffuse sense of unease would only waste resources, diverting people and money not only from important domestic needs, but also, within the armed forces, from those areas where the Soviet Union presents more significant challenges. In East Asia, the Soviet buildup threatens not the United States, but China. Given improvements in U.S.-China relations and more narrow U.S. definitions of its interests in Southeast Asia, the U.S. force posture in the Pacfic could be scaled down, freeing resources for use elsewhere. In the realm of the strategic nuclear competition, both Soviet capabilities and the political consequences of those capabilities are frequently exaggerated. Although some improvements in the U.S. strategic force posture are warranted, a massive response seems inefficient and in some ways counterproductive. In Europe and the Middle East, improving Soviet military capabilities do threaten important U.S. interests and require a clear and strong response. But even here, there are more and less efficient ways of enhancing U.S. military capabilities; concern about trends in the military balance should not cause the neglect of rigorous examinations of proposals on the pragmatic grounds of relative costs and relative effectiveness. Finally, putting into effect the many possible ways of reducing manpower requirements and the growth in military and civilian pay rates would curtail increases in the defense budget resulting from assessed needs to counter the USSR or would at least avoid unexpected increases brought on by inadequate recruitment in the all-volunteer force.

Unfortunately, such an approach has its political difficulties. Sophisticated evaluations of alternative weapon systems and force structures are not persuasive to Congress or the public. Apparently a broad and undifferentiated response is more appealing. The public has stated clearly—in opinion polls, in letters to congressmen, and in its votes during the past year's elections—that it wants the nation's leaders "to do something about the Russians." That is why proposals to improve U.S. military capabilities now receive a sympathetic hearing on Capitol Hill.

If this continues, the U.S. defense budget will increase over the next several years, quite aside from the effects of inflation. In short, 1975 was the year that the arms competition between the United States and the USSR moved forward another ratchet. The Soviet buildup has resulted in a new U.S. buildup, and the competition continues at a higher level. Reversing this trend will require recognition by both nations of its self-defeating nature—recognition that in view of modern military technology and the present nature of the international system, greater expenditures on arms do not necessarily increase security. Indeed, by destabilizing political relations, they may well undermine it.

With such common recognition, arms control negotiations could begin to yield significant results. Although these results would, most importantly, reduce the risk of war and promote greater political and economic cooperation between the superpowers, of particular interest to readers of this book are their potential budgetary effects.

Strategic Arms Limitation

The crucial negotiation is SALT. Although nuclear weapons account for a relatively small share of the two nations' defense budgets, they are the only weapons that significantly threaten the territory and population of both sides. Consequently, their control has implications for broader political relations and for the success or failure of other arms control efforts.

The immediate problem is that the 1972 Interim Agreement to limit strategic offensive weapons expires in October 1977. Should a follow-on agreement not be concluded before then, there would be significant pressure on both sides to step up modernization programs and perhaps to increase strategic force levels. Eventually, if the strategic competition accelerated, pressure to abrogate the 1972 Treaty Limiting the Deployment of Anti-Ballistic Missiles could grow. The budgetary implications of any of these contingencies would be sizable. U.S. officials have mentioned $2 billion to $5 billion as the annual incremental expenditures that would be necessary if the Interim Agreement were to expire without replacement. Building an ABM system would add, at a minimum, another $5 billion annually. And of course the political implications of either development would be grave.

It seems likely that any new agreement would have to follow the guidelines worked out by President Ford and General Secretary Brezhnev at Vladivostok in 1974. The time remaining is probably too short to negotiate a new type of arrangement, and unlike Mr. Carter, Mr. Brezhnev has a vested interest in seeing the labors of 1974 consummated. The Vladivostok accord limits each side to 2,400 strategic missile launchers and heavy bombers, of which 1,320 missiles may carry MIRVs. Adhering to those levels would require no reductions in planned U.S. forces and only minor reductions in present Soviet forces. The few controls on the characteristics of strategic weapons included in the accord would have little impact on modernization programs in either nation. Adding constraints on deployments of cruise missiles and Backfire bombers, a possibility often noted, would still have only minor budgetary impact. In fact, constraints on cruise missiles might lead to higher budgets, in that they would strengthen arguments for buying a large number of B-1 bombers.

Thus, it would be left to SALT III, the negotiations following implementation of the Vladivostok accord, to produce an agreement that might also lead to reductions in strategic budgets. Agreement, for example, to reduce each side's total strategic force levels to 1,320 would bring about savings in operating costs and would permit a reduction in the pace of weapon modernization. For the United States, such reductions could mean annual savings of between $800 million and $5.5 billion at 1978 prices from the level of strategic budgets likely without such agreement.[17] The range is wide because potential savings would depend on which existing forces were cut and which were retained. Phasing out bombers, which are more costly to acquire and operate than ICBMs, would yield much greater savings. In any

17. The calculations leading to the low end of the savings range assume that present modernization programs (B-1 bomber, Trident submarine, and M-X ICBM) would not be affected by the agreement until the late 1980s. They further assume that only ICBMs would be phased out of the force structure to reach the lower ceiling. Under this assumption, the U.S. force would consist of 656 SLBMs, about 400 bombers, and 250 ICBMs. The calculations leading to the high end of the savings range assume that both the B-1 and M-X programs would be sharply curtailed and that bomber force levels would be reduced to about 100.

event, savings are hypothetical; whether they materialized would depend on the effect of the agreement on defense policy in general. If little else changed, reductions in strategic spending could be used for other types of military forces. On the other hand, successful negotiations to cut back strategic force levels so sharply could produce a political atmosphere conducive to unilateral restraint.

Stabilizing the Balance in Europe*

A second negotiating forum of considerable political importance and some potential budgetary consequence is the Vienna talks on mutual and balanced force reductions in Europe. Member states of NATO and the Warsaw Pact have been engaged in these negotiations since October 1973. Although it is encouraging that they have stuck to it for this long, progress to date has been disappointing, basically because the proposals advanced by each side thus far are incompatible.

The Warsaw Pact seeks to preserve roughly the existing balance of forces between East and West, as well as the current balance among members of each alliance. Its proposals thus specify equal reductions, or equal percentage reductions, in manpower for Warsaw Pact and NATO forces in Central Europe, and call for separate ceilings to be placed on the force levels of each country. One proposal, put forth in February 1975, was to simply freeze all forces at existing levels.

NATO argues that the existing East-West balance of forces is unacceptable, and has insisted on a common collective ceiling on ground forces within the agreed geographical area. The last major NATO proposal, made in December 1975, called for a preliminary reduction of 68,000 Soviet ground troops and 1,700 tanks in exchange for U.S. reductions of 29,000 troops, 1,000 nuclear warheads, and 90 nuclear delivery systems—all followed by a second phase reduction to the common collective ceiling of 700,000 ground troops.

Obviously, no agreement can be reached as long as each side remains committed to these positions. Reaching an agreement on asymmetrical reductions—NATO's preference—will be difficult. With no urgent need for Soviet manpower elsewhere, there would seem to be no reason for the Soviet Union to negotiate away its current numerical advantage in Europe. The idea of substituting the withdrawal of some U.S. tactical nuclear weapons for the withdrawal

* This section was prepared by Frederick W. Young.

of NATO ground forces has not been categorically rejected, but the USSR is not likely to find such proposals attractive since nuclear weapons could always be quickly returned to Europe by air. Moreover, the Western European members of NATO would oppose any substantial reduction in U.S. nuclear forces, as they fear it would indicate a weakening of the U.S. nuclear commitment.

The Warsaw Pact position calling for ceilings on the forces of individual countries is probably driven by Soviet fear of resurgent German militarism and Soviet desire to maintain control and influence in Eastern Europe. From this point of view, the highest priority would be to obtain a ceiling on West German forces, although the Soviet Union might conceivably see real, if unstated, advantages in an agreement that restricted the size of Eastern European forces as well. Moreover, the USSR may well view U.S. forces in Europe as a stabilizing influence on West Germany. Ceilings placed on each country would make it impossible to substitute German for U.S. troops; either the United States would remain in Europe or there would be a corresponding loss of NATO capability. Analogously, this reasoning would provide a continuing rationale for Soviet forces to remain in Eastern Europe.

Together, these differences over the principles to guide reductions will make attainment of an agreement difficult. Although compromises are certainly possible, it is essential to explore alternative approaches to stability in Europe; for example, the negotiations in Vienna might be used to ease fears of surprise attack.[18] Such measures might involve the location of observers from an international organization at military installations on both sides, a limit on the size of maneuvers, or restrictions on troop rotation procedures. Under present procedures, for example, the USSR could temporarily increase its manpower in Central Europe by some 100,000 troops enough to mask the buildup for an attack. Indeed, any measure that would significantly increase the warning time before an attack would do more than mutual force reductions to stabilize the military situation in Central Europe. Force reductions degrade the capabilities of both defender and attacker. Steps to increase warning time would differentially weaken the capabilities of any would-be attacker.

18. This suggestion was made by Representative Les Aspin; see *Congressio* *Record*, daily edition, vol. 123 (February 7, 1977), p. H 911–14. Certain provisi of the 1975 CSCE Agreement, known as confidence-building measures, are step this direction.

How the Soviet Union would respond to proposals designed to preclude surprise attacks is unknown. It would see little military advantage in such an agreement since NATO's ability to mount a surprise attack is at best limited. On the other hand, if such proposals were to improve the political situation in Europe without causing a reduction in its forces in Eastern Europe, the Soviet Union might find them worth exploring. By reducing fears of surprise attack, such an agreement would alleviate the principal concern now underlying the U.S. buildup of its NATO forces, and thereby ease pressures on the defense budget. Over the longer term, an improvement in the political atmosphere might result from the agreement and lead to follow-on agreements to reduce force levels.

Naval Arms Control

A third area for arms control with potential budgetary implications concerns the Navy. Here, too, savings are likely to be small, except over a long period. The most promising possibility would be an agreement by the United States and the USSR to limit naval deployments and abolish military facilities in the Indian Ocean region. Soviet spokesmen have mentioned such an agreement favorably, as has President Carter.

Again, the savings are hypothetical. They would be realized only if the forces each side now maintains in the region—and the necessary backup forces—were phased out of their respective force structures. Such a reduction would also permit a slight slowdown in shipbuilding programs, with imputed additional savings. For the Soviet Union, for example, the annual potential value of such an agreement might exceed $500 million.[19]

In all probability, however, neither the United States nor the Soviet Union would be willing to reduce its naval forces directly following such an agreement; and anyway each sees a need for larger naval

---

19. The USSR typically maintains sixteen to twenty ships in the Indian Ocean, operating from bases at Vladivostok and Petropavlovsk. A rough rule of thumb for the U.S. Navy is that it requires three ships in a naval inventory to keep one ship continuously on station in a distant region. According to this rule, the total cost of the roughly fifty to sixty ships necessary to maintain the Soviet Indian Ocean squadron would be at least $6 billion (at U.S. prices). Assuming a twenty-year ship lifetime, an Indian Ocean demilitarization agreement may be said to represent potential annual shipbuilding savings for the USSR of at least $300 million. Operating costs of the squadron are more difficult to estimate, but they would probably amount to another $200 million at U.S. prices.

deployments elsewhere. Still, over the long term, even a limited naval agreement that functioned effectively could reduce requirements for naval forces below the levels that might otherwise obtain. And again, there is the hope that such an agreement could contribute to an improved political atmosphere and lead to other agreements to control naval forces.

Prospects

Paradoxically, the strong U.S. reaction since fiscal 1975 to the Soviet military buildup may have increased the possibilities for successful arms control negotiations. These possibilities are at best tenuous and the negotiations themselves are almost certain to be time consuming and arduous. Nonetheless, a situation in which both East and West are intent on strengthening their military capabilities may also be one in which both sides will most clearly see advantages in negotiating mutual arms restraints.

Successful negotiations of course would do much more than save money. Their primary purposes are to build mutual confidence and reduce suspicion, thereby promoting political cooperation and lessening the risk of war.

Achieving these important objectives, however, will require resolution of the dilemma inherent in present U.S. defense budget planning. In effect, the possibilities for reduced spending in the future may depend on a resolve to continue to spend heavily in the present. Such resolve may be difficult to sustain during the next few years, which are sure to be characterized by sharp competition for budgetary resources and pressure to achieve a balanced budget. This puts a premium on measures to achieve greater efficiency in defense management and on identifying planning criteria that can be used to distinguish between essential, marginal, and whimsical needs for weapons and forces.

In the present international system, the ultimate arbiter remains power; economic and political power most often, but not infrequently military power. In all probability, the Soviet Union can be induced to reach a mutually beneficial accommodation with the West only if it becomes convinced that the United States is willing to take the decisions necessary to compete for this power effectively over the long haul.

CHAPTER FIVE

Employment and Training Assistance

JOHN L. PALMER

THE EMPLOYMENT and training assistance component of the federal budget is particularly important in fiscal 1977 and 1978.[1] In no other area does the Carter administration depart more dramatically from both the Ford administration proposals and the current services budget. This is largely because President Carter's temporary stimulus package emphasizes additional outlays in selective employment-related programs. It may also foreshadow a major long-term expansion of both policy attention and expenditures in this area relative to what would occur had Ford been reelected.

Selective policies to promote employment are increasingly seen as desirable means both of achieving and sustaining full employment without excessive inflationary pressures and of ensuring minimally adequate incomes for families with potential workers. The efficacy of various specific policies, however, is in considerable dispute. Correspondingly, judgments vary considerably on the degree of reliance

1. The term "manpower" has been dropped from official government (and, increasingly, general) usage in favor of "employment and training." There are many possible definitions of what properly constitutes federal employment and training assistance programs. The *Special Analyses, Budget of the United States Government, Fiscal Year 1978* includes, in addition to the bulk of Department of Labor programs, the Work Incentive (WIN) and numerous other minor programs spread across several agencies. The major employment-related programs not encompassed by this definition are the public works programs of the Department of Commerce and the vocational education program of the U.S. Department of Health, Education, and Welfare. Employment tax credits might also be considered to fall into the category of employment and training. Whenever the definition used in this chapter deviates in important ways from that in the *Special Analyses,* it will be made explicit.

that can or should be placed upon such measures. In addition, the primary authorizing legislation for federal employment and training assistance programs, the Comprehensive Employment and Training Act, will expire at the end of fiscal year 1978. For these reasons 1977 and 1978 promise lively congressional and executive branch debate in this area, and the decisions should have a considerable impact on the future course of federal employment and training policies.

Unemployment and the Role of Employment and Training Assistance

By any reasonable standards the labor market performance of the U.S. economy in the 1970s has been inadequate. After nearly a decade of declining unemployment rates, culminating in four straight years of very low unemployment in the late 1960s, the unemployment rate mostly hovered between 5 percent and 6 percent in the early 1970s and then rose to a high of over 9 percent in the peak month of the 1975 recession. Even in mid-1977, nearly two years into the recovery, the unemployment rate is still about 7 percent and is projected to decline at a relatively slow pace.[2]

The major burden for achieving and sustaining low rates of unemployment must, of course, be borne by the broad fiscal and monetary measures that the federal government pursues to facilitate general economic growth. But there is also an important role for selective employment and training policies, both in promoting the quantity and quality of available job opportunities and in enhancing the competitive position of the less advantaged members of the labor force.

The Nature of Unemployment

Although admittedly an oversimplification, it has become commonplace to break unemployment down into three components: frictional, structural, and cyclical. A certain amount of *frictional* unemployment is an essential lubricant to the efficient operation of a dynamic economy. Generally 4 to 5 million people enter or reenter

2. It should be noted, however, that there has been a high rate of growth of employment over the past several years. This has not resulted in commensurately large reductions in unemployment because of large increases in the size of the labor force. This is illustrated by the fact that approximately the same percent of the noninstitutionalized population age sixteen and over was employed in 1966 (56.9 percent), when the aggregate unemployment rate was 3.8 percent, as in 1976 (56.8 percent), when it was 7.7 percent.

the labor market every month seeking employment. Several additional millions who wish to remain working leave their current jobs either in an attempt to improve their position or because an employer no longer requires their services. In both instances, bringing about a good match between job vacancies and workers' skills often requires a modest period of job search. Many millions of workers in the midst of such short spells of unemployment each month can account for several percentage points in the aggregate rate of unemployment.

Structural unemployment exists when, even though there may be sufficient jobs in the aggregate to employ everyone who is in the labor market (taking into account the desirability of some frictional unemployment), the characteristics of available workers are not well matched with employers' requirements for job vacancies. In general, such mismatches are due to imbalances in education, skill, work experience, or geographical location, but their roots can lie in many different specific causes that may vary in importance over time, such as worker displacement owing to shifts in demand or technological change, low productivity that does not warrant payment of prevailing wage rates, rapidly changing characteristics of the labor force, and discrimination by employers.

Who are the structurally unemployed? One way to identify them is to see what types of workers experience considerably greater than average rates of unemployment in a relatively low-unemployment economy. Not surprisingly, such workers are concentrated among the less educated, less-skilled, nonwhite, and less experienced members of the labor force, as well as those who live in economically depressed regions of the country, or whose primary prior experience has been in a rapidly declining industry.

Perhaps most notable and currently discussed, however, is the age and sex dimension of structural unemployment. As table 5-1 shows, unemployment rates for teenagers and young adults are considerably above the average.[3] Although these two groups comprise less than one-quarter of the labor force, they account for over one-half of all unemployment in a 5 percent unemployment economy. Women experience higher rates of unemployment than men do at all age levels

3. Further disaggregation yields even larger unemployment rates. Perhaps the most distressing is that black teenagers living in central cities experience unemployment rates approaching 40 percent, and this does not take into account discouraged job seekers who have ceased to participate in the labor market.

Table 5-1. Structure of Unemployment When Overall Rate is 5 Percent, by Sex-Age Groups[a]

Sex-age group	Official unemployment rate (percent)	Average number of unemployment spells per year[b]	Percent experiencing some unemployment during year	Percent distribution by number of weeks of completed spells of unemployment[c]				
				1-4	5-10	11-14	15-26	27 and over
Males								
16-19	13.9	1.8	24.0	59.6	26.9	7.0	5.8	0.7
20-24	7.3	0.9	24.7	55.9	27.6	7.9	7.4	1.2
25-44	2.7	0.3	12.2	44.2	27.8	10.3	13.2	4.4
45-64	2.2	0.2	8.2	39.8	27.1	10.9	15.5	6.7
65 and over	3.0	n.a.	n.a.	n.a.	n.a.	n.a.	n.a.	n.a.
Females								
16-19	15.2	2.0	25.7	59.8	26.8	6.9	5.7	0.7
20-24	8.4	1.1	22.9	60.1	26.7	6.9	5.6	0.7
25-44	4.9	0.6	13.9	66.0	24.9	5.3	3.5	0.3
45-64	3.1	0.3	9.7	47.6	28.1	9.7	11.5	3.2
65 and over	2.9	n.a.	n.a.	n.a.	n.a.	n.a.	n.a.	n.a.

Sources: U.S. Bureau of Labor Statistics, *Handbook of Labor Statistics, 1975: Reference Edition*; Charles L. Schultze, "The Economics of the Full Employment and Balanced Growth Act of 1976 (S.50)," testimony before the Subcommittee on Unemployment, Poverty, and Migratory Labor of the Senate Committee on Public Welfare, May 14, 1976 (processed), table 1; Bureau of Labor Statistics, *Work Experience of the Population, 1973*, Special Labor Force Report 171 (BLS, 1975). Figures are rounded.

n.a. Not available.

a. Structure of labor force and unemployment in 1973, when the unemployment rate was actually 4.9 percent.

b. Includes those who experienced no unemployment.

c. Estimated for 1973 according to formulas derived by George L. Perry in "Unemployment Flows in U.S. Labor Market," *Brookings Papers on Economic Activity, 2: 1972*, pp. 245–78.

(except at sixty-five and over), with the discrepancy being greatest for those of prime working age.

One probable reason why unemployment among teenagers and women is so high is that their share of the labor force has grown rapidly over the past several decades.[4] These trends are expected to slow (and, in fact, to be reversed for teenagers) in the 1980s and, with gradual adjustments on the part of the employers to the changed composition of the labor force, unemployment among these groups should ease.

Many people have been led to the conclusion that the high rates of unemployment among younger workers and women should be of little social concern because they are often second workers in families (and, in the case of the former, are often in and out of school). But an increasing number of women are the major or sole providers of earned income for their families, and the poor labor market experience of many teenagers may be a major contributor to their employment problems as adults. While the limitations of social intervention in the face of dramatically changing demographic and social forces must be appreciated, the very real and highly undesirable consequences of such concentrations of unemployment cannot be ignored. Furthermore, any unemployment in excess of the frictional amount necessary for economic efficiency reflects idle resources that might be put to productive use and is, therefore, wasteful.

Table 5-1 indicates some other interesting dimensions to the structure of unemployment. Unemployment among teenagers and young adults arises primarily because a large proportion experience frequent short spells of unemployment as they move in and out of the labor market and between jobs.[5] Characteristically, the jobs are low paid and are not good first steps toward higher wages and more secure employment. A smaller proportion of other adult workers experience relatively long spells of unemployment (this is less true of women than men). Since most adult workers experience a spell of unemployment infrequently in a high-employment economy, one can assume that their short-duration spells of unemployment are primarily frictional in nature and not a major social concern.

4. See appendix A.
5. Technically, such unemployment should be considered excessive frictional—that is, more frictional than is desirable from the standpoint of economic efficiency—but it has been lumped in with structural unemployment here since this is generally done in current policy discussions.

Cyclical unemployment is due to an overall deficiency of demand. It occurs when the economy does not generate nearly as many jobs as there are people seeking them. This aggravates the situation for those who would be unemployed anyway for structural reasons, and, in addition, creates substantial new unemployment among experienced workers and new labor force entrants who, under better economic conditions, would experience little or no difficulty in finding and holding suitable jobs. For experienced workers, much of it is in the form of layoffs, often temporary, from jobs of a type they can regain when employment conditions improve.

Much of structural as well as cyclical unemployment is responsive to increased aggregate demand. In fact, strong economic growth is the essential condition for minimizing structural unemployment. The prospects of structurally unemployed workers improve dramatically in times of sustained prosperity since jobs are much more plentiful then. Moreover, discrimination becomes more costly to employers and the growing shortage of skilled and semiskilled workers leads them to provide the necessary work experience, training, and upgrading to unskilled workers. The pool of labor to fill the more casual, low-paying jobs in society begins to diminish; eventually even these jobs have to be upgraded with better wages and working conditions if employers hope to obtain qualified workers for them.

The drawback of a high-pressure economy is that it generates inflation. This process of reducing structural unemployment through aggregate demand alone takes time and is often inefficient. Before it can operate long enough to make satisfactory inroads into structural unemployment, the higher demand may aggravate the rate of inflation. This can happen for many reasons, among them the more rapid bidding up of wages when job vacancies, particularly in skilled occupations, are plentiful. Although it is a matter of considerable controversy, most economists, judging from the events of the past decade, believe that, at least for the next several years, it will be difficult to lower the aggregate rate of unemployment below the 5.0–5.5 percent range solely through conventional methods of economic stimulation without undesirable consequences for the rate of inflation.

The Role of Employment and Training Assistance

Within this broad context, what is the role of employment and training activities—including institutional and on-the-job training, work experience, public employment, and general labor market services[6]—in helping to cope with unemployment? Presumably the primary target of these programs would be those suffering from structural unemployment. Because of the nature of structural unemployment, programs aimed at teenagers and young adults ought to be broadly based, with the goal of reducing job turnover for all who experience high unemployment and providing more substantial assistance to the smaller proportion who will not otherwise become successfully integrated into the labor market at a later age. Programs dealing with adult structural unemployment, on the other hand, should be more narrowly targeted, with emphasis on those suffering or otherwise likely to suffer from chronic unemployment.

By providing appropriate types of job experience, skill training, and other services, such structurally oriented programs could increase the pool of workers for regular jobs that are critical for alleviating supply bottlenecks as the economy expands. In addition, work experience and public employment programs can provide subsidized jobs to those who would otherwise be subject to high rates of unemployment. The benefits of such programs could be twofold: program participants are given an increased competitive edge, improving the distribution of employment opportunities; and there might be a reduction in the degree of inflationary pressure consistent with any given level of employment and output. The latter, in turn, would make it possible to move to lower rates of unemployment faster and to sustain higher aggregate rates of employment than otherwise would be possible.

While there is presumably a long-term need for structurally oriented programs, those designed to deal primarily with cyclical unem-

6. These categories are defined in Congressional Budget Office, "Public Employment and Training Assistance: Alternative Federal Approaches" (CBO, February 1977), p. 14, as follows. Institutional training provides occupational or prevocational skill training, generally in a classroom or other off-the-job setting. On-the-job training provides training for regular job vacancies, generally by payment to public or private employers for the added cost of hiring and training target-group individuals; employers are expected to retain the individual after payment ends. Work experience provides temporary income and employment, usually part-time, primarily for youth and older workers. Public employment can be of many types. The two major ones are work relief, which entails low-skilled, labor-intensive project jobs, usually newly created for program purposes, often involving outdoor work, and often viewed as a direct alternative to income maintenance; and public service employment, which provides more conventional public sector jobs. Labor market services involve many activities, most prominently recruitment, counselling, assessment, and placement.

ployment are needed only temporarily. Public employment and work experience programs (as well as public works) can be expanded on an interim basis to provide jobs for unemployed workers who are expected to fare reasonably well once demand increases. But other methods of economic stimulus (for example, tax cuts or other public expenditure increases) also will reduce cyclical unemployment. Thus, the rationale for employment programs is that they may reduce unemployment faster or have more desirable output, distributional, or other consequences.

Finally, the general labor market services that provide information and other assistance to workers and employers to facilitate the matching of workers to job vacancies can reduce the level of frictional unemployment.

Recent Developments

Federal employment and training assistance programs have been in a constant state of flux for the past fifteen years, during which time they have become one of the fastest growing, rapidly changing, and controversial areas of the federal budget. Outlays have expanded steadily from near zero in 1962 to an expected level of approximately $10 billion in 1977. New legislation has resulted in frequent major program alterations. From 1968 through 1976, Presidents Nixon and Ford frequently vetoed new or larger programs voted by a Democratic Congress. There was a considerable devolution of responsibility to state and local governments as the majority of programs and expenditures were consolidated under new legislation, and the program contents and target populations shifted with varying economic conditions and with the perceptions of Congress and the administration of the principal employment problems.

The Basic Legislation

Employment and training assistance first became a significant federal activity in the post-Depression era under the Manpower Development and Training Act of 1962 (MDTA) and the Economic Opportunity Act of 1964 (EOA). These acts created programs with a multiplicity of highly categorical activities and disparate delivery mechanisms. The fragmentation of delivery mechanisms and decisionmaking authority for the allocation of employment and training assistance funds often made little sense from the point of view of the local labor market. Throughout the late 1960s and early 1970s growing pressures from state and local authorities and increased congressional and administrative concern led to several legislative amendments and changes in administrative practices; these were designed to facilitate greater coordination of the funds expended in local labor market areas through greater "decentralization" and "decategorization."[7] The final result was the Comprehensive Employment and Training Act (CETA), passed in December 1973. Three of its titles continued the type of activities carried out under the earlier legislation and two others make provisions for public employment programs.[8]

CETA–Title I designates general-purpose local governments as prime sponsors to develop a basic planning capacity, receive federal funds, and design programs to fit their own populations and labor market situations.[9] This title represents full decategorization and decentralization and was expected to distribute the vast majority of CETA funds. Title III contains national categorical programs, such as those for migrant workers, native Americans, and for other purposes not amenable to local jurisdictional boundaries. Title IV retains the Job Corps.

The total amount of money expended annually under the earlier legislation had gradually increased to about $1.5 billion by 1973. This expansion has continued under the replacement CETA titles, which reached a level of about $2.5 billion in the initial 1977 congressional budget. Although there was continual tension between the Democratic congressional majority and the two Republican administrations from 1969 through 1976, with the latter wanting less and

7. Decentralization refers to a devolution of responsibility for both the allocation and administration of monies for different program purposes, and decategorization to a loosening of federal restrictions on the nature of the target groups and type of activities.

8. The pure "manpower special revenue sharing" approach advocated by President Nixon early in his first term as part of his fiscal federalism would have given full authority for all programs to local governments. As the result of several years of debate both within the Nixon administration and between it and Congress, CETA does not go nearly this far, although it was a major step in that direction.

9. Jurisdictions must have a population of 100,000 or more. Consortiums of local governments can qualify, and states administer the program for those areas not falling under local prime sponsors. Some 445 states and localities were serving as CETA prime sponsors as of spring 1977. The majority of title I monies are distributed among them by a formula based on area unemployment rates, area poverty rates, and previous levels of federal employment and training assistance funding.

the former wanting more expenditures for these purposes, the differences between them were not major.

Public Employment in the 1970s

New public service employment (PSE) programs contributed the most to the expansion of federal employment and training assistance in the first half of the 1970s, and were a major source of conflict between the administration and Congress. In 1971, Congress passed the Emergency Employment Act authorizing the public employment program (PEP). It was administered on a decentralized basis, with the Department of Labor providing $2.25 billion over a period of three and a half years to subsidize the hiring of currently unemployed workers by state and local governments.

Throughout the late 1960s there had been considerable congressional interest in utilizing large-scale public service employment as a means of dealing with structural unemployment. The public employment program had its roots in that concern, but it was funded at a lower level than Congress desired because of President Nixon's strong objections to this approach. Its passage finally was made possible by the high level of cyclical unemployment in the recession of 1970–71, which provided Congress with the public support to overcome the President's opposition. Although there was some priority given to groups suffering from chronic labor market hardship, the public employment program was implemented so quickly that little time was given to planning, and it was distributed broadly among the unemployed.[10]

CETA–Title II instituted a permanent program patterned after the public employment program, but only at a modest level of funding (about $400 million in 1975), owing in part to the opposition of the Nixon administration. Since the economy was once again back on track, this program was oriented less toward cyclical and more toward structural unemployment, with provision for assisting the transition to regular jobs.[11]

10. Funds were distributed to all local areas, with extra going to those experiencing unemployment rates of 6 percent and above. Federal monies could be used to support wage costs of up to $12,000 a year, with an additional 11 percent available for overhead costs. It was expected that the jobs and pay would be similar to regular state and local government employment, and a "maintenance-of-effort" provision was included in an attempt to require that the subsidized jobs actually represented a net increment to the employment of the administering agency.

11. Funds are distributed to areas with 6 percent or greater unemployment. The

Shortly after CETA was in operation, the unemployment rate began to rise dramatically. In response, Congress passed the Emergency Jobs and Unemployment Assistance Act of 1974, which added a temporary $1 billion annually for public service employment under a new title VI of CETA. Eligibility restrictions in title VI as well as title II were relaxed to the point of inconsequence and transition to regular employment totally dropped as a requirement.[12] While this undoubtedly aided speedy implementation of the programs, it also shifted the emphasis away from structurally unemployed workers before title II was ever implemented. As a consequence, the characteristics of those who obtained the public service jobs varied very little from those of the experienced labor force.

When title VI came up for renewal in 1976, Congress was concerned about both the targeting and the extent to which the monies were reducing the amount of employment that state and local governments otherwise would have financed.[13] These concerns, along with the continued high rate of unemployment, led to an extension and expansion of title VI with several major changes: (1) all new slots from the expansion and at least half of any new vacancies must be filled with persons unemployed for at least fifteen weeks, welfare recipients, or those who have exhausted their unemployment insurance; (2) the family income of prospective participants must be less than approximately 120 percent of the poverty level; (3) the amount of funds that can be spent on nonwage costs was increased from 10 percent to 15 percent; and (4) all new slots from the expansion must be in projects lasting one year or less (as opposed to more conventional ongoing public jobs).

The first two restrictions are an attempt to channel the new jobs to the more needy. The relaxation of the overhead percentage is a recognition of the problems localities were reporting in renting space

maximum salary ceiling is $10,000 rather than $12,000 and the target group is restricted to those unemployed for at least a month, with priority given to the long-term unemployed and those with poor employment prospects.

12. Under title VI the prior length of unemployment restriction was lowered from thirty to fifteen days in areas with unemployment in excess of 7 percent, and the transition guidelines were modified to be only "goals" and not "requirements." The distributional formula for title VI is more complicated than for title II. Some funds go to every area. In addition, 50 percent of the funds are distributed on the basis of area unemployment rates in excess of 4.5 percent, and additional weight is given to areas where the rate exceeds 6.5 percent.

13. This is often referred to as the displacement problem and is discussed further below.

and purchasing supplies and equipment within the previous restrictions. The project orientation and limited time duration represent an attempt both to minimize the displacement of regular jobs and to encourage greater flexibility in tailoring jobs to the more restricted target group.

Other Major Employment and Training Assistance

The other major employment-related program instituted in response to the recent recession was the Public Works Employment Act, which finally became law in mid-1976 over President Ford's veto, which he also had exercised on an earlier version of the bill with a much larger authorization. Under title I of this act, the Economic Development Administration of the Department of Commerce was authorized to spend $2 billion over the next several years on construction grants to state and local governments. To promote speedy expenditure of these monies, Congress required that local jurisdictions initiate construction within ninety days of the grant award.[14]

One final thread of policy development through the 1960s and into the 1970s deserves brief mention. From its inception, the Manpower Development and Training Act contained a small work-experience and training component aimed specifically at welfare (aid to families with dependent children) recipients. This program expanded gradually and in 1967 was incorporated into the work incentive program, which is totally divorced from CETA. It now provides the full range of employment and training services, as well as day care services and a tax credit to employers for hiring AFDC recipients.[15] Since 1972, the work incentive program has also been the vehicle for the work registration and job search requirement applied to many welfare heads of households.

Table 5-2 provides basic data for 1976 on selected employment and training programs. CETA outlays accounted for about $5 billion—well over half of the just over $9 billion attributed to employ-

14. There is a complicated formula for determining which of the grant applications should be funded that gives preference to such factors as geographic dispersion and local unemployment and income levels. The actual allocation of this $2 billion was the subject of considerable controversy because of the apparently irrational results relative to local needs.

15. The tax credit is complicated, but its basic provision is a credit of 20 percent of the workers' wages for the first year of employment.

Table 5-2. Basic Data for Selected Employment and Training Programs, Fiscal Year 1976

Program and approach[a]	Total outlays (millions of dollars)	Person years of service (thousands)	Average length of stay (years)	Cost per person year of service (dollars)	Cost per participant (dollars)
Program					
Comprehensive Employment and Training Act					
Title I: basic allocation to prime sponsors	1,698	448.3	0.35	3,786	1,256
Title II: public employment	544	75.3	0.52	7,226	2,175
Title III					
Migrants and farmworkers	65	6.1	0.15	n.a.	n.a.
Native Americans	61	14.5	0.22	4,185	963
Summer youth employment	459	250.7	0.25	2,380	595
Title IV: Job Corps	181	20.2	0.45	9,321	4,156
Title VI: temporary public employment	1,872	226.6	0.55	8,262	3,906
Community service employment for older workers	47	12.7	2.00	3,387	6,943
Work incentive	307	30.6	0.35	10,300	3,287
Approach					
On-the-job training	487	143.0	0.60	3,492	2,115
Institutional training[b]	907	219.0	0.35	4,210	1,466
Vocational rehabilitation	939	852.0	1.48	1,296	1,921
Public service employment	2,725	299.0	0.53	8,335	4,431
Work experience	1,648	595.0	0.33	2,926	961

Sources: Program data, Congressional Budget Office, *Public Employment and Training Assistance: Alternative Federal Approaches* (CBO, February 1977), p. 51; approach data, *Special Analyses, Budget of the United States Government, Fiscal Year 1978*, tables J-2 through J-6, and J-9.

n.a. Not available.

a. Approach outlays and years of service add to greater totals than do program ones since they include more programs than CETA, community service employment, and WIN.

b. Excludes social services training, which appears in the source (*Special Analyses, 1978*, table J-3), but is not taken into account in the cost calculations reported in table J-9 of *Special Analyses*.

ment and training assistance in the federal budget—with the vast majority being split evenly between the discretionary money allotted to prime sponsors and the temporary public service employment of title VI. There is also a considerable amount of variation in the level of activity and costs of the various approaches to employment and training assistance.

The 1977 and 1978 Budget Options

When President Carter took office in January 1977 he inherited from President Ford a budget for fiscal year 1977 that differed very little from the 1976 budget in the employment and training assistance area, and a Ford proposal for 1978 that would have continued the same pattern, except for a phasing out of the temporary public service employment under CETA–Title VI. Carter quickly requested a series of budget additions for both 1977 and 1978 as part of his economic stimulus package.

President Carter's stimulus package had major budget implications in three areas directly affecting employment: CETA, emergency public works, and an employment tax credit.[16] Tables 5-3 and 5-4 show how the Carter budget for 1977 and the Ford and Carter proposals for 1978 affect the titles of CETA at issue. The most striking difference among them is that President Carter has proposed expanding public employment positions—primarily in the temporary title VI program—by the end of the first quarter of fiscal 1978 to more than double the initial fiscal 1977 level, whereas Ford wished to phase out title VI completely within fiscal year 1978. Since title VI is explicitly a temporary countercyclical measure, even under Carter's proposal the program would be expected to phase out as the unemployment rate drops;[17] it would certainly take several more years than President Ford intended, however. The administration's intention with regard to the future of the increase in permanent public employment under title II of CETA is unclear.

16. The employment tax credit was subsequently withdrawn by Carter along with a proposed $50 per capita income tax rebate; however, since Congress passed a form of such a credit, it is considered in this section.

17. However, statements made by administration officials at a White House press conference on welfare reform in May 1977 indicate that an outlay amount equivalent to the temporary 1978 increases in CETA for countercyclical public service jobs eventually might be proposed to fund a permanent public service employment component of a welfare reform program.

Table 5-3. Budget Proposals and Base for Selected Titles of the Comprehensive Employment and Training Act, Fiscal Years 1977 and 1978[a]
Outlays in millions of dollars; positions in thousands

| | Fiscal year 1977 | | | | Fiscal year 1978 | | | | | |
| | Initial appropriation | | Carter requests | | Current services | | Ford proposals[b] | | Carter proposals | |
Title and program	Outlays	Positions	Outlays	Positions	Outlays	Positions	Outlays	Positions	Outlays	Positions
Title II (public service employment)	400	50	524	100	400	50	...	...	1,016	125
Title III[c] (national categorial programs)	231	74	502	282	231	85	...	...	1,613	424
Title IV (Job Corps)	206	23	255	30	213	23	...	...	471	44
Title VI (temporary public employment)	2,358	260	2,949	500	2,101	260	1,000	130[d]	4,872	600

Source: Office of Management and Budget. Figures are rounded.
a. Releases of the Office of Management and Budget in late spring of 1977 probably will show a small reduction of outlays in 1977 and commensurate increases in subsequent years due to later than anticipated congressional action on the CETA proposals.
b. Where there are major deviations from current services.
c. Excludes summer youth component.
d. The number of positions actually would be 260,000, but because it would be phased out over the year there would be only 130,000 full position-years funded,

**Table 5-4. Details on Proposed Carter Expansion of Selected Programs of Title III
of the Comprehensive Employment and Training Act, Fiscal Years 1977 and 1978**
Expansions in millions of dollars; positions in thousands

	Fiscal year 1977		Fiscal year 1978	
Program[a]	Expansions	Positions	Expansions	Positions
Youth[b]	137	72	863	154
Skill training and improvement program[c]	75	58	250	58
HIRE[d]	24	60	116	92
Veterans[e]	4	3	19	3
Migrant and Native Americans[f]	11	8	56	15
Apprenticeship[g]	20	9	59	17

Source: Office of Management and Budget. Figures are rounded.

a. No details on these programs were available by early May 1977. The descriptions in the footnotes below are based on the author's interpretations of general information released by the administration.

b. Originally proposed under title III, it is now expected that these activities will be authorized by a new title. These programs will be primarily for out-of-school youth aged sixteen to twenty-one who are unemployed, with an emphasis on those also with low incomes or otherwise disadvantaged. The bulk of the money will go to support work relief and work experience type jobs, about one-third for neighborhood and community improvement and maintenance and restoration of parks and other public lands and two-thirds for projects deemed worthwhile by CETA prime sponsors and the secretary of labor. Much of the money will be administered by CETA prime sponsors and distributed partially on a formula basis and partially at the discretion of the secretary of labor. Another large portion will be disbursed through the Agriculture and Interior Departments.

c. Funds will be used to establish high-level, long-term, substantive skill training, through present CETA prime sponsors and with heavy involvement of the private sector in training design and delivery.

d. This program is aimed at increasing private sector employment through the provision of financial incentives to major corporations to hire and train the long-term unemployed. It is patterned after the old JOBS program. The first priority target group will be Vietnam-era veterans.

e. This program will hire disabled Vietnam-era veterans in state employment service agencies to provide outreach services to other members of the same target group and assist their employment efforts. In addition, authority is being sought to provide Vietnam-era veterans priority for 35 percent of the HIRE program.

f. This represents an expansion of the existing mix of programs for these groups. The positions in 1977 and 1978 are in addition to a current services base of 28.5 thousand and 34.3 thousand, respectively.

g. This effort represents a nationally administered program of demonstration projects to provide training, employment opportunities, and related services to workers associated with the trades and to promote the use of apprentice-type procedures in new occupations. It will be focused on private employees with apprenticeable occupations. Some apprenticeship activities are now carried out under title I.

Carter also proposed a sizable increase in national categorical programs under titles III and IV (the Job Corps) of CETA, in some cases for new program activities and in others for activities already being pursued to some extent by local prime sponsors under CETA–Title I.[18] Whether the increase is to be temporary or permanent is unclear.

At the time of this writing, it is apparent that Congress will approve

18. Requested budget authority actually exceeded the estimated outlays for 1977 and 1978 shown in table 5-4 by $1.2 billion for public employment and $760 million in titles III and IV. These amounts are required in the budget authority because of the anticipated program funding patterns, but would not become outlays until 1979.

expansions of CETA very close to those Carter has proposed; in fact, there is support in Congress for even larger increases in CETA, particularly for public employment.

The expansion of public works proposed by Carter was for an increase of $2 billion in budget authority each year for 1977 and 1978 for title I of the Public Works Employment Act of 1976. Congress appropriated the full $4 billion for 1977. Estimated increases in outlays under this title are $100 million in 1977 and $1.8 billion in 1978, with the remaining $2.1 billion to carry over into 1979 and beyond. Since the allocation of the $2 billion in budget authority already existing under this program to state and local governments was so roundly criticized for being insufficiently related to the severity of local unemployment, President Carter indicated that he had instructed the Commerce Department to direct as much of the additional funds as possible into areas of high unemployment.

The final employment-related component of President Carter's original stimulus package was a permanent income tax credit for businesses equivalent to 4 percent of their social security payroll tax payments (businesses were to have the option of taking this or an increase in the investment tax credit from 10 percent to 12 percent). Starting in 1977, employers pay a 5.85 percent payroll tax on the first $16,500 of employees' annual wages, so the maximum amount of this credit would have been about $39 per employee. This tax cut was subsequently withdrawn by Carter, but Congress had already rejected it in favor of a temporary employment tax credit, which it hoped would generate even more employment, providing greater incentives to hire low-wage workers. As finally passed, the tax credit is 50 percent of the first $4,200 of each employee's annual wages ($2,100 maximum) for all such wages in excess of 102 percent of the prior year's level and up to a maximum of $100,000 per firm.[19]

Thus the Carter and Ford administrations have offered very different alternatives for CETA for the remainder of 1977 and 1978 (and, implicitly, for at least a year or two beyond), as well as for two

19. Restricting the credit to wages in excess of 2 percent over the prior year's base is an attempt to direct the subsidy at workers who would not otherwise have been hired by the firm, thereby providing an incentive for such hiring. The $4,200 maximum wage base is intended to create a greater incentive for firms to hire relatively more low-wage workers, and the $100,000 maximum per firm is to insure that large employers do not receive the lion's share of the total credit. To avoid a tax advantage that exceeds the employee's wages, the deduction for wages in calculating business profits is reduced by the amount of the credit.

other specific employment-related policy areas that lie outside of the employment and training component of the federal budget. Consistent with the policies pursued from 1969 through the end of his term, President Ford wished to return the expenditure levels and program emphases of CETA to more or less what they were at the time of its original passage and did not want to make expanded use of public works or employment tax credits. President Carter, on the other hand, had proposed both more public works programs and an employment tax credit, as well as a major expansion of CETA, especially in the public employment titles II and VI and in the work experience and training for youth in the more centralized and categorical programs of titles III and IV. Although Congress has accepted the general thrust of Carter's proposals, it is likely that the Democratic majority would prefer larger expenditures on selective employment-creating measures than Carter has proposed. This is reflected in its rejection of his employment tax credit in favor of a larger one, which was designed in the hopes of promoting faster reductions in unemployment, concentrated among low-wage workers.

Assessing the Budget Options

Since there is substantial agreement on the need for additional fiscal stimulus in 1977 and 1978, any assessment of increasing expenditures for selective employment programs must be made in light of the generally acknowledged alternative—larger general tax cuts. Both strategies are expected to increase the rate of growth of employment and output. What is really at issue in choosing among the various alternatives are the following: How many jobs are created for a given increase in the deficit? How fast is employment increased and with what degree of inflationary pressure? Are the jobs distributed in a desirable fashion? What is the value of the additional output produced? What are the long-run effects on the target groups?[20]

For a given impact on the deficit, selective employment programs generally will create more jobs in the short run than will other public expenditure increases. The latter, in turn, will also create more jobs in the short run than general tax cuts. All three share similar indirect

20. The discussion here does not deal with the magnitude of the stimulus, a controversial topic that is treated in chapter 3. The implied assumption is that, for a given short-term deficit target, there is a trade-off between larger general tax cuts and additional expenditures in selective employment programs.

effects once the additional money is in the pockets of businesses and consumers, but the initial injection of government expenditures directly purchases goods and services and creates some jobs, while tax cuts do not. The more of the initial injection that goes directly into wages and salaries, the more jobs are likely to be created.

Congress appears to have given considerable weight to these relative short-term effects in its deliberations over the desired form of the stimulus. While it is easy to understand the political pressures to maximize the number of jobs for any given amount of budget deficit, the economic desirability of such maximization is often oversold on two grounds. First, the longer-run direct job creation effects of government employment programs are not as great as they are alleged to be. For example, substantially less than half of the expenditures of most public works projects actually go for wages and salaries, and these tend to be for skilled workers earning considerably above the median. Thus, the direct job creation effects of public works expenditures are generally no greater than those of most government expenditures.[21] Public service employment funds, on the other hand, go largely for wages and salaries of a moderate level; however, both common sense and empirical evidence suggest that, overtime, state and local governments use more and more of such federal funds to support jobs they otherwise would have funded themselves. In such instances, federal public service employment expenditures are little different in their effect from additional general revenue sharing, and much of these funds clearly goes for state and local tax relief (whether taxes are actually lowered or merely increased more slowly).

Second, what is important is less the size of the deficit per se than the ability of the budget as a whole to promote a timely return to higher levels of employment under the most favorable circumstances. Many different mixes of fiscally stimulative policies can be pursued to raise total employment to some reasonable target; it is the other effects of these policies that are most important in assessing their merit. These are discussed below for each type of federal employment policy—public works, public service employment, work experience for youth, employment tax credits, and intensive training activities. The implicit comparison in each case, unless otherwise stated, is between the employment policy in question and a broad tax cut that would create an equivalent number of jobs.

21. See Roger J. Vaughan, *Public Works as a Countercyclical Device: A Review of the Issues* (Rand Corporation, 1976), chap. 6.

Public Works

Public works expenditures have several potential advantages. First, they can be channeled to areas where unemployment is particularly severe. Second, a high proportion of the direct job creation effect is concentrated in the construction industry, which is experiencing much higher than average unemployment rates. Both of these factors could contribute to a lower degree of inflationary pressure and more desirable targeting of the additional employment than a general tax cut. Finally, the output produced by public works, such as sewer and water facilities, municipal buildings, streets, and bridges, generally is expected to meet important public needs; in fact, often the federal money facilitates the earlier initiation of a project that eventually would have been undertaken by localities anyway. An indication of the large amount of unmet needs of localities was the over $20 billion in applications the Department of Commerce received within a few months of congressional authorization of $2 billion for the emergency public works program in 1976.

Despite these potential advantages, however, public works have many deficiencies as a countercyclical device. Perhaps most critical is that the timing of the actual expenditures generally lags that desirable on fiscal policy grounds, often by so much as actually to be counterproductive. In recognition of this problem, Congress required that the regulations for the 1976 authorization be prepared within thirty days, that project approval be granted within sixty subsequent days, and that projects must begin on-site construction within ninety days of approval. Similar constraints presumably will apply to the additional $4 billion that Carter has requested. However, although these provisions dictate the time for starting construction, they will not necessarily affect the speed with which it proceeds. Even the administration has projected that only about half of the additional $4 billion will be spent by the end of fiscal year 1978. Based on past experience, this estimate must be considered optimistic.[22]

Desirable as it may be on fiscal policy grounds, attempting to push

22. The predecessor of this public works program was the public works impact program, established in response to the 1970–71 recession in an amendment to the Public Works and Economic Development Act of 1965. Even though it emphasized quick starting and small projects (under $500,000), some projects took at least five years to complete. The average project size for the first $2 billion of the current program is $1 million.

public works expenditures too fast can have detrimental effects on other program objectives. The Department of Commerce had only sixty days to review 25,000 applications for the 1976 appropriation. Under these circumstances, it was impossible to ensure that projects funded actually flowed into areas with the most severe unemployment problems and met important public needs.[23] With the increased emphasis on areas with high unemployment President Carter has stipulated, aided by experience gained from the 1976 project applications, the Commerce Department should be able to obtain better results with the additional authorizations. However, there are severe limitations inherent in the highly complex and time-consuming process, which does not end until the last dollar is actually spent on some construction project in some local community.

Finally, many critics have questioned the extent to which current fiscal stimulus should be aimed at the highly skilled construction trades, which are the primary direct beneficiaries of public works expenditures. Although the unemployment rate in this industry is high, highly skilled unemployed construction workers are probably not the worst off among those without jobs. Moreover, stimulation of the construction industry through more indirect means, such as monetary policy, probably would result in a more diffuse distribution of job opportunities among workers with different levels of skills.[24]

Public Employment

It is often argued that public employment can accomplish several goals, among them the provision of needed additional public services, reductions in unemployment, and beneficial long-term effects on the employment prospects of program participants. It is difficult to pursue all objectives of public employment simultaneously, however, because there are trade-offs among some of them. Under both the public employment program of the early 1970s and titles II and VI of CETA, state and local governments previously were able to spend funds rapidly and to support valuable public services. But this was

23. Recent newspaper articles and congressional testimony have been replete with examples of gross violations of these criteria. See, for example, James C. Hyatt, "The Public Works Controversy," *Wall Street Journal*, February 14, 1977, and "Statement by Phyllis Lamphere on Behalf of the National League of Cities before the House Public Works Committee Subcommittee on Economic Development, February 2, 1977" (processed).

24. And in fact, the low interest rates of late 1976 and early 1977 are fueling a construction boom in 1977.

largely because they were able to select the most qualified workers available and to put them into regular positions in state and local agencies, many of which they otherwise would have been supporting with their own funds—thus freeing those funds for other uses, including tax reductions. Consequently, workers hired under the programs differed very little from those already in the general labor force, and there was considerable uncertainty about how many net new jobs actually were created. From a purely countercyclical point of view, these results are not necessarily unfavorable; but such a program has little to recommend it over general revenue sharing.

The new stringent restrictions in the temporary public employment program (CETA–Title VI) on both target groups and the nature of the work should improve matters. It is anticipated that a majority of the title VI jobs will go to those with poor long-term employment prospects and so result in an increase in the percentage of such workers employed by state and local governments. This, combined with the emphasis on areas with high unemployment, should lead to less inflationary pressure per job created than alternative fiscal measures. In addition, the long-term prospects of program participants and their general target group could be improved by the program if the projects are structured to provide useful work experience and on-the-job training. The fact that the funds must support job slots in projects of limited duration, rather than existing jobs in state and local agencies, will increase the probability that both the jobs and output associated with them are net additions and do not simply displace jobs and output that might have been provided anyway.

These new restrictions have their disadvantages, however. Hiring must be done from a much smaller pool of unemployed workers. State and local governments must initiate new projects or review and select ones from local nonprofit organizations. Needed new services must be identified and a strategy developed for providing them that efficiently employs a heterogeneous and predominantly low-skilled and less experienced labor force. The public services provided by these projects must not displace existing services, yet they must be of substantial social value and provide a work experience that is relevant to job opportunities in the regular labor market. Finally, the transition to regular employment will require new kinds of counseling and placement services heretofore untested. These tasks are formidable, and most will become even more difficult as the unemployment rate declines and the scale of the program is enlarged.[25]

These problems suggest that it would be all too easy to undermine many of the objectives of the new title VI program by expanding it too rapidly or attempting to operate it on too large a scale. There is very little prior experience relevant to the design and implementation of such a program at the federal or state and local level. Ideally, this type of program should have considerable planning behind it, followed by slow and cautious implementation with careful monitoring procedures to allow continuous adjustments in field operations and, possibly, in federal guidelines.

To many critics of public service employment, these are sufficient arguments for permanently limiting the use of CETA–Title VI to a small scale. But it can be argued that it is too popular, holds too much promise, and experience with it is too limited to date, to warrant such a judgment. Nonetheless, sound implementation of an expansion of title VI along the lines President Carter has proposed is likely to be inconsistent with the timing requirements of fiscal policy, and may well exceed the limits of an effective structurally oriented employment policy, even if implemented more slowly. To meet the President's goals for 1977 and 1978, serious consideration should be given to shifting more of the burden to the less restrictive title II; alternatively, the new title VI requirements should be relaxed somewhat. This would imply giving a priority to countercyclical objectives for the immediate future, in which case the program would not be effective as a structural tool and should not be judged a failure for this reason. If, however, the primary objective of title VI is viewed as structural unemployment, the new restrictions should be maintained, but any expansion should proceed slowly and provide for experimentation, monitoring, and feedback.

Employment Tax Credits

The Carter Administration's and Congress's versions of an employment tax credit are very different devices designed for different

25. As the unemployment rate declines, the size of the pool from which program participants must be drawn will also decline, resulting in a public service employment labor force that on average is less skilled and experienced. Also, it is more difficult to avoid displacement of both public and private sector services that would otherwise have been provided in a fuller employment economy. On the other hand, transition to regular jobs might be facilitated.

purposes. President Carter's credit was not intended to generate more jobs than a general tax cut. Its objectives were to: (1) ensure that labor-intensive (small) businesses, which would benefit little from an increase in the investment tax credit, would share in the business tax cut; (2) have a favorable effect on inflation by reducing the cost of labor; and (3) permanently reduce the relative cost of labor, since payroll taxes may discourage employers from using as much labor in the production of a given output as is socially desirable. In terms of these objectives, the administration's employment tax credit had merit, although the amount of the credit—4 percent of the social security tax paid by the employer—was quite small. In addition to these objectives, it would have served fiscal policy needs well, since it could be disbursed quickly and both its size and targeting could be predicted with considerable certainty. The provision of such a small offset to a previously imposed federal tax on labor is, however, a timid step, particularly since the proposal was coupled with an optional increase in the already substantial subsidy to capital.

Congressional interest in a much larger employment tax credit derived mainly from the hope that it would induce greater job creation than an indirect stimulus of equivalent size. Here there are two polar possibilities: a temporary, general, countercyclically oriented subsidy for labor during periods of high unemployment, or a more permanent subsidy for specific groups of workers who suffer high rates of structural unemployment. Various forms were debated, and what emerged from Congress was more of the first type, but with a much larger subsidy for low wages, presumably because of structural unemployment concerns.

The major criticisms that have been made against this form of an employment tax credit are: (1) it will be largely ineffective in directly inducing additional employment; (2) it provides employers with incentives to substitute low-wage, part-time, and temporary jobs for high-wage, permanent jobs at a time when many more good jobs are needed for primary earners; and (3) attempts to try to meet these criticisms have rendered it unduly complex and inequitable, with little net gain.

As an example of the first (and, to some extent, the third) criticism, consider the following. If all labor is subsidized, as it would have been under the administration's proposal, most of the employment tax credit revenues would have been paid to employers who would have hired the same work force anyway. To avoid this problem, the employment tax credit was restricted to only those wages covered by unemployment insurance in excess of 102 percent of the prior year's covered wages for each employer, on the assumption that 2 percent would constitute "normal" growth. But the actual experience of individual enterprises will be quite varied and cannot be expected to cluster around 2 percent. A sizable percentage of the labor force is likely to be employed in firms that would otherwise fall short of 2 percent; these will be ineligible for the tax credit even though they might have been willing to expand their employment to take advantage of it. Another large portion will be employed in firms with considerably more than 2 percent "normal" growth; in such cases a large proportion of the subsidy will go for jobs that would otherwise exist or are not eligible for the credit because of the maximum ceiling. For those eligible employers who might be influenced at the margin, the temporary nature of the credit provides little incentive to utilize a higher proportion of low-wage workers, since there are often substantial fixed costs in altering production methods. Finally, unless they can be confident that there is a market for their products, business firms will have little incentive to expand output and employment, even if the additional labor costs were subsidized. This renders it of uncertain value as a countercyclical tool.

A longer-term subsidy to employers for particular groups of workers with high structural unemployment may be a more useful tool in the arsenal of employment programs. Private employers will continue to provide the vast majority of all job opportunities in the economy; thus any successful strategy for long-term reductions in structural unemployment probably will require major private sector involvement. Such subsidies are subject to similar criticisms as were aimed at the tax credit; however, there are no effective established methods of making deep inroads into structural unemployment. Therefore, it is difficult to escape the conclusion that society should be as willing to experiment on a large scale with this type of private sector job creation as it is about to do with public employment.[26]

26. The results of the work incentive program and welfare tax credits, which are highly categorical, have not been encouraging to date, but a larger incentive for a different population, and with a somewhat different structure, may have more favorable results.

Youth Work Experience

It is difficult to assess this component of the proposed expansion of employment and training assistance because it consists largely of new programs whose guidelines are still being developed. Many of the issues that were discussed above for public employment (and, to a lesser extent, public works) are relevant to the youth programs. For example, a similar trade-off exists between the speed of program implementation for fiscal policy purposes and ability to meet other program objectives. But speed is less crucial in this case, since the amount of money involved is much smaller ($1 billion over 1977 and 1978), and the problem to which the program is addressed will be serious even when the overall unemployment rate is much lower. In addition, while providing goods and services of high social value is desirable, the primary objectives of work experience programs for teenagers should be to provide income assistance where it is needed and to promote favorable long-term employment prospects for the participants.

Two important issues for these youth programs, therefore, are the nature of their targeting within the teenage population and whether the work experience provided will be worthwhile. One of the criticisms of youth programs under CETA and earlier legislation has been that too many of the participants have not been from low-income families and disadvantaged backgrounds. In addition, they were often faulted for doing no more for the long-run employability of the participants than the passage of time would have accomplished. In fact, there is ample anecdotal evidence that many earlier teenage employment programs provided regular paychecks for trivial or no work at all; this will neither help a disadvantaged youth to get a job later nor improve his attitude toward work. It is also unclear how helpful activities such as planting trees in a national forest in Idaho would be to high school dropouts who expect to return to the inner city of Chicago.

Since a large proportion of workers who experience high unemployment as teenagers do find more decent jobs when they get older, it is clear that the mere passage of time ameliorates the problem for them. But for others, the passage of time is not enough. Just how important is the early work experience of youth for their later work behavior and employment opportunities? How much difference can well-designed work experience programs for teenagers make? Which aspects of such programs are more important: the actual skills learned or simply the discipline and self-respect that come from regular work? How can those teenagers for whom it will make a difference in the long run be identified? Very little is known about the answers to these questions.

The addition of large numbers of teenagers to public payrolls will reduce the official unemployment rate with minimal inflationary impact. But the real social payoff will come from paying the wages to those who need the income, while simultaneously providing a work experience that is at worst neutral and at best favorable for long-term employment prospects. Since little is known about how to do this, the new youth programs should be viewed as exploratory efforts that should be expanded, contracted, or otherwise modified over time as experience dictates. Careful program design and a moderate pace of implementation are more likely to yield favorable results than attempts to spend the money very quickly.

Intensive Training Assistance

Of all the employment-related activities now being considered, the expenditure increases proposed for training are the smallest and, with the possible exception of youth work experience programs, the least controversial. President Ford would not have cut these programs back, President Carter has proposed an increase of about half a billion dollars for fiscal year 1978, and Congress has not seriously entertained the possibility of additional expansion. No information was available at the time of this writing on the major new proposed component of President Carter's expansion of skill training (the skill training improvement program). Presumably it will entail the same type of classroom activities that prime sponsors now support with their discretionary CETA money. The other major component of expansion in this area is the doubling of the Jobs Corps.

Skill training programs have provided the longest continuous experience and have been subject to more analysis than any other type of employment program. In retrospect, expectations in the 1960s regarding their effectiveness in increasing the earnings potential of participants appear unrealistically high. Because both descriptive assessments of their benefits and extensive cost-benefit analyses concluded that the programs were not very successful, public enthusiasm for these programs waned in the early 1970s and policy attention turned toward other employment-related activities—most notably public employment.[27]

Several recently completed studies of postprogram earnings indicate, however, that, on average, the programs yield a reasonable rate of return.[28] Whether these results will hold up with large expansions of government-sponsored skill training programs is not known. But, if the programs are carefully targeted, the combination of favorable rates of return and favorable distributional consequences suggests that a small expansion may yield desirable results. In addition, none of the evaluative studies to date has focused on the social benefits generated by training programs that increase the supply of workers in relatively low-unemployment occupations. Such benefits would be realized in the form of higher rates of employment and output with less inflationary pressure.

An important element in the success of skill training programs is the extent to which the training content is geared to the ever-changing mix of occupations required by localized excess demand and by the specific needs of employers. Greater flexibility for participants to shop around for skill training—particularly among successful and market-responsive proprietary institutions—perhaps through the use of vouchers, might promote the first objective. This does not, however, appear to be emphasized in President Carter's program. Greater involvement of private employers in the design and delivery of the programs should make them more suitable for the specific skill needs in the private sector; this apparently will be an emphasis of the skill training improvement program.

Beyond Fiscal Year 1978

The authorizing legislation for CETA was originally due to expire at the end of 1977, but it is expected to be extended for one year at the request of the Carter administration, so that the stimulus package can be dealt with before turning to the longer-term future of CETA. In light of the major expansion and reorientation now scheduled for

27. The excessively high unemployment rates of the 1970s also contributed to the shift.

28. A summary of these is provided in Robert E. Hall, "The Effectiveness of Training Programs in Raising Earnings" (Massachusetts Institute of Technology, September 1976; processed).

CETA over the second half of 1977 and 1978, a strong case can be made for a simple extension of CETA for yet an additional year, both to provide more feedback and to allow the administration more time to develop longer-term plans. Whether or not this is done, several of the issues that must be considered are already evident.

Sorting Out Public Service Employment

Although each individual modification made to the CETA public employment titles over the past several years might have seemed appropriate at the time, the end result no longer makes sense. The permanent title II program was intended to alleviate structural unemployment, but has ended up being used largely for countercyclical purposes. The temporary title VI program, which was originally intended to be countercyclical, now has restrictions placed upon it that are more appropriate for a structural program. These difficulties are illustrated in table 5-5, which summarizes the primary design features appropriate to a countercyclically versus structurally oriented program and indicates the extent to which they are presently embodied in CETA–Titles II and VI.

The danger is that neither structural nor countercyclical objectives will be served well. For example, because of its relatively permanent funding but lax targeting restrictions, the title II program will differ little from general revenue sharing in its eventual effect on state and local employment. Moreover, as was noted earlier, because of the tight restrictions on types of employment and targeting, title VI funds are unlikely to be an effective countercyclical tool. Yet the very temporary nature of the program and the attempts to implement it quickly will severely restrict its effectiveness in alleviating structural unemployment.

It was suggested above that one response to these problems could be to shift more of the burden of the public employment expansion under the stimulus package from title VI to title II, or to loosen the new restrictions placed on title VI. But this is only a stopgap measure; steps should be taken to modify appropriately the basic structure of CETA when its long-term renewal is debated. There are several possibilities for accomplishing this, but the most attractive would be to return title II to its original intent by designing it along the lines suggested under the structurally oriented alternative in table 5-5. Title VI could then be correspondingly redesigned as a temporary countercyclical program, also along the lines suggested in the table.

Table 5-5. Major Desirable Design Features of Structurally and Countercyclically Oriented Public Programs and Extent to Which They are Embodied in Titles II and VI of the Comprehensive Employment and Training Act, as of Spring 1977

Type of program and desirable design features	Extent that features are embodied in CETA	
	Title II	Title VI
Structurally oriented programs		
Permanent funding[a]	Fully	Not at all[b]
Funds allocated to all areas with more than frictional unemployment[c]	Slightly	Almost fully
Narrow targeting on those not likely to fare well in a high employment economy	Not at all	Almost fully
Long-term project orientation[d]	Not at all	Somewhat
Emphasis on relevance of work experience to regular employment opportunities and transitional assistance	Not at all	Slightly
Countercyclically oriented programs		
Temporary funding with level varying inversely with aggregate unemployment rate	Not at all	Somewhat[b]
Funds allocated primarily to those areas suffering from cyclical unemployment	Almost fully	Somewhat
Broad targeting on unemployed	Fully	Slightly
Emphasis on employment that can be effectively and promptly phased in and out	Not at all	Slightly

a. Structural unemployment will be a problem even at relatively low rates of aggregate unemployment. The amount of money expended for this purpose might vary somewhat with the overall rate of unemployment.

b. Title VI is clearly intended to be temporary, and the annual reviews of its expenditure level may cause it to vary inversely with the aggregate unemployment rate; however, an automatic trigger to accomplish this would be more desirable.

c. Even in relatively low-unemployment areas there is likely to be some structural unemployment. The allocation formula could put greater weight on areas with higher unemployment rates (adjusted for size of labor force).

d. Since funding is long term and for the structurally unemployed, special projects are desirable to avoid displacement and to tailor the nature of the work experience to the needs of target groups. Although length of tenure of individuals in programs should be restricted, effective projects will take considerable time to design and implement and should not be forced to terminate.

The Degree of Decategorization and Decentralization

President Nixon's original proposal for "manpower special revenue sharing" represented an extreme move to total decentralization and decategorization. CETA, as enacted, stopped far short of this, but still was welcomed as a major step in this direction by the administration, most state and local officials, and the vast majority of Congress. Title I funds, which can be allocated at the discretion of the prime sponsors, accounted for most of the original CETA appropriations. Over time this concept has been gradually, but severely, eroded, to the point where it now appears that title I will contain less than 20 percent of CETA outlays in 1978. True, the public employment titles have decentralized administration, but both the nature of this activity and the target groups are largely prescribed by the federal government. And all of the proposed expansion of work experience and skill training programs under the Carter stimulus package is highly categorical and funded through the national program titles, even though many of the activities are similar to these now being undertaken by prime sponsors under title I.

This reversion to much greater centralization and categorization has to date aroused very little public and congressional discussion, though interest groups representing CETA prime sponsors are beginning to raise this issue in congressional appearances. Clearly considerable thought ought to be given to this issue when CETA comes up for long-term renewal. This is particularly important because most prime sponsors are just now developing their planning capacities to the point where they can begin to assert effective authority over the allocation of CETA funds. Indications of a permanent reversal in the recent trend toward greater discretion for these prime sponsors could discourage the further development of these capacities. The logical next steps of moving toward an integration of state employment services with the state and local CETA prime sponsor network, as well as greater coordination of other relevant state agencies (such as in the vocational education and vocational rehabilitation areas) with prime sponsors might also be neglected.

It is relatively easy to make a case for strict federal guidelines in designing grant-in-aid programs so as to further national objectives (such as aiding the employment prospects of the disadvantaged and achieving high levels of employment with minimal inflation). It is more difficult, however, to defend the need for such guidelines to prescribe in detail within a broad area such as employment and training assistance the exact nature of the activities that must be undertaken by state and local governments.[29]

Employment and Training Assistance under Welfare Reform

One of the major issues being debated in conjunction with welfare reform is the role that employment and training programs, particularly public employment, should play in ensuring minimally adequate

29. See Charles L. Schultze, "Federal Spending: Past, Present, and Future," in Henry Owen and Charles L. Schultze, eds., *Setting National Priorities: The Next Ten Years* (Brookings Institution, 1976), pp. 323–69, for a discussion of these issues.

levels of income for families with employable members. This subject is discussed more fully in chapter 8; but the potential implications of welfare reform for broader employment and training assistance policies and for CETA should be noted here.

The work incentive program now operates independently of CETA, but it is funded at a relatively low level and is not considered to be very effective. Current discussion of most welfare reform proposals assumes that several billion dollars—coordinated in an appropriate manner with other income assistance—will be devoted to employment and training assistance for the population eligible under welfare reform. This could affect CETA in two ways: the prime sponsors could play a major role in the delivery of such employment and training assistance; and a large portion of current CETA monies could be reprogrammed for the welfare target group.

The desirability of either or both of these outcomes is of major importance for the long-term future of federal, state, and local roles in the development and implementation of employment and training assistance programs. They raise such issues as: how much reliance should be placed on state and local versus federal agencies to administer employment and training assistance programs under welfare reform? Should an employment and training assistance delivery system for the low-income population be separated from the system created for other groups? How large a proportion of total federal expenditures for employment and training assistance should be earmarked for the low-income population? How much emphasis should be put on private sector versus public sector jobs? These concerns obviously are highly interrelated with the redesigning of public employment programs and the degree of decentralization and decategorization under CETA. They must be confronted as both CETA renewal and welfare reform proposals are debated.

Conclusion

In contrast to President Ford, who proposed total reliance on general tax cuts, both President Carter and Congress have put major emphasis on the expansion of existing, and the creation of new, selective employment and training programs to speed recovery from the recent recession. In most cases these programs are intended to serve structural as well as countercyclical goals. It is important to concentrate on structural unemployment as the recovery proceeds in order to reduce the inflationary pressure associated with given levels of output and employment and to promote the long-run employment prospects of those who suffer from chronic unemployment. The requirements of programs designed for structural and countercyclical purposes are generally quite different, however. The countercyclical objective requires that the program be implemented rapidly while the stimulus is needed and be phased out as the unemployment rate declines. The structural objective requires much more methodical program design and implementation, and, if effective, programs should be retained at a substantial level of funding even after the recovery is accomplished. Mixing these two objectives is a risky strategy; it might be better to pursue them through more independent policies.

There is an additional argument for a cautious approach to many of these program areas. In at least three areas—public service employment, youth work experience, and the employment tax credit— the programs favored by Congress represent significant departures in both size and content from any previous efforts. There is, therefore, very little experience or analysis to suggest how such programs ought to be designed or on how large a scale they can operate effectively. In this sense these attempts are experiments. It is to be hoped that, in two or three years, a considerable amount will have been learned to guide future employment policy. This will require an approach to program planning, implementation, monitoring, and analysis not yet strongly in evidence.

CHAPTER SIX

Medical Care Costs

LOUISE B. RUSSELL

A FEW YEARS AGO national health insurance looked like a sure thing for quick congressional action. Many bills, some with the support of major interest groups, had been introduced in the House and Senate, and the issues were being hotly debated. Then somehow the moment passed, and nothing happened after all.

With a new administration, committed in principle to national health insurance, the debate has revived. But this time the approach is more cautious. In the intervening years medical care costs have continued to rise at the rapid rates established in the mid–1960s. It has become clear that the problem is not short term, but chronic, and the overriding issue in health policy is how to solve it. One reason for the more cautious approach is that many people believe the problem of costs must be solved first or national health insurance will only make it worse. Reflecting the lack of consensus about solutions, other people believe that only national health insurance will give the government enough power to bring costs under control.

The dimensions of the problem can be quickly outlined. In fiscal 1976 the United States spent $139 billion on medical care, or 8.6 percent of the gross national product. This was well over triple the $39 billion spent in 1965, when medical care absorbed 5.9 percent of the gross national product. While the fact of increase was not new—

The author thanks Katharine Bauer, Lawrence Brown, Karen Davis, Dorothy Rice, and Stanley Wallack for helpful comments on earlier versions of this chapter.

over the previous decade, 1955–65, national expenditures on health had more than doubled, bringing the GNP share from 4.5 to 5.9 percent—the magnitude of the change was unprecedented.

Through a host of programs, many of them initiated during the 1960s, the federal government contributes to these expenditures, and suffers from the consequences of rising costs. The outlays presented in table 6-1 show that Medicare and Medicaid are the two largest programs in the health budget. Medicaid began on January 1, 1966, Medicare on July 1 of the same year, and their outlays quickly outstripped the original estimates. It is expected that in fiscal 1978 they will account for $37 billion of federal funds, up from $7 billion in 1968, their second full year of operation.

In an attempt to slow the cost spiral, the Ford budget proposed that payments to hospitals and doctors by Medicare and Medicaid be limited to increases of 7 percent in 1978. The Carter administration set this aside and proposed instead a system that would use a formula to link the permissible increase in each hospital's revenues from inpatient care to the rate of inflation in the economy generally. For the coming year the formula would allow an increase of 9 percent (increases in the wages of nonsupervisory employees would not be subject to the limit and other exceptions would be permitted in extraordinary circumstances). The limit would apply to all sources of payment—the federal government, state and local governments, and private payers—and to all short-stay hospitals, except new ones and those run by health maintenance organizations. Limits would also be set on the total amount of hospital investment permitted in each state. The proposed program is intended as the first step in the development of a more permanent system of controls.

If cost control is to be successful, the mechanisms finally selected must be based on a good understanding of the reasons for rising medical costs. While inflation has characterized the entire economy during the last ten years, medical care expenditures have been rising considerably faster than prices generally, as indicated by their growing share of the gross national product. Causes peculiar to the medical sector are at work. The rest of this chapter will discuss the nature of the cost problem in medical care and consider the types of solutions that have been proposed.

The discussion will concentrate on hospital costs. Hospital costs

Table 6-1. Federal Outlays for Health, Selected Years, 1964–78[a]

Millions of dollars

Type of outlay	1964	1968	1972	1976	1978[b]
Health care services	393	7,593	14,538	28,655	39,721
Medicare	...	5,332	8,819	17,779	25,411[c]
Medicaid	...	1,985	4,601	8,568	11,862[c]
All other	...	276	1,118	2,308	2,448
Health research and education ⎫	1,163	1,405	1,952	3,086	3,150
Health planning and construction ⎭		393	443	752	505
Prevention and control of health problems	161	318	541	963	1,117
Total[d]	1,716	9,708	17,471	33,448	44,485

Sources: *The Budget of the United States Government, Fiscal Year 1972*, and issues for 1974 and 1977; Office of Management and Budget, *Fiscal Year 1978 Budget Revisions, February 1977* (Government Printing Office, 1977). Figures are rounded.

a. The outlays in the table are imperfect indicators of federal spending on health since they omit the substantial health-related outlays of the Department of Defense, the Veterans' Administration, and other agencies whose primary mission is not related to health.

b. Outlays projected by the Carter administration.

c. Includes amounts associated with proposed legislation and savings of $695 million for Medicare and $134 million for Medicaid estimated to result from the administration's proposed cost controls.

d. Includes deductions for offsetting receipts.

are the largest item in medical care expenditures, and the fastest-growing: their share of the total, not counting the amounts collected by physicians for care delivered in hospitals, increased from 34 percent in 1965 to 40 percent in 1976. The average cost of a day of care in a short-stay hospital rose from $39.81 in fiscal 1965 to $147.12 in 1976, for an annual rate of growth of 12.6 percent. (By contrast, the consumer price index increased an average of 5.4 percent annually over the same period.) Thus an explanation of the rising cost of medical care must first and foremost be an explanation of rising hospital costs.

The Nature of the Problem

One explanation commonly offered begins with the fact that the Medicare and Medicaid programs were passed by Congress just over ten years ago. A sharp jump in the rate of growth of hospital costs can be dated from 1966, the year Medicare and Medicaid went into effect. Medicare's benefit provisions applied uniformly across the nation from its inception on July 1. Medicaid had gotten off to a quieter start six months earlier and grew rapidly for several years, as individual states initiated programs under the federal-state financing scheme legislated by Congress.

The programs were designed to pay substantial portions of the medical care expenses of two groups of people, the aged and the poor, many of whom had previously had little or no health insurance. Thus, the explanation goes, Medicare and Medicaid created a sudden and very large increase in demand for which the industry was unprepared. Because it takes several years to add hospital capacity and several more years to train doctors, supply was not immediately able to accommodate this large increase in demand. Prices were forced to rise to ration the limited supply.

The inflation induced by the new demand would be, this explanation continues, only a temporary phenomenon. The high prices would attract additional resources, and when, after a few years, the new hospital beds were in place and more doctors had been trained, prices would decline again, or at least rise only as fast as prices in the rest of the economy. Thus the inflation would be a short-run, self-limiting process. The solution was to move additional resources into medical care, and the government could help by undertaking programs to reduce the usual lags in this process. Thinking of this sort was part of what lay behind the health manpower training legislation passed in 1963 and 1964, too late to have any effect on the supply of health manpower before Medicare and Medicaid began.

This theory does not fare well in the light of the events of the last ten years. It is true that hospital occupancy rates increased during the late 1960s, as the theory predicted. But the number of hospital beds, total and per capita, also increased, occupancy rates declined again, and the rise in costs continued unabated. Further, close examination of the cost increases shows that there was a more immediate supply response. From 1950 to 1965, cost per patient day in short-stay hospitals grew at an average rate of 7 to 8 percent a year. And year after year during the period, about half of each annual increase, 3 to 4 percent, was attributable, not to higher prices and wages, but to the growing amounts of resources—labor, equipment, and supplies— used per patient day. From 1965 onward, the rate of growth in cost per patient day increased to more than 12 percent a year, and about half of these larger increases continued to be spent on ever-rising levels of inputs. Thus the rate of increase in the resources used per hospital day jumped to an average of 6 percent a year with the advent of Medicare and Medicaid. While the exact share of cost increases attributable to increasing input levels has varied from year to year, there has been no tendency for the inflow of resources to slow down. The accumulated growth over the decade has resulted in a level of inputs used per patient day that is almost *80 percent* higher than the level of 1966.

This means that, for example, the total number of people employed in short-stay hospitals—which includes those necessary to staff new beds as well as those attributable to higher levels of staff per bed— grew 73 percent between 1965 and 1975, from 1.4 million to 2.4 million. The number of employees per hospital bed increased 35 percent over the same period, from 1.9 to 2.5. Nonlabor inputs increased even faster, as indicated by the fact that labor costs declined from just over 60 percent of total hospital costs in the mid–1960s to 53 percent in 1975.

Thus three things happened. First, there was an immediate supply response, and supply has continued to expand steadily over the years. Second, the bulk of the resources drawn into hospital care have not gone to expand the number of days of care available, as one would expect from the theory, but to increase the intensity of services—that is, the numbers and sophistication of services provided per patient day. Third, in spite of this phenomenal increase in resources, the rise in hospital costs shows no signs of stopping, or even slowing down. It begins to appear that greater supply is not the solution to the problem, but is itself the problem.

There is, however, an alternative explanation that is consistent with the events of the past decade, and what it suggests about the prospects for cost control under the current system is not encouraging. This explanation takes as its starting point the history of all "third-party financing"—private health insurance as well as public programs like Medicare and Medicaid.

The level of third-party financing has increased steadily since World War II. In 1950 third-party payments, public and private, covered about half of all hospital costs; the rest was paid directly by the patient. By 1960 the patient's out-of-pocket payments had dropped to less than 30 percent of the total. Between 1963 and 1969 (the data do not permit a more precise bracketing of Medicare's beginning) this share dropped further, to 18 percent. Third-party financing has continued to expand during the 1970s, and currently only about 10 percent of all hospital costs are paid directly by the consumer.

On average, then, about 90 percent of the cost of hospital care is paid through third-party payers; and because of the way benefits are designed, the figure for many specific items is often 100 percent. For example, under Medicare the patient is required to pay a deductible of $124 for hospital care; after that, virtually all hospital services during a stay of up to sixty days are paid for in full by the program. As a result of such coverage, the out-of-pocket cost of a hospital stay is, for most patients, very low, and the out-of-pocket cost of many hospital services is zero. The third-party payer undertakes an open-ended commitment to pay for whatever services the patient, his doctor, and the hospital administration decide to use at these near-zero and zero "prices."

This incentive structure means that at the point at which decisions are made about the use of resources, the people who make those decisions are able to act as if the resources are free. Rationally they can and do make decisions that bring little or no benefit to the patient, since the resource costs of the decisions—to the people making them—are also little or nothing. And because of the extent to which decisionmaking is shared in medical care, decisions can be made that bring no benefit to the patient or even harm him, if they bring benefits to someone else involved in making the decisions. These benefits may come in the form of more employment in hospitals, higher incomes for medical professionals, or research or teaching opportunities. In sum, there are virtually no economic constraints left to prevent decisionmakers in medical care from doing everything they can think of, no matter how small the benefits nor to whom they accrue; in economic jargon, they are free to head straight for the satiation point. In a complex area like medical care, that point is a distant and moving target.

According to this explanation of the growth in costs, Medicare and Medicaid are only part of a larger problem. They accelerated the transformation of medical care, which was already well under way, from a market in which patients and doctors faced prices that were reasonable indicators of the resource costs of their decisions to one in which—particularly where hospital care is concerned—prices have been nearly eliminated.

Many of the problems that crop up in discussions of medical care

are direct results of this incentive structure, although they are often treated as if they arose from separate causes. They include the use of very expensive forms of treatment that have little or no benefit for the patient, inefficient use of facilities, the provision of unneeded services, the continuing rise in health workers' incomes relative to the incomes of other workers, and outright fraud. There are numerous examples to show that such things are not merely possible in theory, but important in practice.

Intensive care is a case in point. Intensive care is essentially a matter of bringing together in one place more of everything—more nursing time, more laboratory tests and monitoring equipment, more life support equipment like respirators and kidney dialysis machines—for the care of critically ill patients. Its first specific form was the postoperative recovery room for the care of patients recovering from the combined effects of surgery and anesthesia. Next to develop were the so-called mixed intensive care units, which accept patients with a variety of conditions, and separate coronary care units for patients with heart problems. The variety of special units— respiratory units, pediatric units, burn units, and so on—grows larger all the time. Between 1972 and 1975 the number of beds in mixed intensive and coronary care units increased 26 percent; in the latter year they accounted for 5 percent of all beds in short-stay hospitals.

Conservatively estimated, it costs about three times as much to care for a patient in an intensive care unit as in a regular ward. This means that, in 1975, hospital costs were about 10 percent higher than they would have been had intensive care beds been replaced with the same number of ward beds. Put another way, intensive care added about $12.50 to the fiscal 1975 cost of an average day of hospital care ($137.77).

Clearly, intensive care concentrates a great many resources on a few patients. Yet a number of studies indicate that there may be no benefit at all for many of these patients. For victims of myocardial infarction (approximately equivalent to the layman's term "heart attack") some studies find a reduction in mortality rates with intensive care, and at least an equal number do not.[1] A large and carefully

1. Donald Fagin and K. M. Anandiah, "The Coronary Care Unit and Mortality from Myocardial Infarction: A Continued Evaluation," *Journal of the American Geriatrics Society*, vol. 19 (August 1971), pp. 675–86; Andrew P. Klaus and others,

designed study done in Britain assigned patients to intensive care or *home* care, and discovered that the patients kept at home did as well as those in intensive care. Similar doubts have been raised about the value of intensive care for patients with stroke, pulmonary edema (accumulation of fluid in the lungs), and heart conditions other than myocardial infarction.[2]

Further, as with any form of medical intervention, money is not the only cost to be weighed against the possible benefits. Any intervention involves the risk of side-effects and must confer some benefit on the patient to leave him as well off as he would have been without it. Because of the more frequent lab tests and X rays, and the greater use of monitoring and life support equipment, intensive care exposes patients to a higher level of risk than does ward care.

Respiratory therapy is not nearly as large a component of hospital costs as intensive care, but it is growing fast. Hospitals have been organizing departments of respiratory therapy at a great rate in recent years, and between 1969 and 1972, these departments increased their share of costs by 50 percent, to 1 percent of the total in 1972. Individual hospitals report that as many as 25 or 30 percent of their patients receive some form of respiratory therapy during their stay.

Four groups of therapies are included in respiratory therapy: oxygen therapy, humidity and aerosol therapy, chest physical therapy, and mechanical ventilation, including intermittent positive pressure breathing (IPPB). IPPB—a form of treatment in which a respirator assists the patient's breathing, usually in three or four sessions a day of twenty or thirty minutes each—is probably the major item in the workload of most respiratory therapy departments. A 1973 survey found that even small hospitals do thousands of these

"Evaluating Coronary Care Units," *American Heart Journal*, vol. 79 (April 1970), pp. 471–80; Samuel P. Martin and others, "Inputs into Coronary Care During 30 Years," *Annals of Internal Medicine*, vol. 81 (September 1974), pp. 289–93; Robert M. Marshall, S. Gilbert Blount, Jr., and Edward Genton, "Acute Myocardial Infarction: Influence of a Coronary Care Unit," *Archives of Internal Medicine*, vol. 122 (December 1968), pp. 472–75; Graeme Sloman, Mary Stannard, and Alan J. Goble, "Coronary Care Unit: A Review of 300 Patients Monitored Since 1963," *American Heart Journal*, vol. 75 (January 1968), pp. 140–43; K. Astvad and others, "Mortality from Acute Myocardial Infarction Before and After Establishment of a Coronary Care Unit," *British Medical Journal*, vol. 1 (March 23, 1974), pp. 567–69.

2. See references in Louise B. Russell, "The Diffusion of New Hospital Technologies in the United States," *International Journal of Health Services*, vol. 6, no. 4 (1976) (Brookings General Series Reprint 322).

treatments a year: hospitals with 100 to 199 beds averaged 12,000 IPPBs annually, while those with 500 or more beds averaged about 72,000.[3]

People with asthma, bronchitis, emphysema, and other chronic lung diseases make up the largest group for which IPPBs are often prescribed. A recent conference on the use of respiratory therapy for these patients had many sobering things to say, but the criticism of IPPB was perhaps the strongest. The paper that reviewed this therapy summarized the situation as follows: ". . . owing to the lack of evidence to support the widespread application of IPPB and the costs and possible hazards of this modality of treatment, it is recommended that further use of IPPB in patients with stable COPD [chronic obstructive pulmonary disease] be discouraged . . ."[4]

There are many examples of similar phenomena, but a few more will suffice to suggest the range.

It is estimated that 90 percent of the one million tonsillectomies performed on children in 1973 were unnecessary. Probably at least seventy children died from the effects of the anesthesia alone; sixty-three of these deaths would have been avoided if the unnecessary operations had not taken place.[5]

A 1972 survey of hospitals with open heart surgery facilities found that 62 percent of them had done fewer than 100 open heart procedures during the previous year. Aside from questions of the efficient use of capital equipment, this was well below the annual workload of 200 operations recommended by the Surgery Study Group of the Inter-Society Commission for Heart Disease Resources as the minimum necessary to maintain the skills of the surgical team.[6]

Recent congressional investigations have disclosed that people who go to so-called Medicaid mills may be given numerous tests and prescriptions even when nothing is wrong with them, and that Medicaid

3. James P. Baker, "Magnitude of Usage of Intermittent Positive Pressure Breathing," *American Review of Respiratory Disease*, vol. 110 (December 1974), pt. 2, *Proceedings of the Conference on the Scientific Basis of Respiratory Therapy, 1974*, pp. 170–77.

4. John F. Murray, "Review of the State of the Art in Intermittent Positive Pressure Breathing Therapy," in ibid., p. 193.

5. Howard H. Hiatt, "Protecting the Medical Commons: Who Is Responsible?" *New England Journal of Medicine*, vol. 293 (July 31, 1975), p. 237.

6. James K. Roche and James M. Stengle, "Facilities for Open Heart Surgery in the United States: Distribution, Utilization and Cost," *American Journal of Cardiology*, vol. 32 (August 1973), pp. 224–28.

is sometimes charged for services that were never rendered at all. By one estimate, fraudulent bills absorb about a third of the Medicaid dollars spent in New York City.[7]

Mistaken enthusiasms, and even fraud, are part of the human condition and no system can eliminate them completely. This is all the more true in a profession that is moving only slowly away from clinical impression as the major basis for judging efficacy. But the incentive structure of the industry is an important factor. These problems are much more pervasive, and much more expensive, precisely because the incentive structure allows decisionmakers to treat resources as though they were free, rather than forcing them to recognize the costliness of resources and limit their use of them accordingly.

The Current Situation

The incentive structure created by high levels of third-party payment is transforming medical care from a traditional market, in which each patient and his doctor must weigh the possible benefits of care against its cost, to one in which they are able to act as if resources were free. The transformation is nearly complete for hospital care. In effect there is no longer any mechanism to enforce allocative efficiency—that is, appropriate answers to the question: given that resources *are* costly, and that whatever is produced should have benefits for the patient that are in some degree commensurate with the costs, what should be produced, in what quantities, and for whom? For example, how much intensive care should be produced and for which kinds of patients? This is at the center of the cost problem. By comparison, productive efficiency—for example, is intensive care being produced as cheaply as possible—is a minor issue.

If costs are to be controlled, some way must be found to induce medical decisionmakers to weigh resource costs against patient benefits. But before discussing some of the ways that have been proposed to do this, it is appropriate to acknowledge a school of thought that questions why these alternatives should be considered at all. This chapter is based on the assumption that rising costs without a corresponding increase in benefits to the patient are, and should be, widely perceived as undesirable. But there are those who argue that, in reality, very few people share this perception. They claim that the

7. See *Medical Care Review*, vol. 33 (December 1976), pp. 1318–20.

nation prefers a medical care system that treats resources as free and, given the choice between changing the current system in order to control the growth in costs or keeping it and continuing to pay ever-increasing costs, would choose to keep it. This point of view may be correct. But it rests on the questionable assumption that people fully understand the consequences of the current system, in terms of money and in terms of medical risk, and that they understand these to be the consequences of the *system* and neither accidental nor short term.

It is not easy for an individual to figure out how much he pays to support the medical care system, even if he wants to. The amounts are paid out through fringe benefits provided by employers, through federal and state taxes, through the social security payroll tax, and through direct consumer payments. The individual often does not know how much his employer pays for health insurance and has no way of telling how much of his taxes go to finance medical care programs. Because of this, people seriously underestimate the amount they pay for medical care.[8] Thus even an approximate estimate may be useful in setting the terms of the debate.

Consider a family of four, two adults and two children, earning $14,000 in 1975, approximately the median family income. Employer-provided fringe benefits and the employer's portion of the social security payroll tax add $1,750, on average, bringing total income to $15,750.[9] In 1975 the average total expenditure on medical care for an adult between the ages of nineteen and sixty-four was $471.88, and for a child under nineteen, $212.14; these amounts total $1,368 for the family. Further, the earner or earners in the family pay 0.9 percent of their wages, and their employers pay another 0.9 percent, to help support the hospital insurance part of the Medicare program.[10] This adds another $252 to the family's support of the medical care system, for a running total of $1,620.

8. A survey in Britain found that 60 percent of the British public thought that the weekly health insurance tax paid by workers covered all the costs of the National Health Service. In fact, it pays only 8.5 percent of the costs, with most of the rest coming from general taxes. Michael H. Cooper, "Health Costs and Expenditures in the United Kingdom," in Teh-wei Hu, ed., *International Health Costs and Expenditures* (Government Printing Office, 1976), pp. 93–108.

9. Adding fringe benefits to money income assumes that both are equally the cost of labor to the employer and that if, say, health insurance benefits were not provided, an equivalent addition to money income or to some other fringe benefit would be.

10. Ten percent of the proceeds from this tax are used to pay the hospital bills of disabled persons under sixty-five, and these payments are counted a second time

These are not the only expenses, but it is impossible to quantify the others. They include the general federal taxes used to support Medicare—primarily the physicians' insurance part of the program— and that part of state and federal taxes used to pay some of the medical expenses of the elderly poor under Medicaid.[11] Some of these taxes are paid by corporations, and this burden is borne by individuals largely in the form of higher prices. Taxes also pay for other federal and state health activities such as research, vaccination programs, and the support of medical training. Further, the fact that health insurance benefits provided by employers, part of the cost of policies purchased by individuals, and exceptionally high medical expenses incurred by individuals are exempt from income tax, means that taxes on the rest of income are higher. Clearly, 10 percent of income ($1,620 divided by $15,750) is a conservative estimate of the average family's contribution for medical care.

There are two points to be made about this estimate. First, it obviously includes payments that subsidize other groups in the population, notably the poor, the elderly, and the disabled, some of whom would otherwise have to pay disproportionate amounts of their own incomes for care, or go without. But the scope for redistribution is limited; not everyone can be subsidized. The average individual or family will, under any system, have to pay a substantial share of the costs.

Second, the amount is much higher than it would be without the existing incentive structure. What this incentive structure means for the rate of increase in costs over time is suggested by the trend in the share of gross national product accounted for by national expenditures on medical care. This share rose from 5.9 percent in 1966 to 8.6 percent in 1976. Projecting the same change (about 2.5 percentage points in a decade) into the future indicates that the proportion will rise to about 11 percent in 1986, and almost 15 percent in the year 2000. Comparing the more than 10 percent of income paid by the median income family with the national proportion of 8.6 for 1976 indicates that the average family's share (presumably of

in the average expenditures for all persons under sixty-five. Eliminating this double counting would not affect the final estimate significantly.

11. Medicaid payments for those under sixty-five are already counted in the averages for persons under sixty-five.

a higher income) will be well above 15 percent by 2000. These amounts are affordable, but are they desirable?

What Are the Alternatives?

The proposals for dealing with the cost problem can be divided into two groups: those that change the method of payment for medical care in order to change the economic incentives of some or all of the people who make decisions about it; and those that attempt to control directly the quantities of resources used or the quantities of services produced by the industry. Deductibles and coinsurance, health maintenance organizations, and prospective reimbursement are the most important examples of proposals that would change the economic incentives in the industry. The major examples of quantity control mechanisms are certificate-of-need laws and professional standards review organizations.

These alternatives are not mutually exclusive, nor, as the following discussion brings out, is any of them without flaws. A successful program to control medical care costs might make use of several of them.

Economic Incentives

Proposals to change the method of payment attempt to force the people who make decisions in medical care to recognize that resources are costly, either by establishing prices for alternative decisions or by imposing a limit on the total budget of a provider, such as a hospital. In the latter case the regulator does not explicitly set prices for individual decisions. Such prices exist implicitly since if money is spent on one thing there is, under a fixed budget, less left to spend on other things. It is crucial to the success of budget constraint proposals that this fact somehow get translated into prices for individual decisions that are taken seriously by the decisionmakers.

If economic incentives are to be successful in influencing behavior they must have at least the following characteristics. The decisionmaker must know the cost of each alternative *before* he makes his choice. The decisionmaker must gain if the costs of his decisions are low relative to the benefits and lose if the costs are high, and must not be able, at least not routinely, to extricate himself from the consequences of those gains or losses by renegotiating the terms after the decision. And the economic incentives must offer fairly detailed guides to the resource costs of different activities. The purpose of a successful system is to force decisionmakers to ask whether a proposed service is beneficial, first for any patient, and then for the patient in question.

DEDUCTIBLES AND COINSURANCE. A deductible is a specified dollar amount of medical expenses that must be paid by the individual before the third-party payer will reimburse him for any further bills. A coinsurance rate is the percentage of a given expense that must be paid by the patient. Often the design of a program or policy's benefits includes both, although this need not be the case. For example, under the medical insurance portion of Medicare the patient is responsible for the first $60 worth of services incurred during a year, and for 20 percent of all expenses above that amount. Under the hospital insurance part of the program, the patient is responsible for the first $124 of the cost of a hospital stay, but there is no coinsurance.

The logic of deductibles and coinsurance is simple. They constitute a partial return to a traditional market, with ordinary prices as guides for resource decisions. When they apply, the out-of-pocket price of a service to the patient is not zero, as it is when third-party coverage is complete, and the patient must pay some part of the cost of the decisions that he and his doctor make. How large a part depends on the levels at which the deductibles and coinsurance rate are set. Thus the patient and his doctor are encouraged to question whether the likely benefits of a decision outweigh the costs. Since the cost of any alternative is still generally less than its full cost, they will choose some alternatives that would not have been chosen if the patient had to pay the full cost, but equally they will be inclined to reject those alternatives that have little or no benefit for the patient.

If the coinsurance rate applies to all medical bills, the out-of-pocket expense to the patient is reduced, but there is still no upper limit on it; the patient can still find himself burdened with expenses that exceed his ability to pay. The simplest solution, and one that has been proposed often, is to specify a dollar limit on the out-of-pocket expense that an individual or family can incur in a year. Beyond that limit all expenses are covered in full by the third-party payer. A somewhat more complicated solution recognizes that how burdensome any given out-of-pocket expense is depends on the individual's or family's income, and sets the upper limit in terms of a certain percentage of income, say 15 percent. The levels of deductibles and coinsurance rates can also be related to income. For the very poor no deductible or coinsurance need be required at all.

In general, however, deductibles and coinsurance rates can be quite substantial and still be compatible with the need for protection against extraordinarily high medical expenses. It was pointed out earlier that it is impossible under any system to "protect" the average family against the average expenditure for medical care, now more than 10 percent of the median family income. That amount would be no more of a financial burden if less of it were paid in the form of premiums and taxes, and more of it in the form of out-of-pocket expenses for care. And if the altered incentives thus produced succeeded in slowing the rise in costs, the average financial burden would actually be reduced.

Out-of-pocket expenses can clearly change the incentives of the patient. But many medical care decisions are shared with, or even delegated to, the physician, who does not have to pay those costs. Nevertheless, both theory and evidence indicate that the physician's decisions are importantly influenced by the extent of the patient's out-of-pocket expense. First, the cost will influence the patient's initial decision to contact a physician, his decision about the type of physician to go to, and his decision whether to follow the physician's advice. Further, the whole history of medical care costs—which is the strongest case for the effectiveness of coinsurance—shows that, as the out-of-pocket cost to the patient declines, the physician recommends more and more expensive alternatives. For example, a study done in New York in the late 1950s found that when the supply of beds expanded, a disproportionate number of the patients who filled them were drawn from those with Blue Cross coverage.[12] More recently, what changed when Medicare and Medicaid were introduced was not the psychological or scientific aspects of the physician-patient relationship but the level of third-party payment. And costs immediately began to rise more rapidly than before.

Deductibles and coinsurance have several advantages. The incentives they provide apply to the patient and his doctor at the right moment—the moment when decisions about care are being made.

12. Reported in Milton I. Roemer, "Bed Supply and Hospital Utilization: A Natural Experiment," *Hospitals,* vol. 35 (November 1, 1961), pp. 36–42.

They encourage both patient and doctor to consider each time whether the benefits of a proposed treatment are commensurate with the resource costs. And because prices are guides, not laws, they allow considerable flexibility; there is no single "right" answer that must be applied to all patients. Finally, because the incentives apply so often, to so many different people, it is difficult for any one of them to renegotiate the terms in order to avoid the consequences of a decision.

Of course, deductibles and coinsurance can only provide these incentives if they are in effect. Once the maximum out-of-pocket expense has been reached, third-party coverage takes over and the decisionmakers can once again treat resources as if they were free. Thus it is desirable to maintain some economic incentives over as wide a range of expense as possible. For this purpose, coinsurance is preferable to deductibles.

The reasoning behind deductibles is that the initial expenses in a year are nearly certain—almost everyone visits a physician at least once during a year—and there is no value in having protection against them; as the expenses grow larger and less certain to occur, the need for protection increases. But from the point of view of creating good economic incentives, deductibles do not make much sense. They mean that the out-of-pocket expense of the first visit to a physician is greater than that, say, of the tenth, although the resource costs are the same. They mean that the first day of hospital care is quite costly, while the last may be free, although it is surely the total cost that influences the decision to hospitalize, while a positive cost for each additional day would encourage shorter stays. Thus a flat co-insurance rate over the entire range, from the first dollar to the point at which the limit on out-of-pocket expense is reached, would probably offer the best incentive structure. Omitting the deductible would eliminate meaningless differentials in the cost to the patient of different services and would permit the coinsurance to extend over a greater range of expense before running into the upper limit on out-of-pocket costs.

Designing a plan with substantial coinsurance rates would be of little value for cost control if many people, or their employers for them, bought supplementary policies to provide third-party coverage of their out-of-pocket expenses. This would be very likely to happen if the present tax treatment of health insurance premiums were retained. Employer-provided policies are currently treated as a business expense rather than as part of the employee's income and are thus exempt from income and payroll taxes. This allows people to avoid taxes if they, in effect, commit part of their income to medical expenses at the outset, rather than receiving it first as income and subsequently using it to pay medical expenses. Since the out-of-pocket expenses for which an individual would be liable under coinsurance include those initial expenses that nearly everyone incurs, the cost of a supplementary policy would be high relative to the protection it offered (against the difference between the cost of the policy and the maximum out-of-pocket expense). Thus the protection offered would not be a major incentive for buying a supplementary policy. But by the same token, the fact that the expenditures were nearly certain to be incurred would make the tax advantages of such policies very attractive. To avoid ending up once again with the problems of very high levels of third-party payment, supplementary policies would have to be subject to the same taxes as ordinary income.

Finally, the limit on out-of-pocket expenses would, as noted earlier, mean that some medical decisions would still be made as though resources were free. Decisions about resources over this range would have to be made and enforced by some other means. This problem area is potentially important. There are already many expensive procedures that would immediately take expenses past the limit—open-heart surgery and renal dialysis are two examples—and the future holds the promise of more such procedures. The contribution of coinsurance is that it would limit the need for regulation, with all the problems and uncertainties that involves, to this particularly expensive range of medical decisions.

HEALTH MAINTENANCE ORGANIZATIONS. A health maintenance organization (HMO) is an organization of physicians that undertakes to provide, or arrange for, virtually all the medical care required by the plan's subscribers, in return for a fixed annual fee. The original form of the HMO, and still the most common, is the prepaid group practice. Physicians in this type of plan are paid salaries, rather than fees for each service, and work in a central clinic. Some groups own their own hospitals, while others contract with local hospitals for care.

The experience with these plans, and the claims made for them, suggest that the care they provide differs in systematic ways from the patterns observed in the fee-for-service system. Of greatest importance, prepaid groups are believed to make considerably less use of hospital care for their patients, and, secondarily, to provide more preventive medicine. These differences are attributed to the incentives created by the fixed annual payment. It is argued that, because it operates under a fixed budget, an HMO has strong incentives to practice preventive medicine, to detect illness as soon as possible in order to keep treatment costs low, and, when treatment is required, to use the least expensive form that will do the job, in particular avoiding hospital care unless it is absolutely necessary. The reasoning behind this argument has always been weak—insurance companies also work within fixed annual budgets, with premiums being the equivalent of the HMO's annual fee—but the empirical evidence has usually indicated that, in fact, prepaid group practices do have lower hospitalization rates.

In 1970 the federal government became interested in prepaid groups, on the grounds that if they were more widely available they might help to control medical care costs. In 1973 a program was launched to provide start-up funds to encourage the establishment of HMOs. By 1978 the program will have helped to start more than 100 of the approximately 230 HMOs in the country. In the course of the development of the program, the term "health maintenance organizations" was coined in order to include variations in addition to the prepaid group, in particular the foundation plan. Under the latter type of plan subscribers still pay a fixed annual fee, but physicians are paid in the traditional fee-for-service fashion, and are free to choose their office location and form of practice, either solo or group. It was expected that the fixed annual payment would produce the same incentives, and thus the same results, in the foundation as in the prepaid group form of the HMO.

A recent study has investigated the differences in medical care use under HMOs and fee-for-service for a large number of plans.[13] The study was based on the experience of welfare families enrolled in ten different HMOs—eight prepaid groups and two foundations—under the auspices of the Medicaid program. These families were matched with similar families in the same areas, also on welfare, but receiving

13. Clifton R. Gaus, Barbara S. Cooper, and Constance G. Hirschman, "Contrasts in HMO and Fee-for-Service Performance," *Social Security Bulletin*, vol. 39 (May 1976), pp. 3–14.

their medical care from fee-for-service physicians. The results of the study showed that hospitalization rates were indeed much lower for the families enrolled in prepaid group plans than for their fee-for-service counterparts: 46 hospital admissions and 340 days of care per 1,000 population as against 114 admissions and 888 days of care. There were, however, no differences in hospital use between *foundation* subscribers and fee-for-service patients in the same areas. The study also found no important differences between the HMO and fee-for-service groups in the use of outpatient or preventive services, or in the patients' health or satisfaction with their care.

Lower hospitalization rates are a gain simply in terms of the reduced medical risk to the patient, and such startlingly lower rates suggest there should be substantial cost savings as well. But the Medicaid study did not examine the cost results. A study of Medicare enrollees did look at costs, but did not report use rates. This study compared the costs to Medicare of all services, not just hospital care, received by enrollees in seven HMOs with the costs of enrollees living in the same areas who got their care from fee-for-service physicians. The results were not consistently in favor of the HMOs. Three HMOs showed costs considerably below those for the comparable fee-for-service enrollees in both years of the study. Two produced costs that were somewhat higher in both years; and two produced costs that were considerably lower in one year of the study, but about the same in the other.[14]

Because the differences in hospital use showed up for the prepaid group plans in the Medicaid study, but not for the foundation plans, it appears unlikely that the incentives at work are due to the form of payment. The study's authors speculate that the difference arises because the prepaid group physicians are salaried, and thus have nothing to gain financially by hospitalizing patients. Other observers have suggested that the lower rates may be due to purposely restricted hospital capacity in groups that run their own hospitals, to peer review procedures, to profit-sharing arrangements, or to the psychology of small, close-knit groups. The Medicare study suggests that whatever the effective incentives, they may not always operate even in prepaid groups.

14. Peter A. Weil, "Comparative Costs to the Medicare Program of Seven Prepaid Group Practices and Controls," *Health and Society*, vol. 54 (Summer 1976), pp. 339–65.

The frequent successes of prepaid groups give every reason to encourage their development, and to remove the legal and financial restrictions that sometimes impede them. But until the reasons for that success are better established, and with them the ability to produce the same results with each new HMO, there is no basis for making HMOs the cornerstone of a cost control program.

PROSPECTIVE REIMBURSEMENT. The term "prospective reimbursement" refers to those methods of paying hospitals in which the rate to be paid, usually for a day of care, or even the hospital's total budget is set in advance of the time period during which it will apply. Prospective reimbursement schemes are currently being experimented with on a wide scale. The hope that they may offer a solution to the cost problem is based on the hypothesis that the common practice of reimbursing hospitals for all costs actually incurred promotes inefficiency; with the start of Medicare and Medicaid, both of which base payments on retrospective costs, the proportion of hospital revenues paid in this fashion passed 50 percent. Under prospective reimbursement, especially when the hospital must absorb part of any loss and gets to share in any savings, it is reasoned that hospital administrators will have incentives to restrain cost increases by operating more efficiently.

In the Social Security Amendments of 1972, Congress gave the Social Security Administration authority to experiment with a number of reimbursement methods and to waive the usual method of reimbursing for services under the Medicare, Medicaid, and maternal and child health programs, in favor of the method being used in the experiment. Subsequently, the National Health Planning and Resources Development Act of 1974 provided money for grants to help finance a maximum of six state agencies, in order to test their ability to contain hospital costs by setting reimbursement rates.

Several prospective reimbursement plans were already in operation under the auspices of Blue Cross plans or state governments when Social Security received its new authority in 1972. These plans were variations on two basic methods of setting rates: budget review and the use of formulas. Under the budget review method, the reviewing agency examines the hospital's past budgets and its projection for the prospective year. The reviewer may investigate each item in the budget in detail, or he may use a number of guides to identify items that are out of line, either with the hospital's own experience or with that of similar hospitals, and examine only these items in detail. The prospective rate is then set on the basis of the hospital's projected budget, together with any changes in the budget made during the review. By contrast, the strict formula method uses only the hospital's base year costs, not its projected costs, in calculating the prospective rate. The allowed increase over these costs is based on a formula that may incorporate indexes of the general rate of inflation in the area's economy, an automatic allowance for new services, the history of cost increases for similar hospitals, and other factors. Prospective reimbursement plans may also involve elements of both methods with, for example, formula projections used to set the range for acceptable increases in the rates paid individual hospitals.

The first thing the Social Security Administration did with its new authority was to take advantage of the fact that these systems were already in operation and arrange to have some of them evaluated. Four of these early evaluations—of the formula-based system in downstate New York and budget review systems in western Pennsylvania, New Jersey, and Rhode Island—have been completed. The results from these early evaluations have not been particularly encouraging.[15] Statistical tests based on comparing the hospitals in each plan with their own experience before the plan, and with the experience of similar hospitals outside the plan (which usually meant they also had to be outside the state), found that prospective reimbursement had no effect on costs per day, or per admission, in Rhode Island and New Jersey. In western Pennsylvania the number of hospitals in the plan (five) was too small to permit confident conclusions.

Only the downstate New York system demonstrated a significant effect, on both cost per day and cost per admission. But the results must be viewed as tentative. The statistical analysis showed that hospitals in the system started with costs that averaged 25 to 30 percent higher per case than those for similar hospitals in Chicago, Cleveland, and Philadelphia. Prospective reimbursement appeared to reduce these costs by 8 to 9 percent per case. Further, the New York system has generated a large number of lawsuits and appeals so that its ability to control costs over the longer term is not yet clear.

Various reasons have been suggested for this poor showing. In

15. Fred J. Hellinger, "Evaluation of the U.S. Experience in Prospective Reimbursement" (paper presented at the American Public Health Association annual meeting, October 1976; processed).

some plans participation was voluntary. In most a substantial amount of hospital revenue was not subject to the prospective rate. The administration of all of the plans was complicated by the introduction of national wage and price controls. There are a number of experiments in the works—the rate-setting commissions in Massachusetts, Maryland, and Washington State, for example, and a new plan in Rhode Island that begins by setting a limit on the increase to be allowed in total statewide hospital costs—that may give prospective reimbursement a better chance to demonstrate some effect.

    But one observer who has studied many of the existing prospective reimbursement systems concludes that they do not provide the hoped for incentives and are not likely ever to do so.[16] Hospital administrators quickly discover under all the systems that their prospective rates depend, first and foremost, on their past costs. Rather than giving them incentives to cut costs, prospective reimbursement thus gives them every incentive to spend as close to the rate as possible, plus whatever else they think they can justify after the fact, taking care only to avoid extreme situations that might result in costs being disallowed. In fact, the experience in Canada, where budget review has been used for a number of years, seems to show that the review process has reduced the variation among hospitals but has not slowed the rise in costs over the years.[17]

    It seems even more unlikely that prospective reimbursement filters through to the most important decisionmakers in the system—doctors and their patients—in a form that encourages them to ask whether the benefits of a proposed course of treatment are worth the costs. For the most part, rate-setting agencies steer clear of attempting to influence physicians. A few do deal in some fashion with some of the allocative decisions that must be made if costs are to be controlled: in the downstate New York system special appeals are required to get rate increases to cover new services or facilities; Massachusetts will not include these costs in the rate base until after the first year. But other plans concern themselves primarily with productive effi-

    16. Katharine G. Bauer, "Hospital Rate Setting: This Way to Salvation?" in Michael Zubkoff and Ira E. Raskin, eds., *Hospital Cost Containment* (Prodist for Milbank Memorial Fund, forthcoming).
    17. Amanda Bennett, "Canada's National Health Plan," *Wall Street Journal,* December 13, 1976; Robert G. Evans and Hugh D. Walker, "Information Theory and the Analysis of Hospital Cost Structure," *Canadian Journal of Economics,* vol. 5 (August 1972), pp. 398–418.

ciency or try to keep cost increases in line with inflation in general, leaving the allocative decisions to take care of themselves as best they can. None of the programs deals with existing allocative inefficiencies by trying to reduce unnecessary admissions and surgery, unnecessary tests and treatments, and other problems that are already built into the system after so many years of rising costs. Perverse incentives for unnecessary admissions and lengthy stays are, in fact, created by rate penalties for low occupancy. And too often, the injunction to maintain the quality of care while controlling costs works against improvements in the use of resources because it looks to process standards, such as ensuring that a hospital does not discontinue a service or facility, rather than to efficacy.

Stripped of the language of price incentives, prospective reimbursement is simply price regulation. As such, it is subject to all the trials and tribulations to which that particular social institution is heir. These trials and tribulations are shared by the various mechanisms that attempt to control quantities of resources or outputs. Consequently, a discussion of regulation in general will be postponed until after the next section, in which those mechanisms are discussed.

Quantity Controls

Rather than using prices or limits on overall budgets to induce hospitals to produce the "right" configuration of services with the least-cost combination of resources, quantity control mechanisms attempt to enforce these patterns directly. In theory at least, such mechanisms can both deny permission to use certain resources or produce certain services and require the use or production of certain other resources and services.

If controls on resources are to be effective, the regulators must know what inputs are required to produce a particular set of services. And when cost containment is the goal, they must know which is the least-cost set of inputs required to do the job. Further, the decisionmakers in the industry must have incentives that lead them, when presented with a technically correct collection of resources, to produce the desired services (for the right people), and not some alternative set of services. When output is controlled, the incentives must work the other way: the decisionmakers' incentives must lead them to produce the services required by the regulator with the least-cost collection of resources. Either approach requires that regulators have extensive and detailed knowledge of the "right" pattern of outputs and the collections of resources required to produce it, and that they either be lucky in the matter of incentives or have the power and information necessary to manipulate incentives so that the desired connections between inputs and outputs are made.

This is obviously a tall order, one that even the best motivated hospital—let alone hospital regulator—cannot fill perfectly. It is more reasonable to ask whether direct quantity controls can get things moving in the right direction, and whether they represent an improvement in this respect over the situation without controls.

CERTIFICATE-OF-NEED. Certificate-of-need (CON) laws require that proposed investments in health facilities be reviewed by a state agency and approved only if the agency decides there is a need for the investment. New York passed the first CON law, in 1964. By the end of 1970 five states had enacted laws, and, as the rise in hospital costs continued, the number of state laws began to grow rapidly. The details of the different state laws vary, but most cover all types of health facilities and require approval of all new facilities, services, or equipment. Some states exempt projects that cost less than a specified amount, although this exemption often does not apply to projects that increase the bed capacity of the institution.

The Social Security Amendments of 1972 offered federal support for state review of investment projects. Section 1122 of those amendments authorized the Department of Health, Education, and Welfare to deny reimbursement, under the Medicare, Medicaid, and maternal and child health programs, of the capital costs for any project worth more than $100,000, or any project that increased capacity or service, regardless of cost, if the project had not been approved by the appropriate state agency. By mid-1974, twenty-four states had their own CON laws and thirty-nine, including fifteen with CON laws, had contracts with HEW to do reviews under section 1122. Then, in the National Health Planning and Resources Development Act of 1974, Congress made certificate-of-need reviews a requirement for participation in the new planning programs. In ten years, CON had gone from an experiment in a few states to the law of the land.

Evaluation of the effects of such review requirements is based on the early state laws and, to some extent, on the section 1122 contracts. One study of this experience found that many agencies did not consider cost control to be their most important goal; rather, they gave highest priority to improving the quality and distribution of medical resources. Many lacked the kinds of data and review criteria that would seem necessary for good reviews under either objective: in nearly half the agencies, data on acute care beds (the easiest data to get) were at least two years old; other kinds of information—occupancy rates for example—had seldom been collected at all. The criteria for reviewing additions to bed capacity—how many were desirable, of what kinds, in which areas—were usually not well developed. Criteria for reviewing new facilities like X ray and intensive care units were rare in any form.[18]

The study found that over 90 percent of all applications to the agencies were approved. Although the hospital beds approved added only 2 percent to the total supply of beds in the areas studied, nearly three-quarters of the agencies approved projects that, when completed, would bring the number of beds in the area to more than 105 percent of the need projected by the Hill-Burton agency (the state agency that administers federal Hill-Burton funds for hospital construction) for the next five years. Applications for new equipment and services were virtually always approved, in part because of the fallacious notion that only increases in bed capacity are an important cause of higher costs.

Another study of the early experience with certificate-of-need compared hospital investment in beds and in other types of capital across states for the years 1968–72, and came to similar conclusions. In those states with CON laws, the growth in bed supply was reduced, but other kinds of investment increased. The net result was that the levels of total investment were about the same in states with as in states without CON laws.[19] Thus certificate-of-need laws have yet to prove effective at controlling costs. To the extent that they have any potential to do so, they are hampered by the fact that they cover only capital resources, and concentrate on only part of those. Hospitals can find other ways to spend.

PROFESSIONAL STANDARDS REVIEW ORGANIZATIONS. The

18. Lewin and Associates, *Evaluation of the Efficiency and Effectiveness of the Section 1122 Review Process: Part I*, prepared for U.S. Department of Health, Education, and Welfare, Health Resources Administration (Lewin and Associates, 1975; available from National Technical Information Service).

19. David S. Salkever and Thomas W. Bice, "The Impact of Certificate-of-Need Controls on Hospital Investment," *Health and Society*, vol. 54 (Spring 1976), pp. 185–214.

Social Security Amendments of 1972 ordered HEW to designate professional standards review organizations (PSROs) in local or regional areas to review the institutional services prescribed for the patients of the Medicare, Medicaid, and maternal and child health programs. Each organization is supposed to have as its members a large number of physicians practicing in the area. Its principal obligation is to make sure that the institutional services, especially hospital care, provided these patients are medically necessary and of good quality, an obligation which it discharges by reviewing all hospital admissions for necessity, monitoring lengths of stay, and carrying out regular studies to determine whether the care being given agrees with accepted practice.

There has been little experience as yet with the PSROs themselves. A recent study of similar programs that existed before PSROs were created concludes that such evidence as there is, is not sufficient to show that they are effective, either as cost control or as quality control measures.[20] In theory, PSROs have the potential to cut costs by eliminating unnecessary stays and shortening unnecessarily long stays. In practice there is no evidence that the earlier utilization review committees required under Medicare, which had similar potential, actually had any such effects. More generally, PSROs may increase or decrease costs since they may require some services not already being prescribed as well as discourage others that were routinely used before. Their potential effect as quality control measures is equally unclear, the more so since much of what is accepted practice is not based on proven efficacy.

Regulation

During the economic stabilization program, which began in August 1971 with a three-month economy-wide freeze on wages and prices and evolved into a series of controls that were not completely dismantled until April 1974, the rate of growth in the hospital charge for a semiprivate room fell to less than half what it had been during the preceding two years. The rate of growth in physicians' fees was cut almost in half.

Upon closer examination, the accomplishments of the controls are not as impressive as these figures suggest. Most third-party payments

20. Institute of Medicine, *Assessing Quality in Health Care: An Evaluation* (National Academy of Sciences, 1976).

to hospitals are made on the basis of costs, not charges, and the rate of growth in cost per patient day declined only 25 percent, from an average of 13.9 percent for the years 1969–71 to 10.5 percent for 1971–73. Faced with controls on fees, physicians began to bill separately for items that had previously been included in a single fee. Nevertheless, for two years, the share of gross national product going to medical care stood still. Why, then, not impose permanent controls on the medical care industry, or at least on hospitals?

The economic stabilization program was temporary and covered the entire economy during much of the period. The experience with it is thus less relevant in judging proposals to regulate medical care than is the experience with permanent regulation in other industries. Many of these industries—for example, telephones, electric power and gas utilities in many states, and most forms of transportation—have been subject to regulation for decades.

One of the major purposes of all regulation of the public utility type is to keep prices below the level that would obtain in its absence, and this would be its major purpose in medical care. But studies of regulated industries show that prices in these industries are at least as high as they would be without regulation.[21] Where unregulated markets exist, the comparisons are striking: for example, airline fares in California are less than half those for similar routes in the interstate airline market, which is regulated. The only exception to this finding, and not one that inspires confidence after the cold winter of 1977, is natural gas prices. Because prices have been kept artificially high by regulation, there have been numerous attempts by outside firms to enter regulated markets, and the second part of the job of regulatory agencies has been to prevent this.

The explanation for this unexpected result points up a major difference between temporary and permanent regulation. Over the long run, the group that remains most interested and involved in the consequences of regulation, besides the regulatory agency, is the industry itself. It continually keeps its views in front of the regulatory agency. It is the source of most of the agency's information about the industry. It is the quarter from which the agency can most frequently expect challenges to its decisions. Together with the fact that the

21. Roger G. Noll, "The Consequences of Public Utility Regulation of Hospitals," in Institute of Medicine, *Controls on Health Care* (National Academy of Sciences, 1974), pp. 25–48.

regulatory agency, by virtue of its existence, shares responsibility for the industry's failures, these pressures lead the regulator to adopt a cautious and industry-oriented point of view, a point of view not compatible with effective cost control.

To the extent that a regulatory agency does manage to impose prices that are different from those that would exist in the unregulated industry, it elicits a number of undesirable reactions in addition to direct challenges. For example, under the recent controls physicians changed their billing practices to keep their incomes rising in spite of fixed fees. Similar phenomena have been observed under fee regulation in Canada. When rates are set prospectively, hospitals try to spend up to the limit, rather than to use resources more wisely, and rate penalties for low occupancy are credited with inducing unnecessary admissions rather than the elimination of unneeded capacity. The regulatory agency faces the basic difficulty that it is trying to legislate an outcome that runs counter to the incentives of the industry's decisionmakers.

In medical care the almost complete lack of appropriate incentives for decisionmakers means that any agency attempting to regulate the industry has a much larger, more complex job than does the usual regulatory agency. In effect, all the decisions about what should be produced, in what amounts, and for whom, are up for grabs. To deal successfully with these decisions the regulator must know an enormous amount of detail about possible services, production techniques, incidence of disease, and so on. The regulator must be able to second-guess all the important decisions in the industry and somehow enforce those second guesses.

A more fundamental problem with regulation in general, and with such extensive regulation in particular, is that the decisions to be made are not purely technical. They are in part based on values: how much risk is too much, how much is an extra year of life worth, how does its value compare with a reduction in disability for someone else, and so on. In ordinary markets each consumer weighs the risks and benefits of a decision in his own terms. In a regulated medical care market, the regulator that succeeds in imposing some limits on the industry's use of resources will also have to provide guidance as to which areas deserve those resources most.

Regulators do make such value judgments in other industries. For example, by setting airline fares for some routes too low relative to their resource costs and others too high, the Civil Aeronautics Board has created a system of cross-subsidization that results in more flights on low-volume routes, and higher prices on high-volume routes, than would exist in the unregulated market. Another example is the frequent policy of protecting existing firms from the competition of new technologies or production arrangements. Whether or not such value judgments reflect the greater public interest, they have, in practice, worked counter to cost control rather than in favor of it.

In spite of the fact that regulation has not reduced prices in other industries, the idea persists that it will somehow be able to put limits on the uncontrolled expansion of medical care. After all, none of the regulated industries is expanding out of control. The hope is understandable, but there is nothing inherent in the nature of regulation that guarantees its fulfillment.

The limits on industries other than medical care are set, not by regulators, but by the fact that consumers must pay a positive price for their decisions to use the industry's product. Regulators can make some adjustments in the allocation process, and they frequently do. But the scope for this kind of adjustment is limited by the consumer's willingness to pay. The constraints on the size and composition of industry output are economic.

Increasingly in all medical care, and already in hospital care, there are no such constraints. The consumer does not have to ask whether the benefits of an action outweigh the resource costs when those costs—to him, at the moment of decision—are zero. Thus there are no economic constraints on the size and composition of the industry. The industry may look different under regulation, but there is no reason to believe that it will be smaller or grow any more slowly.

Conclusions

The problem of rising medical care costs is the result of the incentives created by extensive third-party payment. These incentives encourage patients and their doctors to behave as though resources were free, with the consequence that the amount of resources used in medical care has grown enormously in the last twenty-five years, and especially in the last ten. The solution is to reintroduce some mechanism that will force those who make decisions about medical care to recognize that resources are costly and to weigh the costs against the benefits of any proposed action.

The history of the last several decades, during which the level of third-party payment has risen to its present heights, indicates that introducing significant rates of copayment for patients would be an effective way to control costs. Health maintenance organizations may also offer some help; they have often been successful in controlling costs, but until the reasons for the successes are understood well enough to allow them to be replicated consistently, HMOs cannot be relied upon as a major element in a cost control program. The various forms of direct regulation that have been experimented with —prospective reimbursement, certificate-of-need, and professional standards review organizations—have yet to show that they can slow the rise in costs, although events under the economic stabilization program suggest that direct regulation of the entire industry may have some effect for a few years. Studies of permanent regulation in other industries, however, indicate that it is not likely to be effective over the longer term.

The cost problem is not a short-term problem of inflation, but a long-term problem concerning the way the nation wants to allocate its resources among different uses. The incentive structure created by third-party financing has an unlimited potential for drawing resources into medical care. If it remains unchanged, the costs of medical care, and with them the budgets of federal health programs, will continue to grow rapidly. This incentive structure is at the heart of the problem of rising costs, and will continue to be whether the third-party payments are channeled through a national health insurance plan or through the network of public and private programs that exists today.

There is, in short, nothing inherent in the nature of a program of national health insurance that guarantees that it will make the cost problem any better, or any worse. Everything depends on the design of the program, and the design problems are the same for a national system as for the present mixed system. Thus the choice between a public and a private, or largely private, system must be based on other considerations—such as uniformity and continuity of benefits, or the ability of the system to respond as conditions change in the future—and on the values the nation attaches to them.

CHAPTER SEVEN

Social Security

ALICIA H. MUNNELL

THE FINANCIAL PROBLEMS of the social security system have received considerable attention in the last few years Large long-term deficits are projected as a result of anticipated demographic shifts and a benefit formula that overcorrects for inflation. The projections have been accompanied by warnings of the more immediate danger that the shortfall in revenues resulting from the 1974–75 recession and a continued rise in disability applications will exhaust the trust funds.

In response to the forecast deficits, President Ford's 1978 budget proposed a series of increases in the social security tax rate to restore short-run balance and recommended that the overindexing of the benefit formula be corrected in a way that would ensure constant replacement rates (ratio of benefits to preretirement earnings) over time. President Carter has suggested a similar plan for correcting the inflation adjustment mechanism but has avoided tax rate increases to stimulate revenues in the short run. Instead, Carter has relied primarily on wage base increases, elimination of the limit on employers' wage base, a small transfer of scheduled tax increases from the health insurance fund, and an infusion of general revenues. The two plans demonstrate that, although social security's financial problems are serious, many workable solutions exist. In fact, much of the difficulty lies in choosing among the various options.

The author is grateful to John L. Palmer and Lawrence D. Thompson for their comments on an early draft of this chapter and to Ann M. Connolly for research assistance.

This chapter explains the options available to restore both short-run and long-run balance to the system, and explores a number of issues in the benefit structure in the light of recent social and economic developments.

The Social Security Program Today

In 1976, the social security program covered over 90 percent of the working population, including the self-employed. More than $75 billion in benefits, financed by current payroll tax contributions from workers, was paid to over 33 million retired and disabled workers and their dependents and survivors. The following discussion of social security focuses on the old age, survivors, and disability insurance portion of the program and omits any discussion of health insurance.

Benefits

The monthly benefits awarded to retired and disabled workers and their dependents and survivors are computed in three stages. The first stage is the calculation of the worker's average monthly earnings (AME) on the basis of taxable wages in covered employment for the years between 1950 (or age twenty-one) and age sixty-two or disability. Five years of lowest earnings and all years of disability may be excluded from the calculation, and years of higher earnings after sixty-two can be substituted for years of lower earnings before sixty-two.

The second stage involves calculating the worker's primary insurance amount (PIA)—the benefit amount payable to a fully insured worker retiring at sixty-five—by applying a nine-bracket benefit formula to the worker's average monthly earnings.[1] The formula multiplies each successive increment of a worker's average wage by a declining percentage (except in one interval). The progressivity of the formula ensures that low-wage workers receive a higher percentage of their preretirement earnings in benefits than high-wage workers.

1. The formula effective in June 1977 is as follows: 145.90 percent of the first $110 of AME; +53.07 percent of the next $290 of AME; +49.59 percent of the next $150 of AME; +58.29 percent of the next $100 of AME; +32.42 percent of the next $100 of AME; +27.02 percent of the next $250 of AME; +24.34 percent of the next $175 of AME; +22.54 percent of the next $100 of AME; +21.18 percent of the next $100 of AME.

The third stage is the determination of the actual benefit paid. This amount usually depends on the relation of the wage-earner to the individual drawing the benefit and the age at which he claims it. A fully insured worker retiring at sixty-five receives a monthly benefit equal to 100 percent of his primary insurance amount; however, a worker can retire as early as sixty-two, with an actuarial reduction in benefits of five-ninths of 1 percent for each month before the age of sixty-five. A dependent spouse, a child, or dependent grandchild receives a benefit of up to 50 percent of the worker's primary insurance amount. If the worker dies, the widow or widower receives 100 percent of his primary insurance amount, while a surviving child or grandchild receives 75 percent. Dependents and survivors can also claim reduced benefits earlier than sixty-five. Wives, divorced wives, and husbands are eligible for permanently reduced benefits at sixty-two. Widows, divorced widows, and widowers can receive permanently reduced benefits as early as sixty.

Monthly benefits and replacement rates for workers in different circumstances are shown in table 7-1. Generally, workers require 60 to 70 percent of their preretirement earnings to maintain their standard of living in retirement. While the social security replacement rates fall short of this figure for workers above the median, the presumption is that most families are not totally dependent upon social security but have private resources available as well.

Since social security payments are meant to replace earnings lost because of retirement or disability, the amount of earned income a person can receive while collecting social security benefits is limited until he reaches seventy-two. This limit is known as the retirement, or earnings, test and is indexed to keep pace with the level of wages. For 1977, a beneficiary can earn up to $3,000 annually, or $250 monthly, with no reduction in benefits. After that, a dollar of benefits is withheld for each $2 of earnings over $3,000.

Coverage

At present, the only significant categories of workers excluded from the social security system are civilian employees of the federal government under a retirement system of their own, some state and local government workers, low-paid or very irregularly employed farm and domestic workers, and unpaid family workers. Railroad employees

Table 7-1. Monthly Benefits and Replacement Rates for Selected Types of Beneficiaries, January 1977

Type of beneficiary	Monthly benefit for worker with median earnings		Replacement rate[a] for worker with		
	Amount (dollars)	As percent of PIA[b]	Low earnings[c]	Median earnings[d]	Maximum earnings[e]
Male worker					
Aged sixty-five	329	100.0	0.582	0.447	0.324
Aged sixty-two	263	80.0	0.466	0.358	0.259
Male worker aged sixty-five, with wife					
Aged sixty-five	493	150.0	0.873	0.671	0.486
Aged sixty-two	452	137.5	0.800	0.615	0.445
Male worker aged sixty-two, with wife					
Aged sixty-five	427	130.0	0.757	0.582	0.421
Aged sixty-two	386	117.5	0.684	0.526	0.380
Widow aged sixty-five, spouse retired at					
Age sixty-five	329	100.0	0.582	0.447	0.324
Age sixty-two	271	82.5	0.480	0.369	0.267
Widow aged sixty-two, spouse retired at					
Age sixty-five	272	82.9	0.482	0.371	0.268
Age sixty-two	271	82.5	0.480	0.369	0.267
Widow aged sixty	235	71.5	0.416	0.320	0.231

Source: Social Security Administration, Office of the Actuary.
a. The ratio of the PIA at award to monthly taxable earnings in the year just before retirement.
b. Primary insurance amount. The entitlement of a single worker retiring at sixty-five is equal to his PIA. All other benefits are calculated as percentages of the PIA.
c. Assumes annual income equal to half the median for males.
d. Assumes annual income equal to the median for all male workers covered under social security. Median income figure for 1975 is preliminary from the Social Security Administration. Median earnings for 1976 are estimated by increasing the 1975 figure by 7.3 percent, which is the factor of increase in average weekly earnings for 1976. See *Economic Report of the President, January 1977*, p. 227.
e. Assumes income equal to the maximum taxable amount each year.

are also not covered directly by social security, but their plan is thoroughly integrated with it, both in financing and benefits.

The number of low-income farm and domestic workers who are not covered is relatively small. Administrative difficulties preclude extending coverage to those groups, though their coverage will increase automatically as the general level of wages rises, since coverage is contingent on a fixed minimum level of wages.

In contrast, the case for extending coverage to federal government employees and the two-fifths of state and local workers now uncovered is compelling, and such a move would greatly improve the equity of the social security program. Under the present system, those workers who are entitled to civil service or state or local pensions can easily achieve insured status (ten years or forty quarters) under social security and receive the minimum social security benefit in addition to their regular pension. These dual beneficiaries profit from the progressive benefit structure, which was designed to help low-wage workers rather than workers whose second career entitles them to benefits.

Extending coverage to federal civilian employees would not involve any serious constitutional or administrative problems. However, the unions and other organizations of federal workers are strongly opposed to such a step, largely because they recognize the bonanza to dual beneficiaries and also because they would have less control over fringe benefits if part of the protection were transferred to social security.

Coverage of state and local workers is more difficult because of the constitutional question of whether the federal government has the right to levy a tax on a state or local government. The issue of state and local employee participation surfaced as a potentially important problem in March 1976, when New York City gave notice that it intended to withdraw 112,000 of the city's municipal workers from the social security program.[2] Widespread withdrawal of state and local systems would significantly aggravate the short-run financial difficulties of the social security system, since revenues would decline with no immediate reduction in benefit liability. Long-run costs would also be affected adversely, since state and local workers generally have above-average earnings and therefore make relatively high contributions per dollar of benefits.

Although the sense of urgency about this problem has declined since New York City decided in January 1977 not to withdraw, the equity issue remains. The problem would be significantly less pressing if the minimum benefit were eliminated and the tilt in the benefit formula reduced. Given the existing benefit structure, however, one possible solution is to extend compulsory coverage directly to the workers and tax them at the self-employed rate, thereby avoiding a tax on state and local governments.[3] The tax treatment of ministers and American citizens employed by international agencies or foreign

2. The notice did not constitute immediate withdrawal, but started the two-year waiting period required under federal law before termination of coverage becomes effective. See the *New York Times,* March 23, 1976.

3. This proposal was originally suggested by Robert J. Myers, *Social Security* (Irwin for McCahan Foundation, 1975), p. 190.

governments provides a well-established precedent for such a move. An alternative would be to tax state and local employees at the normal rate and to finance the employers' portion through general revenues. Another rather different possibility would involve tying revenue sharing funds or some other type of federal aid to coverage of all state and local workers under the social security system. A final option would involve some type of offset so that state and local workers who achieved insured status through a second career received benefits based on their normal rate of pay and would not benefit from the progressivity of the social security program.

Financing

Social security benefits are financed from current payroll tax contributions to the old age and survivors insurance and disability insurance trust funds. The initial payroll tax rate in 1937 was 1 percent, payable by both employees and employers on the first $3,000 of wage income. By 1977, the rate for retirement, survivors, and disability taxes was 4.95 percent each for employers and employees on the first $16,500 of wage income, with the wage ceiling scheduled to rise automatically with the wage level. Hospital insurance contributions raise the overall payroll tax rate to 5.85 percent.

The legislative intent of levying half the tax on the employer and half on the employee was to divide the burden between the two parties. However, most economists now think that, in spite of the intent of the law, the entire tax is borne by the employee (in the form of lower wages than they otherwise would have received).[4]

Since social security benefits are funded essentially by the current flow of payroll taxes, the financing is described as "pay-as-you-go." At the beginning of 1977, the combined old age, survivors, and disability insurance trust funds held assets of only $41 billion, which is significantly less than one year's benefits. However, the lack of a large trust fund should not be a source of concern in a social insurance program. A private pension plan must have sufficient assets to meet all prior and current commitments because it cannot be certain of receiving future premiums. In contrast, the social security program, which relies on the government's taxing powers to meet its obliga-

4. This conclusion is derived from the cost-minimizing behavior of firms. See John A. Brittain, *The Payroll Tax for Social Security* (Brookings Institution, 1972), pp. 39–44, 55–57.

tions, can continue to levy taxes on future generations of workers to pay social security taxes. However, pay-as-you-go financing can lead to short-run problems if economic fluctuations adversely affect receipts or outlays. Long-run financing problems can also arise if there is a significant increase in the size of the beneficiary population relative to the working population. The social security system now faces both these difficulties, as well as having a benefit formula that is over-indexed for inflation.

Financing Strategies for the Short Run, 1977–86

The 1974–75 recession, which combined high levels of unemployment with a decline in real wages, has led to a shortfall in revenues.[5] The recession coincided with a continuing rapid increase in disability beneficiaries that would have depleted disability insurance trust fund revenues even without the downturn in the economy. As a result of the higher outlays for disability insurance and the loss of revenues, the combined funds for old age, survivors, and disability insurance declined by $1.5 billion in 1975 and by $3 billion in 1976. Between 1970 and 1977, trust fund balances have declined from 103 percent of annual outlays to 47 percent.

The Short-Run Deficit

The status of the trust funds in the near future naturally depends upon the future course of the economy. Table 7-2 presents three sets of projections for the funds under alternative economic assumptions.[6]

5. The recession drains the trust funds in three ways. First, employment and real wages were lowered, which directly diminished payroll tax revenues. Second, the unpromising labor market prompted more workers to leave the labor force and seek retirement or disability payments. Third, declining trust funds earn a declining amount of interest income. As the economy emerges from the recession, two of the adverse effects remain: the smaller trust fund earns less interest and there is a permanent loss of real wages caused by the downward shift in the trend growth— that is, while the *growth* of real wages returns to prerecession rates, the *level* of real wages suffers a permanent reduction.

6. The three alternatives assume different patterns and final levels of the percentage increase over prior years in annual average real GNP, average wages, and average CPI, and in the average annual unemployment rate. The initial rates of increase in 1977 are: real GNP 5.4 percent, wages 8.4 percent, CPI 6.0 percent; the assumed unemployment rate is 7.1 percent.

Alternative 1 assumes the largest percent changes in these rates over the time period. Real GNP rises slowly to 5.9 percent in 1979, declines quickly to 3.5 percent in 1982, then falls slowly to 3.0 percent in 1986. The change in the CPI and unemployment rate is steadier; the CPI declines at about 0.6 percent per year to 3.0 percent

If the recovery proceeds at a slow but steady pace, old age and survivors insurance outlays will continue to exceed receipts, and the trust fund balances will decline from 47 percent of annual benefit payments in 1977 to 24 percent in 1980 and will be exhausted in 1983. For disability insurance, outlays will continue to rise so much faster than receipts that the trust fund will be exhausted in 1979.

Temporary declines in the trust funds, which are accumulated as contingency reserves, are the expected consequence of revenue shortfalls during economic downturns. However, the recession has resulted in a permanent loss in real wages and the dramatic growth in the disability insurance program has not been reversed;[7] corrective action is therefore required to restore balance to the funds.

Short-Run Options

Corrective action is needed immediately to bolster the disability insurance trust fund. The most expedient course would be simply to increase the percentage of old age, survivors, and disability insurance revenues going to the disability fund. The hospital insurance trust fund is amply funded for the time being and could also serve as a source

---

in 1982, the unemployment rate falls by 0.7 percent per year to 4.5 percent in 1981 and beyond. The rate of increase in nominal wages declines slowly for several years, then more rapidly to 5.25 percent in 1983 and beyond.

Under alternative 2, real GNP declines slowly until 1980, decreases 1.3 percent between 1980 and 1981, slows again to reach 3.3 percent in 1982, and stabilizes at 2.9 percent in 1985. The increase in the CPI declines in spurts, alternating drops of 0.1 percent and 0.6 percent to level off at 4.0 percent in 1982. The unemployment rate drops at a decreasing rate to 5.0 percent in 1981 and beyond. The rate of increase in covered nominal wages falls 0.3 percent per year to 1979, decreases by 0.7 percent per year to 1981, then levels off at 5.75 percent in 1983 and beyond.

Alternative 3 assumes the smallest but least steady changes in the variables. GNP declines abruptly to 1.7 percent in 1979, increases to 3.4 percent in 1980, and hovers around 3.8 percent after 1981. After a slight decline, the CPI increases to 7.6 percent in 1979, falls to 5.9 percent in 1980 and to 5.0 percent after 1982. The unemployment rate declines to 6.4 percent in 1978, hovers around this level until settling at 5.5 percent in 1984 and beyond. The increase in wages initially declines, revives slightly to 8.2 percent in 1980, then falls sharply to 7.0 percent in 1981, 6.5 percent in 1982, and settles at 6.25 percent from 1983 on.

7. The number of disability beneficiaries has been increasing by approximately 10 percent a year since the early sixties. During periods of high unemployment, the number increases at a somewhat faster rate (11.2 percent in 1975, for example), while during prosperous times the rate of growth averages about 8 percent. The fluctuations in the rate of growth of beneficiaries can be fairly well explained by the movement in the unemployment rate. More difficult to understand is the underlying trend growth rate of 10 percent. Some of the hypotheses put forward to explain the continued rapid increase include the liberalization in the definition of disability, the addition and increasing value of Medicare payments, and reversals on a large backlog of denials.

Social Security **215**

Table 7-2. Estimates of Financial Status of Old Age and Survivors Insurance and Disability Insurance Trust Funds under Alternative Economic Assumptions,ᵃ 1977-87

Amounts in billions of dollars

Calendar year	Old age and survivors insurance		Assets at beginning of year		Disability insurance		Assets at beginning of year	
	Income	Outgo	Amount	As percent of outgo	Income	Outgo	Amount	As percent of outgo
			Alternative 1					
1977	72.5	75.7	35.4	47	9.6	12.1	5.7	48
1978	79.9	83.9	32.2	38	10.9	13.6	3.3	24
1979	88.1	91.9	28.2	31	11.9	15.3	0.5	3
1980	96.5	100.0	24.4	24	12.8	17.2	−3.0	b
1981	103.3	108.2	20.9	20	14.7	19.2	−7.4	b
1982	110.0	116.2	16.1	14	15.5	21.2	−11.9	b
1983	116.8	124.3	9.8	8	16.2	23.4	−17.6	b
1984	123.5	133.1	2.3	2	16.8	25.8	−24.9	b
1985	130.5	142.5	−7.3	b	17.4	28.3	−33.8	b
1986	136.4	152.3	−19.2	b	19.5	31.1	−44.7	b
1987	143.7	162.7	−35.1	b	20.3	34.0	−56.2	b
			Alternative 2					
1977	72.5	75.7	35.4	47	9.6	12.1	5.7	48
1978	79.8	83.9	32.2	38	10.8	13.6	3.3	24
1979	87.7	92.1	28.2	31	11.8	15.4	0.5	3
1980	96.2	100.6	23.8	24	12.7	17.4	−3.1	b
1981	102.8	109.4	19.3	18	14.6	19.5	−7.7	b
1982	109.7	118.4	12.7	11	15.5	21.7	−12.6	b
1983	116.7	127.9	4.0	3	16.2	24.1	−18.8	b
1984	123.9	138.3	−7.3	b	16.8	26.8	−26.7	b
1985	131.1	149.5	−21.7	b	17.3	30.0	−36.7	b
1986	136.9	161.4	−40.1	b	19.3	33.0	−49.2	b
1987	144.3	174.1	−64.6	b	20.0	36.4	62.8	b
			Alternative 3					
1977	72.5	75.7	35.4	47	9.6	12.1	5.7	48
1978	79.7	83.9	32.2	38	10.8	13.7	3.3	24
1979	86.6	92.9	28.1	30	11.7	15.5	0.4	3
1980	94.3	103.2	21.7	21	12.5	17.9	−3.4	b
1981	101.3	113.8	12.8	11	14.4	20.3	−8.8	b
1982	109.0	124.4	0.3	*	15.3	22.8	−14.8	b
1983	117.2	135.6	−15.1	b	16.2	25.6	−22.3	b
1984	125.0	148.0	−33.5	b	16.8	28.7	−31.7	b
1985	132.4	161.6	−56.5	b	17.3	32.2	−43.6	b
1986	138.2	176.2	−85.6	b	19.2	36.0	−58.5	b
1987	145.5	191.9	−123.6	b	19.7	40.2	−75.3	b

Source: Social Security Administration, Office of the Actuary.
* Less than 0.5 percent.
a. See note 6 in text for explanation of alternative assumptions.
b. Trust fund exhausted.

of additional revenues. Either of these measures would avoid payroll tax increases in a period of high unemployment. Another option is a small increase in the disability insurance tax rate. An increase in the rate of 0.35 percentage point, effective January 1978, would prevent the depletion of the fund before 1981. Although a simple shift between trust funds or a small increase in the disability insurance tax rate would solve the immediate problem, a more permanent solution is required for the next decade, since the combined old age, survivors, and disability insurance trust funds will be depleted by the year 1982.

GENERAL REVENUES. The most fundamental question is whether to continue deriving social security revenues exclusively from the payroll tax or to shift part of the burden to general revenues. Underlying this issue is the philosophical rationale of the social security program and its intended effect on the distribution of income. Some argue that social security is best construed as an annual tax-transfer program, which redistributes income from the relatively affluent wage earners to the relatively poor retired. The more common perspective sees social security in a lifetime framework, where payroll taxes are considered compulsory saving for retirement.

The annual view—that social security is part of the federal government's tax and transfer schemes—leads to an evaluation of the tax independent of the benefits, with the conclusion that the payroll tax clearly violates the ability-to-pay criterion for equitable taxation. The tax is levied without provision for the number of dependents, excludes income from capital, and exempts wages over the maximum.

However, the earned income credit introduced into the personal income tax by the Tax Reduction Act of 1975 partly eliminates the burden of the payroll tax on some of the working poor. The credit amounts to 10 percent of the first $4,000 of earned income, after which it is reduced by 10 percent of adjusted gross income in excess of $4,000. But this credit is limited to taxpayers with children (who account for only 56 percent of the nonaged low-income population) and provides no relief for low-income childless couples or single people. Furthermore, limiting the maximum credit to $400 means that a family with two children would still pay a payroll tax on earnings not taxed under the personal income tax (which exempts the first $7,200 of income).[8] Finally, the 10 percent credit offsets only the

8. A family of four filing a joint return with $7,200 in income would claim $3,000 in personal exemptions (four exemptions at $750 each) plus a $3,200 standard deduc-

old age, survivors, and disability insurance portion of the payroll tax; low-income families still pay 1.8 percent of wages for hospital insurance.

Even with an expanded earned income credit, advocates of the annual tax-transfer perspective would favor a more progressive source of revenue to finance social security. General revenues, most of which are derived from the personal income tax, would be preferable on distributional grounds, since the income tax includes unearned as well as earned income in the tax base, applies progressive rates, and makes allowance for dependents. However, the system transfers funds to all covered retirees irrespective of need, and an annual perspective seems at variance with the existing structure.

In contrast, many argue that the present program is best understood as a lifetime compulsory saving program, in which people are forced to save during their working years in exchange for guaranteed income in retirement. In this perspective, where benefits and taxes are considered jointly, the payroll tax with an earned credit can be seen as an appropriate method of financing a compulsory saving program. The earned income credit, however, is essential to the acceptability of the payroll tax; compulsory saving schemes simply do not make sense for low-income families.

Since the present social security system is a compromise between a strictly wage-related saving scheme and a program of income redistribution, it could be argued that a rationale exists for supplementing payroll tax receipts with general revenues. And indeed, there are several precedents for the use of general revenues within the social security system, such as the gratuitous wage credits granted to servicemen, transitional benefits for certain uninsured people, and general revenue financing of some hospital payments.

Two quite different groups have argued against the introduction of general revenues. One group, comprising people associated with social security during its formative years, used to argue that a switch to general revenue financing might mean a break in the perceived link between individual contributions and benefits, thus making social security a means-tested program. This argument has lost force, however, since the principles of social security are now considered well

---

tion. The tax on the resulting $1,000 taxable income would be $138. The tax credit of $35 per personal exemption would bring the family's tax obligation to zero.

enough established for the program to withstand an infusion of general revenues without undermining the earned-right aspect.

More recent opposition to the use of general revenues stems from those who fear there would be more of a tendency to expand social security without the countervailing constituency created by the payroll tax. This view reflects the judgment that increases in social security benefits should have a low priority because of the more pressing needs for general revenues. The argument that general revenues should be used to finance the non-wage-related components of the program is also not very compelling to those who feel that the program should be divested of its welfare function and that benefits should be based entirely on the earnings record of each participant.

Limited use of general revenues has been proposed by President Carter to finance fund deficits from severe recessions. The rationale is that during normal periods social security should be funded fully by the payroll tax, but the responsibility for shortfalls in revenues caused by unemployment rates in excess of 6 percent should be shifted to the government as a whole and financed out of general funds. If this procedure were adopted retroactively it would justify a one-time transfer from general revenues of $9 billion for 1975 and 1976 and probably an additional $3 billion for 1977. Such a move would permit postponement of payroll tax increases until after the economy recovers, but would extend the solvency of the trust funds by only one year. Therefore, this stopgap measure would have to be accompanied by additional annual contributions from either the payroll tax or general revenues.

Infusion of general revenues on a countercyclical basis has the advantage of explicitly limiting the amount of social security revenues to be derived from the general fund. Such a move, however, sets a precedent for general revenue financing and further weakens the link between individual contributions and benefits.

SHIFT HOSPITAL INSURANCE REVENUES. A possibility that avoids direct revenue support is to transfer one of the other financial responsibilities of the payroll tax to general revenues. One proposal, which was advanced by the 1975 Social Security Advisory Council and adopted in part by President Carter, would shift all or some of the 1.8 percent tax for Medicare to general revenues and credit the scheduled increases in the hospital tax rate to the old age, survivors, and disability insurance funds. Since hospital insurance benefits bear no direct relation to contributions or earnings in covered employment, none of the program's underlying philosophies would be violated by such a change. Employment history could still be maintained as an entitlement mechanism to ensure the earned-right principle of the social security system. Transferring one-half of the scheduled hospital insurance tax (1.8 percent in 1977, 2.2 percent in 1978–80, 2.7 percent in 1981–85, and 3.0 percent in 1986) to old age, survivors, and disability insurance would result in a trust fund equal to about 52 percent of annual outlays in 1986 (see table 7-3). President Carter's proposal is to transfer 0.2 percentage point of the scheduled 1978 and 1981 rate increases of the hospital insurance tax to the social security fund. These small transfers would be financed out of hospital insurance trust fund surpluses rather than from general revenues.

Under the Advisory Council's scheme, additional revenues would have to be raised to finance Medicare. However, increases could be postponed until the economy has recovered fully from the recession, since the hospital insurance program is amply funded. The distributional implications of financing it through general revenues compared to simply raising the payroll tax for old age, survivors, and disability insurance depend upon whether the general revenues come from an increase in income taxes, reductions in government spending, or an increase in the federal deficit. While an increase in income taxes is more progressive than raising the payroll tax rate, general revenue funding of hospital insurance benefits that resulted in a reduction in, say, the food stamp program would be quite regressive.

PAYROLL TAX INCREASES. If the payroll tax is to provide all the necessary revenue, it must be increased by raising the tax rate or broadening the wage base, or a combination of the two.

In his fiscal year 1978 budget, President Ford proposed a series of increases in the payroll tax (0.2 percentage point in 1978, 0.6 percentage point in 1979, and 0.3 percentage point in 1980) to raise the old age, survivors, and disability insurance rate from 9.9 percent in 1977 to 11.0 percent in 1980. These hikes are in addition to the increases in the hospital insurance rate (0.4 percent in 1978, 0.5 percent in 1981, and 0.5 percent in 1986) already mandated under current law, thereby raising the total employee-employer tax from 11.7 percent in 1977 to 14.0 percent in 1986. The proposed increases in the old age, survivors, and disability insurance rates would ensure

Table 7-3. Alternative Financing Arrangements for Old Age, Survivors, and
Disability Insurance Trust Funds, Selected Years, 1977–86

Year	Present law	Base increase with rate increase	President Ford's proposed rate increase	Base increase only	Remove base for employers only	Transfer one-half of hospital insurance tax
	Contribution and benefit base (dollars)					
1977	16,500	16,500	16,500	16,500	16,500	16,500
1980	21,000	25,500	21,000	34,200	21,000	21,000
1983	26,100	31,800	26,100	42,900	26,100	26,100
1986	30,900	37,500	30,900	50,700	30,900	30,900
	Contribution rate, employee-employer combined (percent of taxable payroll)					
1977	9.9	9.9	9.9	9.9	9.9	9.9
1980	9.9	10.3	10.7	9.9	9.9	11.0
1983	9.9	10.4	10.9	9.9	9.9	11.25
1986	9.9	10.6	11.1	9.9	9.9	11.4
	Assets of OASI and DI trust funds, beginning of year (billions of dollars)					
1977	41.1	41.1	41.1	41.1	41.1	41.1
1980	26.1	43.5	41.4	43.9	40.6	47.9
1983	−1.0	58.3	54.3	58.0	45.8	74.7
1986	−57.0	69.6	66.2	57.8	34.3	100.6
	Assets at beginning of year as a percentage of outgo during year					
1977	47	47	47	47	47	47
1980	22	37	35	37	34	41
1983	a	38	36	38	30	49
1986	a	36	34	30	18	52

Source: Social Security Administration, Office of the Actuary.
a. Funds exhausted in 1982.

that revenues exceeded outlays through 1986, allowing the fund to increase from its present level of $41 billion to $66 billion by 1986 (see table 7-3).

Raising the payroll tax rate, however, exacerbates the regressivity of the tax system. These tax increases, combined with the possibility of using the payroll tax to finance a national health insurance program, pose the danger of overemphasis on the payroll tax in the overall tax structure. On the other hand, the distributional burden of the payroll tax is not as regressive as it was. The earned income credit reduces the tax burden for low-income families with children. The maximum taxable wage base has more than doubled in the last six years, from $7,800 in 1971 to $16,500 in 1977, making the tax proportional as a percent of wages for a significantly larger segment of the population. Furthermore, many families have two earners and are therefore taxed on earnings in excess of $16,500, which extends the proportionality even further up the income scale.

An alternative to increasing the tax rate is to broaden the taxable wage base. The base is already scheduled to increase automatically in line with the growth of average wages. If the base were raised to $28,800 in 1978 instead of the scheduled level of $17,700 (with subsequent automatic increases, calculated as under the current law), the receipts would yield trust fund balances similar to those under Ford's proposed rate increases (see table 7-3). However, the expansion of the employee's wage base proposed by President Carter ($600 above the scheduled increase in 1979, 1981, 1983, and 1985) is too small to have much effect on the trust funds. While increasing the wage base has more favorable distributional implications, such a move would also have substantial drawbacks. The increased social security taxes would create future liabilities: half the increased revenues accruing from the broadening of the wage base would subsequently be paid out in higher benefits to the affected high-wage earners. These additional benefits would increase the financial burden placed on future generations. In addition, the expansion of social security may have a negative effect on private savings, reducing funds available for capital accumulation.

As an alternative a combination wage base and tax rate increase is also shown in table 7-3. An increase in the wage base to $21,600 in 1978 (with automatic increases thereafter) would require moderate increases in the tax rate to a level of 10.6 percent in 1986. This combination also generates revenues roughly equal to the Ford proposal.

Another possibility, which is also part of President Carter's package, is eliminating the limit on the taxable earnings for the employer but maintaining the scheduled tax base for the employee. This change, even without any tax increase, would yield sufficient revenues to cover deficits at least through 1986, although the trust fund in that year would be only $34 billion, or one-half of the level achieved under President Ford's rate increase. However, maintaining the limit on the employee's wage base can serve as a rationale for not paying higher benefits to those workers earning over the maximum. Advocates of a redistributional social security program might find this scheme an appealing way to finance the short-term deficit, while those who favor a more strictly wage-related benefit program would consider such a further distortion in the ratio of benefits to contributions highly undesirable.

The Timing of Tax Increases

Though a number of alternative financing measures are feasible, there is less leeway in the need for additional financing and the timing of remedial action. The fact that declining trust fund balances are permanent rather than cyclical makes an increase of revenues imperative. However, even a tax hike as modest as President Ford's proposal implies a $7 billion boost in revenues in 1978, a move that is at odds with current fiscal policy requirements. An increase in the tax rate or the earnings base now would retard economic recovery and should be postponed until unemployment has been substantially reduced. Though the short-term deficit need not be financed immediately, there is a time constraint for action set by predictions that the disability insurance fund will be exhausted by 1979. That limit could be extended by a few years, however, if the trust funds were consolidated, because the old age and survivors insurance fund is projected to last until 1983. As an alternative, a transfer from general revenues to compensate for receipts forgone because of the severe recession would also postpone the deadline.

While a shift of revenues between the trust funds or a countercyclical transfer from general revenues avoids raising payroll taxes in a depressed economy, fund assets during the next ten years will be inadequate to act as a buffer in the event of another downturn in economic activity. If social security is to be funded solely by the payroll tax, trust fund reserves should be large enough to withstand a recession without requiring a payroll tax hike when unemployment is high. One study estimated that a reserve equivalent to 60 percent of a year's outlays would be required to satisfy this criterion.[9] Taxes would then have to be raised quickly when the economy recovered in order to restore reserves to the 60 percent level.

A tax increase now would retard the recovery, but postponing the required tax increase means that greater revenues will have to be raised in the future. For instance, President Ford's tax increase proposal would yield a trust fund of $66 billion in 1986. If tax rate increases were postponed until 1981, the old age, survivors, and dis-

9. Paul N. Van de Water and Lawrence H. Thompson, "The Social Security Trust Funds as Contingency Reserves," Technical Analysis Paper 9 (U.S. Department of Health, Education, and Welfare, Office of Income Security Policy, Office of the Assistant Secretary for Planning and Evaluation, July 1976; processed), p. 15.

ability insurance receipts would have to be $5 billion higher annually between 1981 and 1986 to accumulate the same assets by 1986.

Financing Strategies for the Long Run, 1986–2055

In setting social security tax rates, Congress has traditionally followed the principle that estimated future income to the trust funds should be equal to future disbursements. Since 1965, long-range cost estimates have been prepared for a seventy-five-year planning period. These estimates provide useful information to help Congress recognize the long-run consequences of proposed changes and also to identify any developing imbalance between receipts and expenditures.

Long-Run Projections

The 1977 Trustees' Report on the Social Security Administration includes three sets of projections to the year 2055, using three sets of assumptions regarding the fertility rate, the rate of inflation, and the rate of increase in average real wages. As shown in table 7-4, the future costs of the system are extremely sensitive to the assumed values for these factors. Nevertheless, all three sets of assumptions indicate a huge increase in social security expenditures as a percentage of taxable payroll after the year 2000. Since the tax rate is scheduled to increase from 9.9 percent in 1977 to only 11.9 percent in 2011, tax revenues will definitely be inadequate to meet long-term benefit commitments.

The projected cost increases can be attributed to two important factors. The first is the changing demographic structure of the population. Today there are thirty-one beneficiaries for each one hundred workers, while in 2055 it is estimated that there will be forty-eight for each one hundred workers. With a pay-as-you-go system, an increase in the ratio of beneficiaries to workers implies an inevitable matching increase in costs. The second cause of increase in long-run costs is the unintended result of a provision in the 1972 legislation that introduced a double adjustment for inflation into the benefit formula. Additional costs resulting from this technical flaw are avoidable and should not be allowed to cloud the real issues in long-run financing.

DEMOGRAPHIC ASSUMPTIONS. Changes in population are extraordinarily difficult to predict. Population growth depends on three factors—the fertility rate, the mortality rate, and the migration rate. The impact of the migration rate is very small and the mortality rate

Table 7-4. Long-Run Projections of Expenditures of the Old Age, Survivors, and Disability Insurance Trust Funds as a Percentage of Taxable Payroll, under Alternative Assumptions[a], Selected Years, 1977–2055

Year	Expenditures as percent of taxable payrolls under assumption			OASDI tax rates scheduled under current law
	I	II	III	
1977	10.9	10.9	10.9	9.9
1985	11.2	11.6	12.1	9.9
1995	12.1	13.1	14.4	9.9
2005	12.9	15.0	17.6	9.9
2015	15.1	18.9	24.4	11.9
2025	18.1	24.3	34.5	11.9
2035	18.5	26.7	42.0	11.9
2045	17.3	26.6	45.8	11.9
2055	17.2	27.5	49.8	11.9
Average, 1977–2051	14.9	19.2	27.1	10.9

Source: *1977 Annual Report of the Board of Trustees of the Federal Old-Age and Survivors Insurance and Disability Insurance Trust Funds* (GPO, 1977).

a. The assumptions (in annual percentage rates of increase) are:

	I	II	III
Fertility	2.3	2.1	1.7
Real wages	2.25	1.75	1.25
CPI	3.0	4.0	5.0

is reasonably predictable, with a steady downward trend. In contrast, the fertility rate has been subject to wide swings and is very difficult to forecast; at the same time, however, it has an enormous influence on the size of the population.

Since 1800 the fertility rate (number of births per woman of child-bearing age) has declined persistently, although there was a temporary deviation from this trend between 1945 and 1960. Since 1960 the fertility rate has been cut in half, from 3.65 to 1.82 in 1975. The 1977 official projections of the Social Security Administration assume a series of fertility rates varying from 1.7 to 2.3, but their preferred projection assumes that the downward trend in the fertility rate will be checked at a level of 1.65 in 1980 and then rise gradually to 2.1 in 2005, remaining constant thereafter.

The differences in the various fertility rate assumptions have important implications for the size and age structure of the population. With an ultimate fertility rate of 2.3, the population would grow steadily from 226 million in 1977 to 363 million in 2055. In contrast, an ultimate fertility rate of 1.7 would lead to a population peak of 262 million around 2020 and then a decline to 234 million in 2055.

The most significant implication of alternative fertility assumptions for social security, however, is not the absolute size but the changing age composition of the population. The ratio of aged population to working-age population has increased from 11.6 aged per 100 people of working age in 1940 to 19.4 aged per 100 working-age people in 1976. This ratio is projected to rise dramatically as the sizable population born during the post–World War II baby boom starts reaching retirement age after 2010. At that time the working population will be composed of the group born during the period of low fertility that began in the late 1960s. Depending upon the fertility rate assumption, the ratio of the aged to the working population can rise to 0.28 (with a fertility rate of 2.3) or as high as 0.39 (with a fertility rate of 1.7) by the year 2055.

Given the significance and difficulty of predicting the fertility rate, it is important to assess the plausibility of alternative fertility projections. Demographers generally agree that the recent decline in the fertility rate is the continuation of a long-run trend begun in 1800, and that the postwar baby boom was merely a temporary aberration.[10] These expectations are consistent with a series of major developments, all pointing toward smaller families. Birth control information and inexpensive methods of contraception have become more easily available and more widespread. In addition, more people recognize that in an urbanized society a smaller family makes possible the higher standard of living that people have come to prefer. Furthermore, the changing role of women has led many of them to choose increased participation in the labor force rather than spending long periods at home with children. Finally, many people have accepted zero population growth (which requires a long-run fertility rate of 2.1) as a social goal.

While there is general agreement that the fertility rate will remain low, there is less consensus on the level at which the rate will eventually stabilize. Although social security's preferred cost estimates for 1976 were based on a fertility rate of 1.9, the 1977 Trustees' Report assumes an ultimate rate of 2.1. The higher estimate, which corresponds with Census Bureau projections, is buttressed by data from annual surveys of young married women between the ages of eighteen and twenty-four, indicating an average number of expected births of

10. See Lawrence A. Mayer, "It's a Bear Market for Babies, Too," *Fortune*, vol. 95 (December 1974), pp. 134–37.

2.4 in 1971, 2.3 in 1972 and 1973, and 2.2 in 1974. Even with a downward adjustment for those who will remain single, the implied fertility rate is closer to 2.1 than to the Social Security Administration's 1976 projection of 1.9. Therefore, the upward revision seems reasonable, and the resulting cost estimates are probably more realistic than those based on last year's estimate of 1.9.

WAGES AND PRICES. The wage and price assumptions underlying the projections are important because of the automatic adjustment provisions introduced in the 1972 legislation. These provisions require that the benefit table be adjusted to keep up with the increase in the consumer price index and that the taxable earnings base, as well as the exempt amount in the retirement test, be adjusted in line with the increase in average wages.

The rate of growth of average real wages has declined since 1950. From 1950 to 1960 real wage growth averaged 2.3 percent and then fell to a rate of 0.7 percent from 1965 to 1975. Part of the decline can be attributed to the changing composition of the labor force, with an increasing proportion of part-time workers and teenagers. Real wage growth was also affected adversely by the 1974–75 recession. In the future, economic growth should restore normal patterns of real wage increases. As the proportion of teenagers declines and women develop more solid working histories, the proportion of part-time and entry level jobs will decline. With these developments it seems reasonable that real wage growth will increase to the rates experienced before 1965, making 2 percent an attainable goal for the long run. Therefore, the preferred social security projection, which assumes wage growth of 1.75 percent, may be overly pessimistic in terms of wage increases.

The last three Trustees' Reports have used an inflation rate of 4 percent for their central assumption. From 1929 to 1975, the consumer price index rose at an average annual rate of 2.5 percent, but there has been considerable fluctuation within this period. Between 1950 and 1975 the annual increase averaged 3.3 percent, but it averaged 5.5 percent between 1965 and 1975. Inflation is extremely difficult to predict; the determinants are hard to identify and prices are affected by policy as well as exogenous factors. Nonetheless, the 4 percent assumption seems plausible. If the rate of inflation were higher, the future burden would be significantly increased because of the double indexing feature in the current law, which results in rapidly accelerating benefit levels when inflation increases. However, the sensitivity of future costs to inflation would be eliminated once the overindexing is corrected.

The Problem of Overindexing

The 1972 amendments introduced into the Social Security Act a mechanism whereby the benefit formula was adjusted automatically in response to changes in the cost of living. Unfortunately, this adjustment, which is designed to maintain the real purchasing power of benefits, is marred by a serious technical flaw that overcompensates workers for inflation and makes future replacement rates highly dependent on the exact pattern of future wage and price increases.

The automatic adjustment procedure introduces cost-of-living increases by changing the factors in the social security benefit formula. For example, in January 1977 a worker's primary benefit was equal to roughly 138 percent of the first $110 of average monthly earnings, 50 percent of the next $290, 47 percent of the next $150, and so on through six additional brackets. Since inflation during 1976 averaged 5.9 percent, the formula was automatically changed in June 1977 so that each individual's benefit was defined as 146 percent (or 1.059 times 138 percent) of the first $110, plus 53 percent (or 1.059 times 50 percent) of the next $290, and so forth for all the brackets in the formula.

This inflation adjustment works well for those beneficiaries of the social security system who are already retired. For them, monthly benefits increase by the same amount as the cost of living, thus maintaining the purchasing power of their benefits at its original level. At the same time, however, the procedure introduces an unintended overadjustment into the future benefit levels of those who are still working.

This side effect occurs because the same benefit formula is used for currently retired workers and for future retirees, creating what is known as a "coupled" system. For the currently retired, inflation has no effect on the average monthly earnings used in the benefit computation; their average monthly earnings remains fixed at the actual level of their past earnings. But those still in the labor force will, over the long run, get wage increases to compensate for the effects of inflation, and the taxable wage base will be increased automatically in line with the growth in average wages. As a result of the inflation-induced wage increases, these workers will have higher average monthly earnings when it comes time for them to retire and will therefore be entitled to higher social security benefits. In this way, the present adjustment mechanism gives future retirees a double increase in benefits every time the cost of living rises, first from the adjustment of the benefit formula, and second from the higher average taxable earnings.

In actual practice, the impact of the inflation overadjustment is moderated because of the effect of the progressive benefit formula on replacement rates. As an illustration, consider a long period of zero inflation. In this situation, the benefit formula would never change, since the conversion factors in the formula are adjusted only in response to increases in prices. As real wages rise over time, each successive group of newly retired workers would find themselves in higher brackets of the benefit formula, with smaller percentages of their average monthly earnings being replaced by retirement benefits. Eventually, most of the average monthly wage would fall into the highest bracket, which implies a lower replacement rate. In the absence of inflation, replacement rates tend to decline over time as wages rise because of the progressivity of the benefit formula.

The overadjustment for inflation will cause replacement rates to rise whenever prices increase; the progressivity of the benefit formula will cause replacement rates to fall whenever wages rise. The net impact of these two forces on replacement rates depends on whether the wage effect or the price effect is dominant. Table 7-5 shows replacement rates to 2050 under alternative assumptions about the rate of increase in wages and prices.

The depressing effect of rising wages on replacement rates can be seen by comparing two series with the same rate of price increase but differing rates of wage growth. Series A and B both assume 4 percent inflation, but series A assumes real wage growth of 1 percent while series B has real wages rising at 2 percent. This 1 percentage point difference in the rate of wage growth results in significantly lower replacement rates under series B by the year 2050. In that year, the replacement rate with the higher wage growth is 0.667 compared to 0.983 under the low-wage growth assumption, a difference of 47 percent. Comparing replacement rates under series B and C illustrates the effect of the overadjustment for inflation. Both series assume that real wages grow at 2 percent, but the inflation rate is 1 percentage

Table 7-5. Replacement Rates[a] for a Man Retiring at Age Sixty-five, with Average Taxable Earnings in All Years, under Various Assumed Annual Increases in Real Wages and Prices, Selected Years, 1975–2050

	Annual increases			
Calendar year	Real wages, 1 percent; prices, 4 percent (A)	Real wages, 2 percent; prices, 4 percent (B)	Real wages, 2 percent; prices, 3 percent (C)	Real wages, 2 percent; prices, 2 percent (D)
1975[b]	0.434	0.434	0.434	0.434
1980	0.472	0.468	0.468	0.464
1985	0.514	0.495	0.490	0.478
1990	0.548	0.508	0.500	0.482
1995	0.570	0.510	0.494	0.473
2000	0.617	0.533	0.510	0.478
2005	0.661	0.553	0.522	0.482
2010	0.704	0.572	0.530	0.480
2015	0.746	0.589	0.536	0.477
2020	0.785	0.603	0.541	0.473
2025	0.822	0.616	0.545	0.470
2030	0.858	0.628	0.549	0.466
2035	0.891	0.639	0.553	0.463
2040	0.923	0.649	0.556	0.461
2045	0.954	0.658	0.559	0.458
2050	0.983	0.667	0.562	0.456

Source: Social Security Administration, Office of the Actuary.
a. Replacement rate represents the ratio of the primary insurance amount at award (June of year) to monthly taxable earnings in the year just before retirement.
b. 1975 rates are actual.

point higher in B than C. The higher rate of inflation causes the replacement rate to climb to 0.667 by the year 2050, compared to 0.562 under the lower inflation assumption.

The table illustrates one further interesting pattern. When the rate of real wage growth is equal to the rate of price increase, the two effects eventually offset one another and replacement rates become relatively stable. If real wages and prices rise at 2 percent, as they did during the late fifties and throughout the sixties, the replacement rates stabilize around the initial values (see series D). Thus, the legislated inflation adjustments in the formula factors during this period did not destabilize replacement rates, which explains why the procedure raised little concern when it was introduced as an automatic feature in the 1972 legislation.

OPTIONS FOR DECOUPLING. The potentially serious fiscal consequences of the present overindexed system require the adoption of a new procedure to adjust benefits for inflation. To correct overindexing, the system must be "decoupled" to provide separate adjustments for present and potential benefits. Benefits for retired workers would continue to be adjusted by the consumer price index, as under the present law, but benefits for future retirees would use a new indexing mechanism to avoid the present overadjustment.

Creating a decoupled system will inevitably alter the pattern of benefits paid to future retirees. The selection of a particular benefit computation procedure will determine the pattern of replacement rates over time as well as the distribution of benefits among a given group of retirees. The decoupling options are virtually unlimited, which means that it is possible to achieve any level of replacement or any degree of tilt in the benefit formula considered desirable. The following discussion will focus on only two of the alternatives that have been proposed and that may be viewed as the logical extremes.

The 1975 Social Security Advisory Council suggested a decoupling scheme whereby the earnings histories of workers would be indexed by wages to calculate an average monthly *indexed* earnings; the benefit formula would then be adjusted for changes in the cost of living by increasing the break points in line with the increase in average wages, while keeping the percentage factors constant. Once the initial benefit amount for an individual was determined, subsequent increases in the monthly benefit would depend on increases in the consumer price index, as under present law. In 1976, President Ford proposed such a wage indexing scheme, combined with a three-factor formula that would closely duplicate the current rate structure. In May 1977 President Carter suggested a similar decoupling procedure.

An alternative decoupling scheme, proposed by the 1976 Consultant Panel on Social Security created by the Senate Finance Committee, would index earnings histories by the consumer price index and make cost-of-living adjustments by increasing the break points in the benefit formula in line with the increases in prices rather than average wages. This scheme is usually referred to as the Hsiao proposal, named after the chairman of the panel.

The two proposals have very different implications for how fast future benefits grow relative to future average earnings—that is, for the intertemporal behavior of replacement rates. The Advisory Council's proposal would result in constant replacement rates over time for workers at the same relative position in the earnings distribution.

The average worker retiring in 2050 would thus have the same replacement rate as the average worker retiring today, although the average worker in 2050 will be considerably richer in real terms. For example, the average new beneficiary in 1976 had a preretirement wage of about $8,600 and received a social security benefit of about $3,600, yielding a replacement rate of 42 percent. If real wages grow by 2 percent per year, the average worker retiring in 2050 would have preretirement earnings of $37,200 in terms of today's purchasing power. Since under the Advisory Council's proposal the replacement rate for the average worker would remain constant, the worker retiring in 2050 would receive an annual benefit of $16,382 (see table 7-6).

In contrast, the Hsiao proposal would result in gradually declining replacement rates for the average worker. By indexing the break points in the benefit formula by prices, benefits to new retirees do not increase as rapidly as average wages. This proposal allows the progressivity of the benefit structure to lower replacement rates for future generations as workers move up into higher earnings brackets.[11] Under this scheme, the average worker with $37,200 of final real wages in 2050 would receive a benefit of $8,563—a replacement rate of 23 percent.

The Advisory Council and Hsiao proposals can be viewed as alternative interpretations of what it means to replace the same proportion of past earnings for people in the same economic circumstances retiring at different times.[12] The Advisory Council proposal implies that people's economic well-being is determined by their relative position in the earnings distribution, and therefore the replacement rate for the average worker is held constant over time. The Hsiao proposal, however, implies that economic well-being is determined by the absolute level of income in real terms, and therefore replacement rates remain constant for individuals with the same level of real income. This approach assumes that a worker in 2050 with preretirement earnings of $8,600 would have the same spending and saving habits and, therefore, retirement needs as a worker retiring with pre-

11. The result of the Hsiao proposal is that everyone will ultimately be in the highest bracket of the benefit formula, therefore producing a proportional benefit structure. However, the Hsiao proposal represents only one option for allowing replacement rates to decline over time. It would be possible to create a structure with declining replacements that did not eliminate the tilt in the benefit formula.

12. The following discussion draws heavily on the analysis presented in Congressional Budget Office, "Issues in the Financing of Social Security" (CBO, 1977; processed).

Table 7-6. Comparison of Benefits under the Advisory Council and Hsiao Decoupling Proposals for Worker with Average Earnings and for Worker with Same Level of Real Earnings,[a] Selected Years, 1976–2050

Amounts in dollars

Year of retirement	Worker with average earnings						Worker with same level of real earnings					
	Pre-retirement earnings	Annual benefit		Replacement rate[b] (percent)			Pre-retirement earnings	Annual benefit		Replacement rate[b] (percent)	
		Advisory Council[c]	Hsiao	Advisory Council[c]	Hsiao			Advisory Council[c]	Hsiao	Advisory Council[c]	Hsiao
1976	8,600	3,612	3,612	42	42		8,600	3,612	3,612	42	42
1990	11,348	3,698	3,858	43[d]	34		8,600	4,902	3,784	57	44
2000	13,833	6,087	4,288	44	31		8,600	5,590	3,784	65	44
2030	25,056	11,069	6,264	44	25		8,600	7,138	3,784	83	44
2050	37,232	16,382	8,563	44	23		8,600	8,600	3,784	100	44

Source: Congressional Budget Office, "Issues in the Financing of Social Security: A Fiscal Year 1978 Budget Issue Paper" (CBO, January 26, 1977; processed).

a. Projections assume that earnings rise 2 percent faster each year than the CPI and that the fertility rate rises to 2.1.

b. Primary insurance amount at age sixty-two as a percent of earnings in the preceding year.

c. These simulations are based on a "modified theoretical" system described in the 1976 Trustees' Report, which is close to the Ford proposal. See 1976 Annual Report of the Board of Trustees.

d. While the intention was to keep the average replacement rate constant, a technical problem with the method causes it to increase slightly.

retirement earnings of $8,600 today; therefore, the worker retiring in 2050 should be given the same pension amount as a worker retiring today. In contrast, the Advisory Council proposal assumes that a worker retiring with earnings of $8,600 in 2050 will not have the same spending and saving habits as the worker at that level today because he will be much poorer relative to the average; consequently, this worker will require a much higher replacement rate. Under the Advisory Council proposal, this worker would receive 100 percent of preretirement earnings as a social security benefit. Thus, the choice between wage indexing (the Advisory Council proposal) and price indexing (Hsiao proposal) the break points in the benefit formula makes a dramatic difference in the average level of replacement rates over time.[13]

THE COSTS OF THE ALTERNATIVE DECOUPLING PROPOSALS. The Advisory Council proposal provides higher replacement rates than the Hsiao proposal, so naturally it involves higher costs. Under the central assumptions of the 1977 Trustees' Report,[14] the Advisory Council proposal would result in costs of 18 percent of taxable payrolls in 2055 compared to 28 percent under the present overindexed system (see table 7-7). The Hsiao proposal, which allows replacement rates to decline over time, would require expenditures that peak at 12.8 percent of taxable earnings in 2030 and decline to 11 percent in 2055. Since taxes over the seventy-five-year planning period are scheduled to average 10.9 percent, expenditures under the Advisory Council proposal would significantly exceed revenues, although not by as much as under the current system. Under the Hsiao proposal

13. The choice of the index used to construct the average monthly indexed earnings figure is also important because it can significantly affect the distribution of a given level of benefits among individuals with considerably different patterns of earnings histories. Since wages generally rise more rapidly than prices, wage indexing gives greater weight than price indexing to earlier years. Therefore, workers with high earnings at the beginning of their careers but slow growth will do better if earnings are indexed by wages, while workers with rapid growth and high earnings later in life will do better if earnings are indexed by prices. Workers who have their highest wages early in their earnings history include blue-collar workers, whose earnings usually peak early, women who enter the labor force early and then leave, and workers who retire early. People whose highest earnings are likely to occur later in life include white-collar workers, people with long periods of training or education, and women who have children early and join the work force later. Wage indexing thus tends to favor the former group, whereas price indexing will help the latter.

14. The central assumptions include 4 percent inflation, 1.75 percent real wage growth, and a fertility rate of 2.1. As discussed earlier, the real wage growth is probably overly pessimistic, but all estimates prepared by the Social Security Administration are made on this basis.

Table 7-7. Projected Old Age, Survivors, and Disability Insurance Expenditures as a Percentage of Taxable Earnings under the Present Overindexed System and the Advisory Council and Hsiao Decoupling Proposals, 1977-2055[a]

| | Expenditures as a percentage of taxable earnings[b] | | | Combined OASDI tax rate schedule under current law |
| | Present overindexed system | Decoupled systems | | |
Calendar year		Advisory Council proposal	Hsiao proposal	
1977	10.9	10.9	10.9	9.9
1985	11.6	11.5	11.0	9.9
1995	13.1	12.6	10.8	9.9
2005	15.0	13.3	10.3	9.9
2015	18.9	15.5	11.2	11.9
2025	24.3	18.6	12.7	11.9
2035	26.7	19.4	12.4	11.9
2045	26.6	18.4	11.2	11.9
2055	27.5	18.3	10.7	11.9
Average, 1977-2055	19.2	15.4	11.3	10.9

Sources: *1977 Annual Report of the Board of Trustees of the Federal Old-Age and Survivors Insurance and Disability Insurance Trust Funds*, and Social Security Administration, Office of the Actuary.

a. The underlying assumptions are a 1.75 percent rate of growth in real wages, 4 percent inflation, and a fertility rate of 2.1.

b. The Hsiao proposal incorporates a higher maximum taxable earnings, which results in a tax base 3 percent higher than scheduled in the current law.

expenditures would exceed revenues until 2010, after which time the fund would run annual surpluses.

The choice between the Advisory Council and Hsiao proposals involves the basic question of what share of resources should be committed to retirement benefits in the future. The Hsiao proposal has the advantage of committing the nation to a level of expenditure that is known to be affordable. If these expenditures prove inadequate, Congress always has the power to increase benefits beyond the levels guaranteed under this scheme. Congress would also have more discretion in dividing up benefit increases between new and old retirees. Precluding ad hoc benefit increases would mean that once a person retired, his real benefit from social security would remain stable; so those who lived for a long time would fall further and further behind, since they do not share in productivity increases. However, to the extent that benefits are raised beyond those scheduled under the Hsiao proposal, the future costs of the program will also rise beyond those shown in table 7-7.

Those who argue for wage indexing maintain that declining replacement rates would represent a tremendous deliberalization of the well-established concept that social security benefits should keep up with the rising level of wages. They feel that future workers will be willing to bear the higher tax rates in order to ensure the same level of replacement that today's workers receive. Financing the Advisory Council proposal with increased payroll taxes would involve small rate hikes until 2015, at which time the tax would have to be increased to 15.5 percent of payrolls, and then again to 19 percent in 2025. Although this maximum rate represents nearly a doubling of the current levy, it is roughly equivalent to the present payroll tax rates of many European countries. On the other hand, it should be remembered that additional payroll tax levies may be required to finance hospital insurance, and perhaps also a system of national health insurance.

It should be noted that the cost estimates presented in table 7-7 are based on the assumption that the system is decoupled in 1979. If decoupling is postponed for ten years, the costs of the Hsiao proposal would increase by about 1.1 percentage points by 1990 and by 2 percentage points by 2020. Postponing the adoption of the Advisory Council proposal would also increase costs, though by smaller amounts. The cost increases from delaying action occur because replacement rates are allowed to increase for those people who retire under the coupled system. Since the introduction of the automatic adjustments in 1972, the replacement rate for a worker with median earnings has already increased from 0.34 to 0.45. Therefore, while the table seems to indicate that significant problems from overindexing do not arise until 2015 (the difference between the costs of the Advisory Council proposal and the coupled system being less than 1 percentage point until 2005), it is misleading to think that corrective action can be postponed until that time.

Financing Long-Run Costs

While the Hsiao proposal would not require rates beyond those scheduled in the current law, the Advisory Council proposal would involve a substantial increase. The higher costs associated with the Advisory Council proposal lead to questions about two important issues: the timing of tax increases and the possibility of holding down long-run costs by extending the retirement age.

If equity over time were an important criterion, it might be diffi-cult to justify a rate of 10 percent now and 19 percent in 2025, when the ratio of aged to working population will reach its peak. Financing on a pay-as-you-go basis means that current workers will receive a significantly higher rate of return than workers who enter the labor force after the turn of the century. An alternative to pay-as-you-go is a rate rise within the next few years to about 14 percent, thereby spreading the required levy evenly over the period.

An immediate increase in rates would produce substantial sur-pluses, forming a moderate trust fund. If allowed to build up until about 2010, the fund would amount to about three to five years' outgo. After 2010, it would be drawn down to finance benefits. In short, accumulation of a moderate trust fund could smooth out the demographic bulge and keep tax rates relatively constant until 2050.

If pay-as-you-go financing is retained, one way to reduce the high rates associated with the demographic bulge would be to raise gradu-ally the retirement age. Costs in a pay-as-you-go system are extremely sensitive to the ratio of retirees to working population, which in turn hinges on the age at which workers retire. Cost projections are based on the assumption that full benefits are awarded at sixty-five. How-ever, the average life expectancy at sixty-five increased 28 percent between 1930 and 1974, from 12.2 to 15.6 years. Moreover, between 1958 and 1974, the number of days of restricted activity for people sixty-five and over declined 20 percent, from 47.3 to 38.0. This evi-dence of the increased health and life expectancy of the aged and the large projected deficits under the Advisory Council proposal raises the possibility of reversing the trend toward early retirement and raising the normal retirement age, perhaps to sixty-eight. It is estimated that if the retirement age were increased gradually from sixty-five to sixty-eight by one month every six months, beginning in 2005 and ending in 2023, the combined payroll tax rate could be reduced by 1.5 percentage points between 2025 and 2050. Eventu-ally, this extension of the retirement age could reduce costs by as much as 4 percentage points.

The decoupling controversy is one of the most difficult social se-curity issues that any Congress has had to resolve. But regardless of whether the Advisory Council or Hsiao proposal is adopted, action to eliminate the overindexing must be taken soon if unnecessary in-creases in long-run costs are to be avoided.

Issues in the Benefit Structure

While most of the public concern about social security has centered on financing, certain aspects of the benefit structure have also received attention and may become the subject of congressional debate.

The Minimum Benefit

A $10 minimum benefit was introduced in 1935, primarily for reasons of administrative efficiency. Over time, in response to criticism that the minimum benefit was inadequate to meet basic needs, it has been increased more than twice as fast as average benefits. Recently, however, the gradual elimination of the minimum benefit has been suggested by several groups, among them the 1975 Social Security Advisory Council.

The minimum benefit may have performed a useful role in reducing poverty in the past, when state welfare programs did not meet the needs of the elderly. Today, however, the welfare system has been significantly strengthened by the enactment in 1972 of the supplemental security income program, which replaces the old network of state systems with a single, federally financed and operated program of cash benefits to the elderly, the disabled, and the blind. Now that the elderly are guaranteed a basic level of support, the minimum social security benefit is unnecessary since it simply duplicates the benefits of the welfare program.

Furthermore, there is evidence that a large portion of minimum benefits are paid to those who were not primarily dependent on earnings in covered employment during their working years and are not primarily dependent on social security benefits during their retirement years. Minimum benefits are payable on the basis of average monthly earnings under social security of $76 or less. Earnings of this level suggest very weak attachment to the labor force, since a man retiring at sixty-five in January 1977 who worked throughout his life at the prevailing minimum wage would have average monthly earnings of $249.70. Under the present system, workers entitled to other major pensions, such as federal civil service retirement benefits, can easily achieve insured status (one quarter for every year after 1950 or age twenty-one and before age sixty-two) under social security and receive the minimum benefit in addition to their regular pension. In the early 1970s, an estimated 40 percent of those receiving civil service retirement benefits were also receiving social security benefits. The minimum benefit thus often serves to supplement the income of those relatively more affluent retirees who receive other pensions, in direct conflict with its stated welfare objective. The minimum benefit should be phased out because it has been an inefficient welfare device, is inconsistent with a wage-related benefit structure and is a duplication of the welfare function of the supplemental security income program.

Spouse's Benefit

A nonemployed spouse of a retired worker is now granted a benefit equal to 50 percent of the worker's primary benefit. The spouse's benefit is the major source of inequity in the treatment of one-earner versus two-earner families and single people versus married couples, and of women who are divorced after less than twenty years of marriage (and forfeit all benefits based on their husbands' earnings). Whatever the virtues of this treatment in the past, the pronounced trend toward two-worker families and the increased frequency of divorce warrant serious reconsideration of the spouse's benefit.

The inequities in the spouse's benefit follow from the fact that the beneficiary unit and the taxpaying unit are not the same—the tax is levied on the individual, the benefit is awarded to the family. Compare two workers retiring at sixty-five with identical earnings histories, one single and one married with a nonworking spouse aged sixty-five. Both workers paid the same amount in taxes and receive equal primary benefits. However, the married worker receives an additional 50 percent of the primary benefit for support of his spouse, raising his wage replacement rate and giving him more benefits for his payroll tax dollar.

The spouse's benefit also creates a serious inequity between one-earner and two-earner families. Under the current system, a two-earner family could contribute the same amount as a family with a nonworking wife but receive less in benefits. Assume that each spouse in the two-earner family earned 50 percent of the maximum taxable amount in effect each year. If both retired at sixty-five in January 1977, the husband's monthly benefit would be $255.60 and the wife's $265.30, totaling $520.90. (The discrepancy in individual amounts is due to a shorter computation period for women, a discrepancy gradually being eliminated.) In the single-earner family, the husband earned the maximum taxable amount every year and the wife was not employed. If the husband retired in January 1977, this single-earner family would receive a benefit of $619.05 (150 percent of the husband's primary benefit). Thus, while both families contributed the same amount, the one-earner family would receive $98.15 a month or $1,177.80 a year more in benefits than the two-earner family. Another problem is posed by the nonworking spouse who is divorced after less than twenty years of marriage, since under current law she forfeits all rights to the spouse's benefit based on her husband's earnings history.[15]

These inequities—couples versus single people, one-earner versus two-earner families, and divorced spouses—require different types of solutions. The first two can be alleviated by reducing the spouse's benefit, while the third necessitates some type of income splitting. Unfortunately, the proposals made to date deal with only one or two of the inequities and often ignore or even aggravate the third. Furthermore, none of the proposals relates reform in the spouse's benefit to the treatment of survivor and disability benefits. With these limitations in mind, some of the popular suggestions for dealing with the family unit are summarized below.

TAX ON A FAMILY BASIS. One way to eliminate inequities between one- and two-earner couples is to use the family rather than the individual for both taxation and benefit calculations. The primary insurance amount would be derived from the combined earnings of husband and wife up to the maximum taxable amount. Awarding 100 percent of this primary benefit plus the regular wife's benefit to all retired couples would equalize benefits among families with equal total earnings histories, regardless of the number of wage earners. Taxes, too, would be based on family earnings instead of individual earnings, equalizing the taxes of single-earner families and dual-earner families receiving more than the maximum taxable amount. This could be done by allowing multiple-earner families to claim a refund on their income tax returns for social security taxes paid in excess of the earnings ceiling.

15. This treatment seems particularly unjust in view of the fact that if the divorced husband remarries, within one year his new spouse is entitled to full benefits based on his entire earnings record.

ELIMINATE THE SPOUSE'S BENEFIT. A possibility for eliminating inequities between single people and married couples, as well as
between one-earner and two-earner families, is to phase out benefits
for aged spouses and convert to benefits based on individual earnings
records. The proposal discussed by the 1975 Social Security Advisory
Council called for gradually reducing the 50 percent supplementary
benefit to 40 percent in the next six years, to 30 percent six years
later, and so forth until the secondary retirement benefits are completely eliminated in the year 2006.[16] This approach would also result
in a long-run saving to the system of 0.52 percent of taxable payroll.
The largest saving would begin to be realized just after the turn of
the century, when the actuarial deficit is projected to increase sharply
in response to demographic shifts.

While the elimination of benefits for aged spouses may be desirable
to promote equity, such a move would produce considerable hardship
for women who work primarily in the home. If it is decided that the
wife's benefits should be eliminated, some provision must be made
for the retirement income of nonworking wives. One possible alternative would be to allow women to receive benefits on the basis of imputed income for unpaid housework, either by providing earnings
credits to homemakers or by permitting payroll taxes to be paid on the
value of their housework.[17] However, imputing wages to nonworking
homemakers seems undesirable because all workers—full-time, part-
time, single, or married—also perform household chores. There is
little logic to imputing a wage to the nonemployed homemaker without imputing at least some earnings to employed people who work
around the house.

A solution preferable to imputing wages is a mandatory division of
a married couple's contribution credits. Under this scheme, if the husband of a nonworking wife earned the maximum in 1977 of $16,500,
each would be credited with $8,250. The same procedure would be
used for the earnings of a husband and wife who are both employed:
their earnings (up to the maximum) would be added together and di-

16. This pattern was suggested by the Subcommittee on the Treatment of Men
and Women, appointed by the Social Security Advisory Council, but the proposal
for eliminating secondary benefits was not adopted by the entire committee.
17. In 1972, Representative Bella Abzug introduced a bill to amend the Social
Security Act to extend coverage to dependent homemakers for their work at household maintenance. They would receive benefits on the basis of imputed wage credits
rather than on the basis of dependency status.

vided by two, with half credited to each account. Therefore, if the wife earned the maximum of $16,500 in 1977 and the husband earned $7,500, each would be credited with $12,000 ([$16,500 + $7,500]/2 = $12,000) of covered earnings. This approach seems equitable, since the decision on whether or not the wife works is probably made by the family. The nonemployed wife would have a permanent earnings base for future retirement benefits. Even if she should later become divorced she would retain the credits she earned during her marriage.

Without some adjustment in benefit levels, however, eliminating the spouse's benefit and splitting earnings records would involve a drastic reduction in replacement rates for married couples where one spouse is not employed. A small portion of the loss of the spouse's benefit would be offset by the splitting of earnings, thereby concentrating a greater portion of the worker's average monthly earnings in the high replacement rate brackets of the progressive benefit formula. Nevertheless, any sizable reduction in the couple's replacement rate for current workers is probably politically unacceptable.

The Consultant Panel on Social Security proposed a scheme that maintains current replacement rates for couples by allowing a nonemployed spouse to build individual earnings records with additional individual contributions. A nonworking spouse would be assumed to earn 50 percent of the earnings of the working spouse; that 50 percent would be taxed as self-employed income. Eventually, an earnings history would be established for the nonworking spouse of every covered employee. The spouse who retired first would receive a benefit based on his own earnings record until the retirement of both, when the couple could choose between benefits based on individual earnings records or benefits based on the average of the couple's two average monthly earnings.[18]

Allowing couples to average their earnings records upon retire-

18. The family benefit would be divided between the spouses in proportion to the PIAs corresponding to their individual AMEs. Such division would be subject to a minimum of one-third and a maximum of two-thirds. If AMEs had been averaged before the death of a spouse, the surviving spouse would receive two-thirds of the total family benefit. If a spouse died before AMEs had been averaged, the surviving spouse could choose between a benefit based on his or her own AME or on the average of both AMEs. A couple who had averaged their AMEs before obtaining a divorce would continue to receive benefits based on this averaging if they had been married sufficiently long. Since AME averaging can be done only once, if either person remarried no change would be made.

ment provides a more generous benefit to couples than to single retirees as long as the benefit formula is progressive. Thus, while the nonworking wife would be provided for and one-earner and two-earner families treated fairly, the inequity between couples and single retirees with identical earnings records would remain. This imbalance is the inevitable result of averaging earnings records in a progressive benefit structure.

The panel proposal has many advantages, and with a slight modification might also improve the welfare of the nonworking spouse in case of divorce. If the earnings credits of the couple were averaged annually rather than at retirement, each spouse would have a permanent earnings history equal to at least 75 percent of the earnings of the highest-paid spouse.[19] If the couple divorced, the wife would have an independent earnings history on the basis of which she would be entitled to retirement benefits. In the event that one spouse wished to retire before the other, he or she would be entitled to at least 75 percent of the benefit he or she would receive under the current system.

REDUCE THE SPOUSE'S BENEFIT. One final proposal, suggested by Robert M. Ball, former commissioner of social security, involves reducing but not eliminating the spouse's benefit. This suggestion is based on the assumptions that setting the couple's benefit at 150 percent of the single worker's benefit is excessive, and that it is not feasible to reduce replacement rates now for couples. The proposal would reduce the spouse's benefit from 50 percent to 33.3 percent and increase the primary benefit by 12.5 percent. There are several advantages associated with this proposal. It would reduce the importance of the dependent's benefit by increasing the proportion of women who would take benefits based on their own earnings record rather than the spouse's benefit. In addition, raising the primary benefit would increase the money going to single workers and to widows and thereby improve their position relative to couples. Unfortunately, this proposal is quite costly in the long run.

The spouse's benefit is certain to become an increasingly controversial provision as more people consider it an unfair transfer to the

19. During the transition, the mandatory division of the couple's credit on an annual basis would raise a serious problem if the working spouse were older than the nonworking spouse. Consider the case of a male worker aged sixty-five who wishes to retire but whose nonworking wife is too young to collect her benefits. With an annual division, the husband can collect only half the benefits the couple is entitled to and thus may not be able to afford retirement until the wife retires.

single-earner couple from the two-earner couple and the single worker. Concern with the spouse's benefit has increased as the dual-earner family has become more common than the single-earner unit. Working women perceive a small payoff for a lifetime of payroll tax contributions over what they would have received as a dependent spouse. However, any reform of the spouse's benefit will have to provide for the wife who works at home. Especially with the rising divorce rate, some method of splitting earnings will be required to ensure that the nonworking spouse will be entitled to benefits in her own right.

The Earnings Test

Under the social security earnings test, if a beneficiary under seventy-two earns more than the annual exempt amount ($3,000 in 1977, adjusted thereafter with rising wages), benefits are withheld at the rate of $1 in benefits for each $2 in earnings above that amount. Regardless of his annual earnings, a beneficiary may receive full benefits for any month in which he earns less than the monthly measure (one-twelfth of the annual exempt amount).

The earnings test is the most controversial provision of the social security program and is widely regarded as inequitable. Furthermore, provisions that discourage the elderly from remaining in the work force will severely undermine any effort gradually to raise the retirement age to reduce long-run cost increases. Despite its unpopularity, the earnings test has frequently been reviewed and then endorsed by public committees, most recently the 1975 Advisory Council on Social Security. The primary argument for a retirement or earnings test is that it is consistent with social security's standard practice of replacing wage income when a worker retires, is disabled, or dies; eliminating the test would change the nature of the system. A change may be appropriate at this time, but it must be recognized that awarding benefits without regard to labor force activity would represent a dramatic departure from the underlying principle of wage replacement.

The test has been criticized because it does not take into consideration a beneficiary's unearned income, such as dividends, interest, rents, or other pension payments. A person with, for example, $25,000 a year in interest and dividends would qualify for the full benefit, while someone who continued to work full time, earning

$10,000, would have his benefit withheld. However, if the test took into account income other than earnings, it would no longer be an earnings test but an income test. The wage replacement principle would be lost and social security would become more of a means-tested welfare system than a social insurance program.

ELIMINATING THE EARNINGS TEST. The most frequently discussed alternative to the earnings test would be to pay social security benefits to all beneficiaries who reach sixty-five, regardless of their employment status. Such a move would run counter to the basic philosophy of the social security system. However, given the improved health and life expectancy of the elderly and the costs of a large retired population, it may be more important to encourage the elderly to continue to work.

Cost considerations have been an argument against eliminating the earnings test, especially with the likelihood of higher tax rates in the future. Eliminating the test entirely at age sixty-five would result in an additional $2 to $3 billion in the first year and a long-run cost of 0.33 percent of taxable payrolls. With about 110 million taxpaying workers in 1977, the $2 billion to $3 billion extra would require an additional combined employer-employee contribution of $20–$30 for each worker.

LIBERALIZING THE EARNINGS TEST. If the principles of the social security program require at least partial retirement as a prerequisite to receiving benefits, it may be desirable to liberalize the earnings test by either raising the exempt amount or reducing the rate at which benefits are withheld for each dollar of earnings. The 1975 Advisory Council recommended a schedule of withholding for 1977 similar to the following. As under the existing law, no benefits would be withheld for earnings of $3,000 or less, and for all earnings in excess of $6,000, $1 of benefits would be withheld for every $2 of earnings. However, for earnings between $3,000 and $6,000, benefits would be reduced $1 for each $3 earned, instead of the present $1 for every $2. This liberalization would cost about $700 million at 1977 levels, or about 0.04 percent of taxable payrolls over the next seventy-five years. The new test would mean that a couple who received the maximum benefit of $619 in January 1977 would continue to receive at least partial payments until their 1977 earnings exceeded $18,856.

EXEMPT EARNINGS FROM PAYROLL TAX. Some critics have suggested exempting workers sixty-five and over (but not their employers) from the social security payroll tax to partially offset the disincentive of the earnings test. This would probably cost about $1 billion in 1977, although the costs might increase over time as the structure of the population changed. The popular rationale for exempting earnings is to avoid penalizing workers over sixty-five twice, first by withholding benefits and second by taxing earnings. On the other hand, one could argue that various provisions in the law call for these workers to contribute to the system. First, some workers may use earnings after sixty-five to establish credits for social security benefits. Second, workers may substitute earnings after sixty-five for years of lower earnings to derive higher average monthly earnings and, eventually, higher benefits. Third, insured workers receive a 1 percent increase in benefits for each year after sixty-five that retirement is delayed. If the program became an annuity system, however, and benefits were awarded at an agreed-upon age, there would be no logical reason to require employed workers to pay taxes after they qualified for that annuity.

ELIMINATE MONTHLY MEASURE OF RETIREMENT. The present test using a combined annual-monthly measure of earnings creates serious inequities. For example, a beneficiary who earns $19,000 a year and who works regularly throughout the year has all benefits withheld. However, a beneficiary who earns the same amount by working eight months can receive benefits for the remaining four months. Workers in any type of seasonal industry can, upon reaching retirement age, receive some social security benefits during the year even though their work patterns and earnings have not changed.

President Ford included in his 1978 budget the 1975 Advisory Council's recommendation that the monthly measure of retirement be eliminated so that the retirement test would be based solely on annual earnings.[20] Elimination of the monthly measure from the retirement test would result in savings of about $250 million in 1977, or about 0.02 percent of taxable payroll.

EFFECT OF REVISING THE TEST. While it is generally acknowledged that the retirement test discourages the elderly from working, there are no empirical studies that could be used to predict how the

20. The monthly measure should be retained for the first year for which a cash benefit is received so that a beneficiary (as under current law) can receive benefits beginning the first month of retirement, regardless of his annual earnings before retirement.

aged would respond to changes in the exempt amount or the implicit tax rate. More analysis may be required before any reform is enacted. Though eliminating the test might cost as much as $3 billion annually, it is possible that the tax revenues generated in the long run by an increase in labor force participation by the elderly would more than offset the costs.

There is good reason to be concerned about the provision of the social security law that discourages participation in the labor force by people who would prefer to continue working. By limiting available income sources, such a deterrent reduces the welfare of the elderly. The burden falls particularly heavily on those people who have no other sources of retirement income, such as private insurance, pension benefits, or savings. In addition, any provision that encourages a smaller labor force in future years will force a significantly higher tax rate in the long run.

Conclusion

The financial difficulties created by overindexing and recent demographic shifts have startled the public and generated concern that the social security system is not capable of meeting its commitments. This concern is unwarranted. The long-run and short-run financial problems of social security are manageable, but Congress must take action soon.

The short-run problems can be resolved by transferring a major portion of the hospital insurance taxes to the old age, survivors, and disability insurance trust funds. This would retain payroll tax financing for retirement and disability insurance when benefits are related to wage loss, while shifting the funding of hospital insurance to general revenues, which is a more appropriate source. In lieu of this approach, President Carter has recommended heavy reliance on a combination of general revenues and an increase in the taxable wage base. Action must be taken quickly, since the disability insurance fund will be exhausted in 1979 and the old age and survivors insurance fund in 1983.

The long-run problems require that the system be decoupled to eliminate the increase in replacement rates due to overindexing. The Hsiao and Advisory Council proposals would both accomplish this goal, although they have profoundly different implications for the intertemporal behavior of replacement rates. If current rates of replacement are considered desirable, it could be argued that maintaining these rates over time must also be desirable. However, current levels are partially the result of an upward drift since 1972 caused by the overindexing, so a rationale exists for stabilizing them at 1972 levels. In any case, there is the question whether the nation can afford the expenditure required as the ratio of the aged to workers increases dramatically in the next forty years. One interesting implication of the demographic shift is that lower fertility rates, resulting in fewer children per worker, will cause a stabilization or even a decline in the dependency ratio—a measure of total economic burden on active workers. Resources currently devoted to clothing, feeding, and educating children could thus be directed toward support of the elderly.

Regardless of what scheme is adopted, the system must be decoupled soon in order to avoid unnecessary increases in long-run costs. However, whether replacement rates should remain constant or decline over time is a difficult decision, and decoupling is likely to involve prolonged debates in Congress.

CHAPTER EIGHT

Welfare Reform

GEORGE J. CARCAGNO *and* WALTER S. CORSON

WELFARE REFORM is once again occupying the attention of both the administration and the Congress. Although there is near-unanimous agreement that the welfare system should be changed, critics are deeply divided about what form the changes should take. Welfare is a subject that touches some of this society's basic values, such as attitudes toward work and family life, and it consequently arouses strong feelings and equally strong disagreements. President Carter has made welfare reform a major priority of his administration.

In this chapter the current state of the welfare system is reviewed and the various alternative reform proposals are evaluated. Each proposal is analyzed in terms of which of the overall objectives of the welfare system, discussed in the next section, it emphasizes most. This will enable the reader to decide which proposal conforms most closely to the weight he or she assigns to each objective.

Although it is unlikely that any welfare reform will directly affect the budget for fiscal year 1978, budget decisions taken for 1978 may well affect the availability of funds for future welfare changes.[1] For example, if one of the major reform proposals were adopted, additional federal outlays of $5 billion to $25 billion a year would be required, possibly starting as early as fiscal year 1980. Prior-year com-

The authors thank Walter Nicholson, John L. Palmer, and Alice Small for their helpful comments, and Harold Beebout and Robert Scardamalia for providing the data reported in table 8-3.
1. However, if a reform proposal were adopted that required only minor changes in existing programs, such changes could be put into effect for fiscal 1978.

mitments for new programs that would reduce the expected fiscal margin of $30 billion to $46 billion in fiscal 1981 could thus constrain the scope of the reform.[2] Furthermore, program decisions made for the fiscal 1978 budget could either facilitate or hinder efforts to reform welfare.[3] If, for example, new income security programs were added to the system, any future attempts to consolidate welfare programs would be made more difficult, whereas measures to improve the management of existing programs would probably help pave the way for any one of the proposals under consideration.

Objectives of the Welfare System

One symptom of the problems of the welfare system is that overall goals or objectives are not specified in legislation. The collection of programs we now call the welfare system was never designed as a unified system; each program was established with specific goals in mind. There is, however, general agreement that the reduction of poverty is the broad, underlying goal of the system. Each program goes about achieving that goal in a different way, some by providing cash to specific categories of people, others by removing or easing the budget constraints for particular consumption goods (medical care or food, for example). This broad antipoverty goal, however, is not by itself a criterion for an evaluation of welfare alternatives. Subsidiary goals or objectives that focus on how the system operates as well as its end result are necessary for this purpose.

While many system objectives have been identified by welfare analysts, seven are the most important. A somewhat similar set of principles was advanced by President Carter in his May 1977 statement on welfare reform.[4]

2. See chapter 11.

3. Neither the Ford nor the Carter fiscal 1978 budgets proposed major changes in the welfare system. The budget authority request for income support programs totaled $170.2 billion in the Ford budget and $179.8 billion in the Carter revised budget, more than 35 percent of the total federal budget. The bulk of the difference between the two budgets is accounted for by the restoration of reductions proposed in the Ford budget, including withdrawal of the proposed revisions in the food stamp program, continuation of the earned income tax credit in 1978, increases in subsidized housing programs, and continued extension of federal supplemental unemployment benefits to provide coverage to a total of fifty-two weeks.

4. He also stated that the initial cost of welfare reform should be no higher than the cost of present programs. This objective will be very difficult to achieve.

• Adequacy of benefits. The benefits should be high enough to enable individuals with no or low income to gain access to an adequate level of living.

• Horizontal and vertical equity. The welfare system should be structured so that families or individuals in equal circumstances receive equal benefits (horizontal equity) and that families or individuals who have higher pretransfer incomes should continue to have higher posttransfer incomes (vertical equity).

• Work incentives. People who are able to work should find it in their interest to work. Work should result in a higher total income. Self-sufficiency should be encouraged by the system.

• Target efficiency. Benefits should be concentrated on those most in need.

• Supporting the family. Incentives that encourage families to split up or that discourage new families from forming should be minimized.

• Fair treatment of recipients. Recipients should be treated fairly and with the same respect accorded other citizens in dealings with the government.

• Administrative efficiency. The system should accomplish its objectives in an efficient and effective manner at the lowest administrative cost.

Although there is general agreement that these are the appropriate objectives of welfare, very different solutions are proposed to achieve them. This is so for two reasons. First, there is no general agreement on the precise meaning of each objective. What is an "adequate standard of living"? What constitutes "equal circumstances"—should equal circumstances be defined solely in terms of family size and income or should family composition and other factors be taken into account? What form should work incentives take? Disagreement about what each objective means can obviously lead to very different program proposals. Second, some of the objectives are in conflict with one another, and the resolution of that conflict requires that one objective be emphasized at the expense of another. For example, the objectives of adequacy of benefits and target efficiency suggest that adequate benefits should be paid to those with no other income and that no benefits should be paid to people above, say, the poverty level.

Both objectives are in conflict with the goal of preserving strong work incentives, since both high benefits and the high benefit reduction rates[5] needed to prevent spillovers above the poverty line discourage work effort. These conflicts and trade-offs are inevitable. Weights must be assigned to the various objectives before a programmatic solution can be designed. The result is that there is no solution to the problem that can satisfy all objectives equally, for every proposal represents a compromise among conflicting objectives.

The Current Welfare System

Income support for the low-income population is currently provided through over forty separate and varied programs. The most important of these are listed in table 8-1. These programs are of two types: means-tested or welfare programs, such as aid to families with dependent children (AFDC) and food stamps, and social insurance programs, such as old age, survivors, and disability insurance (social security) and unemployment compensation. Although eligibility for social insurance programs is not means-tested (eligibility is usually related to employment history and the current labor force status of the recipient), these programs are an important income source for the poor. Recent estimates show that in fiscal 1976 about one-third of cash social insurance benefits went to those in the lowest quintile of the income distribution; these benefits represented just over 50 percent of the total income received by this group after taxes and transfers.[6] Because of the importance of social insurance, attention must be paid to the interactions of these programs with the welfare system.

The set of programs included in table 8-1 will pay benefits of approximately $185.5 billion in fiscal 1977. This represents an increase of 135 percent in real terms over the figure for fiscal 1968. Over this same period these expenditures have grown as a percent of gross national product from 5.4 to 10.1. Of the total benefits, 27.5 percent

5. The benefit reduction rate is the rate at which the welfare benefit is reduced as income rises.
6. Congressional Budget Office, *Poverty Status of Families under Alternative Definitions of Income,* background paper 17 (CBO, rev. February 1977), tables 2, A-4. For these estimates, cash social insurance programs included OASDI and railroad retirement, unemployment compensation, workmen's compensation, government pensions, and veterans' compensation. Families were classified by income quintiles before taxes and transfers.

Table 8-1. Estimated Benefit Expenditures for Major Welfare and Social Insurance Programs, Fiscal Year 1977

Billions of dollars

Program	Federal	State and local	Total
Welfare	**36.7**	**15.0**	**51.7**
Cash benefits			
Aid to families with dependent children	5.7	4.6	10.3
Supplemental security income	4.7	1.6ᵃ	6.3
Veterans' and survivors' nonservice-connected pensions	3.1	...	3.1
Earned income tax credit	0.9	...	0.9
General assistance	...	1.3	1.3
Total	14.4	7.5	21.9
In-kind benefits			
Food stamps	4.5	...	4.5
Child nutrition and other Department of Agriculture food assistance	3.3	...	3.3
Medicaid	9.7	7.5	17.2
Housing assistance	3.0	...	3.0
Basic educational opportunity grants	1.8	...	1.8
Total	22.3	7.5	29.8
Social insurance	**127.1**	**6.7**	**133.8**
Cash benefits			
Old age, survivors, and disability insurance and railroad retirement	84.1	...	84.1
Special compensation for disabled coal miners	0.9	...	0.9
Unemployment compensationᵇ	15.2	...	15.2
Veterans' and survivors' service-connected compensation	5.7	...	5.7
Workmen's compensationᶜ	...	6.7	6.7
Total	105.9	6.7	112.6
In-kind benefits			
Medicare	21.2	...	21.2
Total welfare and social insuranceᵈ	**163.8**	**21.7**	**185.5**

Sources: Federal expenditures, *The Budget of the United States Government, Fiscal Year 1978—Appendix;* state and local expenditures, U.S. Department of Health, Education, and Welfare, Office of the Assistant Secretary for Planning and Evaluation, "An Overview of the Income Security System," paper 1 (draft), Welfare Reform Analysis Series (Office of the Assistant Secretary for Planning and Evaluation, n.d.; processed).

a. Excludes state administered supplements.

b. Benefits are paid from a federal UI trust fund and are financed by federal and state taxes.

c. Programs are administered by states and usually financed by employers.

d. Lists of federal income security programs often include federal civil service pensions. Pension programs are excluded here since they are qualitatively different from the other income security programs.

will be paid as in-kind benefits, the most important of which are for health and food. For those programs explicitly designed for the poverty population (that is, the welfare programs), 57.6 percent of the benefits are paid in kind. In-kind benefits therefore are extremely important sources of income for the poverty population. Another important characteristic of welfare programs is that 29 percent of the total funds come from state and local governments. Financial problems of these governments have created pressure on the federal government to increase its share of these costs.

In addition to the income security programs, there are a number of employment programs that provide income or services to the poor. Although these programs are generally not means-tested, their focus is on the low-income population. In fiscal 1976 approximately 75 percent of recipients were classified as economically disadvantaged. However, the work incentive program (WIN), which provides placement services, training, or public service employment, is the only program tied directly to the welfare system; able-bodied AFDC recipients with no child care responsibilities must register for this program. Fiscal 1977 budget authority for all training and employment programs total over $9 billion; less than 4 percent of this total is allocated to WIN.

How well does this system work? The results of a recent analysis of the contribution of the welfare system to the alleviation of poverty are reported in table 8-2. Using the poverty line as the dividing line between the poor and the nonpoor, the results show that, before transfers and taxes, 25.5 percent of all families were poor in fiscal 1976. Taking account of all transfer payments and taxes reduced this number to 6.9 percent, or 5.4 million families. These numbers differ from the usual calculations of the poverty population in that they adjust for the underreporting of income in the Current Population Survey and include the imputed value of in-kind benefits. Since it is likely that the value to recipients of Medicaid and Medicare is less than their cost to the government, it can be argued that their value should not be included in this calculation. Removal of these benefits implies that 9.3 percent of all families were poor in fiscal 1976. These estimates show, therefore, that the current welfare system reduces the number of poor from 14.1 percent of all families to anywhere from 9.3 to 6.9 percent.

Table 8-2. Number and Percent of Families below the Poverty Level under Alternative Income Transfers, Fiscal Year 1976[a]

	Families in poverty	
Alternative	Number (thousands)	Percent of all families
No income transfer (before taxes)	20,237	25.5
Social insurance income[b] (before taxes)	11,179	14.1
Social insurance and money transfer income[c] (before taxes)	9,073	11.4
Social insurance, money, and in-kind transfer income[d] (before taxes)		
Medicare and Medicaid excluded	7,406	9.3
Medicare and Medicaid included	5,336	6.7
Social insurance, money, and in-kind transfer income (after taxes)	5,445	6.9

Source: Congressional Budget Office, *Poverty Status of Families Under Alternative Definitions of Income*, Background Paper 17 (CBO, February 1977), p. xv.

a. Families are defined to include unrelated individuals as one-person families.

b. Social insurance programs included are social security and railroad retirement, government pensions, unemployment compensation, workers' compensation, and veterans' compensation.

c. Money transfer income programs are veterans' pensions, supplemental security income, aid to families with dependent children.

d. In-kind transfer income is the imputed value of food stamps, child nutrition and housing assistance, and Medicare and Medicaid.

Description of Existing Welfare Programs

The welfare system is composed of two major cash programs, AFDC and supplemental security income (SSI), and several programs that provide in-kind benefits—food stamps, Medicaid, and housing programs (table 8-1). Of the latter, food stamps and Medicaid are the most important in terms of total dollars currently spent, although one of the housing programs, which provides rental assistance to lower-income families, has the potential to expand greatly in the future. Medicaid, which provides health care coverage for certain categories of the poor, is, in terms of dollars spent, the largest program. While the integration of this program with other components of the income security system is extremely important, it is likely that any reform of the current means-tested transfer system will leave this program largely intact. Its reform will presumably be dealt with as one component of a national health insurance proposal. The discussion in this chapter thus focuses on the three other major welfare programs.

AID TO FAMILIES WITH DEPENDENT CHILDREN. This program, established in 1935 as part of the original social security legislation, is intended to provide aid to needy children who are deprived of parental support by death, incapacity, or continued absence of a parent or, in twenty-seven states (including the District of Columbia), because the father is unemployed. (This latter category of the program is called AFDC-U.)[7] The program is administered at the state or county level, and benefits are jointly financed with the federal government. The federal share in each state ranges from 50 to 83 percent; in some states the counties share in the program costs. Benefit levels and, to some degree, the method of computing benefits are determined by each state.

Benefits paid out and the number of recipients have risen rapidly since the middle sixties. Between 1965 and 1975, total benefit costs rose by a factor of five and recipients by a factor of two and a half. In July 1976, there were 11.3 million recipients; of these, only 5.6 percent fell into the unemployed-father category of the caseload.

SUPPLEMENTAL SECURITY INCOME. This program was begun in 1974 as a federal program to replace state programs for the aged, blind, and disabled. Federal benefits are calculated on a uniform basis throughout the nation. States are required to supplement the SSI benefits for recipients of the old state programs if their benefits would have been higher under the previous program. States can also elect to supplement the benefits for all recipients.

FOOD STAMPS. This program, enacted in 1964, provides benefits in the form of coupons that can be used to purchase only food. Individual households buy the stamps, with the purchase price a function of household size and income. Benefit levels are tied to the price of food and increase automatically with inflation. The benefit level (which is uniform throughout the country, with the exception of Alaska and Hawaii) for a family of four with no other income was $166 per month in January 1977. This program has also grown tremendously since its inception. Starting with 400,000 recipients in 1964, by 1972 there were 11 million, and by 1977, 18 million.

An important characteristic of the program is that it provides coverage to all low-income persons, not just to certain categories of the poor. Except for a portion of administrative costs, the program is fully financed by the federal government.

7. Eligibility for AFDC-U requires substantial prior attachment to the labor force and employment of less than 100 hours per month.

Shortcomings of the Existing Programs

The programs described above, while they have a substantial anti-poverty effect, also create a number of problems in achieving their goals. The current system violates in some way every one of the objectives described above.

Coverage by the system, and in some cases benefits for those covered, is not adequate. Nonaged childless individuals and couples and intact families with children where the father is employed are covered only by the food stamp program. In the twenty-four states without AFDC-U, intact families in which the father is unemployed are also covered only by food stamps. In the twenty-three states where combined benefits for those who are covered by both AFDC and food stamps equal less than 75 percent of the poverty-line income, benefits must be considered inadequate by most standards. The lack of coverage for intact families also means that the system is horizontally inequitable. Increases in earnings can often result in a greater loss of benefits. These "notches" result in vertical inequities because those with earnings above the notches may have lower total incomes than those below. The notches and the high cumulative benefit reduction rates caused by eligibility for several programs create major work disincentives. The payoff for increased earnings can be very small. Although able-bodied recipients of AFDC and food stamps are subject to an administrative work test, it is generally thought to be ineffective. For example, in the last quarter of 1975 only about 15 percent of AFDC recipients in the work incentive program who left did so to become employed. Much of this employment would undoubtedly have occurred in the absence of the program.

The target efficiency of the current system is also thought to be a problem by some. The high deductions from income that are allowed in the eligibility calculations of most of the programs mean that some people with relatively high incomes can still be eligible for benefits. For example, the food stamp program, which pays benefits on a household basis, paid 25 percent of benefits to people with incomes above the poverty line in fiscal 1976. Incentives for family dissolution present in the current welfare system have also been criticized. These incentives result primarily because intact families are generally not covered by the cash benefit system, while single-parent families are covered. However, attempts to estimate the actual importance of this incentive have been inconclusive. The system has also been criticized as being demeaning and stigmatizing in its intrusiveness into even the most intimate details of people's lives. Finally, the current welfare system can be criticized for its administrative inefficiency. Not only are there complex rules and regulations in most programs, but there are also so many different programs.

Misconceptions about Welfare

Certain aspects of the design of the welfare system and even of some of the reform proposals reflect a number of misconceptions about the poor. These misconceptions greatly complicate efforts to reform the system since they may result in programs that do not treat the real problems.

Misconceptions about the Poor

Poor people are poor because they do not work, nor do they want to work. There are several problems with this perception. First, some poor families do receive part of their income from earnings. When classified by prewelfare income, the heads of 13 percent of poor families worked full time and another 22 percent worked part time (see table 8-3).[8] Second, many poor individuals are incapable of working (they are disabled, for instance) or they are not generally expected by society to work (they are children or are sixty-five or over). For fiscal 1978 such individuals are expected to represent 60 percent of the population who live in families with prewelfare incomes below the poverty line—5 percent nonaged disabled adults, 44 percent children, and 11 percent aged.[9] Third, evidence from several controlled experiments designed to measure the work effort of persons receiving financial assistance suggests that, while the introduction of cash assistance will reduce the work done by recipients, the reduction for male heads of household will be on the order of 5 to 10 percent.[10] For wives

8. The aged and disabled are included in these figures. If they were excluded, the percentage of the total working full or part time would increase.

9. Women with children under six are also usually included in the group of people not expected to work. This reduces the number available for employment even more.

10. See Joseph A. Pechman and P. Michael Timpane, eds., *Work Incentives and Income Guarantees: The New Jersey Negative Income Tax Experiment* (Brookings Institution, 1975); and Robinson Hollister, *Incentive and Disincentive Effects of Taxation on Lower Income Groups: The American Experience,* Policy Analysis Series (Mathematica Policy Research, Inc., forthcoming).

Table 8-3. Distribution of the Poverty Population,ᵃ by Employment and Age Characteristics, Fiscal Year 1978

Characteristic of family	Percentage distribution
Families[b] with income[c] below the poverty line	
Weeks worked in year by family head	
Less than 1	65.1
1 to 47	21.9
48 to 52	13.0
Individuals living in families[b] with income[c] below the poverty line	
Age composition of families	
Under eighteen	44.1
Nondisabled, eighteen to sixty-four	40.2
Disabled, eighteen to sixty-four	4.7
Sixty-five or over	11.0

Sources: The Transfer Income Model (TRIM) was used for these estimates with the Current Population Survey of the U.S. Bureau of the Census as the data base. The work was performed by Harold Beebout and Robert Scardamalia of Mathematica Policy Research, Inc., for the authors. The methodology was the same as that used in the Congressional Budget Office study reported in table 8-2.

a. Includes the institutionalized population.

b. Families are defined to include unrelated individuals as one-person families.

c. Income is defined as pretax income from all sources except means-tested transfer programs (welfare benefits). Benefits from social insurance programs are included.

the reduction is considerably larger, but this is not necessarily undesirable, since it suggests that one spouse is choosing to spend more time working in the home. This misconception about poor people's attitude toward work has helped lead to the exclusion of the so-called working poor from coverage by the cash welfare system.

Most poor people are poor for life. Recent data for 1967–72 from a panel study of families show that there is a great deal of movement into and out of the poverty population.[11] Over the six-year period 21 percent of the total population had incomes below the poverty line in at least one year, yet only 2.4 percent were poor all six years. In any one year 8 to 11 percent were poor. Most movement into and out of the poverty population occurred because of changes in family composition, such as marriage, divorce, arrival and departure of children, or changes in the labor force status of family members.

The changes in family composition experienced by the poor imply that a system designed to treat different types of families separately may be complicated to administer and may even induce people to change their family status in order to become eligible.

11. Data from the study are reported in U.S. Department of Health, Education, and Welfare, "The Changing Economic Status of 5000 American Families: Highlights from the Panel Study of Income Dynamics" (1974; processed). The study was conducted by the University of Michigan Institute for Social Research.

Poor people do not know how to spend their money. This view has contributed to the provision of many varieties of in-kind assistance. Such benefits are complicated to administer because they require multiple determinations of benefits and special mechanisms to disburse the benefits; further, by limiting the budgetary choices of recipients, they may be worth less to recipients than their cash value. In fact, studies of the expenditures of low-income families show no unusual patterns. Compared to those with higher incomes, low-income families spend relatively more of their total income on food, clothing, and housing, as one would expect. Analyses of the change in expenditures resulting from increased transfer income also show no unexpected results. In short, the evidence suggests that the poor spend their money about as wisely, or unwisely, as everyone else. A welfare program that directs the consumption decisions of the poor is thus clearly unnecessary as a general policy.

Cheating by welfare recipients is widespread. Many people believe that cheating by welfare recipients is commonplace. An alternative explanation of the many incorrect payments admittedly made is that the rules and regulations are often so complex that it is extremely easy for benefits to be incorrect. In fact, while both the AFDC and food stamp programs have been found to have very high error rates, 27 percent of AFDC cases were in error in July through December 1975 and 46 percent of nonpublic-assistance food stamp cases were in error during the same period; these errors have been attributed to mistakes by the welfare agency as often as to the client. Furthermore, 6 percent of the AFDC cases and 6 percent of the food stamp cases in error were for underpayments, not overpayments. Client error occurred in the AFDC program most often because of a failure to notify the agency of a change in circumstances. These findings suggest that while efforts to reduce abuse and fraud should be continued, a simplification of the rules and regulations will go far toward reducing the incidence of errors.

Misconceptions about the System

The above misconceptions concern the poor and their relationship to the welfare system. There is another set of beliefs and judgments that also inhibit a useful discussion of reform of the welfare system because they are oversimplifications. They relate to the feasibility of reform options and the goals that such reform can be expected to accomplish.

One program can meet all needs. Proponents of universal pro-grams such as a negative income tax sometimes suggest that the ple-thora of existing programs can be swept away and replaced with one program with a straightforward, nondiscretionary benefit calculation. This view ignores the fact that emergency situations may arise that cannot be covered by a single program. It also overlooks the likeli-hood that many states would have to supplement the basic federal benefit to maintain benefit levels. Such supplements might have to incorporate highly discretionary rules[12] and thus be the equivalent of additional programs.

Benefits can be equalized across the country except for cost-of-living differences. This view, which may be appropriate as a long-run goal, ignores the present wide range of benefits. In June 1976, the largest annual amount paid to a family of four on AFDC, plus the food stamp bonus, ranged from a low of $2,556 in Mississippi to a high of $6,948 in Hawaii (the high for the contiguous forty-eight states was $6,132 in New York). This range is far greater than cost-of-living differences would warrant.[13] If one were to try to design a program that made these benefits equal except for cost-of-living dif-ferences, one would either have to make substantial numbers of cur-rent recipients worse off or design a program that would cost more than society appears to be willing to spend. Faced with this dilemma, it is unlikely that there will be equalized benefits in the near future.

Welfare reform will solve the fiscal crisis of state and local govern-ments.[14] State and local governments spend approximately 7 percent of their general revenues on public welfare. State and local officials and organizations such as the National Association of Counties and the National Governors Conference have been strong proponents of welfare reform. By itself, however, welfare reform will not solve their financial problems. The states that presumably stand to gain the most from reform are those with high benefits and high caseloads—typi-

12. It should be mentioned that the two most complete formulations of compre-hensive plans—income security for Americans, first developed by the Joint Eco-nomic Committee, and the 1974 HEW welfare reform proposal, the income supple-ment program—both recognized that multiple approaches may be necessary.

13. For example, a comparison of AFDC benefits in two cities, New York and Houston, for which the consumer price index was computed in July 1976, shows that nominal AFDC plus food stamp benefits in New York were 90 percent higher than in Houston for a family of four. The CPI was almost the same in the two cities, 176.7 (1967 = 100) in New York, 177.4 in Houston. Similar variations would be found in comparisons between other states.

14. For more information on the fiscal crisis, see chapter 9.

cally the large urban states of the Northeast, Midwest, and Pacific regions. It is unlikely, however, that a federal program could completely replace the financial role of these states in public assistance programs. If some sort of federal minimum benefit were established, it would undoubtedly be well below current benefit levels in many states; some form of state supplement would then be required, as was the case with the supplemental security income program. The result is that the savings to many state and local governments would be only some portion of their current expenditures. Furthermore, it is changes in the Medicaid program that would provide the most substantial relief for states, since it is the single largest assistance program.

Finally, it should be noted that programs that reduce state and local expenditures by simply shifting the costs to the federal level still have to be paid for, presumably through higher federal taxes. Whether the residents of a given state come out ahead depends on a number of factors, but it is important to remember that "savings" obtained by shifting responsibility from one level of government to another are not "savings" to the taxpayer.

Basic Issues in Welfare Reform

Much of the disagreement about what reform approach is most appropriate derives from different judgments about two fundamental issues—the form work incentives should take in an income support program and the extent to which specific needs and specific types of people should be served by separate programs. These two questions are basic to the system design, to say nothing of the political acceptability, of a proposal. They also involve deep-seated beliefs about work and welfare and attitudes toward the poor.

Form of the Work Incentive

Most people agree that welfare programs should be designed to encourage work effort. What form the work incentive should take, however, depends very much on one's view of both the attitudes toward work of the recipient population and the availability of jobs for this group. Some people argue that the evidence supports the view that the poor are strongly motivated to work, and so long as the assistance programs provide sufficient rewards for work, program participants will want to work. Because the current welfare system does not encourage work, it should be no surprise that many welfare recipients who could work do not.

Others believe that monetary incentives alone are not sufficient to encourage work effort, and that more direct work requirements are needed. This leads them to the position that able-bodied persons should not receive any welfare benefits at all. Some would arrive at the same conclusion on the grounds that work enhances self-esteem or that this is the approach that most closely conforms to society's preferences.

With regard to job opportunities, some argue that all that is needed is to provide employment through macroeconomic policies that emphasize a low unemployment rate. Others think the structure of the labor market is such that even with high levels of aggregate demand, welfare recipients will have difficulty finding work; so these people would emphasize job creation and training services, perhaps even a guaranteed job program. There are various formulations of the jobs approach, which differ in the level of the wage rate, the benefit reduction rate applied to income of other household members, and the availability of cash benefits for able-bodied recipients.

Consideration of these labor demand and supply issues has led to a range of proposals. At one extreme are plans that favor monetary incentives in the benefit structure combined with expansionary macroeconomic policies. At the other extreme are those that would guarantee a job but no cash assistance to the able-bodied poor. There are also plans in between. One example is to expand the number of public service jobs and require recipients to accept them as a condition of eligibility for income assistance; thus they would still receive an income supplement if family income were low.

While the disagreement has been stated here in its baldest form, as a practical matter the debate will probably turn on the narrower question of the appropriate budget allocation between cash assistance and employment and training programs. This is because in the short run neither of the extremes is a realistic option. The pure incentives approach can be faulted for ignoring both the depth of public feeling about paying benefits to people who can work but do not and the fact that private market jobs have not been provided for everyone who wants one. Training and work experience programs will thus be needed to provide at least some able-bodied people with employment opportunities.

The employment approach must reconcile the desire for jobs with the fact that this approach would provide income to only a small portion of the people in need of assistance. Many of the problems of the existing cash assistance programs would remain unchanged. Further, there would still have to be a program of income supplementation for those who work and have relatively low incomes, either because of low wages or because of large family size. Finally, despite the existence of jobs programs under the Comprehensive Employment and Training Act, the fact is that we have no recent experience with providing large numbers of jobs for disadvantaged people.[15] This means we simply do not know what the impact of providing, say, two million[16] guaranteed jobs would be. Would it force up private market wages? Would people shift from private sector to public jobs? What administrative problems would be encountered? What work would be performed? Would it be of value? How long would it take to create the jobs? These difficult questions suggest that it will be some years before we have the knowledge and the capability to provide a guaranteed job for everyone who wants one or is required to accept one. Thus, the real issue now is to decide how much should be devoted to assistance payments and how much to employment and training programs for the low-income population, rather than whether there should be no job provision or a guaranteed jobs approach.

Degree of Categorization

A related question concerns the extent to which different types of needs and different types of people should be served by separate programs. The current system differentiates along both dimensions: there are programs like food stamps and housing assistance that provide for nutritional and shelter needs, and others like AFDC and SSI

15. See chapter 5.
16. Robert I. Lerman, "JOIN: A Jobs and Income Program for American Families," in *Studies in Public Welfare,* paper 19: *Public Employment and Wage Subsidies,* prepared for the Subcommittee on Fiscal Policy of the Joint Economic Committee, 93:2 (Government Printing Office, 1974), p. 60, estimated that 2.5 million jobs would have to be created to guarantee a job to all able-bodied eligible people. A more recent estimate is that as many as 5 million jobs would be needed. See Department of Health, Education, and Welfare, Office of the Assistant Secretary for Planning and Evaluation, "Leading Welfare Reform Options," paper 5, Welfare Reform Analysis Series (April 1977; processed), p. 2-5. The number of jobs needed depends on the wage rate and the comprehensiveness of coverage.

that serve specific types of people. In addition, other suggested programs include assistance to help defray the costs to the poor of energy consumption, increased housing assistance, and separate programs to provide assistance to those deemed able to work and to those who are unable to work.

The multiple program approach reflects the public's willingness to accept programs that focus on certain needs or certain populations. Programs that provide food or shelter, for example, are viewed more positively by the public, even though they are costly to administer and have many of the features of an income support program. Similarly, certain portions of the population are viewed more sympathetically than others; the aged, blind, and disabled, for example, have received relatively more favorable treatment than other types of people. Separate programs may be needed to achieve the different policy objectives that are relevant to different populations. For example, persons unable to work or not expected to work could receive high benefits with little or no provision for the preservation of work incentives, and those expected to work could receive benefits from another program with a low guarantee and a low benefit reduction rate.

One of the problems with a highly categorical approach is that numerous programs lead to inefficient administration. Proper coordination is difficult to achieve because responsibility for the programs is usually highly fragmented. Furthermore, in-kind programs like food stamps are more costly to administer than a cash program providing equivalent benefits. Another problem is that while the general public may place a high value on in-kind benefits, their value to recipients is less than their cash equivalence.

It is argued that dividing the poor population into those expected to work and those not expected to work will enable those not expected to work to receive more adequate benefits than they do now. The results could, however, be quite different. Among the group not expected to work will be a large number of minority-group, single-parent families with small children; this, indeed, is the stereotypical welfare family that comes to many people's minds when they think of the "welfare problem." It is not obvious that this group, separately identified, will receive more favorable treatment. It is certainly possible that the reverse will be the case. The results would be socially divisive and contrary to the objectives being pursued.

Finally, any approach that divides the population into separate categories must be undertaken with caution. People are too diverse to fit neatly into program categories. For example, while we can make rules about who is expected to work and who is not, many people who would obviously be excused from a work requirement are now employed. Few would argue that they should be discouraged from working. How then would they fit into a system that had a program for them that discouraged work with a high benefit reduction rate? If they were allowed to choose the program with the low benefit reduction rate, what would happen if they become unemployed? How could we justify treating them differently from other people, either other workers or other people not expected to work? In contrast, in a consolidated benefit program, employment and training services could be made available to a subset of the recipients. The objective of furthering employment would thus be achieved without having separate assistance programs administered by different agencies, with the concomitant problems.

Categorical programs may also provide people with the opportunity to alter their circumstances to fit into one category or another. For example, one of the criticisms of the AFDC program is that it establishes incentives for family breakup to establish eligibility.

Reform Alternatives

Numerous proposals for reforming the welfare system have been advanced in recent years. For ease of explanation they are presented here in three groups. The distinguishing characteristic of each group is the extent to which its proposals involve changing the structure of the existing system.[17]

Minor Restructuring

One group of analysts argues that the problems with the welfare system can be solved within the current structure. They do not view the problems as serious enough to warrant major restructuring of the

17. The cost estimates for the various plans are from Congressional Budget Office, *Budget Options for Fiscal Year 1978* (Government Printing Office, 1977); Office of the Assistant Secretary for Planning and Evaluation, "Leading Welfare Reform Options"; "Statement of Secretary Bob Bergland, U. S. Department of Agriculture, before the Committee on Agriculture, House of Representatives, April 5, 1977," USDA 907-77 (1977; processed); and Congressional Budget Office.

system or its replacement with a completely new program. Minor restructuring might involve either redirecting the current system or improving administration.

REDIRECTING THE CURRENT SYSTEM. The major changes needed in the present system are improvements in work incentives and in the target efficiency of benefits. To achieve the first objective direct work requirements are proposed. In California an approach of this nature was tried on a limited basis in the early 1970s; it required some recipients to participate in work relief programs in order to receive benefits.[18]

Several proposals have been advanced to channel benefits to the neediest recipients. An example of these proposals was contained in the national welfare reform act of 1975, a bill that was not reported out of committee in the Ninety-fourth Congress. This bill would have prohibited AFDC benefits for strikers and children over seventeen, reduced and standardized work expense deductions, required non-needy persons in the household to contribute support to AFDC families with whom they were living, and, most important, limited eligibility to those families whose gross income was less than 150 percent of family needs.[19]

As compared to current AFDC policy, the national welfare reform act of 1975 would reduce expenditures in fiscal 1978 by $1.4 billion ($800 million of the saving would be federal and $600 million would be saved by states and localities). While similar proposals have been made to alter the food stamp program, more ambitious changes— which are discussed in the next section—have been proposed by the Carter administration.

There are two major problems with the approach that emphasizes redirection of benefits. First, it ignores a number of problems in the current system. Equity issues are not addressed. In particular, no attempt is made to increase benefits or services for groups that are inadequately covered by the current welfare system. Although many do not approve of cash benefits for intact families, it is necessary to recognize that families with full-time earners can be poor. Some provision, either supplemental income assistance or employment services, must be made for them.

18. For a description of this approach see State Department of Social Welfare, *Welfare Reform in California . . . Showing the Way* (State of California, 1972).
19. In AFDC each state sets a standard of need for each family size.

Second, the conflict between work incentives and target efficiency is not recognized. Plans to provide income cutoffs for eligibility while improving target efficiency create major work disincentives. A person could be working and receiving AFDC or food stamps and still have an income just below the cutoff level; an increase in earnings to above the cutoff would make them ineligible for benefits and so decrease total income. Even if the direct work requirements in these proposals were effective in putting those with no jobs to work, those who are already working and have low incomes would not be helped by these proposals.

MANAGEMENT INITIATIVES. Most observers of the welfare system agree that the current system is an administrative mess and is too complicated to be administered well. A number of measures for improving administrative efficiency have been proposed. These include simplifying the system by standardizing certain key items across programs (such as the definitions of income, allowable assets, and work-related expenses) and by streamlining the eligibility process, eliminating overlapping administration, and maximizing the use of common data.

While improvements in efficiency are important, their impact is severely limited if there are no structural changes to the system. Better administration cannot, therefore, be considered a long-run solution to the welfare problem. However, improved management is something that can be undertaken while other reform options are discussed and, perhaps, enacted.

Incremental Reforms

A number of changes can be made to fill gaps in coverage and thus make the system more equitable. Proponents of this approach argue that it is politically feasible and for that reason is to be preferred, in the short run, over the major reform proposals discussed in the next section.[20] They also emphasize the flexibility a multiple program approach provides.

A number of individual changes can be made, some involving modest amounts of additional funds and others requiring substantial amounts. While some of the changes represent a sharp departure from

20. A discussion of this approach is found in Richard P. Nathan, "Alternatives for Federal Income-Security Policy," in *Qualities of Life* (Heath for Third Century Corporation, 1976).

certain features of the current system, they are included here because they do not fundamentally alter the existing categorical structure. Incremental reform strategies can, of course, be developed that include several changes in one package.[21] The following are among the more important suggestions.

ESTABLISHING A NATIONAL MINIMUM AFDC BENEFIT. The current wide variation in AFDC benefit levels among states cannot be accounted for by cost-of-living differences. The result is that many families who are poor by national standards receive no assistance in many parts of the country. Permitting the states to establish their own AFDC benefit levels has another result as well. It means that the federal government, which shares in the costs of the AFDC program, has no control over the distribution of its expenditures among states. Thus federal dollars may be going to support a family whose income is above the poverty line in one state while a much poorer family in another state receives far less assistance.

Establishing a federally financed national minimum AFDC benefit would alleviate these problems, while providing some level of fiscal relief to the states. State supplementation could be mandated to ensure that benefits are maintained in states where they are higher than the minimum. The total incremental cost of a national minimum set at three-quarters of the poverty-line income is estimated to be about $2.3 billion in fiscal 1978.

EXTEND AFDC-U. AFDC could be made into an income support program for both intact and single-parent families by extending AFDC-U to all states and eliminating the requirement that fathers must work less than 100 hours per month to be eligible. The net cost of providing national coverage in this manner is estimated to be $1.5 billion to $2.5 billion a year.

CHANGES IN THE FOOD STAMP PROGRAM. The Carter administration has proposed to restructure the food stamp program by standardizing deductions,[22] lowering income limits for participation, establishing a fixed benefit reduction rate of 30 percent to apply to net income, and eliminating the purchase requirement and disbursing only the bonus value. These changes would improve target efficiency

21. Because of interactions among programs, the net budget impact of an incremental package will be slightly less than the sum of the costs of each incremental reform.
22. The proposed deductions are $80 a month plus 20 percent of earnings.

by reducing benefits to high-income families and make it easier for the lowest-income families to participate in the program since they will no longer have to purchase stamps. The Carter proposals would also eliminate one of the basic reasons for having an in-kind program —the discipline it imposes on recipients to spend their income in a particular way. Since virtually every household with income other than food stamps will spend more on food than the bonus value, the program would no longer impose a major constraint on expenditures. This line of reasoning leads one to argue either for retaining the program with a purchase requirement or for replacing it entirely with a cash benefit.

It has been estimated by the administration that the net cost of this proposal is approximately zero. Standardizing deductions reduces costs by $400 million a year, but this is offset by cost increases resulting from increased participation of eligible people in response to the elimination of the purchase requirement.

EXPANDING IN-KIND BENEFITS. One way to fill gaps in the current system would be to expand in-kind benefits by adding a housing allowance. This would subsidize the rental costs of the low-income population, either through direct subsidies to landlords or through some form of voucher similar to food stamps. A typical formulation would be to pay rental costs in excess of 25 percent of income of families living in housing designated as meeting minimum standards. While a housing allowance program already exists (the rental subsidy program in section 8 of the United States Housing Act as amended), it has provided only limited assistance, primarily because of start-up problems at the local level where it is administered. The expenditures could be increased by relaxing some program restrictions and by more aggressive implementation.

If section 8 or other similar housing allowances were fully operational, the net cost would be $4 billion to $6 billion a year (in 1974 dollars), assuming only 30 to 50 percent of those eligible would actually participate.

WORK BONUSES. Some type of work bonus—through either a wage subsidy or an earnings supplement—has also been proposed to fill gaps in the current system. A wage subsidy augments hourly wages by paying some portion of the difference between a target wage and the recipient's actual wage. An earnings supplement increases earnings by paying a benefit equal to some percent of earnings. To limit costs, the supplement is phased out above some earnings level. An example of an earnings supplement is the earned income tax credit under the individual income tax. The credit is 10 percent of family earnings up to $4,000 for families with children. Above that level the benefit is phased down at a rate of 10 percent of adjusted gross income. The benefit thus falls to zero at $8,000.

A program of this type can be designed at virtually no net cost or at a cost of billions of dollars. The choice is a function of available funds and the allocation of benefits between those who are employed and those who are not.

LIMITATIONS OF THE INCREMENTAL APPROACH. Criticism of any reform proposal obviously depends on one's viewpoint. Thus, proponents of minor restructuring fault the incremental approach as going too far, involving as it does major expansions in benefit programs. Those who believe it to be more appropriate to make major changes in the structure of the current system argue that the political feasibility of the incremental approach may be overstated. Some of the proposed changes, such as a housing allowance, are very costly, and others involve a major change in some programs, such as the establishment of a federally financed and administered minimum AFDC benefit. The political difficulties that would be encountered in seeking to enact these changes are likely to be as severe as those that would be encountered with a more comprehensive reform package.

The incremental approach can also be costly. If it absorbed a substantial share of the fiscal dividend, more fundamental reform would be put off to the distant future. The incremental approach would complicate an already overly complex system. Adding more programs would compound management problems and offer families even more opportunities to receive high cumulative benefits and face high cumulative benefit reduction rates.

In defense of the approach, its proponents ask whether the more fundamental reform that would be postponed is really necessary. If the gaps in coverage can be filled by adding or expanding programs, why pursue the goal of having a more comprehensive package? Furthermore, if some of the management improvements discussed earlier are introduced, and the new programs are properly integrated with the existing ones, administrative efficiency could be improved.

Comprehensive Reform

The costs of doing nothing or proceeding incrementally are high. If nothing at all was done the problems of the system would continue; in fact, the pressures are so great that it is probably impossible to do nothing. The result would be further unplanned expansion of the system, thus worsening its problems. With incremental reforms, there would be a further proliferation of programs and the continuation of many of the existing problems.

The specific proposals under the comprehensive approach can be divided into three groups: cash assistance with or without a jobs component; jobs programs with minimal reliance on cash assistance; and programs aimed at different populations on the basis of whether or not they are expected to work.

These three different types of proposals precisely mirror the positions taken on the two major issues discussed above—the type of work incentive and categorization. Guaranteed employment appeals to those who emphasize work to relieve poverty; while a multiple program approach appeals to those who wish to preserve work incentives for people who are expected to work and adequate benefit levels for people who are not. A consolidated program of cash assistance appeals to those who emphasize the importance of treating people in an equitable manner.

COMPREHENSIVE CASH ASSISTANCE WITH EMPLOYMENT PROGRAMS. Three major comprehensive cash assistance plans have been developed: the income supplement program (ISP), developed by the Department of Health, Education, and Welfare; the income security for Americans plan (ISA), developed under the direction of Congresswoman Martha W. Griffiths by the Subcommittee on Fiscal Policy of the Joint Economic Committee of Congress; and the proposal of the staff of the National Governors Conference.

The income security program and income security for Americans plan share a number of basic similarities.[23] They provide cash income supplements to all low-income people, without regard to family

23. For full details, see Department of Health, Education, and Welfare, Office of the Assistant Secretary for Planning and Evaluation, "Income Supplement Program: 1974 HEW Welfare Replacement Proposal," technical analysis paper 11 (1976; processed), and *Income Security for Americans: Recommendations of the Public Welfare Study,* Report of the Subcommittee on Fiscal Policy of the Joint Economic Committee, 93:2 (GPO, 1974).

composition. Most existing means-tested programs would be eliminated (although supplemental security income would remain under the ISA proposal). If a federal agency administered the basic payment, some fiscal relief would be provided to most states. Both plans have a link to the positive income tax system, the ISP by tying benefits and break-even levels to the value of exemptions and the standard deduction, and the ISA through a tax credit. Both plans seek to limit benefit reduction rates in order to preserve work incentives. A work test requiring recipients to register with state employment services can be a feature of both plans. An expanded public service employment or other jobs program would be fully consistent with either proposal, although such a program would probably be limited in scope because of the financial requirements of these transfer programs. One possibility would be to channel existing job program funds to the low-income population.

Net costs for ISP and ISA are approximately $8 billion in fiscal 1978, assuming benefits in each plan are set at about 75 percent of the poverty-line income. Using existing job program funds to benefit the low-income population as part of such proposals would represent no increase in budget outlays and would reduce transfer program costs to the extent that income from jobs programs would count in the transfer program's benefit calculation.

The proposal of the staff of the National Governors Conference represents, in some respects, the logical extension of the incremental reform approach. A uniform national benefit would be provided for all families with children, the food stamp purchase requirement would be eliminated, and substantial fiscal relief given the states. The states would continue to be involved in program administration, and there would be a public service jobs component. The program thus limits coverage to families with children and leaves the existing administrative structures largely unchanged. The net fiscal costs would be $5 billion to $10 billion in 1974 dollars ($6.5 million to $13 million in 1978 dollars), depending on the size of the job program, increases in program participation, and the amount of labor force withdrawal resulting from the high benefit reduction rates in the plan. The cost to states would fall by about $2 billion.

The perceived shortcomings of the comprehensive cash assistance approach depend, again, on one's perspective. Some would find the cost to be excessive, others would argue that it is politically infeasible.

Other criticisms include the following. It is target inefficient, since the need to build work incentives into a program with a high basic benefit means payments are made to families above the poverty level. It may discourage work effort, because the high basic benefit needed to provide an adequate level of living for those with no other income, as well as the high benefit reduction rates, may discourage some people from working. It may distort the private labor market, since in low-wage areas the program may force wages up.

Proponents of the comprehensive approach argue that any program that aids the working poor will be somewhat target inefficient if monetary work incentives are to be preserved. They point to the experimental evidence and other studies[24] to support their view that the work disincentive effects will be of manageable size. Finally, it must be admitted that the program could force up wages in certain areas, although the benefits are low enough that this should affect relatively few jobs.

EMPLOYMENT PROGRAMS WITH MINIMAL CASH ASSISTANCE. The notion that able-bodied persons should be given a job instead of a cash payment has popular appeal, because it both reduces welfare costs and emphasizes the work ethic. Various proposals of this type have been suggested.[25]

One possibility is to guarantee a job paying, say, $3.50 an hour ($7,200 a year) to all families with children in which there is a family member who is expected to work.[26] To be eligible, family income[27] must be below the poverty level; the job would substitute for an income maintenance payment. For families with an employed parent, larger earned income tax credit and food stamp benefits would be available as an income supplement. For families where no one is expected to work, cash assistance would be provided through a federalized AFDC program, with benefits set at 75 percent of the poverty-line income.

This plan is distinguished from other job plans by its relatively

24. See, for example, Leonard Goodwin, *Do the Poor Want to Work? A Social-Psychological Study of Work Orientations* (Brookings Institution, 1972).

25. See, for example, Arnold H. Packer, "Categorical Public Employment Guarantees: A Proposed Solution to the Poverty Problem," in *Studies in Public Welfare*, paper 9, pt. 1: *Concepts in Welfare Program Design* (1973), pp. 68–127, and Lerman, "JOIN: A Jobs and Income Program for American Families."

26. This is an updated version of the Packer proposal cited in note 25.

27. Defined as total family income minus the applicant's earnings, unemployment insurance benefit, earned income tax credit, and the household's food stamp benefit.

high wage rate. Thus, two obvious criticisms—that it will be costly (the plan described above is estimated to have a net cost of $30 billion to $40 billion a year) and that it will have a serious impact on the private labor market (where many jobs pay less than $7,200 a year)—can be dealt with by lowering the wage rate; the wage rate in the jobs and income (JOIN) program, for example, was set at $4,600 for families with children in 1975. The lower the wage, however, the greater the need for income supplementation to provide an adequate income level for larger families.

Critics of the jobs approach raise a number of questions. First, since the wage guarantee is related only imperfectly to family income and family size, large families would still need some form of income supplement. Second, there is a "notch" in the program: eligibility for the guaranteed job continues until family income from other sources exceeds the poverty level; at that point the entire guaranteed job earnings are lost. This creates an incentive to keep family income below the cutoff level so as to be eligible for a job. Third, dividing the population into the appropriate categories is difficult and produces inequities. Fourth, the impact of establishing a program providing 4 million to 5 million[28] guaranteed jobs is unknown. How will it affect wages in the private market? What behavioral incentives will it establish? There is little past experience to guide decisionmaking, since recent public jobs programs have been much smaller and generally did not involve people who would typically be eligible for welfare assistance. (The current programs employ about 310,000 persons a year.) Fifth, the administrative problems would be severe. How can a large number of new jobs be created? Who would supervise the workers? If a long period is needed to build up to five millions jobs, how would they be allocated in the short run? Sixth, what would be the effect of substantially increasing the public sector? Would workers produce as much in government jobs as in conventional jobs, assuming there is a shift from jobs in the private market to the government jobs?

It must be pointed out that many of these uncertainties derive from the fact that there has been much less research on how to design and implement jobs programs than on the effects of income assistance programs. The difficulties cited above thus do not reflect inherent problems of the jobs approach, but rather the absence of data that

28. Fewer jobs would be required if the wage rate were lower or if eligibility for jobs were restricted to certain family types.

would enable us to predict better the impact of the program. An obvious conclusion is that more resources should be devoted to experimentation with a jobs program for the welfare population.

MULTIPLE PROGRAM SYSTEM. Another reform proposal seeks to achieve the goals of income support and the provision of employment opportunities through three programs aimed at specified groups that are thought to have different requirements: those unemployed and expected to work, the working poor, and those not expected to work. The proposal is sometimes referred to as "triple track."

For the unemployed, the unemployment insurance system would be expanded to cover those who exhaust their benefit rights and to new entrants and reentrants to the labor force. These persons would be eligible for a special unemployment assistance benefit. It would be set at 75 percent of the poverty-level income, would be means-tested, and would vary by family size. Eligibility would be cut off when family income exceeded 125 percent of poverty-line income. Food stamps would be continued, although the purchase requirement would be eliminated. The special unemployment assistance benefit would have a strict work requirement.[29]

The working poor would receive benefits from the reformed food stamp program and the earned income tax credit, which would be expanded to cover single persons and childless couples. For those not expected to work—primarily single-parent families with children under twelve[30]—a reformed welfare program would provide coverage. Other families could also be covered by this program because of incapacity, age, and family care responsibilities. Employment and training programs as well as child care and social services would be expanded to enhance the client's chances of employment. The food stamp program would continue and a national federal minimum benefit in AFDC would be set at 75 percent of the poverty-level income.[31] The net cost of the program is estimated in 1974 dollars to be $11 billion to $20 billion ($14 billion to $16 billion in 1978 dollars).

Critics of this approach emphasize the difficulty of separating the

29. In another version the special unemployment assistance benefit would be a nonmeans-tested fixed benefit. Family income would be considered only at application and would have a cutoff at 150 percent of poverty. Earnings of the recipient would reduce his benefit dollar for dollar.
30. The aged, blind, and disabled would continue to be covered under SSI.
31. In some versions food stamps would be cashed out for the welfare track.

population into categories. There is also disagreement as to whether identifying a group of people who are not expected to work will reduce the stigma of welfare, particularly since many people with similar characteristics are employed.

Supporters of the approach argue that building it into the unemployment insurance system would lend the program additional support because of the favorable public attitude toward social insurance. However, unemployment insurance has come under increasing criticism recently as cases of abuse have been brought to public attention; to greatly expand its coverage by adding a welfare component might bring it even more criticism. Supporters also argue that by placing responsibility for employment problems in the Labor Department rather than with the welfare system, the plan introduces a more appropriate division of responsibility and relieves the welfare system of the burden of finding jobs for people expected to work.

Conclusions

It is apparent that no welfare program or set of programs can fully achieve all the objectives of the welfare system. Conflicts among the objectives require difficult trade-offs to be made when designing a new system. Even so, the existing welfare system must be judged to be deficient. It is inequitable, it discourages work, the benefits in many states are inadequate, it creates incentives for family breakup and disincentives for family formation, it is demeaning and stigmatizing, and it is difficult to administer well.

Similarly, any reform proposal will be judged deficient in some respect, particularly when there is disagreement on desired objectives or on the weights to be attached to them. Some of the basic characteristics of the alternative reform proposals are summarized in table 8-4. If the evaluation of the existing system summarized above is correct, the minor restructuring proposals must be regarded as leaving most of the problems unchanged, although steps to improve administrative efficiency are compatible with any of the proposals and should be pursued. As to choosing among the others, it may be useful to recall the discussion of the work incentive and categorization issues. If the basic decision is how to allocate resources between reform of assistance programs and the creation of government jobs, then the fiscal limitations, the uncertainties about the impact of a very

Table 8-4. Basic Characteristics of Alternative Proposals for Welfare Reform, Fiscal Year 1978

		Characteristics				
		For a family of four[a]			Change from current system in net cost (billions of dollars)	Other major programs in the welfare system that would be retained
Alternative	Target population	Benefit level	Break-even level	Work requirement		
Minor restructuring						
National Welfare Reform Act of 1975[b]	Primarily one-parent families with children	Varies by state	150 percent of benefit level	Registration and acceptance of employment and training	−1.4	Food stamps, supplemental security income
Incremental reform						
Establish a national minimum benefit for aid to families with dependent children	Primarily one-parent families with children	AFDC plus food stamps to equal 3/4 of the poverty line	Poverty line	Registration and acceptance of employment and training	2.3	Food stamps, SSI
Extend the unemployed-father portion of AFDC	Intact families with unemployed father	Varies by state	Varies by state	Registration and acceptance of employment and training; active job search required	1.5–2.5	Food stamps, SSI
Change food stamp program	Universal	$2,100[c]	$8,500[c]	Registration and acceptance of employment and training	0.0	Aid to families with dependent children, SSI

Add housing allowance	Universal	Rental costs in excess of 25 percent of income	...	Not specified	4.0–6.0[d]	AFDC, SSI, food stamps
Comprehensive reform					
Income supplement program	Universal	$4,325	$8,650	State administered work registration	7.8[e]	None
Income security for Americans[f]	Universal except for SSI eligibles	$4,440	$6,800[g]	None	8.4[e]	SSI
Employment programs					
Unemployed	One- and two-parent families with children	$7,200	Poverty level	Public service employment job is only benefit	30–40[h]	Food stamps
Working poor[i]	One- and two-parent families with children	Not applicable	$10,000	Not applicable	30–40[h]	Food stamps
Families (with children) on welfare[j]	Single-parent families with children under six	75 percent of poverty level	100–125 percent of poverty level	None	30–40[h]	SSI
Multiple program systems					
Unemployed	Universal, one family member unemployed	75 percent of poverty level	125 percent of poverty level	Registration for employment and training and acceptance of job offer after first 30 days	11.0–16.0[h]	Food stamps

Table 8-4 (continued)

		For a family of four[a]				
Alternative	Target population	Benefit level	Break-even level	Work requirement	Change from current system in net cost (billions of dollars)	Other major programs in the welfare system that would be retained
Working poor[i]	Working poor	Not applicable	$12,000	Not applicable	11.0–16.0[h]	Food stamps
Families (with children) on welfare	Single-parent families with children under twelve or two-person families with a temporarily disabled adult	75 percent of poverty level[k]	75 percent of poverty level[g]	None	11.0–16.0[h]	Food stamps, SSI

Sources: Congressional Budget Office, *Budget Options for Fiscal Year 1978* (Government Printing Office, 1977); U.S. Department of Health, Education, and Welfare, Office of the Assistant Secretary for Planning and Evaluation, "Leading Welfare Reform Options," paper 5, Welfare Reform Analysis Series (April 1977; processed); idem, "Income Supplement Program: 1974 HEW Welfare Replacement Proposal," technical analysis paper 11 (1976; processed); "Statement of Secretary Bob Bergland, U.S. Department of Agriculture, before the Committee on Agriculture, House of Representatives, April 5, 1977," USDA 907-77 (1977; processed); Congressional Budget Office.

a. Benefit levels and break-even levels are for federal benefits except for the National Welfare Reform Act of 1975 and the extension of aid to families with dependent children unemployed-father portion.

b. Proposed in the Ninety-fourth Congress (H.R. 5133, S. 1719), but not reported out of committee.

c. Adjusted from current levels for expected inflation.

d. Change in cost for calendar year 1974.

e. Includes tax relief.

f. Originally developed by the Joint Economic Committee; submitted to the Ninety-fourth Congress (H.R. 14031, S. 3000).

g. Actual break-even level would be higher owing to deductions from income. In the multiple program system, $600 a year would be deducted.

h. Net cost for total multiple system package—that is, for the unemployed, the working poor, and families (with children) on welfare. These costs were estimated for calendar year 1974 rather than fiscal year 1978.

i. Expanded earned income tax credit would provide benefits to all working poor.

j. Food stamps are not available for this group.

k. Food stamps would bring benefit up to the poverty level.

large government employment program, and the lack of experience in administering one suggest that a prudent approach would be to institute structural reforms of the cash assistance programs and increase somewhat the number of public employment jobs. Simultaneously an effort should be made to improve knowledge about how these programs would work and what their effects might be.

The decisions on the categorization issue are, if anything, more subjective. A system with multiple programs that serve overlapping populations presents a more complex set of administrative problems than does one with fewer programs. Do the presumed benefits of categorization offset this? The argument that the categorical approach is more politically acceptable because in-kind benefits are viewed more favorably than cash benefits or that certain groups are viewed with more sympathy than others is difficult to evaluate, particularly if one assumes that active public leadership can alter public opinion. As for the argument that many objectives imply the need for many programs, consideration must be given to the difficulties inherent in categorizing the population and the inequities that are likely to result. The strongest argument for categorization is that special programs are needed for those who are able to work. This could also be achieved, however, by a consolidated program. We would argue that categorization also poses the risk of making welfare even more stigmatizing than it is, for we are not as confident as the supporters of some categorical approaches that a large group of single women with small children in a program for unemployables will be viewed with compassion.

The weight of the argument thus falls toward the consolidated program approach. Whether this is also a politically acceptable approach remains to be determined.

CHAPTER NINE

The Cities

RICHARD P. NATHAN *and* PAUL R. DOMMEL

OVER THE PAST TWO DECADES, direct payments from the federal government to local governments have increased more than sixfold as a percentage of the revenues local governments raise on their own—from 2 percent in 1955 to 13 percent in 1975—and the upward trend continues. Both the Ford budget and the Carter budget revisions for 1977 and 1978 contain policy changes with important implications for cities. This chapter looks at urban conditions, the problems of cities, and the role of the federal government in relation to them.

Conditions and Problems of Cities

In discussions of core city problems, the question is often asked, revival for whom? What is the role of the inner city? Who will live there? Who will work there? Who will shop there? Often the way these questions are asked and the answers given suggest a stereotype of pervasive decay and hopelessness that reflects conditions in some cities and in some areas of others. However, the picture must not be overdrawn. Urban hardship is a localized infection, confined to certain cities and within these cities to certain areas that have been characterized in recent years by a rapid process of deconcentration. The

The authors gratefully acknowledge the research assistance of James W. Fossett. Helpful comments were provided by Philip M. Dearborn, George E. Peterson, and Robert D. Reischauer.

picture many of us carry in our minds of vast, densely populated slum areas is by no means the whole picture.

As suburbs grow and inner-city school problems are compounded, the easy answer that the inner city should be abandoned has become more fashionable. The purpose of this chapter is not to argue for a certain level of resources or type of new program, but to shed light on the nature and complexity of the problems of hardship cities and to suggest the wide variation of policy responses that are possible on the part of the federal government.

An analysis of urban conditions and the problems of cities requires a definition of terms.

Definition of Urban

The Census Bureau defines an "urban place" as a community of 2,500 or more population. Douglas, Wyoming (pop. 2,677), for example, is an urban place. According to this definition, about 70 percent of the population live in urban places, but many of these, like Douglas, do not fit the usual image of urban.

There is also what the Census Bureau calls an "urbanized area," which includes at least one central city of over 25,000 population and the surrounding closely settled territory. About 60 percent of the population live in these areas, which more closely fit our image of what urban means.

Finally, there is the standard metropolitan statistical area (SMSA), which is the most frequently used, but in many ways least accurate, term of reference for urbanization. A metropolitan area includes an "urbanized area," plus, in many cases, some immediately surrounding territory that is more rural than urban. About two-thirds of the population live in metropolitan areas.

Regardless of what definition is used, ours is an urban nation and will remain so, though there are modest signs of change. Between 1970 and 1973, for instance, the metropolitan area population increased by 3 percent; but in the same period the nonmetropolitan population increased by 4.2 percent.

What Is a City?

The term "city" can also be used in ways that cause confusion. To some a city means a very big city, perhaps above 500,000 in population. By this definition there are just twenty-seven cities in the

United States, and they contain 15 percent of the total population. The number of people living in these big cities is growing, but their share of the total population is declining; they constituted 15.6 percent of the population in 1970 and about 18 percent in 1950.

Those concerned about the often undefined or poorly defined "urban crisis" tend to focus on the central cities of SMSAs. Currently there are 375 central cities having 31 percent of the nation's population, their size ranging from under 20,000 to nearly 8 million. Like big cities, central cities collectively have a shrinking share of the national population. However, to focus only on urban problems in central cities overlooks the problem of troubled suburban cities.

A third way of defining a city is to use a population cutoff much lower than the big city level, perhaps 50,000. If this is done, there are 397 cities, including both central and suburban cities. Using this definition, cities also have a declining share of the population— 34.8 percent in 1973 compared to 37.2 percent in 1960—despite the fact that the number of cities above 50,000 in population increased in this period.

According to all three of these definitions, cities contain a minority and declining portion of the nation's population. However, the overall picture obscures significant points, as, for example, the fact that major regional population shifts are occurring.

Decline of the Northeast Quadrant

The most evident regional shift is the growing share of the national population contained in the southern and western states, while the "northeast quadrant," composed of the northeast and north central regions, is declining. Up until very recently, the majority of the nation's population lived in these two regions; the northeast quadrant accounted for 53.7 percent of the population in 1960 but declined to 49.6 percent in 1976.

This regional shift has its counterpart in metropolitan area population changes. Although the population of metropolitan areas has been increasing in the aggregate, there have been declines in some of the largest metropolitan areas, particularly in the northeast and north central regions. During the period 1960–70, only one (Pittsburgh) of the twenty largest SMSAs lost population. However, between 1970 and 1974, the number of losers among this group increased to five (New York, Pittsburgh, Cleveland, St. Louis, and

Seattle), with four of these being in the northeast quadrant. Of the fifteen SMSAs that gained population between 1970 and 1974, the seven in the northeast quadrant had a mean growth rate of 0.85 percent. On the other hand, for the eight metropolitan areas in the South and West that grew in this period, the mean growth rate was 7.2 percent. Essentially the same pattern emerges for cities; population declines tend to be greatest among the older and generally larger cities of the northeast and north central regions.

Other Characteristics of Declining Cities

A decline in population would not be a problem per se unless it was associated with problem conditions for the cities affected. One such condition that is particularly serious for declining cities is their relative old age. Census data are available for all cities on housing built before 1939. For central cities and suburban cities of over 50,000 population in 1973, the proportion of the housing built before 1939 was 29.8 percent for those that gained population and 58.4 percent for the losers. Although comparable census data are not available, knowledge of the cities in which Brookings field research has been conducted indicates that an aging housing stock is associated with the deterioration of related physical facilities—streets, schools, sewer and water facilities, parks.[1]

There is also a relation between population decline and major economic variables, as shown in table 9-1 for the decade 1960–70. Declining cities had a per capita income level $300 lower than growing cities in 1970; housing values were nearly $3,000 lower. It can also be seen that between 1960 and 1970 per capita income increased almost 5 percent faster in the growing cities than in the declining cities, and home values increased nearly 6 percent faster in the growing cities.

Composite Urban Conditions Index

In the foregoing discussion three factors have been used as indicators of city problems—population decline, old age, and economic condition. A report on the block grant program for community de-

1. This field research was conducted as part of a Brookings study of the community development block grant program. See Richard P. Nathan, Paul R. Dommel, Sarah F. Liebschutz, Milton D. Morris, and Associates, "Block Grants for Community Development" (U.S. Department of Housing and Urban Development, 1977; processed).

Table 9-1. Characteristics of Cities above 50,000
Gaining and Losing Population, 1960–70

Population change, 1960–70	Population change, 1960–70 (percent)	Black population, 1970 (percent)	Per capita income		Median house value	
			Amount, 1970 (dollars)	Percent change, 1960–70	Amount, 1970 (thousands of dollars)	Percent change, 1960–70
Population loss (n = 150)	−6.7	17.3	3,062	57.0	15.9	32.5
Population gain (n = 339)	20.5	10.2	3,354	61.7	18.8	38.2

Sources: Calculated from U.S. Bureau of the Census, *County and City Data Book, 1962* (Government Printing Office, 1962), and *County and City Data Book, 1972* (Government Printing Office, 1973).

velopment put these three variables together in a composite urban conditions index for 489 central and suburban cities of over 50,000 population.[2] When the mean for this urban conditions index is set at 100, a total of 196 cities, or 40 percent of the 489 cities ranked, have a rating above this level. There are 123 cities (including 11 suburban cities) that have an index rating of 150 or more. These cities, to varying degrees, are considered in this analysis to face urban hardship conditions. Eighty-three (67 percent) of the cities with an index above 150 are in the northeast quadrant. This represents more than a third of the central and suburban cities in the two regions; conversely, only 16 percent of the southern and western cities studied are in this relative hardship group.

In terms of size, the incidence of hardship tends to be greatest among the very largest cities. Whereas 25 percent of all cities are above 150 on this urban conditions index, 45 percent of all cities of above 500,000 population are in this relatively high hardship group. Table 9-2 shows the forty-four cities of above 100,000 population in 1970 that rank above 150 on the index. The twenty-nine cities ranking above 200 can be said to have the strongest combined indicators of relative hardship conditions. The last column of the table shows that the higher-ranked cities tend to have high minority populations.

2. The index is constructed as follows:

$$\text{Urban conditions index} = \frac{\dfrac{\text{Percent pre-1939 housing}}{\text{Mean percent pre-1939 housing}} \times \dfrac{\text{Percent poverty}}{\text{Mean percent poverty}}}{\dfrac{100 + \text{rate of population change}}{100 + \text{median rate of population change}}}$$

See ibid., chap. 12.

As for their finances, the fact that spending for what the Census Bureau defines as "common functions" is higher and has been rising much faster for the higher-ranked cities further aggravates their problems. Increasing costs mean an increasing tax burden for those who remain in the city; they can either continue to bear the burden or leave, as have many others before them. If they leave, the resource base is further diminished, but the costs only range from fixed to increasing. Thus, the tax burden becomes still higher on a shrinking population base, which tends to be increasingly composed of lower-income persons.

Other studies have compared the conditions of large central cities relative to their own suburbs.[3] From this perspective, too, there is a pattern whereby the central cities that are most disadvantaged relative to their suburbs are concentrated among older and larger cities in the northeast and north central regions. The marked city-suburban disparities in those two regions are to a large extent a product of city boundaries established in the late nineteenth century, boundaries that at the time reflected the extent of urban settlement but now encompass mainly the poverty-impacted core of the metropolitan area. Conversely, most of the central cities that compared favorably with their adjoining suburban areas in this analysis are newer, spread-out cities located in the South and West.

Several lessons can be drawn from these analyses. It is important to recognize that the United States does not have what can be called a *"national* urban crisis." Many large cities are well off. Moreover, most city dwellers live in suburbs or in relatively small cities. What we face, in short, is a situation in which some—though by no means all—central cities and a few large suburban cities are experiencing what can be called "urban crisis *conditions.*"

The Diversity of American Federalism

One of the major difficulties in formulating federal policy to deal with these conditions is the complexity of the structural arrangements that exist for providing services in urban areas. This point can best be made by illustration. According to the measures of relative hardship presented in table 9-2, the city governments of New York and Chicago (the nation's two largest cities) confront urban problems of

3. Richard P. Nathan and Charles Adams, "Understanding Central City Hardship," *Political Science Quarterly,* vol. 91 (Spring 1976), pp. 47–62.

roughly equal severity. Chicago has an index rating of 201; New York's is 180. Their response to these problems, however, has been quite different. Table 9-3 presents comparative per capita data for several major financial items for the two cities in fiscal year 1975. New York City received and spent almost five times as much per capita as Chicago.

Closer examination, however, reveals that much of this disparity is due to differences in the structural arrangements for the provision of services rather than to differences in the relative size of the public sector. The data displayed in table 9-4 make this point, correcting for these structural differences by including the expenditures of other local governments providing services to Chicago residents in the functional categories where financial disparities are pronounced.

New York City was one of only three units of local government operating within the city boundaries in 1972, and the only unit with property taxing authority. By contrast, there were 500 units of local government in Cook County (which overlies Chicago), 475 of which had the authority to collect property taxes. To contrast the structural differences further, the Illinois state government was more active in the direct provision of services during this same period, spending $15 more per capita than New York State.

Structural differences are particularly important in the two categories where the expenditure disparity is largest, education and welfare. The New York City school system and university system are both city agencies funded with city revenue. In Chicago, by contrast, both the city school system and institutions of public higher education are independent of the city government. As table 9-4 shows, the Chicago city school district spent almost as much per capita for local schools as New York. While local expenditures on higher education were substantially lower in Chicago, it should be noted that the state maintains a major branch of its university system in Chicago, while the New York State university system does not operate a major campus in New York City.

Comparisons of welfare spending are more complex. New York City is a county for purposes of administering the federally aided public assistance programs, making it subject to the New York State requirement that counties pay half the total state-local share under these programs, whereas the state of Illinois pays the full amount of the state-local share under federally aided welfare programs.

Table 9-2. Characteristics of Forty-four Cities with Population above 100,000 and More than 50 Percent above the Mean on the Urban Conditions Index, Various Dates, 1960–70

City	Urban conditions index[a]	Population, 1970	Population change (percent) 1960–70	Population change (percent) 1970–73	Percent pre-1939 housing, 1970	Poverty population, 1970 (percent)	Nonwhite and Spanish population, 1970 (percent)
St. Louis, Mo.	351	622,236	−17.0	−10.9	73.9	19.7	42.3
Providence, R.I.	333	179,116	−13.7	−5.1	80.7	17.8	10.8
Camden, N.J.	333	102,551	−12.5	−2.5	70.0	20.8	46.4
Newark, N.J.	321	381,930	−5.7	−4.6	68.4	22.1	62.2
Buffalo, N.Y.	292	462,768	−13.1	−8.1	85.7	14.8	21.9
Cleveland, Ohio	291	750,879	−14.3	−9.7	73.3	17.0	40.9
Trenton, N.J.	288	104,786	−8.2	0.0	81.0	16.3	40.7
New Orleans, La.	274	593,471	−5.4	−2.6	49.4	26.2	49.8
Pittsburgh, Pa.	260	520,117	−13.9	−8.1	74.4	15.0	20.8
Savannah, Ga.	260	118,349	−20.7	−10.9	39.9	25.8	46.6
Chattanooga, Tenn.	257	119,082	−7.8	41.0[b]	48.3	24.5	36.0
Boston, Mass.	257	641,071	−8.1	0.0	77.2	15.3	20.8
New Haven, Conn.	252	137,707	−9.4	−4.5	69.2	16.5	30.7
New Bedford, Mass.	246	102,477	−0.7	−0.7	80.8	15.1	4.8
Paterson, N.J.	228	144,824	0.8	−1.3	70.5	16.3	35.7
Cincinnati, Ohio	226	452,524	−10.2	−5.6	59.3	17.1	28.7
Jersey City, N.J.	226	260,545	−5.7	−3.2	78.9	13.5	28.2
Baltimore, Md.	224	905,787	−3.5	−3.1	60.0	18.0	47.9
Hartford, Conn.	223	158,017	−2.6	−5.9	67.0	16.2	36.6
Albany, N.Y.	221	115,781	−10.7	−3.4	74.7	13.2	12.5

City		Population					
Youngstown, Ohio	220	140,909	-15.5	-5.0	67.4	13.8	28.3
Cambridge, Mass.	219	100,361	-6.8	-1.8	79.7	12.8	10.5
Birmingham, Ala.	218	300,910	-11.7	-2.7	42.7	22.5	42.6
Philadelphia, Pa.	216	1,950,098	-2.6	-4.2	69.5	15.1	35.6
Scranton, Pa.	213	102,696	-7.1	-3.3	86.6	11.4	1.0
Syracuse, N.Y.	210	197,297	-8.7	-6.4	70.8	13.5	12.2
Rochester, N.Y.	205	296,233	-7.0	-6.5	79.5	12.0	19.2
Chicago, Ill.	201	3,369,357	-5.1	-5.2	66.5	14.3	41.5
Detroit, Mich.	201	1,513,601	-9.4	-8.0	61.8	14.7	46.2
Berkeley, Calif.	197	116,716	4.9	-3.4	57.1	18.1	37.0
Louisville, Ky.	195	361,958	-7.4	-7.1	53.2	17.0	24.4
San Francisco, Calif.	188	715,674	-3.3	-4.0	66.9	13.6	42.6
New York, N.Y.	180	7,895,563	1.5	-2.9	62.1	14.7	33.3
Duluth, Minn.	176	100,578	-5.9	-2.9	72.6	11.4	1.5
Oakland, Cal.	176	361,561	-1.6	-3.4	53.3	16.2	50.6
Minneapolis, Minn.	174	434,400	-10.0	-12.2	68.1	11.5	7.2
Springfield, Mass.	170	163,905	-6.1	3.2	64.4	12.4	16.1
Canton, Ohio	167	110,053	-3.1	-3.2	66.2	12.2	14.2
Erie, Pa.	158	129,231	-6.7	0.3	66.8	11.0	6.8
Worcester, Mass.	156	176,572	-5.4	-1.3	74.4	9.9	3.3
Washington, D.C.	155	756,510	-1.0	-3.0	47.0	16.3	74.3
Salt Lake City, Utah	155	175,885	-7.2	-1.1	52.1	13.8	9.6
Spokane, Wash.	154	170,516	-6.1	+1.6	53.6	13.5	3.8
Dayton, Ohio	154	243,601	-7.4	-12.3	52.1	13.7	31.7

Sources: Same as table 9-1, and U.S. Office of Revenue Sharing, *General Revenue Sharing: Final Data Elements, Entitlement Period 6* (Government Printing Office, 1976).
a. For definition of urban conditions index, see note 2 above.
b. Chattanooga's population gain was due in large part to a series of annexations in 1971–73.

Table 9-3. Per Capita Amounts of Selected Revenue and Expenditure Items,
New York City and Chicago, 1974–75
Dollars

Item	New York City	Chicago
General revenues	1,677.57	340.63
Property taxes	349.00	98.53
Intergovernmental revenue	884.51	106.80
General expenditures	1,522.37	310.20
Education	356.53	11.85
Highways	26.71	30.36
Public welfare	377.63	5.84
Health and hospitals	212.01	14.99
Police protection	91.58	77.41
Fire protection	38.86	25.65
Sewerage	46.81	8.09
Other sanitation	36.55	20.66
Parks and recreation	19.80	3.14
Housing and renewal	81.95	3.82
Total Debt	1,934.64	411.12
Long-term, full-faith, and credit	1,044.72	96.26
Other	889.92	314.86

Source: U.S. Bureau of the Census, *City Government Finances in 1974–75*, GF75, no. 4 (GPO, 1976),
table 6.

The city government of Chicago accounted for less than 10 percent of total spending by local governments for services to its citizens
in the seven functional areas included in table 9-4, while the city of
New York accounted for nearly all such spending. That cities vary
widely in the way in which they organize and finance the provision
of services is not a new observation. However, it is in this context
that the role of the federal government and its budget in aiding cities
must be considered.

The Federal Role in Aiding Cities

Although there are no programs in the federal budget that provide
funds only to cities, there are many that aid cities along with other
types of local governments, particularly counties and townships. In
recent years the amount and number of federal grant programs that
aid localities has increased markedly. Between 1952 and 1972, there
was, in fact, a doubling in the localities' share of total direct federal
payments to state and local governments, as shown in table 9-5. Most
of the increase over this period is accounted for by growth in grant

Table 9-4. Per Capita Expenditures, Chicago and New York City, and of Local Units Furnishing Services to City of Chicago, by Function, 1974–75
Dollars

Function	Local unit furnishing services to Chicago	Local unit	Chicago area City of Chicago and local unit	New York City
Local schools	Chicago City School System	321.92	333.77	356.53
Higher education	City Colleges of Chicago	13.39[a]	13.39	63.33
Parks and recreation	Chicago Park District	31.12	34.26	19.80
Sewerage	Metropolitan Sanitation District	29.88	37.97	46.81
Health and hospitals	Cook County Health Department	24.69	39.69	212.01
Housing and renewal	Chicago Housing Authority	29.25	33.07	81.95
Welfare	Cook County Welfare Department	1.09	6.93	377.63

Sources: U.S. Bureau of the Census, *City Government Finances in 1974–75*; idem, *Local Government Finances in Selected Metropolitan Areas and Large Counties, 1974–75*, GF–75 no. 6 (GPO, 1976), and idem, *Census of Governments, 1972*, vol. 4, *Government Finances*, no. 1: *Finances of School Districts* (GPO, 1974), table 9.
a. 1971–72 expenditures.

Table 9-5. Federal Payments to State and Local Governments and
Share to Local Governments, Selected Fiscal Years 1952–75

Fiscal year	Federal payments to state and local governments (millions of dollars)	Percentage of federal payments to local governments
1952	2,585	9.1
1956	3,347	9.6
1960	6,994	9.2
1964	10,097	11.7
1968	18,053	12.6
1972	33,584	18.2
1974	42,854	28.3
1975	49,628	28.6

Sources: U.S. Bureau of the Census, *Governmental Finances*, selected years, and idem, *Summary of Governmental Finances*, selected years.

programs for education, the environment, and community development. Even more striking is the fact that from 1972 to 1974 the proportion of federal payments received by local units rose by another 50
percent, accounted for primarily by the enactment of the general
revenue sharing program.

Two main types of federal grants to localities can be distinguished.
Formula grants are distributed according to an automatic allocation
system specified in law or regulation; project grants are provided on
the basis of individually approved projects meeting the appropriate
federal requirements.

Until the advent of general revenue sharing in 1972, almost all
formula grants provided by the federal government were made to
state governments for fairly narrowly defined purposes. However, the
trend in recent years, which was a major theme of the New Federalism of the Nixon administration, has been toward broader-purpose
formula grants, with a substantial proportion of these grants going
to local governments. Two-thirds of all general revenue sharing payments are made to local units; all block grants for community development and 70 percent of those for the manpower block grant
program are paid directly by the federal government to localities.

These new and broader grants were adopted in large measure as
instruments of political decentralization, as a means of increasing
the discretion of the recipient units, and to reduce the influence of
federal officials on state and local policymaking.

There is considerable significance in this dual shift toward greater reliance on formula grants and the direct allocation of federal grants to local units. In terms of their political effect, the increased reliance on direct grants to localities represents an important modification of the original concept of American federalism. Traditionally, local governments in the United States have been regarded as "creatures" of the states, and thus not on the same legal footing as the states for purposes of their relationships with the federal government.

The Spreading Effect

The shift from project grants to formula grants and the increase in the amount of funds provided under formula grants to localities can also be seen to have had a spreading effect. Whereas project grants could be targeted on a few units or disproportionately paid to certain units, formula grants treat all localities the same with respect to the economic and social characteristics specified in the distribution formula. This, of course, has been one of their selling points—that they are evenhanded and that as a result funding can be anticipated in advance. This spreading effect has significance in relation to urban hardship conditions. It has tended to benefit suburban governments and small cities that previously were not aided, or not aided appreciably, under federal grants. The resulting reduction in the relative proportion of federal grants made to other cities—particularly large cities—may be said to be good where these cities do not face hardship conditions and yet received relatively high levels of federal aid. Furthermore, the inclusion of suburban governments (by no means a homogeneous group) can be argued to be desirable as a means of aiding poor suburbs and of stimulating richer suburban governments to deal with social needs—for example, by providing training, jobs, housing opportunities, and public facilities for minorities and lower-income groups.

But this relative decrease of funds to the larger cities can also be criticized, especially in the case of larger cities facing urban hardship conditions. In 1968, 62.2 percent of all federal grants for cities went to cities of over 500,000 population; the corresponding figure for 1975 was 44.3 percent. On the other hand, the shares for cities of under 500,000 population rose. Cities of 100,000–499,999 population received 17.5 percent of all federal grants to cities in 1968 and 22.9 percent in 1975; the share for cities under 100,000 rose even more, from 20.3 percent in 1968 to 32.8 percent in 1975.

Table 9-6. Grants to Local Governments under Ford and Carter Budgets,[a]
by Major Federal Programs, Fiscal Year 1977

Millions of dollars

Program	Ford budget outlays	Carter budget outlays	Increase
Revenue sharing[b]			
General revenue sharing	4,540	4,540	0
Countercyclical revenue sharing	838	1,458	625
Block grants			
Community development	2,250	2,250	0
Comprehensive Employment and Training Act, Title I[c]	1,015	1,015	0
Other[d]			
Wastewater treatment construction	4,430	4,430	0
Emergency public works	791	987	196
CETA, Titles II and VI (public service jobs)	1,931	2,431	500
Urban Mass Transportation Administration grants	1,773	1,773	0
Spend-down of programs folded into community development block grants	1,169	1,169	0
Other job training and employment assistance	1,075	1,403	328
Federally impacted schools aid	791	791	0
Community Services Administration funding	494	494	0
Airport development assistance	308	308	0
Emergency school assistance	269	269	0
Economic development assistance	188	188	0
Rural water and waste disposal grants	163	163	0

Sources: *Special Analyses, Budget of the United States Government, Fiscal Year 1978*; Office of Management and Budget, *Fiscal Year 1978 Budget Revisions, February 1977* (GPO, 1977); idem, Budget Review Division, "Grants-in-Aid in the Revised 1978 Budget" (OMB, 1977; processed). The CETA figures are estimated from U.S. Department of Labor, "News," USDL 76–1346, 76–1426, 76–1499, October 22, 1976, November 22, 1976, and December 17, 1976, respectively.

a. Excluding grants estimated at under $100 million.

b. Two-thirds of estimated total outlays; there are some exceptions to the two-third rule in states affected by special limitation provisions in the law.

c. Estimate excludes consortium incentives.

d. Some of these programs make small grants of undetermined amounts to state governments. Except for CETA, figures are for total outlays.

The Array of Federal Grants for Localities

Although there is a tendency to view federal grants in terms of their proliferation and duplication, local-aid funds are concentrated in a few programs and functional areas. Table 9-6 shows all federal grants under which at least $100 million is estimated to be provided to local governments for fiscal year 1977, under both the Ford and Carter budgets. The table includes sixteen major programs and program areas, which account for an estimated 90 percent of all direct federal

Table 9-7. Ford and Carter Budget Authority and Outlays for
Major Local-Aid Programs, Fiscal Year 1978

Millions of dollars

Program	Ford budget	Carter budget	Change
Countercyclical grants			
Local public works			
Budget authority	3	2,000	1,997
Outlays	803	2,800	1,997
Public service employment			
Budget authority	400	5,871	5,471
Outlays	1,400	5,888	4,488
Revenue sharing			
Budget authority	0	1,550	1,550
Outlays	0	1,550	1,550
Other grants			
Sewage treatment construction			
Budget authority	4,500	4,500	0
Outlays	5,160	5,160	0
Urban mass transit[a]			
Budget authority	492	492	0
Outlays	2,059	2,159	50
Community development			
Budget authority	4,554	5,311	−757
Outlays	5,112	5,195	83
Local public works and development			
Budget authority	1,619	1,742	123
Outlays	1,535	1,535	19
Employment and training			
Budget authority	2,838	4,256	1,418
Outlays	2,912	4,747	1,835

Source: Office of Management and Budget, *Fiscal Year 1978 Budget Revisions.*
a. Grants by Urban Mass Transportation Administration only.

aid to localities.[4] Overall, the Carter administration has proposed increases in outlays to state and local governments of $2 billion in 1977 and $10 billion in 1978. A more comprehensive comparison of the Carter and Ford budgets for local aid in 1978 is presented in table 9-7, which shows both authority and outlay figures. To summarize the main points brought out by the two tables, it can be said that the Carter revisions for 1977 and 1978 make some changes, but not many, in spending for local assistance; these increases are very large

4. Federal programs such as income support grants and the Law Enforcement Assistance Administration's block grant, which "pass through" aid to local governments by an initial allocation to the states, are excluded from this table.

but tend to be limited to those required to implement the administration's economic stimulus package.

How do major federal aid programs for localities relate to the urban hardship conditions discussed earlier? Distributional issues are of immense importance in this context. Unless the amount of funds available for federal programs to aid localities were significantly increased, changes in allocation systems to place greater emphasis on relieving urban hardship conditions would require reductions in the amount of funds available for other cities, typically smaller and suburban cities with higher income levels and better economic prospects. Yet these communities, like all local governments, are hard hit by inflation.[5] They are as a result increasingly sensitive to ways in which federal funds can ease their fiscal pressures. Moreover, they have demography on their side. Growth of the suburbs and their representation in the House of Representatives has resulted in stepped-up, and increasingly successful, demands on the part of these governments to obtain federal grants. Meanwhile, central cities facing hardship conditions, which have been losing population, tend to be concentrated in the northeast and north central regions, which lost eight seats in the House under the reapportionment based on the 1970 census.

Several ameliorating factors offset these negative ones. Since not all cities with hardship conditions are central cities (some are older suburbs), since not all are located in the northeast quadrant, and since many wealthier suburban communities depend upon central cities for jobs and cultural amenities, there is a possible base for political support for federal policies focused on urban hardship conditions that goes beyond the boundaries of the old central cities. Furthermore, to the extent that older and declining cities have disproportionately high levels of unemployment, poverty, and deteriorated housing, federal programs designed to deal with such conditions can, or at least should, be expected to focus assistance on these cities.

Major HUD Programs

The federal agency that relates most closely to cities is the Department of Housing and Urban Development; its two largest activities

5. David Greytak and Bernard Jump, "The Effects of Inflation on State and Local Government Finances, 1967–1974," Occasional paper 25 (Syracuse University, Maxwell School of Citizenship and Public Affairs, 1975).

to aid cities are community development and housing. The Ford administration's budget for 1978 recommended increases in both areas; the Carter administration, in turn, transmitted budget revisions that would make further outlay increases.

COMMUNITY DEVELOPMENT. In 1974 a new law was passed to consolidate seven previously established federal grant programs for community development into a single block grant to be distributed by HUD, in part under a new formula allocation system and in part on a discretionary basis. The seven "folded-in" grants subsumed under the new program are urban renewal, model cities, water and sewer facilities, open spaces, neighborhood facilities, rehabilitation loans, and public facility loans. Some 2,500 local governments received such block grants for community development in 1975.

President Ford's budget for fiscal 1978 proposed two important changes in this program. It urged raising the authority level by $252 million to $3.5 billion, and also recommended a revised formula for allocating these funds to give more aid to hardship cities. The new formula, similar to that proposed in the recent Brookings report for HUD on this program, is a "dual formula," retaining the existing three-factor formula and at the same time introducing a new second formula.[6] Under the dual-formula approach, eligible jurisdictions receive aid under whichever formula (the original formula or the new one) entitles them to the higher amount of funds.

The original formula contained in the Housing and Community Development Act of 1974 is based on population, overcrowded housing, and poverty (double weighted). Under this formula, when fully implemented, the share of all central cities would decline from 71.8 percent under the folded-in programs to 42.2 percent in the sixth year of the block grant program. The northeast quadrant's share would decline similarly, New England's share falling from 9.9 percent to 4.7 percent and that for the Middle Atlantic States from 22.7 percent to 17.4 percent. The Ford administration's proposed new alternative formula, for example, uses population decline, the proportion of population living in poverty, and the number of pre-1939 housing units as formula factors (pre-1939 housing reflects physical need, a dimension of urban need not included in the original formula). The net effect is to increase the funds going to older and declining cities, and to the northeast quadrant generally.

6. See Nathan and others, *Block Grants for Community Development*, chaps. 5 and 6.

The Carter administration also proposed revisions in this program. It recommended a supplementary block grant fund of $400 million in the form of discretionary "action grants" for major projects in needy cities. Also proposed was a dual formula for the basic allocation system, with the new formula consisting of poverty, pre-1939 housing, and "growth-lag," defined as the difference between the population growth (or decline) of each eligible city and the national average growth rate for all entitlement cities. Like the Ford administration's dual formula, this proposal has a significantly stronger urban focus than the allocation system in the current law.

HOUSING. Widespread concern about the slow recovery of the housing industry from the 1974–75 recession resulted in pressure on the federal government in 1976 to expand the level of its housing programs. From 1971 through 1973, housing starts for the nation exceeded 2 million annually; in 1974 they were 1.34 million and in 1975, 1.16 million. The Ford budget submitted in January 1977 proposed 400,000 assisted housing units for fiscal year 1978, an increase of 165,000 units over 1977. Most of these subsidies were proposed to be provided through section 8 of the United States Housing Act as amended, a housing assistance program under which a payment is made for the difference between the fair market rent of dwellings occupied by eligible families and 25 percent of their income. Unlike the other programs considered in this chapter, section 8 funds are paid to both private developers and local governments. Assistance is available for new housing, rehabilitated housing, and existing housing.

The inclusion of existing housing, which in 1977 accounted for 38 percent of all section 8 approvals, raises important policy issues. For one thing, it means that a considerable portion (possibly as much as half) of the 165,000 new section 8 units proposed in the 1978 Ford budget would not be for new construction. The inclusion of so many existing units undermines the stimulation of new construction as one of the purposes of housing assistance programs.

The second domestic policy issue raised by the inclusion of so many existing units under the section 8 program relates not to housing policy but to income-security policy. Because section 8 funding is limited, many families with the same or lower income levels than families in existing housing units that happen to be subsidized do not receive this form of income assistance. As contrasted to subsidies for new housing units, the problem of horizontal inequity created here cannot be offset by the fact that new housing construction is being stimulated. The justification of subsidies for occupants of existing housing units rests much more heavily on an income-security rationale. Proposals for welfare reform—including a universal housing allowance available to all poor families—have been advanced in part as a means of reducing the unfairness of current housing assistance programs.

Federal housing programs are related to still another area of domestic policy, civil rights. The Housing and Community Development Act of 1974 requires that, as a condition of receiving block grant funds for community development, recipient jurisdictions develop a "housing assistance plan" indicating their housing needs (including units for persons expected to reside in the community) and how they propose to meet these needs. Experience to date under the block grant program indicates only minimal efforts to develop and implement housing assistance plans.[7] Here again, the question of distribution is raised. Should federal housing subsidies be concentrated in the inner city or spread out in the metropolitan areas in order to achieve spatial deconcentration of income groups, an objective of the block grant program?

President Carter's budget proposals call for 400,000 assisted housing units both in 1977 and 1978, and a change in the mix to give more emphasis to conventional public housing and section 8 subsidies for existing housing units for lower-income families. Nearly $9 billion in increased budget authority and $124 million in increased outlays are requested for 1978.

Meeting Capital Needs

The federal government provides grants under a number of programs for certain kinds of construction projects undertaken by local governments, and also assists them in borrowing for routine capital purposes. In recent years the trend in federal grants for capital purposes has been away from large-scale construction and toward smaller projects. Critics of this trend toward shorter-term and more dispersed urban development activities have recommended that federal policy be changed to assist large-scale construction projects.

7. Ibid., pp. 64–67, 393–97.

Some have suggested changing the block grant program for community development by grafting onto it a new section resembling the conventional urban renewal program. (The Carter administration's proposal of supplementary "action grants" moves in this direction.) Others have proposed an urban development bank to assist local governments in financing public and private economic and community development projects. Still another approach involves federal tax credits for investments in areas of urban distress.

Traditionally, local governments have relied on the private market to raise funds for capital purposes of a more routine nature, with the interest received by lenders being exempt from federal taxation. Most cities—New York is the major exception—have avoided relying extensively on borrowing for operating purposes. As opposed to the recommendations to provide assistance for relatively large-scale capital development projects, a number of related types of federal aid have been recommended to help cities meet their regular capital needs. Some have urged that temporary assistance, such as that provided under the New York Seasonal Financing Act, be offered to a wider range of cities. Another approach is that in addition to the tax exemption, the federal government guarantee state and local bonds, with the guarantee available to units facing especially serious fiscal pressures and willing to subscribe to the conditions under which the guarantee would be made available.

A more widely favored approach is for the federal government to give local governments a taxable bond option. Under this approach, states and localities would have the option of using a taxable debt instrument on which the federal government would pay part of the interest cost (somewhere between 30 and 50 percent) in exchange for eliminating the federal tax exemption. Major arguments in favor of the taxable bond option are that it would encourage institutional investors otherwise not attracted by the federal tax exemption to enter this market, and at the same time enable the federal government to subsidize state and local borrowing on a more efficient basis. This is a proposal of long standing; both the Ford and Carter administrations have recommended this approach, and support for it appears to be growing.

Revenue Sharing

The general revenue sharing program enacted in 1972 for five years was extended for three and three-quarters years in 1976. The

new law distributes $6.85 billion per year to some 39,000 general-purpose units of state and local government; two-thirds of these funds are paid to local governments.[8]

A second form of revenue sharing—countercyclical revenue sharing, also enacted in 1976—is proposed to be extended to 1982 as part of President Carter's economic stimulus program. This program, triggered at 6 percent unemployment nationally, distributes funds according to the general revenue sharing formula, adjusted by the level of unemployment locally.

The revenue sharing program provides another good illustration of the way in which formulas under federal grants affect older and declining central cities. Despite an overall advantage of approximately two to one for central cities as compared to suburban units under revenue sharing, there is agreement among analysts of the program that some large central cities with particularly serious hardship conditions are discriminated against under the current formula. Specifically, a 145 percent ceiling on local allocations contained in the act (no local unit can receive more than 145 percent of the average per capita payment to localities in its state) discriminates against central cities like St. Louis, Philadelphia, and Baltimore, which do not have an overlying county government. If the *combined* allocations of shared revenue for a central city and its overlying county government exceed 145 percent, but both the city and county shares are below this level, the ceiling does not apply. It only applies to individual units; coterminous city-counties (as in the three cases above) are therefore the jurisdictions most likely to be affected. Ironically, the tradition of local government in the northeast quadrant is such that it is precisely the oldest, most disadvantaged municipal governments that are likely to feel the pinch of this requirement. In 1975, the Ford administration proposed raising the 145 percent ceiling to 175 percent, but the renewal law passed in 1976 did not do so.

Beyond the problem of the ceiling are more fundamental questions of whether the formula for distributing both general and countercyclical revenue sharing funds should give greater emphasis to urban hardship. This could be done by adding formula factors such as density, age of housing, and rate of population change (inverse) that tend to favor hardship cities. In addition to changing the basic for-

8. For a history and description of the new law, see Richard P. Nathan and Charles F. Adams, Jr., and Associates, *Revenue Sharing: The Second Round* (Brookings Institution, 1977).

mula, other possibilities, not considered in 1972 or 1976, include introducing a new dual-formula approach (as proposed for the community development block grant) or an automatic supplement limited to jurisdictions that exceed specified threshold levels on indicators of economic and social need.

The Ninety-sixth Congress, which convenes in 1979, will again need to consider general revenue sharing legislation. President Carter has consistently recommended eliminating state governments from eligibility on the grounds that their needs are less acute than those of most local governments, although he did not propose that this be done in 1977 in the extension of the countercyclical revenue sharing program. There are both substantive and tactical reasons for keeping the states in the revenue sharing picture, given their central role in determining the boundaries, functions, and finances of local units. However, should state governments be eliminated from the program, opportunities would be opened for distributing the freed-up funds on a basis that gives greater attention to the urban hardship conditions of local governmental units.

Other Federal Grants to Localities

Of the programs listed in table 9-6, eight have not yet been discussed. The urban or hardship focus of four of these programs is examined in this section.

EMPLOYMENT AND TRAINING BLOCK GRANT. Title I of the Comprehensive Employment and Training Act (CETA) allocates funds to state and local governments acting as prime sponsors for a variety of employment and training activities previously operated as project grants. Cities and counties of over 100,000 population are eligible to act as prime sponsors, along with consortia of local governments. All prime sponsors, including state governments, are required to submit plans for the expenditure of Title I funds, which must be approved before programs can be funded.

Again, the composition of the formula is of key importance for the cities. Eighty percent of the funds provided under CETA–Title I are allocated among prime sponsors according to three factors: half on the basis of each prime sponsor's share of the previous year's funding, 37.5 percent based on each sponsor's share of total national unemployment, and the remainder based on the number of adults below an agency-defined poverty line. No unit may receive less than 90 per-

cent of its previous year's funding or more than 150 percent. The floor provision is especially important for cities.

Under this formula a number of larger and older cities have been losing funds. Overall, the prime sponsor cities' share of CETA–Title I funds declined from 25 percent under the programs consolidated into this title to 22 percent in 1976. In 1976, two-thirds of the cities required special payments to bring them up to the 90 percent floor. County governments (including many that are highly urban) have been beneficiaries under CETA; their share of funds increased from 13.5 percent before CETA to 16.3 percent under the formula in 1976. The major source of these shifts in funding has been the formula's reliance on the number of unemployed, rather than on the concentration on the disadvantaged under the earlier programs. The relatively high poverty line used by the Department of Labor also tends to reduce the advantage of the older cities. The CETA authority expires in September 1977; the Carter administration has requested a simple one-year extension.[9]

MASS TRANSPORTATION. There are three major sources of federal funding for urban public transportation. Two are programs operated by the Urban Mass Transit Administration (UMTA); the third consists of diversions from the highway trust fund. The cumulative federal share of projects funded under these three programs was $7.1 billion as of October 1976.

The two programs administered by UMTA are currently operating under $11.8 billion of authority enacted for the six-year period 1974–80. Estimated outlays under the two programs in 1977 are $1.8 billion. Approximately $7 billion, or about two-thirds of the total UMTA grant authority, is budgeted for project-type grants, where the federal government pays up to 80 percent of the net cost of capital acquisitions (rights-of-way and rolling stock). Nearly one-third of these project grants have been made for bus purchases; the remaining 70 percent has been split almost equally between construction of new rail systems and the expansion of existing systems.[10] The funding distribution of these project grants shows a high concentration in a relatively small number of cities. Three-fourths of these

9. Formula information and distributional data for this section was provided by the National Academy of Sciences monitoring project on the CETA program.

10. Congressional Budget Office, *Budget Options for Fiscal Year 1978* (GPO, 1977), chap. 7.

funds were obligated for eight cities as of September 1976, largely for rail systems. Thirty-two urbanized areas received 91.6 percent of these capital grant commitments. Of these thirty-two areas, the central cities of fifteen scored above 150 on the urban conditions index, approximately the same proportion as that of all cities above 500,000 population. Within this group, however, there is little relationship between relative hardship ratings and the level of funding received. Baltimore, Boston, Philadelphia, and Pittsburgh (all above 150 on the index) received substantial shares of the reservations allocated for these project grants, while Buffalo, Cleveland, and St. Louis (the three highest-ranked cities in table 9-2 that received project funding) received relatively small amounts of funding.

The federal government also provides formula grants for public transportation (about $4 billion in authority, with current projects of approximately $600 million a year) to some 248 urbanized areas. The formula allocates one-half of the available funds on the basis of population and one-half on the basis of population weighted by density. Grants are made to one public body in each area; the state acts as recipient for areas under 200,000 population. The Congressional Budget Office estimates that over 90 percent of these funds have been used for operating subsidies and that these funds are equal to about 20 to 25 percent of the deficits of existing public transit systems.

To summarize, federal support of mass transit operations has been heavily focused on capital support in a relatively small number of cities; operating subsidies have been spread more widely. However, the effectiveness of these funds in relieving urban hardship is difficult to gauge because the ultimate benefits may go disproportionately to higher-income suburban areas and residents.

PUBLIC SERVICE EMPLOYMENT. Grants to local governments for public service employment under Titles II and VI of CETA represent two-thirds of federal outlays for public service employment in fiscal 1977. (The remaining one-third is paid to state governments.) Total federal outlays for public sector jobs have expanded dramatically in the past three years—from $400 million in fiscal 1974 to $2.7 billion in fiscal 1977—as economic conditions have worsened. Under Title II, as initially enacted, funding for public sector employment was to be concentrated in areas of high unemployment; positions were reserved for the disadvantaged and long-term unemployed. Under Title VI, more emphasis was placed on counter-cyclical goals. Countercyclical considerations were given further prominence in 1976 by the passage of the Emergency Jobs Program Extension Act.

The last two Ford administration budgets recommended phasing out Title VI. The Carter administration's economic stimulus package, however, recommends an additional $940 million in authority and $700 million in outlays for Titles II and VI for the remainder of fiscal 1977 and further increases in funding in 1978.

The effectiveness of these programs in providing funds to urban hardship areas has been reduced by worsening economic conditions and the use of these titles to further countercyclical goals. This situation has been particularly marked with respect to Title II. Under the initial legislation, prime sponsors were eligible for funding if their area had an unemployment rate of 6.5 percent or more, and funds were allocated on the basis of the prime sponsor's share of the total number of unemployed. However, increased unemployment has made almost all prime sponsors eligible under this program, requiring that funds be spread among a large number of recipients and thus lessening its impact for hardship cities.

Title VI funding is more responsive to variations in the severity of unemployment. Half the funds are distributed according to the sponsor's share of total unemployment; one-quarter according to the share of unemployment in excess of 4.5 percent; and one-quarter according to the share of unemployed in subareas with unemployment greater than 6.5 percent. One recent evaluation of Titles II and VI concludes that CETA public service employment programs have been successful "to a modest extent" in concentrating programs in SMSAs with substantial unemployment, but less successful in channeling funds to areas that have experienced major declines in employment as a result of the recent recession.[11]

EMERGENCY PUBLIC WORKS. The emergency public works program enacted in 1976 has been the subject of considerable controversy. The allocation of funds was based on a list of factors in the legislation to be defined by the administering agency, in this case the Economic Development Administration (EDA). One feature of the law that was especially important was the two-pot allocation system.

11. Michael Wiseman, "Public Employment as Fiscal Policy," *Brookings Papers on Economic Activity, 1:1976,* pp. 67–104.

The agency was required by law to allocate 70 percent of the available funds to jurisdictions with unemployment rates above the national average and 30 percent to jurisdictions below the national average but above 6.5 percent. EDA initially anticipated that this 70–30 division could be made on the national level, since it did not expect a large volume of applications for the 70 percent portion. Contrary to expectations, however, enough applications for the 70 percent pot were received to exhaust total allocations in every state, while a relatively small number of applications was received for the 30 percent funds.

As a result, EDA decided to make the 70–30 split on a *state*, rather than a national, basis. Once applications were scored, applications for the 70 percent pot competed against each other at the state level. As a result of the large number of applications, this competition was intense; many jurisdictions with substantial unemployment rates received no funds at all, while applicants for the 30 percent pot, where competition was much less intense, received relatively large grants in spite of their low unemployment rate. In New Jersey, for example, the unemployment cutoff for funding from the 70 percent pot was 11.37 percent. No applicants with unemployment rates between the national average and this figure received any funding, while applicants with rates between 6.5 percent and the national average received funding from the 30 percent pot.[12]

While full data are lacking, it would appear that two groups of beneficiaries emerged as a result of the operation of the allocation process for emergency public works funding in 1976. Most very large and high-hardship cities tended to do reasonably well under the scoring procedure for applications, since they were likely to have both a large number of unemployed persons and a high unemployment rate. Smaller governments, on the other hand, appear to have benefited from the 30 percent pot and their ability, through another controversial ruling, to claim areas outside their borders as part of their project areas. Under this ruling, prosperous suburban communities were able to claim the unemployment rate of contiguous central cities

12. EDA also decided to adopt a system of "benchmarks" to prevent funds from being concentrated in a small number of units. Under this procedure, which also has a spreading effect, no unit could receive a higher share of state emergency public works funds than its share of state or county unemployment. Regardless of a project's score relative to projects requested by other units, it was not funded if the unit's benchmark allocation had been exceeded.

on their applications. Middle-sized cities and those experiencing moderate hardship appear to have been disadvantaged by the procedures for calculating both the number of unemployed and the rate of unemployment.

The Congress has recently made a number of modifications in the procedure for allocating public works funding that help to rectify the problems discussed here and increase the amount of support going to urban hardship areas. New legislation eliminates the 30 percent pot and requires modifications in the procedures used for scoring applications that discriminated against many large cities.

Welfare Reform and the Cities

Welfare reform, however defined, is an important issue for cities. It is especially important for central cities. The poverty rate for central cities (14.4 percent) was twice that of suburbs in 1974. Moreover, the incidence of welfare benefits is generally higher in the older and declining cities of the northeast and north central regions. This does not mean that the budgets of these central cities are directly burdened; welfare is more likely, even in these regions, to be a state or county responsibility. A basic choice in framing the urban policies of the federal government is that between providing financial assistance to jurisdictions and pursuing an "income strategy" concentrating on aid to individuals in the form of income transfers (both cash and in-kind). There are three dimensions of welfare reform that bear on the issue of relieving urban hardship: benefit levels, coverage, and fiscal relief.

BENEFIT LEVELS. Since welfare benefit levels in the northeast and, to a lesser extent, the north central region tend to be relatively high, any provisions in a welfare plan to establish a minimum benefit level would have little effect on many persons in these regions who are already receiving assistance. Setting such a national minimum— for example, under the aid to families with dependent children (AFDC) program—while it may be desirable for social policy reasons, would primarily benefit people in other regions of the country.

COVERAGE. On the other hand, changes in the coverage of federally aided welfare programs could have much more of an impact on the hard-pressed cities in the northeast quadrant. Coverage, for example, could be extended to more of the working poor and the disabled, as well as all poor families with unemployed fathers, and perhaps also single persons and childless couples.

FISCAL RELIEF. Although it is the states that benefit most directly from fiscal relief under welfare reform, some counties and a few central cities (notably New York, Denver, and Washington) would also be likely to benefit. An important consideration for urban policy applying to fiscal relief under a welfare reform plan is the question of whether some or all states should be required to pass through a portion of this aid to local governments, and if so, which ones and on what basis. Two views have been advanced on this question. One would pass through fiscal relief according to the proportion of welfare spending by particular local jurisdictions. Another would pass through a fixed proportion of fiscal relief funds to all localities in a manner reflecting their welfare caseload, the rationale being that this population is a high-cost group for the provision of public services generally.

President Carter has set in motion a review process to examine welfare reform options. Whatever approach is ultimately taken—whether it be to establish a new system or institute a series of incremental changes in existing programs—the impact of welfare reform in relieving the human and fiscal problems of hardship cities needs to be evaluated according to this three-part framework.[13]

Basic Choices for National Policy

Just because urban hardship exists does not necessarily mean that new federal programs should be initiated, or old ones expanded, to aid hardship cities. This point is often made in the following terms. Most people do not choose to live in old and densely populated cities with high-rise life styles. The growth of new areas and new settlement patterns (both in suburbs and increasingly in small cities) reflects individual choices, which are perfectly appropriate, and in fact desirable, in a democratic society. The role of the old inner cities, it is argued, has to change and in fact is changing; public policy should not swim against the tide. Juxtaposed to this view, other observers of the urban scene advocate new federal programs to revitalize inner cities as centers of commerce and culture, as well as residential places

13. For a detailed discussion of alternative approaches to welfare reform, see chapter 8.

for a cross-section of income groups. There are innumerable positions in between these two poles that would involve a shift of national policy to put more or less emphasis on relieving urban hardship. Many who favor a shift in national policy to relieve urban hardship have as their purpose not necessarily to restore inner cities to some notion of past grandeur, but, in varying degrees, to give these cities a better capability to adjust to changed conditions and take advantage of opportunities for growth, revival, and new development.

It is important to remember that the troubled cities are not without hope. Revival is already occurring in many areas; some areas of these cities have long been healthy; other neighborhoods and areas in which urban problems have been especially severe are emptying out, with the result being large tracts of vacant or little-used land in the inner city. Increasingly, urban development efforts are being concentrated on transitional areas with growth potential and on efforts to stem further migration from the city, particularly on the part of commercial activities.

The essential question is how much we should do, and how we should do it, to concentrate development and rehabilitation activities in these older and declining cities in order to speed the revival process where it is underway and take advantage of new opportunities for development by channeling program funds and capital into these communities.

Although local initiative and state government efforts have immense importance in this context, the purpose of this chapter has been to focus on the ways in which federal policy can relieve urban hardship. This includes both the amount of federal resources to be allocated and the way in which they are to be deployed.

Many issues relating to countercyclical expenditure programs, as well as ongoing federal aid programs that affect local governments, come to the fore this year because so many of these programs expire in 1977—the block grants for community development, employment and training, and law enforcement, in addition to the emergency public works and countercyclical revenue sharing programs.

In particular, President Carter's countercyclical package, as this analysis shows, involves substantial additional funds for localities. Although these funds for the most part are channeled through countercyclical programs, there is every reason to expect that efforts will be made by both state and local officials to continue these higher levels of expenditure beyond the current recovery phase. A fundamental question is raised by these programs. If they were to become, in effect, permanent (or very long-term) programs, would we want the federal government to play as extensive a role as this would mean in some cities? Especially in cities such as Chicago or Cleveland, where the city government itself accounts for a relatively small share of public spending, the total amount of federal aid received under programs for public service employment or the revised block grants for community development program could amount to as much as one-third of the city government's operating budget.

Alternative Strategies

Beyond decisions about the level and distribution of funding under existing programs are important questions as to the types of urban programs that the federal government should be using. There are five basic ways in which federal strategy could be changed to place greater emphasis on helping to relieve urban hardship conditions, both in inner cities and older suburbs. Although there are trade-offs among them, these five strategies are not mutually exclusive; they can be combined in many ways.

A STRATEGY OF MULTIPLE FORMULA CHANGES. The existence of a fairly small number of large-scale federal programs that aid localities suggests that unless or until bold new spending initiatives are adopted, a strategy of multiple formula changes may be the best short-term solution for those who seek to increase help for cities. Such a strategy involves seeking out opportunities across the spectrum of federal domestic programs for existing programs to be modified, and in some cases expanded, to deal more effectively with urban hardship conditions. Considerable attention, for example, is being given currently to alternative allocation systems under the block grant program for community development. Likewise, a recent proposal to add passenger ridership as a formula factor in the allocation of grants for the operation of mass transit systems is an indication of interest in addressing formula grants to urban need. Similar opportunities exist for modifying the distribution formulas for other grant-in-aid programs.

THE CATEGORICAL GRANT APPROACH. A second approach for changing federal policies to deal with urban hardship conditions would be to fall back on a heavier emphasis on categorical grants as the best means of channeling funds to areas with urban needs. (The term "categorical grants" is used here to refer to grants to local governments or groups for fairly narrowly defined purposes.) The debate on this question involves the highly political question of whether federal grants enacted by Congress and allocated by federal officials would increase the funds going to cities with hardship conditions or whether, on the other hand, the growth of the newer suburbs in population and poltical power would result in, at best, a marginal improvement in the distribution of new categorical grant funds, but with lessened certainty and allocative efficiency. There is already evidence that the Carter administration may start down the road to re-categorization. Major initiatives have been advanced for youth employment and special action grants for community development, in the latter case as a supplement to the existing block grant program.

TARGETING ON SELECTED FUNCTIONAL AREAS. A third possible approach for strengthening the urban emphasis of federal policy is to allocate a larger proportion of federal grant funds to selected functional areas that are particularly important in the inner city. This approach bears a close relationship to the re-categorization strategy just discussed, although in this case block grants, as well as categorical grants, could be relied upon to alter the functional-area mix of domestic programs and increase the relative importance of programs that help to relieve urban hardship. In addition to the block grants for community development, other possibilities for altering the functional mix of federal aids include public service employment, mass transit, and public works programs.

NEW PROGRAMS FOR THE CITIES. Opportunities also exist for more far-reaching changes. Despite their diminishing political base, some spokesmen for large cities have called for a new national commitment to urban redevelopment in the form of a Marshall Plan for the cities. Such proposals have not been as seriously or vigorously advanced in recent years as they once were, perhaps reflecting changing demographic conditions, or perhaps a current conservative mood on spending issues.

More likely than a large new grant program to revive the inner city is a lending program along the lines of an urban development bank, or "Urbank." The Carter administration is currently working on such a proposal; thus, important issues as to the functions and operations of an urban development bank are soon likely to be at the forefront of discussions of urban policy. These issues might include the following. Should such an institution provide general financing assistance or focus on major development projects in hardship cities? If the latter, how large a subsidy is required to shift capital development projects to these cities? What kinds of credit facilitation techniques should be used—guarantees, interest subsidies, both? What should be used for collateral? (One possible approach is to use escrowed community development block grant funds as collateral for bank-approved projects.) How can private funds be tied into this program? Should such a bank include, as many have proposed, rural development, energy development, fiscal relief?[14]

AN INCOME STRATEGY. The fifth area of federal domestic policy of importance for cities is welfare policy, defined broadly as the transfer of resources (both cash and in-kind) to needy persons, as opposed to grants to jurisdictions. (Expanded public service job programs as an alternative to assistance payments are part of this option.) The design issues in this area and the time and resources needed to set up a program are such that initiatives cannot be expected to emerge quickly, even if an incremental and phased welfare reform strategy is adopted this year. Nevertheless, the problems for national urban policy created by the diversity of functional assignments and financial responsibility in American federalism can be seen as reasons for supporting income and employment strategies to aid needy individuals directly, as opposed to grants-in-aid to local governments. Both welfare reform and health insurance, two issues currently being widely debated, provide opportunities for emphasizing transfers and jobs for individuals in dealing with urban needs.

Public versus Private Sector Effects

One other major choice needs to be mentioned. The Carter budget revisions for 1978 propose substantial increases in federal grant programs for countercyclical purposes, much of which will aid hardship cities. Some of these benefits will have an impact on the public sector, some on the private. Additional revenue sharing funds, for example,

14. A recent round table discussion of urban fiscal experts held at the Brookings Institution revealed both a high level of uncertainty and difference of opinion as to the role such a new financing institution should play and a consensus on the need for better definitions than have been offered to date of the way it should operate. "Round Table Discussion on Urban Development Banking," transcript (Brookings Institution, March 1977; processed).

can be used to hold down or cut taxes, as well as to increase local government spending.[15] Likewise, federal funds for public service employment can be used for substitution purposes (often despite provisions to the contrary) to pay the salaries of employees already on the payroll. Welfare programs and community development programs, on the other hand, can have a greater effect on the public sector in the sense that a relatively higher proportion of these funds is likely to add to the level of public spending.

Whether or not differences in effect between the public and private sectors have important policy implications depends, of course, on the goals attached to individual grant programs. For a program of general fiscal assistance (such as revenue sharing) this distinction may not be critical to its effectiveness. However, for other programs, such as those aimed at promoting public sector employment or job training, the question of the additive or stimulative public sector impact may be considered an important determinant of program effectiveness.

This issue, however, is not as open and shut as it may seem. Substitution effects are not necessarily bad; they offer a means of relieving the fiscal problems of older and declining cities and of local governments generally. Public service employment funds, for example, can be an important means of providing fiscal relief; there is considerable evidence that this has been the case of CETA public service employment funds in a number of hardship cities. A new law passed in 1976 seeks to reduce the substitution effect of public employment programs by requiring measures to designate these funds for special projects for new jobs for the disadvantaged. Still another view of this issue regards the stimulatory effect of some federal grants to local governments as excessive. For example, in some cases, matching requirements can result in a net drain on local revenue, as in the case of project grants from the federal government for sewage treatment plants and related kinds of major capital facilities.

The Future for Hardship Cities

The decline in the population of older cities and the commensurate rise in the population of the suburbs, combined with the overall shift

15. See Nathan and Adams, *Revenue Sharing: The Second Round,* for an analysis of the private and public sector impacts associated with revenue sharing and a general review of the "fungibility" issue as it relates to federal grants.

in population to the Sunbelt region, produce what in the final analysis is a political question. Will there be majorities to support strategies for domestic policy that seek in some measure to shift resources to hardship cities? There are both social and economic reasons for advocating such a policy. Socially, the issue is whether and how the national government should help deal with concentrations of the poor in the older core cities. Economically, the issue is whether the costs of abandoning these cities and their infrastructure are greater than the costs of aiding a revival process. Currently there are signs that the domestic policy of the federal government is changing for both reasons in a way that involves greater attention to what we have termed "urban crisis conditions." Whether this trend will continue and how far it will go remain to be seen.

CHAPTER TEN

Energy

MILTON RUSSELL

THE INCREASE in energy prices in 1973–74, the critical shortage of natural gas in 1976–77, the continuing increase in oil imports from potentially unreliable sources, and the fear that the world is running out of energy have created a national preoccupation with energy matters. The proposals announced by President Carter on April 20, 1977, represent one in a series of efforts to formulate and articulate measures that respond to the energy situation. But energy policy, as Presidents Nixon and Ford discovered, is not enacted by presidential edict. The Congress, the judiciary, the states, and the private sector all interact with the executive in establishing the framework within which importers, consumers, and producers of energy operate. The Carter proposals are a new element in a continuing process; even if they do not prevail, they are important in that they will provide a focus for the ensuing debate.

President Carter's program, which would have very widespread effects, emphasizes conservation and conversion away from oil and natural gas. The cornerstone of the program is gradually to require most consumers to pay the replacement cost of energy. Through raising energy prices, encouraging consumers to insulate, and imposing an automobile tax and rebate scheme to facilitate attainment of existing mileage efficiency standards, the President hopes to lower

This chapter benefited from extensive review by colleagues at Resources for the Future. Research assistance was provided by Thang Long Ton That.

317

the growth in energy consumption from 3–4 percent a year to 2 percent in 1985. Still, additional energy supply will be required, and Carter's program is predicated on efforts to obtain it from coal and nuclear power. These sources are also expected to provide some of the energy now supplied by oil and natural gas. Under the program, domestic oil and natural gas production will not be maximized— that is, their price to producers will remain controlled below the replacement cost. The switch from oil and gas is to be achieved by inducing or requiring industry and electric utilities to convert to coal and encouraging utilities to bring more nuclear power on line, primarily by reducing licensing delays. President Carter plans to avoid trading off environmental quality for more energy supply by maintaining or strengthening environmental and safety standards while offering government support for developing clean-up technologies. The result would be higher energy costs but a cleaner and healthier environment. The program includes doubling the ultimate size and speeding completion of the strategic petroleum reserve as the chief immediate response to the insecurity of the level of oil imports. By 1985, however, the goal is to reduce imports to a level where their interruption would pose no substantial threat.

Energy Problems

There are three separable but related energy problems: energy costs have risen, energy costs may rise substantially in the future, and sudden cost increases, such as would be imposed by an interruption in oil supplies from abroad, would be seriously disruptive. Energy costs are important because higher costs of acquiring any commodity reduce real output and hence real income—the converse of increases in productivity. An increase in energy costs, however, is additionally harmful because other goods and services are not good substitutes for energy. This means that consumption patterns are affected and the productivity of the capital stock directly reduced. The more rapid the increase in energy prices, the greater are these secondary effects— hence the special concern about the effect of an oil embargo.

The first problem, the recent turnaround in energy costs to the United States, was caused by the action of the oil exporters. In this country, as in most of the rest of the world, oil is the dominant substitute for other fuels, and the incremental supply of oil is imported.

Table 10-1. Prices Received by Producers for Major Energy Fuels, Selected Years, 1950-76

Constant 1976 dollars[a]

Year	Coal (dollars per short ton at mine mouth)	Natural gas (cents per thousand cubic feet at wellhead)	Domestic crude oil (dollars per barrel at wellhead)	Saudi Arabian crude oil (dollars per barrel, 34° API, f.o.b.)
1950	10.83	14.5	5.62	n.a.
1955	9.40	21.7	5.77	n.a.
1960	9.04	27.0	5.55	2.95
1965	8.41	29.5	5.42	2.52
1970	10.36	28.3[b]	5.26[b]	2.10
1971	11.35	29.2	5.44	2.66
1972	11.77	28.6	5.21	2.83
1973	11.60	29.3	5.29	3.95
1974	18.00	34.7	7.85	12.31
1975	10.13	46.5[c]	8.02[c]	11.21
1976	20.00[e]	58.0[e]	8.18[p]	11.51

Sources: Coal, gas, and domestic oil, U.S. Bureau of Mines, *Minerals Yearbook*, relevant annual issues, and idem, *Minerals and Materials: A Monthly Survey* (January 1977), pp. 17, 19, 21; 1976 figures are from Bureau of Mines; Saudi Arabian oil, Petroleum Industry Research Foundation, *Vertical Divestiture and OPEC: A Critical Examination of the Arguments for Vertical Divestiture of U.S. Foreign Oil Operations* (PIRF, January 1977), p. 9.

n.a. Not available.

e Estimate.

p Preliminary.

a. Calculated from the official wholesale price index for all commodities.

b. Reduction in the depletion allowance from 27.5 percent to 22 percent (1969 Tax Reform Act) lowered after-tax return and thus the effective price.

c. Narrowed applicability of the depletion allowance lowered after-tax return and thus the effective price.

Consequently, when the world oil price rose, the value of domestic substitutes for it increased as well. The replacement cost and hence value of energy consumed in the United States thus rose with the world oil price, whether or not domestic energy prices were allowed to follow[1] (see table 10-1). Had the oil exporters not chosen to exact monopoly returns, the cost of energy might still have risen over time (assuming depletion of the world resource base outpaced improvements in energy supply technology), but the increase would have come more slowly and predictably and led to an orderly transition to alternative energy sources and to a gradual change in consumption patterns.

The second problem is that energy costs may rise still more. Of

1. The apparent cost of domestic energy production and use has also risen because of increased expenditures to improve environmental quality and to protect human health and safety, which were formerly absorbed by those directly affected rather than by energy consumers.

fundamental importance to energy costs over the next ten to fifteen years is the behavior of some of the oil-exporting countries. These nations, though only loosely organized in the Organization of Petroleum Exporting Countries as a cartel, have thus far exhibited a collective purpose in acting to keep the imported oil price to U.S. refiners at about the same level since 1974 (in constant dollars). In the longer run, however, it is domestic developments that will be decisive in affecting overall energy costs. Domestic coal, nuclear energy, and new technologies will play ever-increasing roles in energy supply. In the latter years of the century, the prime determinant of energy cost will be whether a limitless or at least very large supply of energy is known to be potentially available and what its costs will be.

The third problem is that sharp jumps in the price of oil because of an attempted embargo or other interruption of supply by exporting countries would have a disruptive effect on consuming nations.[2] The probability of this happening is lessened by the dependence of oil exporters on the industrialized nations. The exporters must continue to sell oil in order to meet current consumption and security needs, to broaden their industrial bases, and to preserve the prosperity of the importing countries where their surplus funds are invested. Consequently, the threat of an embargo on oil sales by all OPEC countries is virtually nonexistent, and the chances of an economically motivated long-term embargo by any one exporter are small. An embargo on sales to selected countries would be almost impossible to enforce.

Nonetheless, the possibility remains that one or more oil-exporting nations might reduce oil shipments so much that world oil supplies would fall, creating shortages and higher prices. The large international financial reserves now held by some oil exporters could also be used to punish or reward other nations through shifts in balances among financial centers. The prospective economic effect of an oil supply interruption or financial market manipulation lessens the willingness of the United States and others to pursue foreign policies that might antagonize oil exporters. This concern adds a special international dimension to energy policy.

2. There have been four such incidents: the first associated with the attempted nationalization of Iranian oil production in 1951–54, the second with the closure of the Suez Canal in 1956–57, the third with the Arab-Israeli war of 1967, and the last with the 1973 Arab-Israeli war. Only the last diminished world oil supply, since before 1973–74 adequate surplus capacity existed in the United States and elsewhere to offset declines in shipments from the Middle East.

Underlying all these issues is the difficulty in making the trade-offs between output and environmental quality, health, and safety required in obtaining and using energy. The ultimate effects of energy production and consumption are sometimes unknown and often poorly understood. Much uncertainty exists even about such basic questions as the long-term climatic effect of fossil fuel use. And it is equally difficult to evaluate the benefits—including those to the environment and to human health and safety—to be derived from the higher levels of economic output that more energy use makes possible. Nonetheless, the policy issue is clear: to the extent there is a conflict between energy and other objectives, the benefits from achieving more of each must be weighed and a decision reached. The difficulty comes in identifying the conflicts and weighing the alternatives. Since values and goals differ, this decision ultimately depends on the political process.

Special Issues in Energy Policy

Two domestic issues have dominated the recent energy policy debate: the effect of energy choices on inflation, employment, and income distribution and the special case of natural gas.

Inflation, Employment, and Income Distribution

The economy does not respond instantaneously or completely to changes in the relative prices of goods and services. Any sharp increase in primary energy prices thus raises the general price level and temporarily increases unemployment, and, as well, alters the distribution of income.

The ultimate size of the effect on the general price level of changes in primary energy prices or taxes depends on the mechanisms at work in the economy. While there is some disagreement among economists on this point, it seems likely that energy price increases would not be completely offset by declines in other prices; and the inflationary effect would probably not be limited to a one-time shift upward in the price level equal to the direct contribution of higher energy costs. This means that the price-level effect is an important consideration in energy policy.

However, the size and importance of the price effects of energy policy changes can be overstated. First, primary energy costs make up only a fraction of the price of consumer energy services—about one-half for gasoline, one-third for natural gas, and one-tenth for coal converted to electricity. Thus large proportionate price increases at the source are relatively much smaller as seen by the consumer. Second, primary energy is a small part of the overall economy—only about 5 percent of gross national product. Direct consumer expenditures for delivered energy services were only 6.2 percent of personal consumption expenditures in 1976, up less than 1 percent from the lowest level of the past quarter century. Finally, the economy regularly sustains price fluctuations in other sectors where, just as they would in energy, they induce reallocation of productive resources and restructuring of consumer demand patterns. Policy-induced energy price changes should be viewed within this context.

Price increases for domestically produced energy transfer income, and thus purchases, among sectors and change the composition of the labor skills demanded, but they need not raise unemployment permanently. Higher prices for imported energy similarly transfer income and wealth abroad: national output shifts toward goods and services for immediate export and toward capital investment, taking up the slack created by jobs that disappear elsewhere. The adjustment process requires expansionary federal policies to maintain full employment during the transition, given that other prices do not immediately fall. There is no reason to suppose, however, that long-run unemployment levels would be affected by energy price increases, even though real wage rates could be depressed.

This macroeconomic analysis offers scant comfort to those adversely affected by changes in energy prices or energy policy. Greater employment opportunities in one sector do not automatically provide jobs for those who lose their jobs elsewhere, and the value of the human capital associated with some jobs, like the value of particular capital assets, is directly reduced. No policy can reverse the net economic loss from higher energy costs, but there are numerous policies, some already in operation, that can alter its distribution and lessen the losses associated with adjustment to it. Unemployment compensation, for example, aids in this transition.

The income distribution effects of energy price increases are constrained by income maintenance programs and the progressive tax structure. Most income maintenance programs automatically increase benefits when price indexes rise, leaving those affected about as well off as before. Purchases of energy, including energy embedded in capital and services, are slightly less than proportional to income though lower and middle income groups spend a higher proportion of their income on direct energy purchases than do those who are better off.[3] Thus, the major distributional problem higher energy prices pose is that they lower the real income of the poor. If minimum welfare levels are to be maintained, real expenditures, not energy consumption, should be protected; hence the income support instrument should not be such that payments depend on the amount of energy consumed after the price increase.

The increased income and wealth of energy producers and other beneficiaries represent the other side of the distribution issue. These increases draw more labor and capital into energy-producing activities, leading to more domestic energy output. In the process, extraordinary returns are eliminated, except for capital gains and the extra rent due to the higher value of resources in the ground. Any special tax aimed at appropriating a portion of the gains from energy price changes should be placed on the added value of such existing energy resources. Otherwise, the tax will discourage the production of additional energy, leaving output lower and encouraging additional imports.[4]

The Natural Gas Shortage.

The critical natural gas shortage of 1976–77 resulted from a 24 percent increase in winter heating demand over 1975–76, made more serious by a long-run disequilibrium in the market for natural gas sold for resale in interstate commerce. The country coped with the short-run crisis through transfer of gas among pipelines, relaxation of price and other controls, substitution of other fuels, and reduced consumption by means of voluntary reduction in use and forced closings of plants, schools, and businesses.

The natural gas shortage is a case study of the potential for disruption when the need for adjustment to higher energy costs is camouflaged and response delayed. Because natural gas prices have been held down, more has been consumed, leaving less available for the

3. Robert A. Herendeen and Jerry Tanaka, *Energy Cost of Living,* CAC document 171 (University of Illinois at Urbana-Champaign, Center for Advanced Computation, 1975).
4. See the discussion of taxation below.

future. The lower prices have also meant that less of the resource base has been explored and developed. The decline in available reserves has forced some consumers to do without. Future demand for natural gas has been increased by the lower prices because long-lived gas-specific capital equipment has been installed. Thus, serious disequilibrium now exists between the amount of gas demanded and the amount the industry is capable of supplying, not only at its current controlled price, but at its long-run equilibrium price as well. This disequilibrium is superimposed over what appears to be the rising cost of gas, which will not level off until either the delivered cost of gas is greater than that of alternative fuels so that consumption shifts to other fuels, or new gas sources (perhaps synthetic gas or imported natural gas) become economic at the higher domestic natural gas price.

Complicating this whole situation is the division of the field market for natural gas into regulated and unregulated segments. In the regulated interstate markets, high-priority existing consumers, such as residential users, have both security of supply and low prices, while other consumers get no gas at all. In the unregulated markets in the gas-producing states, on the other hand, everyone can get gas, and the price consumers pay, while higher than that in the regulated market, is lower than it would be if interstate consumers who are now forced to do without could bid for the supply. The expectations created by this division have led to different consumption patterns in each market, the implications of which must be considered in future policy decisions.

Optimal adjustment toward a long-run equilibrium in the natural gas market would affect both production and consumption. Deregulation of natural gas that had not previously been consigned to interstate markets would be one means to achieve this adjustment. On the supply side, deregulation would prompt new exploration and more intensive development of known reservoirs. At a higher price, the amount of gas marketed would also be increased because the amount wasted, used in the field, or used for producing petroleum would fall owing to its higher value. Finally, decontrol and the rising prices it would induce would encourage the development of synthetic natural gas and the expansion of liquefied natural gas imports at rates that would minimize total energy costs to the economy.

On the demand side, the gradually higher price resulting from deregulation would increase the value produced by the gas actually brought to the market. Substitution of other fuels for gas would be encouraged, thus freeing gas for use where its special characteristics were most valuable. Such opportunities are greatest in currently un-controlled intrastate markets, where most of the industrial consumption of gas takes place. Natural gas prices in those markets are more nearly in equilibrium with those of other fuels, and hence a relatively small rise in the gas price will result in voluntary fuel switching, espe-cially in uses such as petroleum refining and electric generation. Only if all gas prices rise will new patterns of use and investment in conser-vation be encouraged for all consumers, even those who cannot switch to other fuels. Decontrol would allow each consumer flexibility to adjust fuel use and consumption patterns so as to ensure that no gas was used except in such a way that it made a maximum contribution to meeting human wants.

Despite the harmful effects on some consumers, gradual decontrol of natural gas would reduce the cost of energy to the economy, not increase it. In essence, the higher prices and fuel switching occasioned for some consumers would make gas supplies available to those for whom the alternatives are worse.[5] The inefficiencies and inequities of the present system are disguised, but its benefits to some are large and obvious. In contrast, decontrol would bring obvious losses to some but widely dispersed and less readily visible benefits to the economy generally. On the whole, the economy would benefit from the more efficient use of energy and other resources that decontrol would bring.

The Carter proposal is not for decontrol. It would extend price controls to all natural gas, make them permanent, raise the controlled price for some gas that is now regulated, and impose a tax on some gas uses. It goes part of the way toward achieving a more efficient use of resources, but in some ways it makes the situation worse than it is at present. If the Carter proposal is enacted, producers would prob-ably explore for and produce less gas than they do now; almost cer-tainly they would produce less than if prices were decontrolled. A special tax-rebate scheme for some industrial uses of gas will encour-age switching to other fuels as it raises gas prices nearer replacement

5. Decontrol would also transfer "rent" from consumers who obtain gas at less than its replacement cost to owners of the right to produce gas. See the discussion of energy taxes below for comments on a possible means of reducing the windfalls involved in decontrol of new gas prices.

costs. But gas consumers not covered by that phase of the program will pay less than the replacement cost of the fuel they use; if they are allocated supplies, those in the previously unregulated markets will pay less than under the existing system. Further, the expected future price of gas to nonindustrial consumers will be reduced. Conservation will be discouraged.

In short, these proposals will not eliminate the gas shortage; they will partially disguise it and extend it to the markets that are now uncontrolled. In addition, they will remove the market test for supplemental gas supplies and encourage investment in uneconomic facilities and processes.

Policy Instruments with Small Budget Impact

Energy is produced and consumed predominantly in the private sector; hence much of federal policy is exercised through instruments that affect final energy use and output decisions only indirectly. While such influence may be large, its direct effect on the federal budget is small. Policy instruments with small budget impact include some that affect energy prices, some that alter energy supply more directly, and others that change the amount of energy consumed.

Federal energy price controls exist alongside substantial private discretion in energy matters. Unlike the usual market condition where output and consumption are directly connected through price, these elements are somewhat separated under existing energy policy, yet shortages do not develop. This peculiar arrangement can exist because of the role played by imported petroleum as the balancing supplementary source of energy. Foreign oil is allowed entry in unlimited quantities at the world price, and hence domestic oil prices can be held below world market levels without rationing. The situation with natural gas is somewhat different because imported oil and gas can make up only part of the gap; rationing is required in the price-controlled market. Thus the major energy-sector result of existing oil and natural gas price controls is higher levels of oil imports than would exist without them.

If the level of oil imports is perceived as a problem in itself, however, and imports are to be reduced, the situation changes markedly. The energy system loses its ability to adjust to price controls, and the government must be more directly involved in determining energy use and production. Under these conditions, a choice among policies implies selection of the combination of prices, incentives, and restraints that leads to the mix of oil imports, energy consumption, and domestic energy production desired by the government.

The same relationship exists with regard to adjustments of energy consumption and production in the future. When energy prices are not allowed to reflect future scarcity of energy resources, adjustment of future energy consumption to the availability of energy requires explicit government direction. The private sector will no longer automatically bring forth new energy sources through exploration, development, and research to meet future demands; likewise, future demand will no longer automatically be affected by changes in consumption patterns and energy-using capital stock in response to expected energy prices. Again, explicit government decisions are required on prices to be set, research and development to be funded, and changes in consumption to be induced.

Policies Affecting Prices

Government power may be used to set energy prices above or below the real cost of energy to the economy as measured by the value of the resources expended in its acquisition. Prices are held below costs by controls or subsidies for energy production, and raised above costs by taxes on energy consumption.

The thrust of the Carter proposals on energy prices is to raise them gradually to most consumers through taxes and special measures, while controlling the price of most oil and gas produced domestically. This policy mix is intended to lower oil imports by reducing oil consumption; it does not provide much incentive to increase domestic oil and gas supply. To obtain the target oil import level, energy consumption must therefore be kept lower, and coal and nuclear power use higher, than it would be through a policy mix that relied on deregulated prices, assisted as necessary by general taxes on oil and gas consumption and subsidies to energy production.

The regulatory approach espoused by Carter will require a set of policy instruments to direct energy consumption by fuel form, geographic region, and end use. Energy use patterns would thus be responsive to political decisions. In the proposals announced so far, economic incentives (through taxes and subsidies) rather than specific rules and regulations predominate among these instruments. A more market-oriented policy would rely more on domestic supply, and would require less government direction of the energy sector, although income distribution and macroeconomic issues would require more attention.

Crude oil prices are currently regulated through a complex structure that seeks to differentiate oil produced through investment made before the 1973–74 price increases from that produced pursuant to investment decisions made since. In practice, any quantity of oil less than the amount flowing from a reservoir in the base period is considered "lower-tier" oil and gets a lower price, while quantities above that amount are "upper-tier" oil, which gets a higher but still controlled price. "Stripper" oil, defined as oil from wells whose open flow has fallen below ten barrels of oil a day, is not subject to price controls; it is classed as upper-tier oil in calculating the composite price for regulatory purposes.

The price of lower-tier oil has not been changed since 1973; the price of upper-tier oil is set so that the composite price is equal to the amount allowed by statute. Under existing law, the statutory composite price rises gradually in real terms, and the President is free to escalate the rate of increase unless Congress disapproves. Mandatory controls lapse in mid-1979, though the President retains the discretion to limit oil prices until 1981. Price treatment of crude oil from the Alaskan north slope has not been settled. Even if no controls were imposed, however, the Alaskan wellhead price would probably be below the upper-tier price because of the high pipeline transportation charges that must be absorbed before that oil can enter markets in competition with OPEC oil. Table 10-2 shows the estimated wellhead price allowed upper-tier and lower-tier oil since 1973, and compares it with the average domestic wellhead price (including stripper oil) and the refinery acquisition cost of imported oil.

The major policy issue concerning crude oil price controls is whether to have them at all, and at what level prices should be set. Ignoring for the moment the additional domestic energy supply that would come forward if controls were eliminated, abolition of crude oil price controls would remove the substantial enforcement and compliance costs of the program. In addition, it would remove losses in potential petroleum output due to uncertainty about future regulatory decisions and climate and to the distortions created by the controls themselves. The present multiple price system leads to the use of more

Table 10-2. Oil Prices per Barrel, 1973-77

Constant 1976 dollars[a]

| Month and year | Domestic wellhead crude oil | | | Imported crude oil[c] |
	Lower tier	Upper tier	Average[b]	
August 1973	5.00	5.00	5.00	5.75
December 1973	6.49	12.27	8.37	10.61
1973	5.29	5.29	5.29	n.a.
1974	5.75	11.58	7.85	14.31
1975	5.26	12.58	8.02	14.57
1976p	5.13	11.69	8.18	13.47
January 1977p	5.03	11.13	8.27	13.73
February 1977p	5.00	11.00	8.25	13.96

Source: Federal Energy Administration.
n.a. Not available.
p Preliminary.
a. Calculated from the official wholesale price index for all commodities.
b. Includes some oil not controlled due to exceptions in legislation.
c. Refiner acquisition cost, which includes transportation from the port of entry to the refinery.

real resources in producing a given amount of oil than need be used. Producers have no incentive to spend more than $5.00 to produce another barrel of lower-tier oil, but every incentive to spend much more for a barrel of upper-tier oil. Hence some lower-tier oil is left in the ground, while more resources than would be required to get it are expended in getting oil from an upper-tier source (and still more in replacing it with imported oil). Permanent retention of controls, with the addition of yet another higher-priced but still controlled tier for "new" oil, as President Carter proposes, would substantially increase administrative costs and open the prospect for more frequent disputes and greater distortion and inefficiency in production. On the other hand, the Carter proposal of a wellhead petroleum tax, which would equalize in stages the cost of all petroleum to refiners, would simplify controls by eliminating the need for the current array of complex and tortuous special provisions designed to prevent inequity among refiners who now buy different proportions of regulated and unregulated crude oil.

Given controls of any sort, the higher the price of oil, the greater the quantity produced domestically and the lower the amount imported. The nation gives up resources equal to the full cost of oil purchased abroad; at the same time, to the extent that domestic production can be increased at the same price, some of those resources are not actually used up but represent rents and profits that can be taxed away or reinvested in further production. There is thus a net economic loss to the nation when oil is imported that could be produced domestically at the same price. Hence, if there are to be controls, the higher and more certain the crude oil price allowed producers, the lower the penalty the controls will impose on the economy.

The prices of some petroleum products are also controlled at the refiner and reseller level, volumes of product transferred between parties are regulated, and parties are required to remain linked in buyer-seller relationships unless formal approval is obtained from the Federal Energy Administration. These highly detailed, complex, and cumbersome regulations were adopted at the time of the 1973–74 shortage and have since been frequently expanded, adjusted, and amended in a mostly futile effort to lessen their more wasteful effects. This system has, of course, improved the position of the special interests that have the skill and political influence to affect the decisions reached. In a report issued in late 1976, an interagency task force reviewed the operations of the Federal Energy Administration and recommended removal of these regulations, on grounds that they were counterproductive in normal supply periods because they raised prices to consumers, lowered competition, and imposed substantial administrative and compliance costs (about half a billion dollars a year) on the economy.

In the discussion of existing natural gas price and allocation controls above, it was shown that the domestic supply of energy (gas) has been reduced by controls. In addition, energy (oil) imports have been increased. Thus the cost to the economy of energy as a whole has been increased. Since the higher energy cost has been paid in part through the inability of some consumers to get gas at all, the level of economic output has probably been depressed more than it would have been by price increases, which would have balanced supply and demand. Other resources have been used inefficiently as adjustments have been made—including industry location changes —because of this particular regulatory system with its multiple price structure and differential availability of gas.

Petroleum and natural gas price and allocation controls have been maintained because of their presumed effects on income and wealth distribution, on the level of economic activity, and on inflation. Additional domestic supply and a more productive use of resources have thus been traded off for lower energy prices to consumers. Table 10-3

Table 10-3. Prices Paid by Consumers for Major Energy Fuels, Selected Years, 1950-76

Constant 1976 dollars[a]

Year	Gasoline[b] (cents per gallon)		Fuel oil[c] (No. 2, cents per gallon)	Electricity[d] (dollars per million Btu)	Natural gas[d] (dollars per million Btu)
	Excluding tax	Including tax			
1950	47.5	63.3	n.a.	20.00	2.01
1955	45.6	61.9	n.a.	16.53	1.91
1960	40.4	59.9	28.9	13.92	1.92
1965	37.4	56.2	29.0	11.90	1.82
1970	36.0	52.3	27.1	9.02	1.55
1971	35.4	51.2	27.6	9.03	1.58
1972	33.3	49.2	26.8	9.13	1.62
1973	34.4	49.7	29.1	8.94	1.60
1974	46.7	60.5	41.6	9.57	1.64
1975	48.1	60.6	41.2	10.00	1.79
1976e	47.4	59.5	41.8	10.23	1.98

Sources: Gasoline and fuel oil, American Petroleum Institute, *"Basic Petroleum Data Book"* (processed), sec. 6, tables 4 and 5, and for 1976, API, Department of Statistics; electricity and natural gas, American Gas Association, *Gas Facts, A Statistical Record of the Gas Utility Industry: 1975 Data* (AGA, 1976), pp. 111 and 115, and for 1976, AGA, Department of Statistics.

n.a. Not available.
e Estimate.
a. Calculated from the consumer price index.
b. Regular grade, price at the pump.
c. Annual average retail price including all applicable taxes.
d. Residential use.

shows that, partly because of price controls, unit energy prices to consumers in real terms have not risen substantially since the 1973–74 surge imposed by OPEC, and have not kept pace with the rise in energy replacement costs. The failure to consume less energy is consistent with energy prices that have not risen much in real terms. It is also consistent with unit energy costs that have fallen relative to real income. Gasoline, electricity, and natural gas prices are lower or about the same as they were in 1950, when income levels were substantially lower.

The petroleum and natural gas price and allocation systems have benefited some economic interests. "Small" refiners, some entrenched petroleum product wholesalers and retailers, northeastern energy users, high-priority interstate natural gas consumers, and intrastate natural gas consumers are among those favored at the cost of other energy-producing, distributing, and using interests and of the economy as a whole. Joining them in support for controls are those who believe that the effect of controls is to improve the lot of lower-income groups and to lessen unemployment and inflation.

Policies Affecting Supply

The federal government can affect energy supply directly by research and development (discussed below), environmental quality and human health and safety policies, energy import and export policy, and leasing and production policies for mineral deposits on federal lands.

Environmental and safety issues have been especially important in delaying development of Alaskan and Outer Continental Shelf oil and gas resources, in slowing the deployment of nuclear power, and in reducing the use of coal. In the future they may be even more important in reducing energy supply from oil shale, coal gasification, and coal production. Supply reduction has come directly through prohibitions and regulations and indirectly through the uncertainty and cost engendered by slow, changing, complex, and somewhat unpredictable decision processes. This last is susceptible to reform, and President Carter has promised better administration and requested improved procedures, including some that would lead to less delay and more certainty in decisions, and thus more production. The fact remains, however, that energy production and use inevitably affect the environment, so a trade-off cannot be avoided. The energy-environment trade-off is also affected by the remainder of the energy policy mix. For example, to the extent that prices charged by energy producers are allowed to rise, they can afford to produce more while still meeting environmental requirements. President Carter's goal of maintaining or improving environmental quality and safety is thus inconsistent with holding energy prices to producers down; the two can be reconciled only through other policies that lower consumption still more, or else by relaxation of the import target.

Direct restriction of oil imports has been suggested to reduce dependence on OPEC oil, but this would raise the cost of energy to U.S. consumers just as taxes and conservation measures do. In essence, this would mean that OPEC's threat to withhold oil would be defused because we had already imposed the loss upon ourselves (though in a way that would avoid the extra cost of a sudden impact). Still, the full cost of importing oil is not now met by the price paid for that oil.

Private buyers are not induced to make preparation for possible supply restrictions, and that cost is thus not passed forward in the price of oil. A tariff or charge to cover these security costs would eliminate this subsidy and restrict imports as well.

Natural gas imports from abroad present difficult policy problems. For at least the foreseeable future, any foreign source of gas supply would tend to be linked to a single gas transportation and distribution system because of the special technology involved. If one supplier refused to continue to sell gas, no other would have excess capacity to make up the difference. The market power of the gas exporter would thus be very great; by refusing to deliver he can impose actual physical shortages on importers, at a cost to him merely of the delay in receiving payment for gas in the ground. The likelihood of economic or political pressure through threats of gas supply reduction would be lessened if the exporting country bore more of the burden of any interruption. That burden would be more evenly divided if the gas exporter owned both the gas liquefaction plant and the tankers used for transportation, and thus lost productivity of invested capital as well as suffered delay in obtaining income from gas sales. Vulnerability would also be lessened if the consuming system relied on the imported gas for only a portion of its supply. The Federal Power Commission's authority over natural gas imports could be used to make their approval conditional upon meeting these and other security-enhancing criteria.

The rate of exploitation of the mineral deposits controlled by the federal government is important in affecting energy supply because at present the most promising potential supply sources are found on federal lands. Leasing policies are thus among the most important determinants of mid-term production of oil, gas, and coal.

Policies Affecting Demand

Federal conservation actions can usefully be divided into those which lead energy users to do what they would do in any case if it were not for informational or institutional impediments, and those which require less energy to be used. In the first case, when energy users are given the information they need to balance the life-cycle cost of more energy-efficient against less energy-efficient appliances, or of space conditioning cost with and without insulation, they may choose the energy-conserving route. Without that information, lower initial cost may sway them to buy the less energy-efficient item or not to make energy-conserving investments. Alternatively, when institutional barriers to energy-saving practices—such as excessive minimum lighting standards or air flow for buildings—are removed, consumers again can follow their preferences and save energy at the same time. An important measure proposed by President Carter along the same lines would require individual metering of energy service to apartments and businesses. With individual metering, consumers can save money when they save energy, and are thus induced to do so.

The issues involved in requiring or subsidizing lower levels of energy use are more complex and controversial. Mandatory conservation measures are, in effect, selective energy price increases, taxes, or subsidies. They lead to the substitution of other resources for energy (more insulation in homes, for example) or to loss of satisfaction as consumers are unable to follow practices or obtain goods they want (such as higher speeds on highways, or larger cars). Such measures affect the distribution of the costs of less energy use and raise costs, through requiring more use of other resources. An alternative instrument, combining prices with a general energy tax, would induce consumers to use energy efficiently in all its applications and to reduce energy use on the basis of individual estimates of its benefits. Mandatory measures, in contrast, apply only to some energy applications and represent the government's view of what uses should be curtailed. Measures requiring fuel switching (for example, electric generation from oil and gas to coal) to reduce consumption of oil and natural gas fall in this class of actions; they may be thought of as taxes to achieve a reduction in use of a fuel form by one sector alone.

Preference for the use of mandatory conservation measures instead of using a price and tax instrument to reduce demand implies that government should redistribute well-being through use of energy measures, or else that, given some level of energy consumption, private decisions about the way it is used are inferior to those of government. In practice, however, the choice of mandatory conservation measures may follow from the view that a preferable alternative is politically impossible, but that the reduction in energy use is nonetheless worth its cost.

Policy Instruments with Large Budget Impact

Federal energy policy instruments can also have a significant effect on the budget in their application to energy consumption, domestic energy production, and oil imports. Expenditures, especially for energy research and development, have been rising rapidly. The strategic petroleum storage program may cost as much as $15 billion over the next few years. On the other hand, energy excise taxes already amount to about $5 billion a year, and tax proposals offered by President Carter could lead to as much as $70 billion moving through the Treasury in 1985. Table 10-4 summarizes the major items of budget authority and budget receipts in the Ford and Carter administrations' submissions to Congress before Carter's April 20, 1977, energy message.

The Strategic Petroleum Reserve

Oil-exporting nations have the power and have demonstrated the will to restrict oil exports. Such restrictions could raise the effective price of oil (paid partially, perhaps, in shortages) sufficiently to be economically disruptive. Furthermore, the United States cannot insulate itself from the problems of its more vulnerable trading partners should their oil supplies fall. Fear of such disruptions tends to constrain the diplomatic freedom of the United States and weaken its allies. Hence, minimizing the potential disruption occasioned by the action of oil exporters is a major U.S. policy objective. One means of furthering that goal is through creation of a strategic petroleum reserve; another is membership in the International Energy Authority which provides for sharing of shortages in an emergency.

The reserve would be drawn on to supplement private inventories, consumption reductions, and energy supplies from other sources if supplies from established exporters were restricted.[6] This program was authorized by the Energy Policy and Conservation Act of 1975, which required 150 million barrels of stored oil by December 1978

6. Decisions about the use of the reserve in an emergency would be difficult. Premature use would leave the nation exposed to serious harm if the supply emergency outlasted the oil reserve. Excessive restraint in using the reserve, on the other hand, would lead to unnecessary hardship. The 1973–74 embargo period was characterized by such restraint; private inventories of oil actually increased in response to the allocation decisions adopted. Clear decision rules are difficult to formulate but probably should be established before any emergency and should remain secret.

Table 10-4. Budget Authority and Budget Receipts, Selected Agencies and Programs Affecting Energy, Fiscal Years 1976–78

Millions of dollars

Agency and program	1976 actual	1977 estimate	1978 Ford submission	1978 Carter submission
Budget authority				
Federal Energy Administration	466	646	2,449	3,856
Programs	153	155	258	344
Strategic petroleum reserve	313	491	2,191	3,512
(plus allocation from naval petroleum reserve)	...	44	502	502
Energy Research and Development Administration (nonmilitary)	2,833	4,454	5,461	5,373
Direct energy research	1,858	3,010	4,015	3,921
Uranium enrichment	384	783	719	719
(plus enrichment revenues)	629	699	966	966
Basic research and technology development	320	373	430	430
Other	271	288	297	303
Geological Survey	273	316	354	354
Bureau of Mines (mines and minerals)	159	166	161	161
Federal Power Commission	37	43	43	43
Mining Enforcement and Safety Administration	84	97	106	106
Total budget authority	**3,851**	**5,721**	**8,573**	**9,892**
Including allocation from naval petroleum reserve and enrichment revenues	4,480	6,464	10,041	11,360
Budget receipts				
Rents and royalties				
Outer Continental Shelf	2,662	2,600	3,100	3,400
Other[b]	393	390	529	529
Excise taxes[c]	4,358	4,944	5,126	5,126
Total budget receipts	**7,413**	**7,934**	**8,755**	**9,055**

Sources: *The Budget of the United States Government, Fiscal Year 1978*, and ibid., *Appendix;* Office of Management and Budget, *Fiscal Year 1978 Budget Revisions, February 1977;* Federal Energy Administration, "Budget Amendment, Fiscal Year 1978: Submission to Congress" (processed); U.S. Energy Research and Development Administration, "Narrative Highlights: FY1978 Budget to Congress" (n.d.; processed), and ibid., "Revised FY1978 Budget to Congress" (February 1977; processed); and data from ERDA, Office of the Comptroller. Figures are rounded.

a. Subject to further revision on the basis of the April 20, 1977, message.
b. Primarily energy.
c. Highway and airport trust fund receipts and excise tax on gasoline.

and about 500 million by 1982, and authorized storage of up to 1 billion barrels.

Crude petroleum can be stored in a few large installations and, in an emergency, withdrawn for refining and distribution, or else petroleum products can be stored in dispersed locations near final markets. The crude oil option is substantially less expensive and does not result in significant regional differences in security. It has been favored in all official proposals.

The proper ultimate size of the reserve is conceptually clear but operationally difficult to determine. The storage program should be of such a size that the present discounted cost of the incremental storage would be equal to the present expected value of the incremental disruption that it prevents. While impossible to quantify precisely, this optimal size would be substantially smaller than the estimate of the largest future net supply reduction. The Ford budget envisioned 500 million barrels by 1982, while President Carter proposes acquiring this amount by 1980, and 1 billion barrels by 1985. The budget effect of the more rapid buildup is striking: it would cost $1.3 billion more for fiscal year 1978.

The capital cost of the storage facilities is about $1.50 per barrel, or $1.5 billion for the billion-barrel program. The actual cost to the national economy of the oil fill, regardless of the source of purchase or its apparent cost, is determined by the price of imported oil at the time the oil is stored, because imported oil is the incremental source of petroleum. Based on 1977 prices, 1 billion barrels would cost about $14.5 billion; the 1954 amendments to the Merchant Marine Act, which require that 50 percent of goods purchased by government be transported by American ships if they are available, could add substantially to this amount. On the other hand, if the oil were acquired at an average price reflecting the controls that now exist on domestic oil, the budget appropriation would be lowered by about $3 billion.

Decisions about the size of the reserve should be based on its true cost. That cost does not include the possible subsidy to U.S. shipping (which should be charged against whatever function it is presumed to serve). It does include oil fill at world prices, reduced neither by the subterfuge of using naval petroleum reserve receipts (about $0.5 billion in fiscal 1978) nor by acquiring price-controlled oil. The annual cost of the strategic petroleum reserve after it is completed would include small maintenance expenditures ($10–$20 million) and about $1.5 billion as the opportunity cost of carrying the investment at the usual 10 percent rate.

Energy Research and Development

Energy research and development is concentrated in the Energy Research and Development Administration, though some activities are found elsewhere in government. The proportion of total effort devoted to nonnuclear programs has been growing since the agency was formed; the overall level of effort has risen substantially. Total energy research and development requests remained about the same in President Carter's February budget revision as in the original Ford 1978 budget (see table 10-5).

THRUST OF THE CARTER BUDGET. Compared to previous budgets, the Carter budget for energy research, development, and demonstration moves toward nearer-term results, toward development and demonstration, and away from research with more distant results. The emphasis is more on reducing demand and less on increasing energy supply. On the supply side, the focus is on additional expenditures for more technically certain and near-term measures, rather than less technically certain, more distant, but potentially more effective technologies.

The near-term focus of the Carter research and development budget is necessary given the other elements of his energy program and the concern for reducing dependence on imports. Unfortunately, however, there is a lag in the effect of many research and development efforts on energy production and consumption because of the low rate of turnover of capital stock and the slow adoption of new processes. Moreover, even with controlled prices, some of the effort devoted to near-term, almost commercial projects replaces expenditures that would be undertaken by the private sector if not preempted by the actual and threatened federal presence. Hence the net effect of federal expenditures of this sort is smaller than the sum of expected direct results from the specific programs. These factors make careful selection and management of the near-term research and development program critical, and imply that it may require larger federal expenditures than might otherwise be anticipated.

It is uncertain whether the federal energy research and development budget can grow enough to fulfill the role it is forced to play by

Table 10-5. Budget Authority for the Energy Research and Development Administration, Selected Programs, Fiscal Years 1976 and 1977, and Ford and Carter Submissions, 1978

Millions of dollars

Program	1976 actual	1977 estimate	1978 Ford sub-mission	1978 Carter sub-mission[a]
Total	1,654	2,643	3,598	3,499
Research and development for energy conservation	76	161	160	318
Electric energy systems and energy storage	39	60	58	90
Transportation	13	28	36	86
Improved conversion efficiency	7	24	33	56
Buildings and community systems	12	27	22	52
Fossil energy development	426	483	893	940
Coal	362	409	504	527
Petroleum and natural gas	43	43	53	72
Oil shale and in situ technology	21	31	42	42
Solar energy development	115	290	305	305
Thermal application	44	94	55	100
Solar electric applications	64	172	224	176
Geothermal energy development	31	55	88	88
Fusion power development	247	416	513	433
Liquid metal fast breeder technology	505	686	855	656
Clinch River breeder reactor	170	238	235	150
Other	335	448	620	506
Nuclear fuel cycle and safeguards	167	406	636	611
Fuel cycle	54	217	380	380
Uranium resource assessment	18	36	65	a
Support of nuclear fuel cycle	26	76	140	a
Waste management (commercial)	13	105	175	a
Safeguards	16	31	41	41
Advanced isotope separation technology	30	47	57	52
Uranium process development	64	110	159	139
Other fission	87	146	148	148

Sources: U.S. Energy Research and Development Administration, Office of the Comptroller, and ERDA, "Narrative Highlights," cited in table 10-4. Figures are rounded.

a. Subject to further revision.

the Carter energy program. There will be strong competition for the budget dollar and considerable resistance to expanding the proportion of total output going to the public sector. If the energy and development budget does not grow adequately, rising proportions of it would be required to support current energy requirements, and lesser amounts would be available for research of the sort that could smooth the transition to new energy sources. The possible long-term consequences of the emphasis in the Carter energy research budget program are thus important. Unless substantial increases in future budget expenditures are realized, lower short-term energy prices are being traded off against possible disruptively higher future energy costs. These implications are explored below.

CRITERIA FOR RESEARCH AND DEVELOPMENT DECISIONS. The goals of energy research and development are to lessen the prospective cost of performing the functions energy performs—getting energy cheaper and using less of it for each unit of output—and shifting use away from natural gas and imported oil. These goals include making energy production and use safer and less damaging to health and the environment.

Federally sponsored research and development should complement, not substitute for, that performed in the private sector. Otherwise, energy costs are shifted from energy consumers to taxpayers, and energy consumption becomes subsidized. Federal expenditure on energy research and development is most productive when it is used to support activity that yields social benefits that are not capable of being realized through private-sector operations.

The proper framework within which to approach federal energy research decisions is to compare the present value of the future cost of a project with the discounted present expected value (including contributions to security) of the difference between the future cost of all energy if the project is pursued and if it is not. Thus the wisdom of initiating or abandoning any one project depends in part on which others are pursued, and with what success. The fact that a technology would be adopted when developed (because it would be cheaper) does not by itself indicate that it should be pursued; it may cost more to develop than it is worth. It also follows that as one project moves closer to success, the value of all other projects declines because their expected contribution to lowering future energy cost falls. The timing of prospective expenditures, prospective contributions to lowering energy costs, and the rate of discount chosen are also critical in making decisions regarding research and development programs. What all this means is that all energy research and development decisions must be considered simultaneously, and reexamined frequently. Recent decisions about the breeder reactor illustrate this point.

THE BREEDER REACTOR PROGRAM. The breeder reactor program has been the largest single energy research and development effort pursued; it was budgeted at almost $700 million in fiscal year 1977. The breeder reactor, as its name implies, creates more fuel than it uses up. In the liquid metal fast breeder reactor the reactions that produce heat for electric power also convert nonfissile uranium-238 (99.3 percent of the total) to plutonium-239, which can be used in other reactors. The breeder reactor thus utilizes an energy technology that, in principle, could place a cap on future escalations in the cost of energy.[7]

The danger of the proliferation of nuclear weapons capability is regarded by most experts as the major issue concerning the liquid metal fast breeder reactor, since the plutonium it produces can be used to make nuclear weapons. The difficult questions are the extent to which U.S. refusal to deploy this technology will reduce the rate of nuclear weapons spread to additional nations, the effect that reduction would have on the prospects for world peace, and the economic and other costs at which that effect would be achieved. Thus, uncertain costs and benefits must be weighed. President Carter's decision to delay indefinitely deployment of plutonium breeder technology, and the rationale for that decision, is consistent with the view that, while the proliferation danger avoided might be small, the cost advantages of the plutonium breeder would probably be even smaller for some time to come. The decision not to deploy thus should be reconsidered if the underlying assumptions prove wrong. Meanwhile, it has important implications for other parts of the energy development effort, as well as for breeder reactor research itself.

The potential advantage of the plutonium breeder over the uranium light water reactor depends on lower nuclear fuel cost offsetting higher reactor cost. Without the breeder, nuclear power costs will rise with fuel costs. Light water reactor fuel costs depend upon the cost of uranium and the cost of enriching (concentrating) its fissile isotope U-235 from the 0.7 percent level found in nature to the 3 percent required. While little is known with adequate certainty about the dimensions of the domestic or world supply of uranium, the Nuclear

7. Other alternatives are possible, but the liquid metal fast breeder reactor technology appears more certain and nearest to deployment. Prototype breeders of this type are now operating abroad, and experience with them appears to promise technical and economic success.

Energy Policy Study Group[8] concluded that enough uranium was reasonably assured to permit postponement of deployment of plutonium breeder technology without a significant cost penalty. The decision to defer planned deployment of the breeder, then, adds urgency to the task of ascertaining how much uranium will be ultimately available, at what cost, and on what time schedule. It also makes research aimed at lowering the cost of mining and processing poorer-grade ores more important.

The amount of natural uranium required to produce a given amount of power in a light water reactor depends upon the degree to which separation and concentration of its fissile isotope is carried. The smaller the proportion of fissile material left in the main body of the uranium after the separation process, the less uranium must be found and mined to produce a given amount of electricity, but the greater the separative work, and hence enrichment capacity, required. The amount of separative work rises disproportionately as the proportion of the fissile isotope recovered rises. Consequently, research and development directed at lowering the cost of isotopic separation is made more important by the breeder decision, as are additions to enrichment capacity.

Another area affected by the breeder decision are those actions that influence the growth in electricity demand to be met by nuclear power. The more rapidly electricity demand grows, the more rapidly uranium costs will rise, and the higher the cost of delay in the deployment of the fuel-efficient breeder reactor. Additionally, the greater the growth rate in electricity demand, the less feasible is reliance upon unproven alternatives to existing technology. The breeder decision thus implies increased value for research to reduce electricity demand, to increase the ability to use coal, and to find nonelectric alternatives to which to switch demand from oil and gas. It suggests expanded exploration of other nuclear options, such as the thorium cycle, and efforts to make the plutonium breeder more benign through institutional and technological developments that will allow its energy potential to be realized safely. In effect, one opportunity to lower prospective energy costs has been delayed for now—the corollary is that the value of opening other options is raised.

8. *Nuclear Power Issues and Choices,* Report of the Nuclear Energy Policy Study Group (Ballinger for the Ford Foundation, 1977).

Outside the United States, energy choices are more limited, so the relatively small advantages—including contribution to energy independence—claimed for the plutonium breeder here are much larger abroad. The only effective way the United States can now restrain plutonium proliferation through electricity production is to offer other nations an economic alternative to it. Consequently, the final effect of the breeder decision is to increase the potential contribution to world peace from developing exportable energy technology and resources that may be deployed with safety in other nations. As a minimum first step, the United States must be seen to be a reliable supplier of enriched uranium, and to achieve this end, additional enrichment capacity is required.

THE FUSION PROGRAM. The fusion reactor, like the breeder reactor, offers the possibility of an effectively limitless source of power. Fusion research decisions are illuminated by two factors. First, the technology may not work; if it works, it is unlikely to be available until well into the next century; and, even if it is finally available, its costs may prove so high or its environmental or other attributes so harmful as to preclude its use. Thus the United States cannot afford to depend on fusion technology. Second, fusion technology is competitive with the fission breeder and with other energy sources on which long-term dependence might be placed. If fusion were developed fast enough and proved satisfactory, electricity demand could possibly be met without using breeder or other advanced nuclear fission technology and without discontinuous jumps in electricity costs.

However, fusion technology is not yet at the stage where its development can be substantially speeded simply by increasing the level of research effort. Basic scientific questions remain to be answered, essentially in sequential steps. The fusion program, budgeted at $433 million for fiscal year 1978, more nearly approaches basic than applied research.

THE FOSSIL FUEL PROGRAM. Fossil fuels, imported and domestic, provide the great bulk of the energy used in the United States and will continue to do so through at least the remainder of this century. While domestic coal deposits are large and the use of coal is increasing, domestic petroleum and natural gas reserves are much smaller in relation to their rate of use. The objectives of the federal fossil fuel program, which is funded at almost $1 billion in the Carter budget, are to increase domestic production of petroleum and natural gas, increase the utilization of coal, and facilitate the use of oil shale.

The proper role and scope of the fossil fuel program depends importantly on other parts of the government's energy policy and on the potential availability of oil imports. If prices of oil and natural gas are allowed to reach market-clearing levels, most of the socially attractive research and development opportunities for supply enhancement and increased use of coal and oil shale would be exploited in the private sector. If they are not, government action may be necessary to avoid undue supply shortfalls and unnecessary reliance on imported oil. If oil imports could be relied upon to respond to economic rather than political forces, they would appear to be a less costly supply alternative than synthetic liquids or gases, perhaps for some decades, even if domestic production were not encouraged. Again, necessary government support of research and development in synthetic technologies would be limited. Existing price controls, President Carter's proposed program, and the political aspects of reliance on oil imports, however, may have together added sufficient uncertainty to intermediate-term energy supply and demand as to dictate a more activist role for government-sponsored research in this area.

The petroleum and natural gas supply enhancement program would reduce oil imports modestly in the intermediate term and lessen the pressures that would otherwise accompany the decline in domestic oil and gas production. It would not, however, much affect oil cost to the consumer because that depends on the world price of oil, of which additional U.S. production would be a small part.

The coal program has different implications. First, if environmentally benign, safe, and economical coal conversion to electricity could be increased, deployment of alternatives, including the breeder reactor, could be delayed at a lower cost. Second, economically attractive conversion of coal to synthetic liquids and gases would delay the switch of end-use technologies away from these fuel forms. To be most useful, information on these possibilities should be available by the time when fuel switching would have to begin and when decisions on deployment of the breeder reactor or other new nuclear technologies would need to be reassessed—that is, by about 1990. Present technologies are not competitive at current prices, and opportunities for basic research remain.

There are two major implications of this analysis. One is that research and development effort expended on more effective use of coal in electric power plants is both important and timely, and its results would quickly be put into practice in the private sector. The other is that deployment of current-generation synthetic gas and liquid fuel plants could be achieved only through large subsidies. If it were not for natural gas price regulation and uncertainty about the price and availability of imported oil, such deployment would be obviously undesirable. Under existing circumstances, however, it may be worthwhile to demonstrate existing technology even while concentrating on developing advanced processes for future use. These demonstration projects would provide information on costs and operating experience in case they had to be used, and also could yield information on environmental, social, and other effects common to future technologies. Consequently, support of limited demonstration of technologies known to be uneconomic need not pass the tests required for a decision to deploy such technologies on a large scale. The important element in the decision to demonstrate a technology should be the project's potential information contribution, not its early contribution to fuel supply or its individual economic viability.

SOLAR ENERGY. The solar water heating and space conditioning program is designed to reduce the demand for conventional energy sources in the near future. This technology must overcome serious economic and institutional barriers before it can make a noticeable impact on energy use. Its commercial acceptability depends mostly on the cost of competing conventional fuels, and is thus hindered by price controls on oil and gas and by electric utility rate structures that do not present consumers at the margin with the full replacement cost of electric energy. Among the institutional problems that must be resolved are restrictive building codes, the lack of legal status of rights to the sun, and the lack of a supply and maintenance infrastructure. President Carter has requested more state-of-the-art solar technology demonstration units than were sought in the Ford budget. The additional units will not utilize markedly improved technology, nor will they provide much information on how the general public will react to solar heating and how it can be integrated into existing communities and energy delivery systems. From the point of view of achieving national energy goals, the benefit from this $45 million doubling of the solar heating and space conditioning budget is largely symbolic; it demonstrates a commitment to the solar idea, not to solar energy use itself.

Electricity production from the sun absorbs the bulk of research expenditures on solar energy. Budget requests were $172 million in fiscal year 1977, and even though reduced substantially in the Carter February budget revision, remained at $176 million for fiscal 1978. The issue with solar electric power is not technical feasibility but economic viability. This solar electric research effort is premised on the view that this option should be maintained for the future. The Carter administration, by withdrawing most of the authorization request for a scale-up of a solar electric installation, adopted the position that demonstration projects are not ripe for full-scale funding now.

Neither of these solar energy programs is expected to make much difference in energy sources even by the turn of the century. The rapid growth in research and development for all the solar programs has come as a result of intense public and congressional pressure. There is widespread agreement among energy analysts that expenditures have heretofore been rising faster than the funds could be efficiently used.

CONSERVATION. Federal energy conservation activities supported by the Energy Research and Development Administration have three goals: improved operation of central station electric systems, increased application of electricity to replace petroleum, and reduced overall energy consumption. The first two of these goals have been pursued primarily along traditional lines emphasizing fundamental research and efforts with more distant potential results. These programs have grown, and the Carter budget requests for 1978 are up 50 percent from fiscal 1977 levels.

Though portions of the proposed energy conservation research program are devoted to developing cost-effective technology that could not be created privately, a substantial amount of the effort is quite different in nature. The Carter budget reverses earlier decisions that research devoted to narrow industrial applications should be the primary responsibility of the industries benefited and of their capital equipment suppliers. Federal support is proposed for developing processes and technologies to save energy, and money, for specific firms and industries. The budget also includes funds to support deployment of technologies and processes already near adoption by the private sector.

Two issues are raised by programs of this nature. First, by engaging in activity that is in the interest of private firms to do anyway, the government is not adding to the total research activity. Indeed, such programs may discourage private activity when expectations are raised that delay will result in future federal subsidization. Second, federal support of these activities reduces the funding available for the more general and longer-term research that government is uniquely able to carry out.

The activist position that the Carter budget takes on industrial and near-term technologies largely explains the sixfold increase in Energy Research and Development Administration conservation expenditures between fiscal 1976 and 1978. Federal Energy Administration conservation programs have increased even more markedly, with the eightfold 1978 increase over 1976 explained by essentially the same shift toward a more activist set of criteria for programs.

Tax Options

Tax instruments are a central part of the energy policy mix proposed by President Carter. Taxes can form a wedge between the prices received by energy producers and those paid by consumers. Tax expenditures[9] alter the relative cost of different activities and thereby influence consumer and producer behavior. Extensive use of the tax instrument provides a means by which private incentives for efficiency in energy use can be retained, though the levels of energy use and of domestic production is determined by government.

Special energy taxes are not designed to gather revenue but instead to affect private-sector behavior. Revenues thus must be returned to the private sector, but not through measures that encourage energy consumption. The tax expenditure mechanism can absorb revenues in a way that furthers the goals originally sought, as can subsidies that encourage domestic energy production or conservation.

TARIFF ON IMPORTED OIL AND NATURAL GAS. A tariff on imported energy would raise its cost to consumers. If accompanied by

9. See appendix B for an explanation of this term and for a discussion of the effect of tax expenditures on the budget system.

decontrol of domestic oil and gas, a tariff would increase domestic supply because at the higher price more would be produced. In any event, it would lead to less consumption of imported fuels and more consumption of domestic coal and nuclear power, which it would make relatively cheaper. If levied at a rate designed to compensate for the insecurity and other external costs of imported oil, a tariff would transfer those costs (not increase them) from taxpayers to domestic energy consumers, and perhaps to foreign oil producers.[10] For example, a levy of $1 a barrel, or roughly 2.5 cents a gallon, would yield revenues of approximately $3 billion in fiscal year 1978, based on an 8-million barrel a day import level. This amount would more than cover the annual cost of a 1-billion barrel strategic petroleum reserve. A tariff would also make domestic consumers pay more nearly the replacement cost of the energy they consume.

A "BTU" TAX. An overall energy consumption tax would not distinguish between energy obtained from essentially benign (environmentally and internationally) sources and energy from sources that present uncompensated risks. Its justification is that it would reduce the amount of energy consumed in the present, leave more energy to be consumed from depletable sources in the future, and in this way lower the prospective increase in the future cost of energy. Implicitly, the rationale for a Btu tax assumes that the present cost of energy does not already incorporate the discounted value of consuming in the future the energy saved now. This assumption in turn implies that the OPEC price is too low—that the scarcity value of oil is not now fully being captured. There is no persuasive evidence for this view.

PETROLEUM AND NATURAL GAS TAX. An alternative to the nondiscriminatory Btu tax would be a wellhead tax on petroleum and natural gas to equalize its cost with that of imports. A declining tax initially set to make average domestic prices equal to world prices could be combined with phased complete decontrol of petroleum and decontrol of natural gas prices as contracts expire. This combination would eliminate existing consumer windfalls from fuel priced below its replacement cost without creating equal windfalls for producers. It would also promote efficiency in the allocation of resources by

10. Such a tariff would reduce the potential monopoly rent available to OPEC. If oil exporters are now maximizing their return from oil sales, after the tariff was imposed they would find a decrease in price appropriate; if not, they are not now maximizing revenue, and their optimal potential price increase would decline.

requiring consumers to adjust to the rise in energy costs. The tax and controls would be simultaneously removed over a period of time keyed to the investment lags in energy production, minimizing windfalls to producers from existing investment while maximizing the incentive to bring production into being for the future.

President Carter has proposed a related scheme for oil, but has not followed the windfall revenues approach. In his proposal consumer windfalls from oil price controls would be removed over a three-year period through a rising wellhead tax on oil.[11] Prices received by producers would be regulated indefinitely, however, at 1977 control levels (in real terms) for production from existing producing properties. This latter provision will discourage new investment to increase production from known fields and hence will reduce output, as a pure windfall tax would not. Under the Carter proposal, oil from newly discovered reservoirs would be price-controlled indefinitely at the 1977 world level in real terms; prices would be allowed to rise from the 1977 upper-tier regulated level over a three-year period. Oil from stripper wells would be allowed the world price, as would some other high-cost production. Oil producers would thus receive four separate prices for identical oil, depending largely on when wells were drilled.

Potential revenues from a windfall gains tax such as that described above would be substantial, indicating that the existing subsidy to energy consumption is also large. At a nominal output level of 10 million barrels a day of petroleum (oil and natural gas liquids) and perhaps a $6 per barrel difference between the cost of imported oil with a security tariff and the current average price of domestic oil, this tax would amount to about $22 billion in the first year and then decline. The tax in the first year under the Carter proposal would be substantially lower, but would rise over the next two years and then change with each change in the world oil price and with the amount of oil produced in each category.

A TRANSPORTATION FUEL TAX. Substantial support has developed for a tax on motor fuel used for transportation. President Carter has proposed a variant of a motor fuel tax, a tax on gasoline that, starting in 1979, would rise or fall by 5 cents a gallon depending

11. However, the price to residential fuel oil consumers is retained below the oil replacement cost by rebating to them, on a dollar for dollar basis, the wellhead tax collected on oil converted to residential fuel oil.

on whether or not gasoline consumption in the previous year exceeded or fell below given targets.

A tax limited to gasoline would lead to inequities and distortions; for example, it would not affect automobiles and light trucks that use diesel fuel. Any effort to cover diesel automobiles, or to exclude light trucks that use gasoline, would be administratively complex and open to evasion. In addition to these problems, it is difficult to understand the energy-related rationale for a transportation fuel tax that does not cover all fuels used in transportation, including fuel for trucking, air travel, buses, and trains. Even with a general tax, the largest effect would remain on personal automobiles, which use about 70 percent of the fuel used for transportation. And an equal per-gallon tax on all fuel would still provide an incentive for using the more energy-efficient modes of transport. It should be noted, however, that a transportation fuel tax would be more discriminatory among regions, sectors, and life-styles than would a tax on all uses of energy, or even a tax on petroleum.

If the decision were made to discourage transportation uses of energy, a motor fuel tax would be more efficient than would such alternatives as more rigorous standards for fuel efficiency in vehicles or a tax-rebate scheme for new automobiles based on fuel economy. A motor fuel tax affects all vehicles, not just new ones, and it affects fuel use decisions at the margin. It would lead to a changed use pattern for the existing vehicle fleet in that low miles-per-gallon vehicles would tend to be used less (by multicar owners and by transfer among owners) and high miles-per-gallon vehicles more. Further, each decision to travel (and driving patterns as well) would be affected, as would modal choices. Essentially the same reasoning leads to the conclusion that lower tax revenues would be needed to save a given number of gallons of petroleum over the next ten years with a constant, initially higher tax rate than with one that started lower and then escalated. The broader-based the tax, the lower the rate (and hence the distortive effect) needed to achieve energy saving goals. Other considerations, such as avoiding massive taxes and rebates, are also important, however, and they may require the use of instruments that are less efficient with reference to energy goals but more satisfactory overall.

A TAX REBATE BASED ON MILES PER GALLON. The Carter administration has proposed a tax to discourage the purchase of new vehicles that get fewer miles per gallon, and a rebate of that tax to lower the relative price of cars that use less fuel. If enacted, this proposal would provide economic incentives to meet the already established automobile efficiency standards, and thus would help shift the transportation capital stock toward the use of less fuel per mile driven. It would not reduce the transportation services demanded of those vehicles, nor of the existing fleet, for the reasons discussed above.

TAX EXPENDITURES. Tax expenditures through percentage depletion on oil and gas production flow largely to underground resource owners and do not have much effect on petroleum or natural gas supply. The immediate tax write-off now allowed some exploration and development expenses, on the other hand, does increase cash flow to the exploration sector and increases the return to it, with positive effects on petroleum and natural gas supply. The latter instrument thus meets the test of being specific to the function it is designed to affect. Because oil prices are determined by OPEC actions and by government controls, the greater oil supply does not lower consumer prices. Thus tax write-offs increase domestic oil supply but not consumption, and hence lower oil imports. The situation is somewhat different with regard to the uncontrolled natural gas market, where the effect of write-offs is partially to lower prices because it increases supply.

The Carter administration has proposed a number of other tax expenditures to induce investment in energy-conserving equipment, to reduce energy consumption through insulation, to induce conversion of oil and gas-using facilities to coal, and to increase use of solar energy. These measures would achieve energy-related goals by transferring some of their cost from one energy sector to another and from the energy sector to taxpayers as a whole. In most of these cases, the tax expenditure would have the same effect as alternatives such as a change in the controlled price or a direct subsidy. Thus, whether tax expenditures or more direct or general measures should be used depends on administrative or political considerations, not on the desirability of the goals they may achieve.

Overview

The nation faces three energy problems, and while they will not go away of their own accord, none of them need seriously threaten the maintenance of our prosperity or national security—if appropriate policies are adopted. The problems are: possible short-run economic disruptions caused by restriction of oil supply by foreign nations; the increase in the relative cost of energy due to OPEC actions, to the gradual exhaustion of traditional energy resources, and to enhanced concern for the environment; and the need to move, over the next several decades, from an economy based on cheap oil and natural gas to one relying on more abundant energy sources. The goal of energy policy is to minimize the effect of these problems so as to increase current and prospective national welfare. Reducing energy consumption, increasing domestic energy production, and reducing oil imports are intermediate goals through which these ends are sought.

The only exceptional element in this trio of problems is the insecurity of the oil supply. The other problems are no different in kind, though arguably in degree, from those faced by this and other economies throughout history. Because energy use is so pervasive, however, and because its rising cost was communicated from abroad and in such a dramatic fashion, the necessary adjustments have been painful to endure and politically difficult to accept.

The policy required to minimize the current cost of energy is consistent with that appropriate to other aspects of the economy. It consists mainly of allowing changes in relative prices to perform their allocative and incentive function, with government serving to cushion the adjustments so that the burden—and the benefit—does not remain disproportionately with some economic sectors or groups. The cornerstone of the Carter energy conservation program—that energy prices to consumers should equal the replacement cost of energy—reflects this policy, though failure to extend similar treatment to energy production will hamper achievement of short-run energy goals. It may also lead to subsidies and inefficiencies that drain away resources that could better be used elsewhere. Even with energy prices reflecting energy costs, however, there would remain a role for government in developing cheaper means to produce energy and in finding ways by which consumers can satisfy their wants while using less of it.

The era of primary dependence on oil and natural gas is not over, but its end appears more nearly in sight than it was a decade ago. It will come more rapidly if policies are adopted that dampen incentives

to continue the exploration and technological development neces-\
sary to exploit fully the resource base. The shape of the energy future
is being determined by the options now being opened—and closed.
Fortunately, there appears to be time to examine alternatives carefully (though not interminably) before irreversible commitments are
made. The nation will depend on coal, the light-water reactor, and
oil imports for most of its energy growth through the rest of this century. Effort must be devoted to making these sources secure, economical, safe, and environmentally benign. Since these goals are to some
extent contradictory, trade-offs will be required.

The more distant energy future is less certain. New technologies
will be meshed with new institutions and patterns of living. The lead
times are so long that attention needs to be devoted now to future
requirements in order to lessen the possibility of disruptive changes,
such as those which have had unstabilizing economic and political
effects over the past few years.

The greatest energy risks lie in the immediate future. They arise
from world dependence on oil exports from a few nations, most of
which are located in a politically unstable part of the world and are
not fully integrated into the world economy. Without that integration,
constraints on disruptive behavior are weak, and the threat to other
oil-importing nations, if not the United States, is potentially overwhelming. Beyond the usual efforts to achieve international stability,
the United States can reduce this risk by encouraging integration of
the oil exporters into the world economy. If it is to do this the United
States must be prepared to participate freely in trade and capital
transactions, including those relating to energy. And this means that
the United States requires energy security—from stockpiles and
added energy production capacity—so that it can play a confident
role in international affairs. It also is necessary that it maintain an
open economy in which others, including the oil exporters, can expect to participate.

For the longer run, it is critical for the United States to develop the
energy technology and resources with which the transition from primary dependence on oil and gas can proceed. In order to minimize
the incentive of oil exporters to reduce oil supplies the United States
should act so that it is seen to be willing to share its technology and
resources with others, including the present oil exporters, in the
future.

CHAPTER ELEVEN

Budget Prospects and Process

ROBERT W. HARTMAN

PRESIDENT CARTER, in his election campaign and in his first months in office, has indicated that he will attempt to coordinate policies and to limit spending by setting budgetary targets and by implementing a new budget process. In this chapter, the long-term budget outlook of the Carter administration is reviewed and the new budget process—zero-base budgeting—is evaluated as an instrument in reshaping government priorities.

PART I. PROSPECTS FOR ATTAINING PRESIDENT CARTER'S GOALS

During President Carter's current term in office, he will initiate budgets for fiscal years 1979 through 1982. In his campaign for the presidency, Carter outlined explicit economic, social, and budgetary goals for fiscal year 1981, the last budget he will propose before the 1980 election. He stated that he favored, and expected to achieve, the following goals: limiting federal spending to about 21 percent of gross national product; achieving an unemployment rate of about

The author was aided by helpful comments on earlier drafts from Frank deLeeuw, Arthur Hauptman, Darwin Johnson, Bruce MacLaury, Arthur Okun, John Palmer, Robert Reischauer, David Rowe, and John Schillingburg. Data were generously provided by staff members of the Office of Management and Budget and the Congressional Budget Office. Nancy Osher contributed research and editorial assistance.

4.5 percent; balancing the federal budget; and initiating about $60 billion worth of new and strengthened social programs and tax cuts.

These goals were attacked not so much for any intrinsic faults but because their consistency was questionable. How could all these good things be achieved simultaneously? Is this a list of dreams or a reasonable plan? From the vantage point of the fall of 1976, Carter's social and economic goals seemed to be quite consistent with his self-imposed goal of a balanced budget for fiscal 1981. The key to making all the new President's goals consistent is the assumption that full employment will be restored by fiscal 1981. Using a 4.5 percent full-employment unemployment rate, and assuming that real output at full employment grows at 3.75 percent a year between fiscal 1976 and 1981 and that inflation averages about 5.5 percent a year,[1] full-employment gross national product would be about $2.90 trillion in fiscal 1981.

A $2.90 trillion economy in 1981 could easily allow the attainment of the goals laid out by Carter in 1976: federal revenues would be approximately $633 billion, about 21.8 percent of gross national product;[2] if federal spending were held to 21 percent, it would total about $609 billion, which would be more than covered by estimated receipts, allowing about $24 billion of tax cuts to balance the budget; federal spending already committed under existing law (current services outlays) would be $531 billion, leaving "room" for about $78 billion of new spending.[3]

1. A common inflation series is used throughout this chapter. It is based on Carter administration forecasts for 1977 and 1978 and House Budget Committee "high growth path" assumptions thereafter (see appendix A).

2. Up from 18.7 percent of actual GNP in fiscal 1976 because personal income taxes rise more than proportionately to national income, because corporate profits taxes were very low in 1976, and because of already legislated increases in social security and unemployment taxes. For derivation of receipts estimates at full employment under various assumptions about productivity and the full-employment unemployment rate, see appendix A.

3. Throughout this chapter, the budget margin—the gap between projected receipts and current services outlays—is divided into a spending increase component and a tax cut component by setting both receipts and outlays at 21 percent of full-employment GNP. Establishing a firm percentage of GNP as a limit on federal spending is obviously an oversimplified way of expressing the intention of "limiting the size of the federal government." It ignores the composition of federal spending (such as purchases of goods and services versus transfer payments), movements in relative prices of public and private goods (see chapter 2), and the fact that tax expenditures, not counted in federal outlays, are often a direct substitute for them (see appendix B). Nonetheless, for purposes of discussion, setting some expenditure target (in relation to output) is more helpful than simply assuming that all of the budget margin would be used for federal spending (because the receipts will be

Thus, in the 1976 campaign, Carter could reasonably promise to achieve his goals for the federal budget. Since that time, however, two factors have arisen to make the budgetary outlook less optimistic: revised estimates of potential gross national product and President Carter's 1978 budget revisions and commitments.

Revisions in Potential GNP

As explained in appendix A, the Council of Economic Advisers has lowered its estimate of how much gross national product would be produced at any given level of the unemployment rate. The principal reason for this revision is that since about 1966 growth in output per man-hour in the economy has declined sharply from the average of the postwar period. Even when corrected for the effects of the business cycle, the council maintains that productivity growth has declined very substantially. As a result, estimates of potential output in fiscal 1981 under the new productivity assumptions are more than 4 percent below earlier estimates based on more favorable productivity assumptions.[4] In addition, the council has estimated that the changing age and sex composition of the labor force ought to raise the unemployment rate designated as the full-employment unemployment rate. The rate used in the new CEA estimates is 4.9 percent in fiscal 1976, falling to 4.8 percent by 1981, as the proportion of adult males in the labor force begins to rise again by that time.[5]

Revised estimates of full-employment gross national product in 1981 are about $2.77 trillion, about $127 billion below the earlier Carter estimate. This cut in projected GNP would result in a gloomier

---

there) or that it will all be returned to taxpayers (because it belongs to them for private use, unless a special tax is levied to finance a new program). Each of these polar positions on the uses of the margin has its advocates; the division used here is the one advocated by President Carter during his election campaign.

4. The new CEA projections also incorporate revisions in the GNP accounts to reflect prices prevailing in 1972 rather than in 1958, the previous benchmark year. Since sectors with fast output growth tend to have falling relative prices, this revision also lowers measured real growth.

5. These new rates are estimated by assuming that the full-employment unemployment rate was 4.0 percent in 1955 and that the unemployment rates of various age-sex categories remain fixed at the 1955 level. The full-employment unemployment rate rises over time solely because the proportions of the labor force concentrated in high-unemployment-rate age-sex cells is greater than in 1955. If adjustments were also made for worsening relative unemployment rates for women and teenagers, the rate would rise to 5.4 percent in 1976.

picture for President Carter's goals. Federal revenues in 1981, at a 4.8 percent unemployment rate, would be about $598 billion, a drop of over 5 percent below previous estimates. Limiting federal spending to 21 percent of GNP in 1981 would imply a spending total of $582 billion, about $27 billion below the target estimated last fall. Tax cuts would be only $16 billion. Current services outlays would not be very different from those estimated in late 1976—about $532 billion.[6] Thus, the elbow room for greater federal spending would only be about $50 billion.

While the revised CEA potential output series gives heavy emphasis to reduced productivity growth during the past decade, it does not significantly change previous estimates of growth in the labor force. Since the 1960s labor force participation rates of adult women, in particular, have increased substantially. If these increases continue, it is possible that the added real output stemming from the larger labor force will offset declining productivity growth. In a recent paper, George L. Perry[7] constructs a model of potential U.S. output that incorporates these recent labor force trends. As a result, Perry's estimate of full-employment[8] gross national product in fiscal 1981 is $2.85 trillion, midway between the Carter campaign estimate and the revised CEA series. Under Perry's full-employment output in 1981, federal receipts under the tax laws President Carter inherited would total about $619 billion (21.7 percent of GNP). This would provide enough revenues to balance the budget at about $598 billion (21 percent of GNP), provide a $21 billion tax cut, and initiate about $66 billion in new programs.

These revisions of potential output clearly affected budget decisions made in the early days of the Carter administration. The revised CEA estimates (which were available at the time Carter made his initial fiscal 1978 budget revisions) implied less room for new undertakings than was indicated during the campaign. The shrunken receipts estimates meant limited flexibility to lower taxes permanently. Whatever long-run estimate of full-employment gross national product is embraced by the Carter administration (at this writing it

6. This estimate corrects for the slightly higher outlays at a 4.8 percent, rather than 4.5 percent, unemployment rate in 1981.

7. "Potential Output and Productivity," *Brookings Papers on Economic Activity, 1:1977.*

8. Perry's full-employment unemployment rate is 5 percent, slightly above the revised CEA estimate.

Table 11-1. Outlays and Receipts for the Current Services and Ford Budgets, Fiscal Years 1978 and 1981

Billions of dollars

Item	1978	1981[a]
Outlays		
Current services	445.4	531.5
Proposed Ford reductions	−12.4	−31.3
Proposed Ford increases	+7.0	+26.7
Ford budget	440.0	527.0
Receipts		
Current tax laws extended	409.5[b]	595.7
Proposed Ford reductions	−16.3	−46.3
Proposed Ford increases	+1.7	+14.2
Ford budget	394.9	563.6
Budget margin or deficit (−)		
Current services	−35.9	64.2
Ford budget	−45.1	36.6

Sources: Office of Management and Budget and author's estimates.

a. Based on the Council of Economic Advisers 1977 revised series of potential gross national product; see appendix A.

b. Includes reestimates made in February 1977.

has explicitly adopted none), the revisions of the Ford budget were made with the more constraining long-run view of potential output in mind.

President Carter's 1978 Budget Revisions

President Ford's proposed 1978 outlays included substantial increases above current service levels in national defense and several other areas, which were more than offset by proposed reductions, especially in manpower, income security, and health programs.[9] In addition, President Ford proposed a large permanent tax reduction and a continued reduction of individual income taxes in future years to limit the average tax rate to the level it would reach in 1979. At the same time, he proposed increases in social security taxes.

Table 11-1 summarizes the future implications of the Ford budget proposals. His projected 1981 budget[10] limited federal spending to

9. See chapter 2.

10. President Ford projected an unemployment rate in fiscal 1981 of about 4.8 percent, under the revised CEA potential output assumptions. Thus the debate about the 1981 outlook is about "potential" GNP as well as actual GNP. The projected budget data for President Ford's proposals have been adjusted for higher inflation rates to make them comparable to other data used in this chapter.

about 19 percent of gross national product, slightly less than the amount projected under current law, despite huge defense increases (nearly half of the $26.7 billion in increases by 1981 was for national defense), by proposing reductions in current entitlement programs. At the same time President Ford countenanced a large reduction in federal receipts by 1981—to nearly 20 percent of gross national product in that year—because his long-run program apparently did not anticipate any major social initiatives.

President Carter's 1978 budget revisions were, therefore, severely constrained. The new President had to ask for a reversal of most of the Ford budget reductions, which were mainly repetitions of earlier cutbacks he had criticized in the campaign. But he was not ready to reverse most of Ford's proposed increases, including most of the critical defense plans, after only a few days in office. In short, Carter's dilemma was that he was committed to a substantial increase in the 1978 budget deficit to spur the economy, and yet had to raise revenues above President Ford's program to have a shot at a balanced budget in the future.

A glance at the long-run implications of the Ford proposals in table 11-1 indicates that undoing his proposed reductions and accepting some of his increases would alone raise 1981 expenditures beyond Carter's limits even without any stimulus program. Accepting permanent tax cuts to stimulate the economy would drive receipts below Carter's spending target in 1981.

The long-run implications of President Carter's 1978 budget revisions are summarized in table 11-2. Defense spending in 1978 was reduced slightly, but no explicit decision was made about future outlays; the estimate in the table eliminates all real growth in defense purchases beyond 1978. By reversing most of President Ford's budget reductions, especially in the labor, health, and income security areas—many of which were designed by the outgoing President to save huge sums of money in the future—President Carter implicitly drove up 1981 outlays into the $550 billion range. For this reason, every attempt was made in designing the 1978 stimulus package and other budget revisions to limit the future spending implications of the new proposals. Nevertheless, the Carter budget revisions added nearly $25 billion to the Ford proposals, driving up the 1981 spending base to about $552 billion.

On the tax side, a similar eye to the future conditioned the new

Table 11-2. Carter Revisions to the Ford Budgets, Fiscal Years 1978 and 1981

Billions of dollars

		1981	
		Revised Council of Economic Advisers estimate[a]	*Perry estimate*[a]
Item	*1978*		
Outlays			
Ford budget	**440.0**	**527.0**	**527.4**
Stimulus program	+7.5	+0.9	+0.9
Defense changes	−0.4	−5.2	−5.2
Reestimates of uncontrollable programs, net[b]	+2.0	+5.4	+5.4
Reversals of Ford proposals and all other changes			
Education, training, employment, social services	+2.7	+3.9	+3.9
Health	+1.3	+9.0	+9.0
Income security	+3.8	+10.5	+10.5
All other	+5.7	+0.3	+0.3
Carter budget revisions	**462.6**	**551.8**	**552.2**
Receipts			
Ford budget	**394.9**	**563.6**	**578.9**
Reversal of Ford tax proposals and reestimates	+15.4	+34.2	+39.7
Stimulus program: personal tax cut	−5.6	−4.6	−4.6
Carter budget revisions	**404.7**	**593.2**	**614.0**
Budget margin or deficit (−)			
Carter budget revisions	**−57.9**	**41.4**	**61.8**

Sources: 1978 data, *The Budget of the United States Government, Fiscal Year 1978*, and Office of Management and Budget, "Current Budget Estimates, April 1977" (processed); 1981 data, ibid., and Congressional Budget Office, backup sheets for data in House Committee on the Budget, *First Concurrent Resolution on the Budget: Fiscal Year 1978*, H. Rept. 95–189 (Government Printing Office, 1977), and author's estimates.

a. See appendix A.

b. Unemployment insurance, social security, and interest.

administration's strategy. President Ford's permanent tax changes were dropped. The stimulus program originally featured a tax rebate concentrated entirely in fiscal 1977, an optional business tax cut in the form of an investment tax credit presumed to terminate in 1980 (both later dropped), and individual income tax cuts that had the virtue of not exhibiting an increasing revenue drain over time.[11] Thus, the Carter tax revisions restored most of the revenue to the federal

11. See discussion in chapter 3.

Table 11-3. The Carter Budget Outlook under Alternative Assumptions, Fiscal Year 1981

Amounts in billions of dollars

Basis of estimate	Outlays		Receipts		Margin of receipts over outlays	Use of margin, assuming budget in balance at 21 percent of GNP	
	Amount	Percent of full-employment GNP	Amount	Percent of full-employment GNP		Spending increase	Tax reductions
Old estimates of potential output, 4.5 percent full-employment unemployment rate, mid-1976 spending levels and tax laws[a]	531	18.3	633	21.8	102	78	24
Adjusted for new estimates of potential output and full-employment unemployment rate[a]							
Revised Council of Economic Advisers series	532	19.2	598	21.6	66	50	16
Perry series	532	18.7	619	21.7	87	66	21
Adjusted for Carter fiscal 1978 budget revisions							
Revised CEA series	552	19.9	593	21.4	41	30	11
Perry series	552	19.4	614	21.6	62	46	16
Adjusted for payroll tax proposals							
Revised CEA series	552	19.9	604	21.8	51	30	21
Perry series	552	19.4	625	21.9	72	46	26

Sources: Appendix A and author's estimates. Figures are rounded.
a. The old and new estimates are explained in appendix A.

tax base that President Ford would have eliminated. Projected revenues for 1981, however, are heavily dependent on which of the new full-employment targets President Carter adopts. Under the revised CEA estimates, receipts would be $593 billion, while the Perry estimate of potential output would yield $614 billion.

President Carter's Social Security Proposals

On May 9, 1977, the Carter administration proposed far-reaching changes in the social security tax laws. Aside from some proposals that transfer monies from one government account to another, several proposals would have a significant impact on fiscal 1981 federal revenues.

The administration proposed $10.6 billion in payroll tax increases. First, raising the payroll tax base for employers to the entire amount of wages and salaries in three steps between 1979 and 1981 would add $9.2 billion to federal receipts in fiscal 1981. Second, increasing the tax rate on the self-employed from 7.0 percent to 7.5 percent in 1979 would raise $0.4 billion in 1981. Third, increasing the wage base subject to employee payroll taxes by $600 above currently scheduled increases in both 1979 and 1981 would raise federal receipts by $1.0 billion in 1981.

The Implications of the Budget Choices

The transformation of the budget outlook facing President Carter is summarized in table 11-3. From what seemed, in the fall of 1976, the relatively easy task of deciding how to allocate as much as $78 billion in new spending among competing social programs has evolved the more difficult task of squeezing social priorities into the $30 billion to $46 billion spending room above current service levels. The new President's revision of President Ford's final budget accounts for $20 billion of this shrinkage, while the revised full-employment gross national product estimates, in lowering the spending target, supplied the rest.

The new estimates of potential GNP and the tax cuts proposed in Carter's budget revisions cut the 1981 revenue potential to nearly 21 percent of GNP. However, his social security tax proposals have hiked revenue potential in 1981 back up to the point where a net tax reduction of $21 billion to $26 billion would still be consistent with balancing the budget. While the prospects of achieving the new administration's aims are considerably less sanguine than they were during the campaign, it does appear that new spending programs combined with tax cuts totaling about $60 billion may still be feasible.

Adjusting the Budget Projection Assumptions

This bare outline of budgetary prospects must be qualified in several ways. Many alternative procedures for projecting outlays and receipts are possible; unfortunately, many of these qualifications make the budget outlook worse, not better.

Outlays

First, in projecting 1981 budget outlays implied by current programs, many arbitrary and politically unrealistic assumptions are made. For example, the projections discussed thus far adjust federal spending for anticipated inflation only in those programs where such adjustments are required by law.[12] If outlay increases were so limited, there would be a steady erosion in the purchasing power of federal grants-in-aid that are not indexed, such as aid to education, and a decline in real services in nondefense operating programs, such as the national park service. If all these other programs were adjusted to maintain the 1978 level of real services, an additional $15 billion in spending would be required in 1981.[13]

Second, the projections made here delete some $5 billion in 1981 outlays that represent real growth implied by President Ford's national defense program. The debate on defense spending has narrowed to *how much* real growth we need.[14] It is probably prudent to

12. Principally entitlement programs that are indexed and pay for federal employees. In addition, this chapter uses the practice of the Office of Management and Budget of adjusting procurement and operations and maintenance programs in the Department of Defense for inflation because appropriations for these programs include estimates of anticipated inflation.

13. These adjustments include maintaining the 1978 value of grants and other federal purchases, a cost-of-living increase for veterans' benefits, and the effect of these adjustments on federal interest costs. The estimates are from the Congressional Budget Office, reported in backup sheets for House Committee on the Budget, *First Concurrent Resolution on the Budget: Fiscal Year 1978*, H. Rept. 95-189 (Government Printing Office, 1977).

14. See chapter 4.

Table 11-4. Effect of Alternative Assumptions on the Budget Margin, Fiscal Year 1981
Billions of dollars

Item	Use of margin[a]	
	Spending increase	Tax reductions
Total margin implied by Carter's 1978 budget revisions and payroll tax proposals	30–46	21–26
Alternative assumptions		
Adjust for inflation in nonindexed programs	−15	...
Adjust for real growth in defense spending as in Ford budget	−5	...
Adjust individual income taxes		
Limit taxes to 9 percent of GNP	...	−42 to −48
Eliminate rate increase due to inflation occurring after 1978	...	−21 to −22

Sources: Line 1, table 11-3; other lines, Congressional Budget Office and author's estimates.
a. The first entry is implied by the revised CEA estimate of potential GNP and the second by Perry's estimate.

plan to use some of the elbow room in the budget for these inflation and defense adjustments (see table 11-4).

Receipts

The projections of taxes in budget planning exercises always start with the revenue implications of existing tax provisions; this has been done here, modifying 1981 receipts only for President Carter's increased standard deduction and payroll tax proposals.

These projections are probably an unrealistic view of likely congressional behavior, however. Individual income tax receipts would grow from 8.9 percent of gross national product in 1978 to about 10.5 percent in 1981 if current laws are unchanged, because inflation and recovery will raise average effective tax rates. In the past, upward drifts in personal income tax rates have been offset by tax reduction laws. President Ford's budget followed this precedent by proposing to freeze effective tax rates at the level they would reach in 1979 (about 9 percent of GNP). This would result in a reduction in taxes of $42 billion to $48 billion by 1981,[15] pushing the new administration's receipts well below its target for a balanced budget at 21 percent of GNP in 1981. Even limiting tax reductions to eliminating

15. The smaller reduction is implied by the revised CEA estimate of potential GNP and the larger by Perry's estimate.

the higher tax rates due solely to post–1978 inflation would necessitate a tax cut of $21 billion to $22 billion by 1981 (see table 11-4).

Summary

The upshot of these adjustments to the budget outlook can be summarized as follows. On the spending side of the budget, if President Carter is to limit spending to 21 percent of full-employment gross national product in 1981, new program initiatives will be limited to $10 billion to $26 billion unless inflation adjustments are withheld and real defense growth is stopped. The only other way to find resources to finance new initiatives—such as welfare reform, which alone could cost $25 billion[16]—is to cut back expenditures on existing programs.[17] President Carter hopes to do this with the aid of a new budget process, which is evaluated in the second part of this chapter.

On the receipts side of the budget, the goal of budget balance is equivalent to limiting taxes to 21 percent of gross national product.[18] Existing tax laws, supplemented by President Carter's payroll tax increase, would yield receipts about $25 billion above that percentage. This excess in receipts, however, is just about the amount necessary to provide a tax cut offsetting the individual income tax rate increases produced by inflation between 1978 and 1981. This, in large part, explains why President Carter strongly opposed permanent tax cuts in the early days of his administration. In order to make a strong tax reform palatable, the President will need every spare dollar for tax reduction (over and above any gains from reform). The 1981 excess is big enough for one (but only one) significant tax cut; any larger tax cut would eat into the shrinking spending margin.

Questioning the Basic Economic Assumptions

The budget projections, and the conclusions drawn from them, are only as good as the assumptions on which they are based. Many people would question some of the underlying assumptions about in-

16. See chapter 8.
17. If the Carter administration chooses to support a large-scale national health insurance program, most of its costs would have to be financed through new taxes.
18. President Carter's energy tax proposals are potentially so large that it is impossible to integrate them with an overall budget plan. The package includes provisions to rebate all taxes collected, and thus becomes a separate balanced budget. In any event, Carter's campaign promises on the budget ignored energy taxes and rebates.

flation and the ability of the economy to reach full employment under a balanced budget target.

Inflation

The price increases assumed in this chapter show a steady decline from about 6 percent between fiscal years 1977 and 1978 to 5.1 percent a year between fiscal 1979 and 1981. But a case could be made for changing these assumptions, either up or down.

The case for revising the inflation adjustment upward is straight-forward. As the unemployment rate drops from the 7.0 percent range in mid-1977 to the assumed 5.0 percent range in 1981, one would normally expect that labor and product markets would tighten. An optimistic view would be that markets are so slack at the start of the period that tightening would have no appreciable effect on the rate of inflation. But "no appreciable effect" implies a constant inflation rate (about 6 percent throughout the fiscal 1978–81 period), not the decelerating rates assumed in the present projections. Further, according to this view, if one adds to the tightening of demand the administration's energy tax proposals, and the likelihood that world commodity prices will rise as the industrial economies simultaneously recover from slack conditions, the chances for a decelerating inflation seem small.

The contrary view—that the inflation rate will be lower—is taken by the Carter administration. When the administration announced its anti-inflation program in the spring of 1977, it also enunciated the goal of reaching a 4 percent inflation rate by the end of 1979. The case for such deceleration of inflation, despite a return to full capacity in labor and product markets, is based on several considerations. First is the belief that the mid-1977 inflation rate is still echoing the double-digit inflation rate of 1974. As 1974 recedes in the memory of labor-management negotiators and as relative wages and prices adjust to the big hike in energy prices, the underlying inflation rate could recede. Second, it is argued that price advances in slack markets, characteristic of the 1975 recession, are partly due to business fears of the reimposition of price controls in some form. The Carter administration's anti-inflation program carefully avoids any hint of price controls in the future.[19] If this policy, therefore, has the intended psychological effect on price setters, inflation could be trimmed.

19. See chapter 3.

Third, efforts are underway both domestically and internationally to create buffer stocks of various commodities, which could moderate at least the most extreme upward movements in prices (for instance, coffee) that contributed to inflation in the past. Finally, it is argued that even though aggregate demand in the U.S. economy is moving up to eliminate slack, the fact that the administration is planning to accomplish this through a balanced budget would decelerate inflation. This claim is based on the belief that a dollar's worth of demand from government sources is inherently more inflationary than a dollar's worth of private demand.[20]

The implications of these alternative inflation assumptions for the budget projections are widely misunderstood. For example, although achieving President Carter's goal of 4 percent inflation would be welcome news for the economy, it would, ironically, reduce the budget margin. This is because federal revenues are much more responsive to inflation than are outlays in programs automatically adjusted for inflation. If inflation were held to 4 percent beginning in early 1980, the projections of federal revenues by fiscal 1981 would fall by $16 billion, while outlays in indexed programs would decline by only $7 billion. This would reduce the margin between receipts and outlays by $9 billion out of the $51 billion to $72 billion estimated in table 11-3. If the anti-inflation program succeeds, in other words, providing $60 billion in additional expenditures or tax cuts and still balancing the budget would be considerably more difficult. Conversely, any quickening of inflation would pour receipts into Washington faster than indexed programs would ship them out, thereby at least temporarily improving the federal deficit.[21]

The major conclusion that ought to be drawn from this is certainly not that inflation is good—only a single-minded goal of balancing the budget could produce that answer—but rather that an unanticipated change in the rate of inflation requires a rethinking of budgetary and economic goals. This point will be considered after outlining the debate over the unemployment rate assumptions.

20. A variant on this point is that even if there is no difference in the inflationary impact of public versus private demand (as most economists believe), as long as major corporation leaders believe that deficits are *the* cause of inflation, they will act accordingly and raise prices even in weak markets, until they observe budget balance.
21. How Congress would adjust programs that do not have automatic inflation adjustments could reverse these effects, but such reactions are problematic and would take time.

Unemployment

The projections discussed earlier in this chapter assumed that a full-employment economy would be reached by fiscal 1981, despite the administration's intention to move from a very stimulative budget in 1978 to less stimulative fiscal policy with a balanced budget in 1981. The question is whether moving to a balanced budget in 1981 is compatible with demand sufficient to sustain full employment in that year.

DEMAND PESSIMISTS. One group of pessimists argues that this scenario will not work because private demand will not take up the slack created as the federal government's demand growth ebbs. This view is largely based on the observation that the real growth rate over the period 1978–81 required for full employment, especially when coupled with the recovery phase of the business cycle from 1975 to 1977, would imply an unprecedented period of rapid growth of output, greatly in excess of the average rates in either the 1960s or early 1970s. Thus, for example, under Perry's definition of full-employment gross national product, annual real growth would have to average 6.2 percent between 1978 and 1981.[22] While this rate would represent a postwar high, it is important to remember that never in the 1960s or early 1970s did the economy start so far below its potential—however measured—as it was in 1975 and 1976. So an uncommonly strong growth rate would be built on an uncommonly large reserve of unused productive capacity. Such a situation is unprecedented all around, and historical averages do not help much in predicting whether such rapid growth is feasible.

A more sophisticated version of the thesis that the nonfederal sector's underlying demand is too weak to compensate for a more restrictive fiscal policy is based on an analysis of these other components of demand. Aside from federal purchases of goods and services, aggregate demand consists of consumption, investment, state and local government spending, and net exports. If federal spending on goods and services rises yearly at a real rate of 2.7 to 3.6 percent,[23] while real gross national product must grow at a 5.2 to 6.2 percent rate,

22. The average annual growth requirement for the revised CEA version of potential output is 5.2 percent.
23. This is the annual rate of growth of total federal outlays in 1978–81 needed to reach 21 percent of GNP in 1981 under the revised CEA and Perry series, respectively. "Real" rates here mean deflated by the GNP deflator.

some or all nonfederal demands must grow faster than real GNP. With federal individual income taxes rising rapidly, real consumption is likely to grow even less than real GNP. This means that the burden of filling the aggregate demand gap falls disproportionately on domestic investment (about 14 percent of GNP in 1976), state and local spending (about 13 percent), and net exports (about 1 percent).

Although net exports would boom if the members of the Organization of Petroleum Exporting Countries accelerated spending out of their balance-of-payments surpluses, the net export sector is too small to supply the needed rises in demand to replace a shrinking federal sector. State and local government spending does not hold out much hope either. The major forces that drove up these expenditures in the past (growth of school and college enrollments and the catch-up effort in public employee wages) have waned, and these governments are under pressure to enlarge budget surpluses to provide for future pension liabilities.[24]

In the end, the attainment of full employment by 1981 under a balanced budget depends on a buoyant level of private domestic investment. Specifically, it appears that real investment expenditures would have to grow about 4 percent per year faster than real gross national product (depending on exactly what assumptions are made about other spending sectors) in order to sustain a fully employed economy in 1981.[25] Such a growth of investment is not out of line with postwar experience. In the 1961–65 upswing, for example, the annual rate of growth of real investment exceeded that of real gross national product by over 4 percentage points per year, about what would be required in a 1978–81 upswing. Alternatively, if investment were to grow at 10 percent a year in 1978–81, the ratio of investment to gross national product (under Perry's estimates) in fiscal 1981 would be about 15 percent,[26] well under the ratio in calendar year 1973, the last boom year.

24. See Henry Owen and Charles L. Schultze, eds., *Setting National Priorities: The Next Ten Years* (Brookings Institution, 1976), chap. 9.

25. This exercise can be continued ad infinitum. One can argue that inventory investment cannot grow in excess of GNP for any length of time and that residential construction is already booming in the base year, so that all the stimulus must come from plant and equipment spending. While this conclusion is qualitatively correct—business fixed investment is the key sector—the chance of error in estimating it by successive removal of best guesses in other sectors is great.

26. This assumes that the ratio of real investment to real GNP in 1978 will be the same as in 1976, which is probably a lower bound.

Thus, it is by no means inconceivable that nonfederal demand will grow fast enough to make up for a tightening federal budget and produce a fully employed economy. Whether such rapid growth materializes will depend on many factors, not the least of which is cooperation from the monetary authorities in preventing a tightening of the cost and availability of credit. But assuming such monetary ease is problematic; the pessimists' case cannot be ruled out.

DEMAND OPTIMISTS. The pessimistic position essentially argues that if the economy were to approach full employment, the amount of saving that the private sector (including here state and local governments and the foreign sector) wishes to undertake will exceed private investment demand. The opposite view is that as full employment is approached, private investment demand will exceed private saving. There will then be increased bidding for labor, capital, and other resources and inflation will accelerate before full employment is reached. According to this view, the underlying strength of private demand will first show itself as a "shortage of capital," with willing investors unable to find funds to borrow as full employment is approached.

This description of the state of nonfederal demand fits previous postwar episodes of full employment much better than the alternative view. The full-employment economies of 1955, 1966, and 1973 were all followed by increased rates of inflation and credit squeezes; in all three of these years the federal budget in the national income and product accounts was very close to being in balance. There is, of course, no certainty that future instances of full employment with a balanced budget will set off such inflationary forces, but any energy program that forces retrofitting of buildings, conversion to new energy sources, and rapid replacement of gas guzzlers would increase the prospects for this kind of strong private investment demand.

Budget Making under Uncertainty

The uncertainties about the economic assumptions underlying the budget projections discussed in this chapter cannot be resolved now. In reality, economic forecasting is in no position now to predict the weakness or strength of demand in fiscal 1981 or to pinpoint the inflation rate that will follow from any given unemployment rate. There is inadequate evidence now to reject the kinds of assumptions behind the projections laid out above. And yet the President and the

Congress must make decisions now that will affect the budget several years hence. The trick to rational budget planning is to retain enough flexibility, as to both goals and budget commitments, to allow for reassessment of plans as more information becomes available.

Thus, the early decisions of the Carter administration—to limit revenue losses and to minimize the long-run spending effects of initial decisions—were based on the supposition that there was relatively little spending room in the future and that future tax revenue should be saved for tax reform. This strategy seems warranted on the basis of the budget projections already discussed. But, as noted, the economic assumptions may be wrong.

As time passes, new information about the economy will become available. On the one hand, the nonfederal economy may prove weaker than expected: unemployment may not drop off and incomes may not rise as anticipated. Such an outcome would make both reaching full employment and balancing the budget less likely. The administration will, in that case, have to choose what is more important to the nation; balancing the budget is by no means the obvious choice. Indeed, if nonfederal demand proves to be so weak, a good case can be made for planning a deficit at full employment. This would mean boosting spending or increasing tax reductions above initial plans. There is no reason to make such a policy shift now; but since such a change is not unlikely to be needed it is a mistake to commit the nation to a balanced budget in such a way that future revisions cannot be made.

On the other hand, accumulating evidence may indicate that while unemployment rates are declining according to plan, inflation is higher than expected. If high rates of inflation seem to be due to a general buoyancy of demand as a 5 percent unemployment rate is approached, the proper fiscal policy would call for planning a budget surplus at that level of unemployment, allowing government savings to supplement private savings and alleviating inflationary pressures.[27] This kind of revised budget plan (which is equivalent to aiming for budget balance at a higher unemployment rate than the one originally designated as the full-employment unemployment rate) requires that

27. Planning for a full-employment surplus may be favored on other grounds as well. The share of private investment in full-employment GNP can be increased by pursuing an easier monetary policy combined with a tighter fiscal policy. To the extent that one believes that there are institutional and tax forces driving investment below its socially optimal level, such a change in mix of policies would be warranted.

the spending side of the budget not be so fully committed as to make future expenditure slowdowns impossible. It also implies that some flexibility on the tax side be maintained: all the planned tax reductions should not be committed in advance.

Worst of all, if inflation were to proceed at a more rapid pace than initially assumed and high unemployment persisted as well, a thorough reworking of economic policies as well as budgetary goals would be called for. Under such a persistent "stagflation," the mild anti-inflation program of the Carter administration would certainly have to be reconsidered. Aggregate fiscal policy alone cannot remedy stagflation. In the light of the economic outlook after anti-inflation policies were adjusted, there would be every reason to revise the goals set for budget balance and federal share of gross national product that were based on assumptions that failed to materialize. Once again, the time to make these decisions is when the evidence is in—not now.

This concept of a continually revised budget plan is in contrast to the only two alternatives possible for dealing with the uncertainty of the economic future. One is to forget planning altogether and base current budget decisions on short-term fiscal considerations only. This strategy is very close to what the federal government has done in the past. It leads to adoption of programs with unexpected future consequences and to spending programs in times of recession whose only virtue is speed. In short, it means abandoning the conscious setting of priorities.

The second strategy is to develop budget plans according to a worst-case set of assumptions—to act as if there were a weak nonfederal sector and a very poor trade-off between inflation and lowering unemployment. Such assumptions would probably mean raising unemployment rate targets (say, to 5.5 percent) and proceeding very cautiously on any spending programs for the long run. This strategy has the virtue of being almost sure of self-fulfillment. If the federal government pulls in its reins drastically, unemployment is sure to remain high, although price rises will probably be less than the worst-case projection. This approach really implies throwing in the towel on achieving economic and social goals.

Thus, given the alternatives, and despite the uncertainty of the assumptions, the long-view approach taken by the Carter administration seems to represent a reasonable way to make budget decisions.

Table 11-5. The Budget Outlook, Fiscal Years 1978–81
Amounts in billions of dollars

Item	1978	1979[a]	1980[a]	1981[a]
Outlays				
Current policy[b]	463	496	528	567
Target level[c]	463	500–504	540–549	582–598
As percent of GNP	22.6	22.0	21.5	21.0
Receipts				
Current policy[d]	405	465–470	530–542	604–625
Target level[c]	405	457–461	516–525	582–598
As percent of GNP	19.8	20.2	20.6	21.0
Planning margin or deficit (−)				
Current policy	−58	−31 to −26	2–14	37–58
Target path[e]				
Spending room	...	4–8	12–21	15–31
Tax reduction	...	8–9	14–17	21–26[f]
Actual surplus or deficit (−)	−58	−43	−24	0

Source: Author's estimates, as explained in notes. Figures are rounded.

a. The first entry is implied by the revised CEA estimate of potential GNP and the second by Perry's estimate; see appendix A.

b. Based on data from Congressional Budget Office, backup sheets for data in House Committee on the Budget, *First Concurrent Resolution on the Budget: Fiscal Year 1978*, adjusted to include inflation adjustments for nonindexed as well as indexed programs.

c. Estimated by charting a constant annual rate of growth of outlays or receipts to reach 21 percent of GNP in fiscal 1981.

d. Estimated from GNP using constant real growth from fiscal 1978 to 1981 of 5.2 percent and 6.2 percent to reach revised CEA and Perry potential outputs, respectively, and price assumptions from appendix A. Receipts have been adjusted to include President Carter's proposed increased standard deduction and his social security tax increase proposals made in May 1977.

e. Spending room or tax reduction is the difference between the target level and current policy estimates of outlays or receipts.

f. Based on difference between current policy and target level receipts before rounding.

But it is the first step; the budget plans will need continual revision and the budgetary goals, including budget balance, will need continual reevaluation. The next step for the Carter administration will be the fiscal 1979 budget, which promises to be a very difficult one.

The 1979 Budget

The Carter administration will submit its first full-fledged budget for fiscal 1979 in January 1978. Table 11-5 presents estimates of the numbers behind the decisions that will have to be made in the course of preparing that budget. "Current policy" outlays—including inflation adjustments for nonindexed as well as indexed programs (see table 11-4)—are projected to rise to $496 billion in 1979.[28] Receipts will depend on how well the economy recovers. Table 11-5 illustrates the path of receipts assuming a smooth recovery from fiscal 1978 to both the Council of Economic Advisers revised potential output and Perry's estimate of potential output in 1981, with the former showing lower receipts due to lower expectations of output growth.[29] Current policy receipts include President Carter's increased standard deduction and social security tax increase proposals.[30] Under these assumptions, the budget deficit would range from $26 billion to $31 billion in fiscal 1979.

If a current policy budget were pursued through 1981, a surplus ranging from $37 billion to $58 billion would occur. Since the Carter administration has called for a balanced budget at 21 percent of gross national product in 1981, spending programs above current policies of $15 billion to $31 billion would be undertaken and tax reductions of $21 billion to $26 billion would be in place by 1981. A "target level" for outlays and receipts can therefore be estimated by charting a constant growth path so that each reaches 21 percent of GNP in 1981. This implies an outlay total of $500 billion to $504 billion and receipts of $457 billion to $461 billion in 1979 (table 11-5).

Thus, as the Carter administration decides during 1977 what levels to propose in its fiscal 1979 budget, its choices are quite constrained. If the economy proceeds on the course assumed in these projections, 1979 outlays might include $4 billion to $8 billion in new initiatives above existing programs.[31] Even this amount of spending room could be eroded by congressional action to raise the administration's 1978 outlay proposals, by delays to fiscal 1979 in spending for the new public works and public service employment programs, by any provision for real defense growth, and by any catching up of expenditures in programs that exhibited a shortfall in fiscal 1977.

28. The noncompulsory inflation adjustments are $4 billion, $9 billion, and $15 billion in 1979, 1980, and 1981, respectively. The current policy estimates do not include real growth in defense expenditures.

29. Real GNP is assumed to grow at an annual rate of 5.2 percent in the revised CEA estimates and of 6.2 percent in the Perry estimates between 1978 and 1981.

30. The social security proposals add $2 billion, $6 billion, and $11 billion for fiscal years 1979, 1980, 1981, respectively.

31. This is the difference between the target level of outlays of $500 billion to $504 billion and current policy outlays of $496 billion. It is shown as "spending room" in table 11-5.

In any event, the fiscal 1979 outlay target that is consistent with the administration's long-run plan does not leave much room for new initiatives. Moreover, the 1979 target outlay level represents growth of 8–9 percent over fiscal 1978, a considerable slowdown from the 13 percent increase in the previous fiscal year.

On the receipts side, a smooth path to budget balance in fiscal 1981 would allow $8 billion to $9 billion in tax reductions in 1979. This raises two problems for the Carter administration. First, the initial reaction to President Carter's $11 billion tax rebate proposal suggests that a tax cut of this size will be derided as inadequate. Since the political chances of the administration's tax reform package will probably be dependent on the net tax reduction accompanying it, this limited tax reduction flexibility may jeopardize tax reform. There will thus be pressures to enlarge the tax reduction in fiscal 1979. But this raises the second problem: if both outlays and taxes are keyed to budget balance in fiscal 1981, the actual budget deficit in 1979 will be $43 billion.[32] Even though this deficit is consistent with a balanced budget in 1981, the administration will have a tough time explaining why, in the second fiscal year after 1977, its deficit is down by only about $6 billion.

The economy never performs exactly as anticipated. The planning budget shown in table 11-5 can be used to illustrate how the administration might react to changes in the economy. If recovery proves sluggish in 1977, one would expect an acceleration of the timetable for new spending initiatives and tax reductions. Such changes might jeopardize the prospects for a balanced budget in fiscal 1981, but they would help in meeting the goal of reaching full employment by that year. On the other hand, in the course of planning the fiscal 1979 budget the economy may improve more rapidly than expected and inflation may turn up. In that case, one would expect a strong push from the White House to restrain the 1979 budget to somewhere near current policy levels, postponing tax reductions and new programs to later years. Such a move would make it unlikely that $60 billion in new initiatives could materialize by 1981.

One matter of concern—though it is endemic to the federal budget process—is that all these budget decisions will have to be made

32. This deficit results from 1979 receipts and outlays of $461 billion and $504 billion, respectively, in the Perry estimates, and $457 billion and $500 billion, respectively, in the revised CEA estimates (table 11-5).

by late 1977, yet the proper fiscal policy depends on forecasts of the economy as late as September 30, 1979, the end of fiscal 1979. This means that the President must try to chart a course to his long-term goals using imperfect instruments under conditions of poor visibility.

PART II. NEW DIMENSIONS IN THE BUDGET PROCESS

President Carter's difficult budget choices over the next few years would be eased if the future costs of existing programs were lower. In that case, the administration could propose a higher level of spending for new programs (or for high-priority old programs) at any desired level of total federal spending. This section evaluates President Carter's choice of a budget process to help weed out low-priority expenditures and contrasts it with other new developments in federal budgeting.

The Composition of Current Services Spending in Fiscal 1981

Before discussing the process to be used to identify areas of budgetary saving, it is important to understand the composition of the $552 billion in spending projected for fiscal 1981 after President Carter's 1978 budget revisions (table 11-3). A useful way to divide up that total is to look first at the 1978 spending level of $463 billion and then at the projected increase in outlays from that level.

The shares of President Carter's 1978 budget, according to type of spending, are shown in table 11-6. Whatever process is used to examine the existing budget base ought to be well-suited to an intelligent examination of transfers, grants-in-aid, and national defense programs, for these represent 80 percent of current spending. Unfortunately, there is some reason to question whether the new executive branch budget process for examining the budget base is well adapted to these types of spending.

The other component of the projected $552 billion in spending for 1981 is the *increase* of $89 billion in expenditures under existing programs between 1978 and 1981. Table 11-7 lists the principal components of these changes. Four broad program areas account for virtually all of the projected spending increase, with the rest of the

Table 11-6. Composition of Budget Outlays by Type of Spending, Fiscal Year 1978

Type of outlay	Amount (billions of dollars)	Percent of total
Transfer payments[a]	200	43
Grants-in-aid[b]	56	12
National defense	113	24
Net interest	32	7
Other federal operating programs	62	13
Total	463	100

Sources: Office of Management and Budget, "Current Budget Estimates, April 1977," and author's estimates.
a. Office of Management and Budget's "nondefense payments for individuals."
b. Excluding those supporting transfer payments.

budget consisting largely of offsetting smaller increases and decreases.

Social security accounts for 35 percent of the projected expenditure increase. About half of this projected rise is due to the automatic cost-of-living indexation of beneficiaries' monthly payments and half to the growing numbers and higher earnings histories of incoming beneficiaries. Medicare and Medicaid account for another 21 percent of rising expenditures. The key factors in this increase are the expected rise in medical care prices and, especially for Medicaid, a projected large increase in utilization of higher-cost services over the period. Federal employee pay and retirement programs account for 22 percent of expected outlay growth. Since employment is projected to remain approximately constant during the period, all of the rise in pay is attributable to growing wage rates, based on comparability to private sector pay. Retirement costs are subject to the same factors as social security.

National defense increases make up 33 percent of the projected increase in federal spending between 1978 and 1981. Pay increases and pensions for retired personnel (not including veterans pensions under the Veterans Administration) account for about 11 percent of total federal outlay growth. Most of the remaining 22 percent is attributable to inflation in existing purchases and to an accelerated rise in these purchases as a result of the rapid appropriations increases since 1975.[33]

One approach to cutting into the projected 1981 budget base is to focus on the increases in spending between now and then, on the

33. See chapter 4.

Table 11-7. Components of Increase in Federal Outlays, Fiscal Years 1978–81

Item	Increase, 1978–81	
	Amount (billions of dollars)	Percent of total
Total outlays, 1978	463	...
Plus: sources of increase		
Social security	31	35
Medicare and Medicaid	18	21
Federal employees pay and retirement	20	22
Civilian agency pay	5	5
Department of Defense pay	7	8
Civilian retirement and disability and military retirement	8	9
National defense (net of pay and retirement)	20	22
Reduction in unemployment compensation and in countercyclical programs	−13	−14
All other	13	14
Total	89	100
Equals: projected 1981 outlays	552	...

Sources: Congressional Budget Office and author's estimates.

premise that it is politically easier to *prevent* a spending increase than to take away something already in hand. The listing of projected spending increases suggests possible fruitful areas for paring, such as price and cost controls in health programs and changes in the rules governing federal employee pay and in determining social security benefits. The national defense sector is so huge that the simple inflation adjustment for purchases accounts for over $10 billion in outlay growth, not to mention whatever might be added later for real growth. Apparently, such a selective approach to trimming the budget was rejected by the Carter administration in favor of a comprehensive view of federal spending.

Zero-Base Budgeting

Zero-base budgeting (ZBB) is the name given to a technique of budgetary decisionmaking developed in 1969 for a large corporation. The technique has been used by several state and local governments, notably Georgia, where Governor Carter adopted the process in the preparation of his 1973 budget.

The essence of zero-base budgeting is that it forces program managers to define a minimum level of effort (below the current level) and incremental levels of effort above the minimum for each program. These levels of effort are then ranked by management in decreasing order of priority to indicate the agency's willingness to undertake various levels of effort in each program as the agency budget rises. A cutoff line is established and levels of effort above the line are approved. Those below the line are not funded. If the minimum level of effort of any program falls below the budget line, that entire program is wiped out.

In an executive order dated February 14, 1977, President Carter directed the heads of executive departments and agencies to implement this zero-base budgeting process in the fiscal year 1979 budget. The initial directive to federal agencies[34] specifies that each "decision unit," the program or organizational entity for which budgets are prepared, prepare the following materials.

Decision unit overview. Among other things, this includes a statement of major objectives, the "ultimate realistic outputs or accomplishments expected," as well as a description of the feasible alternative ways of accomplishing them. The method proposed for the budget year is identified, and expected accomplishments of the decision unit are described, using both quantitative and qualitative measures of results.

Decision packages. In addition to identifying information, each decision package must contain an activity description, resource requirements, a short-term objective, and a statement of impact on major objectives. These packages must show the added service at each level of effort, including the following: Minimum level, defined as the level below which the activities can no longer be conducted effectively; this must be below the current level (unless operation below that level is impossible). Current level (unless the total requested for the decision unit is below the current level): a concept similar to the current services level described in chapter 2. The decision unit estimates the budget required to maintain the current year level of activity. When appropriate, it may also include a level or levels between the minimum and current levels; and any additional increments desired above the current level.

Ranking sheet. Each review level prepares a ranking sheet that lists the various levels of minimums and increments in descending

34. The following is paraphrased (or quoted directly) from Office of Management and Budget, "Zero-Base Budgeting," Bulletin 77-9 (April 19, 1977; processed).

order of priority to submit to the next higher review level. Higher level review may result in the addition or deletion of decision packages and the revision of decision packages or rankings. Some or all of the initial decision packages may be consolidated.[35]

Advantages

The advantages of this approach are that it will allow agencies, the Office of Management and Budget, and the President to see the consequences of funding programs below current service levels and to replace some currently built-in costs with new programs or large increments in other existing programs. The process in principle gives no special preference to "old" budget dollars in their competition with "new" ones. Advocates of zero-base budgeting frequently contrast it with "incremental budgeting," which, they contend, takes the current service level as a given base, and considers only positive increments to the base. To some extent this picture of incrementalism does represent how budgeting has been done in the federal government.[36] By treating all parts of the budget comprehensively and equally, zero-base budgeting may uncover unnoticed waste and avoid the special advantages that may have accrued to old standby programs.

Many of the other advantages that are claimed for zero-base budgeting do not seem to require its elaborate ranking format, but may still be of value. One such claim is that ZBB improves the information that managers need to make budgetary decisions.[37] Another is that ZBB integrates planning, budgeting, and operational decisionmaking into one process. Finally, by requiring that a common methodology be followed all the way down to the lowest levels of each agency, zero-base budgeting offers the prospect of involving more people in

35. There are some hints of flexibility in OMB's approach. Although all agencies in the executive branch whose budgets are subject to presidential review are required to go through the same zero-base budgeting exercise, selected special issues will be identified by the agencies for more traditional studies (issue papers) when decision packages are not appropriate. These will also influence budget decisions.

36. One feature of past budget practice that limited rigid incrementalism was that the dollar estimates of current service levels were regarded as inaccurate. ZBB may, ironically, strengthen an incremental approach by furnishing better current service estimates.

37. According to about two-thirds of the budget analysts in the government of the State of Georgia, ZBB has brought about such an improvement. George S. Minmier and Roger H. Hermanson, "A Look at Zero-Base Budgeting: The Georgia Experience," *Atlanta Economic Review*, vol. 26 (July–August 1976), p 9.

budgeting and taking advantage of the expertise of program managers.

One purported advantage of zero-base budgeting in the operation of state and local governments is quite inapplicable to the federal budget. ZBB is suited to "allowing for quick budget adjustments or resource shifts during the year, if necessary when revenue falls short."[38] This advantage presumably stems from the ease of moving the budget cutoff line up the priority listing, eliminating the lowest ranked programs.[39] In the federal government, however, revenue shortfalls do not necessitate spending level cutbacks, because, unlike state and local governments, the federal government has no requirement for a balanced budget. (Indeed, a revenue shortfall caused by a weak economy is often a reason to raise spending.) Moreover, budget adjustments during a year generally mean going back to Congress for revised appropriations. A President, unlike a business executive, cannot reprogram funds.

Disadvantages

Several criticisms about the suitability of zero-base budgeting for the federal budget process have been made.[40]

WASTE OF MANAGERIAL RESOURCES. A great deal of top management's time in the federal government is spent on the budget; changes in the budget process that improve the efficiency of that time are therefore valuable. The executive branch has been moving toward economizing on decisionmaker's time by taking the current service level as the base of the budget, concentrating executive attention on small changes (positive *and* negative) from that base. Zero-base budgeting, in principle, spreads managerial time over each dollar in a program's budget. But the gain in discovering a very inferior program (one whose minimum level is ranked low) must be weighed against the possible loss of executive time that might better be spent in careful study of small changes from the current service base.

38. Jimmy Carter, "Zero-Base Budgeting," *Nation's Business*, vol. 65 (January 1977), p. 26.
39. In fact this does not seem to be the experience in Georgia where changing budget levels in 1974 and 1975 led to the submission of entirely new decision packages. See Minmier and Hermanson, "A Look at Zero-Base Budgeting," p. 9. Peter A. Pyhrr seems to claim the opposite; see "The Zero-Base Approach to Government Budgeting," *Public Administration Review*, vol. 37 (January–February 1977), p. 7.
40. Many of these issues are raised by Robert N. Anthony, "Zero-Base Budgeting Is a Fraud," *Wall Street Journal*, April 27, 1977, p. 26.

In practice, however, because an overwhelming majority of programs are not really under serious challenge and will not be scaled back to zero, the zero-base budgeting process in federal agencies is quite likely ultimately to be reduced to examining the same small changes in the base that traditionally constitute executive review of the budget.[41] This would mean that the budget process would essentially be dealing with the traditional issues, but at a high cost in resources spent in compiling comprehensive lists and in scarce managerial time diverted from relevant decisions.

INAPPROPRIATENESS. It is significant that all the successes claimed for zero-base budgeting are in *direct* operational programs, in which a state government or a business actually delivers a service (such as vocational rehabilitation). This is because it is relatively easy to define an output (people of various types rehabilitated), to analyze alternative methods of attaining the output (institutional training, television courses, vouchers to purchase training), and to define levels of effort associated with the levels of output. Programs can be successfully studied one at a time because they produce results independent of other activities. Zero-base budgeting helps this kind of analysis by isolating how much extra output the government can provide for an increment of cost, and it may aid in identifying duplicative programs.

But most of the domestic federal budget is spent on *indirect* operations, such as transfer payments and grants to state and local governments. These are not as well-suited to the zero-base budgeting approach. Grants, for example, are interdependent; how much Washington pays for state and local education should be dependent on how much it pays for state and local health care assistance, since both grant programs are partly designed to offset the fiscal burdens of state and local governments. Moreover, there are no clear "minimum levels" or discrete increments comparable to those in direct operating programs; the minimum level of general revenue sharing, for instance, is zero, and each dollar above the minimum constitutes a possible program level. Transfer payments are similarly sensibly analyzed in terms of an overall policy of alleviating poverty and compensating for income variations, such as those occasioned by

41. This is acknowledged by Peter Pyhrr, the developer of ZBB. He points out that at Texas Instruments, top management concentrated on funding levels between 70 and 110 percent of the current year's expenditure. Peter A. Pyhrr, *Zero-Base Budgeting: A Practical Management Tool for Evaluating Expenses* (Wiley, 1973), p. 96.

unemployment. Building a coherent transfer payment budget involves constructing a mosaic of food stamps, Medicaid, AFDC, unemployment compensation, social security, and so on that is consistent with the overall policy. Consequently, it would not make sense for the Department of Agriculture, which operates the food stamp program, to rank increments in spending in that program against agricultural research, but not against increments in social security, which is run by the Department of Health, Education, and Welfare. This is an inherent problem of government organization, not by any means unique to zero-base budgeting, but the insistence of the new process on making rankings at every level heightens the difficulty.

For the major operating program of the federal government, national defense, the emphasis of zero-base budgeting on examining basic objectives is a helpful characteristic, but its failure to emphasize a multiyear approach to spending (discussed below) may limit its usefulness in military procurement, research, and construction programs.

GAMESMANSHIP. Another difficulty, again inherent in the budget process but possibly more acute with zero-base budgeting, is that agencies may try to tailor their budget requests so that reductions are difficult to make. A story is told that when the Department of the Interior was asked what would have to be given up if its budget were cut by 5 percent, the secretary responded, "We'd have to close the Washington Monument." Under ZBB, there is every incentive to load questionable functions into the minimum level (highest priority) part of a decision package set and position the politically most attractive activities in the zone where the agency manager thinks a higher-level decisionmaker will actually be trading off one program against another. This kind of gamesmanship can obviously be overcome by astute oversight as budgets pass through bureaus, agencies, departments, and OMB, but especially because of the newness of ZBB and the flood of new forms, oversight may not be very keen for some time to come.[42]

MYOPIC BIAS. Finally, zero-base budgeting focuses on the budget for the upcoming year; in so doing, it diverts attention from the

42. For an imaginative example of how a bureaucrat might turn ZBB into an exercise to maximize his budget, see James Q. Wilson, "Zero-Based Budgeting Comes to Washington," *The Alternative: An American Spectator*, vol. 10 (February 1977), p. 5.

long-run consequences of current actions (very important in defense, construction, and entitlement programs) and the need to regulate current-year decisionmaking by future-year goals. While, in principle, a budget process encompassing both ZBB (intensive examination of existing programs) and multiyear budgeting (which tends to emphasize examination of increments and future-year goals) is conceivable, it is very difficult to make such a procedure comprehensible and workable.[43] In terms of the goal of identifying program reductions that eliminate waste and are politically feasible, there is much to be said against the myopia of the ZBB approach. Large changes in program funding in a single year almost always cause dislocations—people lose entitlements they had come to expect, or states are faced with prospective budget deficits as a result of abrupt federal fund cutbacks—which is a major reason why so few programs have been eliminated in the past. By contrast, a multiyear approach has a chance to reduce the growth in the program base. In fact, before the decision to implement zero-base budgeting was announced, there was every reason to expect a shift in both the executive branch and Congress to multiyear budgeting.

Multiyear Budgeting

In a report issued on January 19, 1977, the Office of Management and Budget recommended to the Congress that "The Federal Government . . . have appropriations requested and enacted in the context of explicit longer-range plans. Specifically, target amounts should be included in the budget, but not enacted as appropriations, for the two years beyond the budget year. Also, the Congress should include target amounts for these years in their concurrent resolutions."[44] The Congressional Budget Office later endorsed the same principle.[45]

The primary motivation for these proposals is not explicitly to find

43. In Georgia, ZBB originally did require managers to make projections of decision package costs. Pyhrr, however, recommended that the requirement be abandoned, except in unusual cases. See Pyhrr, *Zero-Base Budgeting*, pp. 132–33. The OMB bulletin on ZBB does require multi-year data, but it is not clear how the future costs are to be reflected in current year decisions.

44. Office of Management and Budget, "A Study of the Advisability of Submitting the President's Budget and Enacting Budget Authority in Advance of the Current Timetable" (January 19, 1977; processed), pp. 5–6.

45. Congressional Budget Office, *Advance Budgeting: A Report to the Congress* (Government Printing Office, 1977).

ways to reduce the size of the budget. Rather, multiyear budgeting is intended to force all federal decisionmakers—agencies, the President, and the Congress—to develop current budgets in terms of long-range goals and constraints and to ensure that the future impact of current year decisions is fully understood. In providing a budget process that is amenable to reducing the budget base, multiyear budgeting has some advantages.

Setting out a multiyear plan, as was done in the first section of this chapter, inevitably turns attention to those components of the base that are growing either rapidly or by large amounts. This can help in identifying where the budget can be reduced without taking away existing benefits.

Multiyear budgeting would facilitate some radical reforms by allowing packaging of reform proposals. In a multiyear context, the political drawbacks of eliminating programs are lessened; the gradual phaseout of a grant program can be coupled with phasing in a new (or expanded old) program. Elimination of an operating program—for example, procurement of a particular piece of military hardware—can be linked to a new program—a better piece of hardware—so as to minimize dislocation in nonfederal institutions. Multiyear budgeting provides a mechanism for such joint actions because it constitutes a form of budgetary commitment by the executive branch of the federal government—that is, a functioning multiyear budget would show the policy decisions made by the administration and how they planned to implement them. This makes it possible to "guarantee" (barring some unforseen circumstance) that, although program X will be phased out, program Y will, over time, compensate most of those who suffer from the termination of program X. Such combined packages may represent a feasible method for getting the political backing necessary for enactment of program reductions.

On the congressional side, the proposal to include expenditure targets for future years in each congressional concurrent resolution should hold back the most egregious types of uncontrolled spending. For example, in the past large new entitlement programs were often started late in a year, thus showing small initial costs. If expenditure targets for future years were already on the books, such an entitlement program could be challenged by recourse to the targets. While this procedure would not be foolproof—the future target is as likely to be amended as the offending program—it could pave the way for more conscious forward planning in the Congress and the restraint such planning exerts on untoward spending growth.

Sunset Laws

Senator Edmund Muskie and others have proposed the Sunset Act of 1977. This law would require that each program of the federal government be reauthorized[46] at least every five years, that such reauthorization be based on a comprehensive and simultaneous review of other programs in its budget function or subfunction (such as national defense or public assistance), and that if a program is *not* explicitly reauthorized, it automatically terminates (fades into the sunset). The law also would apply to federal tax expenditures—the special tax treatment for certain types of income or expenditure. The Carter administration is supporting the sunset act, with some proposed amendments.[47]

The sunset law is intended to concentrate attention on the fundamental rationale for a program or for a whole governmental function, rather than on incremental changes in it. But, unlike zero-base budgeting, the sunset law would be divorced from the budget process proper. In the legislative context, this separation is appropriate because basic policy is supposed to be made in the authorization process, not in the budget or appropriations phase. An attractive feature of the sunset approach is that it would allow taxes and outlays for a particular function to be jointly reviewed and evaluated, thus encouraging trade-offs between the programs of different agencies and between different mechanisms (tax expenditures or spending) for achieving the same objective.

The principal difficulty with the sunset approach is that it is too comprehensive. To reexamine, from the bottom, every budget func-

46. An authorization is legislation that establishes the legal authority for the federal government to engage in an activity. Once an activity is authorized, "budget authority"—usually an appropriation law—may be passed and the activity undertaken.

47. See "Statement of Bert Lance, Director of the Office of Management and Budget, on the Sunset Act of 1977, before the Senate Subcommittee on Intergovernmental Affairs" (OMB release, March 22, 1977; processed). Interestingly, one of the administration's objections to the bill is that the requirements for information "may overload the Executive branch with requests at the same time that it is attempting to carry out the annual zero base budgeting efforts" (ibid., p. 4).

tion every five years means examining anywhere from 1,000 to 100,000 programs or activities.[48] This would spread very thin the available analytical manpower to perform the evaluations and might consume a disproportionate amount of congressional time. On the other hand, there are government activities and tax features that have gone unexamined for many years, and sunset laws may be the only way to bring them out of the closet.

Selectivity as a Guide for Program Review

One lesson ought to be learned from this review of budgeting processes: the federal government and its budget are very complex and varied. This means that the appropriate method for finding budget reductions should be specially designed approaches in different areas.

One promising way to restrain the growth of the federal budget is to get at the causes of the major expenditure increases built into current programs. This requires careful study and evaluation in those few programs or expenditure categories that exhibit the large increases.

Waste, duplication, and inefficiency in existing programs may require radical rethinking of governmental roles and functions. Such comprehensive reviews should be undertaken on a selective basis where there is a priori knowledge of inefficiency. Such selectivity would concentrate top-level managerial time on promising ventures. In the executive branch, this can probably best be achieved through full-scale reviews of selected activities, with the full participation of the departments, OMB, and the President. In the Congress, sunset provisions may be required in certain areas where legislation is rarely reviewed in order to provoke the needed reexaminations. Most programs, however, are reexamined regularly by Congress, and comprehensive sunset laws do not seem necessary, nor is annual rejustification of the fundamentals of programs required across-the-board in budget reviews.

Taking a long-run approach to federal spending and taxing is essential for budget control and implementation of new priorities. The most serious defect in current budget procedures is the absence

48. The low estimate is by supporters of the legislation and the high one from the Senate Rules and Administration Committee, which is critical of the proposal. See Richard E. Cohen, "Taking Up the Tools to Tame the Bureaucracy: Sunset Legislation," *National Journal*, vol. 9 (April 2, 1977), p. 518.

of a multiyear context for presidential proposals or congressional budget resolutions. This can be remedied by a multiyear federal budget, the first step of which could be a presidential budget encompassing three fiscal years and congressional action to incorporate the last two of these years' budgets into its concurrent resolutions.

Studies and changes in the budget process will at best allow the government to identify less urgent expenditures and come up with better alternatives. One of the dangers of an excessive focus on process changes is that it deflects interest and energies from policymaking.[49] In many areas of federal spending, knowledge of wasteful and duplicative programs already exists; the difficulty in terminating such weak programs is that special interest groups influence the executive branch or the Congress, or both, to maintain them. The political strength of these groups has been the major stumbling block to progress in making government more efficient. Thus, any process for identifying wasteful tax provisions or spending programs will need a political follow-up by a strong-willed president.[50] President Carter's early proposals to terminate a number of water resource programs may be a clue to his determination to spend some political chips on efficiency. Buried in OMB's directive on zero-base budgeting is a hint of what may be its real purpose; one of the objectives listed is to "provide a credible rationale for reallocating resources, especially from old activities to new activities." Taken in this sense, zero-base budgeting may be just a way for the President to demonstrate the fair and evenhanded way he came to his budgetary decisions. Whether zero-base budgeting will be a political success in persuading the Congress and the public to reorder national priorities remains to be seen.

49. The fear that process may overwhelm policy in the Carter administration is provocatively argued by Jack Knott and Aaron Wildavsky, "Jimmy Carter's Theory of Governing," *Wilson Quarterly*, vol. 1 (Winter 1977), pp. 49–67.
50. The relations between budget process and expenditure reduction are spelled out in greater detail in Robert W. Hartman, "Next Steps in Budget Reform: Zero-Base Review and the Budgetary Process," *Policy Analysis*, vol. 3 (Summer 1977).

CHAPTER TWELVE

Reflections on Administrative Reorganization

HERBERT KAUFMAN

As MANY OF THE PRECEDING CHAPTERS indicate, opportunities for fresh program initiatives by the new administration are limited. Money for them is not at hand. Little can be raised by cuts in existing service levels because the security and stability of the nation and the benefits and advantages of countless special interests would be adversely affected by deep reductions in ongoing programs; the opposition would be insurmountable. At the same time, substantial real increases in government expenditures are not likely because of President Carter's declared determination to achieve a balanced budget by the end of his first term.

Under these conditions, the vision of freeing significant sums by reducing waste in government and using the savings to finance new programs without cuts in old ones, more taxes, or large deficits is especially appealing. The endless crusade against governmental inefficiency and complexity has therefore taken on renewed intensity.

Reorganization of the executive branch is a commonly advocated weapon against inefficiency and complexity, but it is not the only one. Changes in public policy can also be effective. Improvements in administrative management, budgeting, personnel administration, standard operating procedures, methods of purchasing, incentive systems, and other techniques of handling the day-to-day business of the executive branch can increase efficiency and simplify operations. But compared to reorganization—the creation of new administrative organizations on a grand scale, the regrouping of old ones, the termination of outmoded units and the redistribution of their functions among others, changes in the degree of autonomy enjoyed by existing bodies, and other such transformations of structure—they are often seen as superficial, trivial, and politically unrewarding. Thus, when reformers strive to make government simpler, more efficient, and less costly—to get it "under control"—they tend to go the reorganization route. Yet reorganization is not self-evidently the most promising means to achieve efficiency, simplicity, and reduced cost.

The Frustrating Quest for Efficiency

The standard reorganization strategies for rationalizing and simplifying the executive branch often clash with one another. Many consequences of reorganization, it must be admitted, cannot be tracked; some claims made for specific strategies, and some of the charges against them, rest on nothing more than faith or prejudice or self-interest. Logically and empirically, however, various strategies appear to contribute as much to exacerbation of the problems of executive organization as to their solution. The probabilities of net gains, if any, seem very small. Reviewing the list of standard prescriptions for organizational improvement explains why.

Standard Prescriptions

Although myriad detailed proposals have been advanced to make the executive branch more orderly, symmetrical, and efficient, they all turn out to be variations on one or another of the following seven basic prescriptions.

1. Limit the number of line subordinates over whom any executive is assigned jurisdiction (commonly referred to as "the span of control"). This practice presumably avoids the dilution of leadership and keeps the executive from losing touch with what his subordinates are doing simply because there is too much to keep track of. It also allows immediate subordinates to check in with the boss as frequently as they feel they must in order to find out whether they are in compliance with his or her wishes. And it frees executive time for reflection about broad policy matters and for coping with external relations.

2. Group related functions under a common command. Otherwise, coordination is difficult to achieve and redundancies cannot be eliminated. Moreover, leaders with responsibility for a diversity of functions frequently find themselves at the mercy of their more specialized nominal subordinates.

3. Furnish executives with ample staff assistance so that they are provided with evaluations of subordinates' performance apart from those supplied by the subordinates themselves, with personal sources of information other than the formal hierarchy, and with capacity to work up their own programs and policies. They also need close, trusted, personal emissaries to interpret and expand on policy statements and orders because executives are usually too preoccupied with other demands to perform this function themselves. Forty years ago, the President's Committee on Administrative Management proclaimed emphatically, "The President needs help."[1] At least from that time forward, it has been an axiom of public administration that staff assistance lets an executive multiply his influence in his organization. Executive reorganizations at all levels have consistently increased such staff.

4. Authorize executives to reorganize fairly freely the agencies and units under their command. With such authority, executives would be able not only to take the initiative to rationalize the structures they head, but also to negotiate from positions of strength with the officers below them. In a pluralistic governmental system, bureau chiefs often effect political alliances that make them quite independent of their nominal superiors. Under these conditions, superiors generally need all the implements they can gather to exert the power of their offices.

5. On the other hand, *reduce* the vulnerability and obligations of certain agencies and agency heads to political leaders. Stability of policy is often considered vital to investment and advance planning; if policies were to be reversed every time there was a change of parties or of leaders within parties, the uncertainty could have depressing effects on economic development and growth. Furthermore, politicians are vulnerable to demands for special consideration and special advantages by constituents whom they hesitate to offend. To impede

1. The President's Committee on Administrative Management, *Administrative Management in the Government of the United States* (Government Printing Office, 1937), p. 5.

political oscillation and favoritism, many public servants have been granted security in office, permitting them to resist political pressures more readily than easily removable personnel can. Organizational designs are often fashioned with this end in view.

6. Decentralize administration. This strategy is sometimes adopted to promote efficiency, effectiveness, and responsiveness by empowering field officers to take action on their own, and thus to deal quickly with matters in their bailiwicks. Because of their knowledge of local circumstances, their judgments are said to stand a better chance of fitting local requirements and of convincing residents that local interests have been respected. Decentralization thus combines speed and adaptability and the possibility of controlled experimentation. It is therefore commonly recommended by critics of governmental cumbersomeness, coldness, and delay.

7. Increase public participation in the administrative process. Underlying this strategy is the premise that if people affected by governmental decisions and actions take part in the formulation of such measures, no interest will be overlooked or neglected and no significant consequence unanticipated. Few claims are made for the efficiency of such procedures, but responsiveness and, to a lesser extent, effectiveness can allegedly be improved in this fashion, thus diminishing the feeling that government is out of control.

Most of the techniques of reinforcing public participation in administrative decisionmaking are procedural rather than organizational. That is, decisionmakers are obliged at various points to afford opportunities to the public to express views on pending matters and to challenge judgments and policies already adopted. But there is also a structural means to this end—namely, giving an interest group an agency of its own, with a chief having a central role in government decisions affecting that group. It may be an entirely new agency or an older one elevated in status after separation from another organization in which it occupied a subordinate position. In either case, it provides the group with a representative in higher circles and a defender of its interests.

All these measures have been recommended as steps on the road to a better administrative system. They are meant to enable leaders to simplify structure, streamline procedure, coordinate action, build cohesive work forces, reward the diligent, expel the deadwood, motivate the staff, rationalize their organizations, and stay attuned to the populace, thus lifting government to higher levels of efficiency, accomplishment, and humanity. They have therefore had considerable influence on federal structure.

The Prescriptions Have Been Followed

These doctrines of administration lie behind some familiar features of the federal executive branch.

1. Limiting the President's span of control and grouping related functions were among the principal reasons for establishing the Department of Defense, the prototypal "superdepartment" encompassing two ordinary departments previously at the cabinet level (War and Navy) and a new one of the same rank (Air Force). Similar considerations also gave rise to the Housing and Home Finance Agency, later to become the Department of Housing and Urban Development, which pulled together some of the scattered operations constituting the government's urban and housing programs and policies. Within departments, corresponding developments took place, with new administrative levels, such as the National Oceanic and Atmospheric Administration and the short-lived Social and Economic Statistics Administration in the Department of Commerce, interposed between secretaries and groups of bureaus.

2. Staff assistance for executives resulted not only in the Executive Office of the President, which was created in 1939 and experienced very rapid growth almost continuously from that time on, but in corresponding multiplication of deputy secretaries, under secretaries, assistant secretaries; assistants and deputies to all these new lieutenants; and staff units (legal counsel, public relations, congressional relations, personnel, administrative management, housekeeping services, budgeting, policy planning, and others) in virtually all departments. There are reasons why the Congress might sometimes feel uneasy about this trend. For one thing, it means increases in the size and cost of the executive branch. More importantly, it interposes officials oriented toward the President between congressional committees and "their" bureaus. Nevertheless, the doctrines of administration have been honored; the growth of staff has proceeded steadily.

3. Reorganization authority for executives at the presidential level was granted in generous measure during both world wars and the

Great Depression[2] and in more circumscribed grants at other times. The first Reorganization Act was passed in 1939, was superseded by the First War Powers Act during World War II, then reappeared with some modifications in 1945, and was reenacted regularly thereafter until it was allowed to lapse in 1973. Reinstating it was one of the first things President Carter requested of the Congress.

The reorganization acts of the past enhanced presidential managerial power by reversing the roles of the Congress and the President. They provided for the executive to submit reorganization plans that would automatically take effect with the force of law unless the Congress, which could not amend them, vetoed the proposals by voting them down within sixty days. They permitted the President "to appeal directly to the full membership of either house for support in a floor vote within a stipulated time on the package as he put it together, bypassing both the leadership and the legislative committee seniors if they are unsympathetic."[3] As a result, 86 of the 109 plans submitted from 1939 on succeeded.[4]

The Congress was always cautious about this delegation of power. It never made the legislation permanent, instead granting the authority only for limited periods, after which it had to be reenacted. Every act since 1964 excluded from the delegation authority to create or eliminate cabinet-level departments, thereby requiring regular statutes for these purposes. Some also restricted the number of plans to a maximum of one every thirty days, confined each one to a single subject, and forbade the establishment of new legal authority by means of plans. Early versions required negative votes in both houses to defeat a plan; later, a negative vote in either house was made sufficient. Despite the restraints, however, an eminent student of the re-

2. In World War I, sec. 2 of the "Lever Act" of 1917 (40 Stat. 276) and the "Overman Act" of 1918 (40 Stat. 556) conferred on the President broad powers of agency creation and reorganization for the duration of the war plus a period afterward. In the Great Depression, Title IV of the Economy Acts of 1932 (47 Stat. 382, 413–15) and 1933 (47 Stat. 1489, 1517–20) authorized extensive transfers, consolidations, and redistributions of executive agencies by executive order of the President (subject in the earlier statute to veto by either house of the Congress) for a limited period of time. In World War II, Title I of the First War Powers Act, 1941 (55 Stat. 838) similarly authorized sweeping reorganizations of "any executive department, commission, bureau, agency, governmental corporation, office, or officer" during and shortly after the war.

3. Harvey C. Mansfield. "Federal Executive Reorganization: Thirty Years of Experience," *Public Administration Review*, vol. 29 (July–August 1969), p. 341.

4. Office of Management and Budget, "President's Reorganization Authority" (OMB, April 1977; processed), app. 3, p. 4.

organization process, Harvey C. Mansfield, concluded that "reorganization plans have proved a serviceable device for shifting bureaus, realigning jurisdictions, regrouping activities, and upsetting some ties of influence."[5]

President Carter requested not only restoration of the 1971 law that had been permitted to lapse, but some additional powers as well. He proposed a four-year life for the legislation instead of a two-year authorization. He sought to eliminate the requirement that each reorganization plan treat only one subject. He called for omission of any limitation on the number of plans that could be submitted in a given period. And he asked for authority to amend a plan within thirty days after submission, to let him respond to congressional objections. A challenge by the chairman of the House Government Operations Committee requiring an *affirmative* vote by both houses to turn a plan into a law was easily turned back, but the President did not get everything he requested. The enacted bill contains only a three-year life span, the restriction on subject matter, legislative procedures to facilitate floor votes (thus preventing committees from bottling up resolutions of disapproval), exclusion of independent regulatory commissions from the executive's reorganization power, and a provision limiting to three the number of plans pending in the Congress at one time. Still, the President got the main authority he wanted.[6]

At the cabinet level, most department heads already enjoyed broad legal authority to redesign their organizations. Following the recommendations of the first Hoover Commission, a series of successful reorganization plans and some statutes vested in these and a few other officials all the authority given by law to the bureaus and subordinates under them, authorized them to redelegate those powers at will, and permitted them to transfer records, property, personnel, and, to a limited extent, funds within their own departments. Indeed, the logic of reorganization was pushed even further at this level than at the presidential level.

4. Insulating administrative agencies from politics was the major premise behind the original "independent" regulatory commissions,

5. Mansfield, "Federal Executive Reorganization," p. 341.
6. For a comparison of the various proposals for the reorganization act, see American Enterprise Institute for Public Policy Research, *The Executive Reorganization Act: A Survey of Proposals for Renewal and Modification* (The Institute, 1977). The statute is Public Law 95–17, April 6, 1977.

the autonomy of the Federal Reserve Board, and the merit system and job protection for the civil service. More recently, members of the Civil Service Commission, who originally served at the pleasure of the President, were given staggered terms of six years; a professor of administrative law suggested new protections for the commissions;[7] some experts called for the transformation of certain administrative tribunals into full administrative courts;[8] and a reorganization committee recommended that the merit system be expanded "upward, outward, and downward."[9] Even with added protections, none of these institutions can be made totally immune to political pressure. But because of the safeguards around them, they are in a better position to resist such pressures when they want to than they would be without their special shields. Few architects of government expect more than that.

5. Decentralization has had a spotty record within the executive branch (as distinguished from intergovernmental relations, where, through revenue sharing and block grants, the federal government recently returned to states and localities some of the discretion over their affairs it had acquired).[10] Executives have not been disposed to delegate power freely to their subordinates, nor have subordinate administrators been any more generous with *their* subordinates. In any case, citizens applying for agency benefits or other actions do not ordinarily accept adverse decisions at lower levels, but push their cases upward through administrative and political channels in the hope of securing favorable judgments. Still, students of government continue to urge administrative decentralization with great regularity, and now and then a modest step in this direction is taken by this agency or that.[11]

7. Bernard Schwartz, *The Professor and the Commissions* (Knopf, 1959), chap. 7 and pp. 266–69. For a contrasting view, see Emmette S. Redford, "The President and the Regulatory Commissions," *Texas Law Review,* vol. 44 (1965–66), pp. 288–321.

8. Commission on Organization of the Executive Branch of the Government, *Legal Services and Procedure: A Report to the Congress* (Government Printing Office, 1955), pp. 87–88. See also its Task Force report on the same subject and of the same date, pp. 246–56.

9. President's Committee on Administrative Management, *Administrative Management,* p. 7.

10. See James A. Maxwell and J. Richard Aronson, *Financing State and Local Governments* (3rd ed., Brookings Institution, 1977), chap. 3, esp. pp. 71–76.

11. The Department of Housing and Urban Development, for example, adopted a plan of reorganization in 1969 and 1970 that called for decentralization to field

6. Participation by the public in administrative decisionmaking became such a rallying cry in recent years that many people do not realize it has a long history in our government.[12] There are agencies that represent specific groups (the Departments of Labor, of Agriculture, and of Commerce, for instance, and the Veterans' Administration). There have been administrative boards made up of representatives of various interests, and advisory boards that give interests a voice in policy making. Even prior to enactment of the Administrative Procedure Act in 1946, but more so since then, provisions were made to obtain the views of people affected by impending administrative legislation and adjudications before these decisions became final. To be sure, unorganized interests, which for a long time included such large groups as consumers, the poor, and women, were comparatively ineffectual in pressing their views on administrative actions, and recent efforts to redress the balance may well begin a new chapter in the history of administrative organization and procedure. If so, however, it will be a chapter in a very long book; organizing for interest-group participation is nothing new.

The structure of the federal executive branch is thus in large part the product of the standard prescriptions for better administration. Abstract doctrine has been established in practice.

General Contradictions in the Prescriptions

One of the first things close examination discloses is that the standard prescriptions for reorganization tend in opposite directions. The first four standard prescriptions push power upward in hierarchies, building leadership strength and exerting a centralizing thrust. The last three impel power outward and downward; theirs is an impulse toward dispersal of authority.

Some people maintain that the tendencies are not opposed at all. The making of broad policies, they say, can be centralized while the

offices and established new area offices within regions to carry out the plan. Decentralization was also among the reasons for establishment of common regional boundaries and common headquarters cities for many departments and agencies; see Harold Seidman, *Politics, Position, and Power: The Dynamics of Federal Organization* (Oxford University Press, 1970), pp. 59–61, and *United States Government Manual, 1976/77* (GPO, 1976), app. D. See also Martha Derthick, *Between State and Nation: Regional Organizations of the United States* (Brookings Institution, 1974), chap. 7.

12. Avery Leiserson, *Administrative Regulation: A Study in Representation of Interests* (University of Chicago Press, 1942).

administration (or "execution" or "implementation") of those policies can be decentralized and dispersed. Although the old distinction
between policy and administration, argued most cogently by Frank
Goodnow early in this century,[13] had fallen on hard times by the third
quarter of the century, it has never been invalidated. There are still
many who subscribe to the view that an organization can concentrate
policy formulation while devolving administrative responsibility.

On the other hand, if policy is defined as what is actually done
rather than what is said or intended, policy and administration cannot
be separated in practice, and the contradictory thrusts cannot, by this
definition, be reconciled. Theorists of this persuasion[14] hold that
leaders who stay aloof from the nitty-gritty of their organizations'
operations soon find themselves exercising less and less influence over
the actions of those below them. If, however, they endeavor to shape
policy in practice by controlling the administrative behavior of their
subordinates, they obviously are directing things from the center.
Thus, policy and administration being closely intertwined, centralization and decentralization cannot be pursued simultaneously. To get
control of policy, it is necessary to get control of administration. If
administrative discretion is decentralized, policy follows close behind.
Organizations cannot have it both ways, and it would be futile to
attempt to apply all seven techniques of organizational improvement
at once to a given set of circumstances. Choices must be made. Difficult trade-offs cannot be avoided.

Specific Mutual Negations and Hidden Costs

To be more specific, grouping related functions under a common
command wars with the separation of agencies from the hierarchy of

13. Frank J. Goodnow, *Politics and Administration: A Study in Government*
(Macmillan, 1900), esp. chap. 4. The distinction had been drawn earlier, though not
argued so fully, in Woodrow Wilson, "The Study of Administration," *Political
Science Quarterly*, vol. 2 (June 1887), pp. 197–222; reprinted in vol. 56 (December
1941), pp. 481–506.
14. Luther Gulick, for example: "Much of the actual discretion used in administration is used at the very bottom of the hierarchy, where public servants touch the
public. The assessor who walks into the home and sees the furniture and the condition
of the house, the policeman who listens to the motorist's story, the health inspector
who visits the dairy, the income tax auditor who sees the return and interviews the
taxpayer—all these people are compelled to exercise more discretion, and more important discretion from the point of view of the citizen, than many other functionaries
much farther up in the organization. While this is the actual situation in badly organized and poorly directed administrative units, it cannot be completely eliminated
even in the best." "Politics, Administration, and the 'New Deal,'" *Annals of the
American Academy of Political and Social Science*, vol. 169 (September 1933), p. 62.

the executive branch in order to protect them from political pressures. Coordination and control are increased by hierarchy, but political favoritism and other forms of special consideration are facilitated when organizational barriers to these practices are removed. Some students of administration are so appalled by disclosures of such abuses that they advocate making the barriers around many agencies higher and stronger. Each standard prescription has advantages, but it is impossible to get the advantages of both at the same time.

Similarly, increasing participation by agency clientele in agency decisionmaking opens the way for narrow political interests to exert powerful influence on administration. Indeed, if it is coupled with separation from the executive hierarchy and resolute decentralization, it can be tantamount to turning important sectors of the government over to special interests. It is certainly at the opposite end of the scale from taking politics out of administration and keeping administration out of politics. And it also conflicts with the implications of keeping the span of control narrow.

Reinforcing agency autonomy so as to stiffen resistance to efforts at improper intervention by politicians likewise runs afoul of the strategy of allowing executives to reorganize fairly freely. Independence and its benefits come at the expense of reorganization authority and *its* advantages, and vice versa. There is no way to avoid this trade-off.

And so it goes. Limiting the span of control in a large organization produces a "steeper" hierarchy with more administrative layers, thereby insulating leaders from front-line realities and slowing the process of reaching decisions. It also contributes to the emergence of superdepartments, and of superagencies within departments, which impedes capture of the superadministrators by a single set of narrow interests, but imposes on them such a wide array of responsibilities that they are often at a disadvantage in dealing with their more specialized subordinates. At the same time, superdepartments are created by downgrading ordinary departments, making departmental leadership posts less attractive to many prospective heads.

Grouping agencies or activities by common purpose renounces the advantages of grouping them by target clientele, by area, or by process (not to mention by other purposes). Decentralizing by delegating discretion to lower echelons jeopardizes coordination and consistency, and risks entrapment of field offices by local private and political interests.

The insulation devised to exclude politics from administration at all levels itself entails some significant costs. Government officers and employees with substantial job security sometimes come to regard elected officials and political executives as amateurs, birds of passage, and opportunists compared to career public servants who know their programs and dedicate their lives to them. Under these circumstances, it would be natural for some careerists to feel that instead of bending to every shift in political winds, they should occasionally use their staying power to outlast their political superiors and make their own policies prevail.

Even building up executive staff assistance, once regarded as self-evidently beneficial, can impose heavy charges on the system if allowed to proceed unchecked. In the Watergate inquiries and their aftermath, it became clear that platoons of staff assistants can isolate an executive from currents of opinion and discontent in the country, from the rest of the government, and from his own line lieutenants, the members of the cabinet. Meanwhile, staff members often muddy the waters of administration by intervening in the operation of departments and agencies in the name of their chief, who may know nothing of their adventures.

It was more than thirty years ago that Herbert A. Simon pointed out that administrative principles are like proverbs in that they come in mutually contradictory pairs.[15] "Look before you leap," but "he who hesitates is lost." "Haste makes waste," but "strike while the iron is hot." "Absence makes the heart grow fonder," but "out of sight, out of mind." "Clothes make the man," but "all is not gold that glitters" or "don't judge a book by its cover." The analogy is still apt. There is wisdom and truth in both parts of each pair. The genius of the reorganizer is to know which trade-off to make at a given time.

Real Payoffs

Obviously, no reorganization is inherently right or wrong. No given administrative pattern will invariably increase efficiency, effectiveness, or responsiveness. In particular circumstances, identical organizational arrangements may produce diametrically opposite effects while radically different arrangements may produce identical effects.

15. Herbert A. Simon, "The Proverbs of Administration," *Public Administration Review*, vol. 6 (Winter 1946), p. 53.

It All Depends, declared Harvey Sherman in his book by that title.[16] One can hardly quarrel with that.

None of this means, however, that there is no point to reorganizing. On the contrary, the consequences of reorganization are frequently profound. But the profound, determinable consequences do not lie in the engineering realm of efficiency, simplicity, size, and cost of government. Rather, the real payoffs are measured in terms of influence, policy, and communication.

Effects on Influence

For example, reorganization redistributes influence. If the Arms Control and Disarmament Agency had been set up in the Department of Defense instead of as an independent unit, it seems likely that the advocates of arms limitations would have had less impact on policy than they did. Policy recommendations to the President and the Congress filtered through the armed services community would almost certainly have been unlike the proposals emerging from an agency with a different perspective on the world, a different mission, and a different set of priorities. Moreover, the conduct of negotiations over disarmament and arms limitations would probably not have been as vigorous, patient, or perseverant under execlusive Defense Department auspices.

Similarly, if environmental protection were scattered among environmental protection units in other agencies instead of being lodged in the Environmental Protection Agency, chances are the views of environmentalists would have been swamped by oil interests in the Federal Energy Administration, air and highway interests in the Department of Transportation, coal interests in the Department of the Interior, and so on. Within the policymaking councils of the government, the environmentalists' voices would have been muffled, if not silenced.

Consumer groups are demanding a separate consumer agency for the same reason. Consumer units dispersed among producer-oriented agencies, they are convinced, would not carry much weight; they want

16. *It All Depends: A Pragmatic Approach to Organization* (University of Alabama Press, 1966), esp. chap. 2. See also Seidman, *Politics, Position, and Power;* Peri E. Arnold, "Reorganization and Politics: A Reflection on the Adequacy of Administrative Theory," *Public Administration Review,* vol. 34 (May–June 1974), pp. 205–11; and Herbert A. Simon, Donald W. Smithburg, and Victor A. Thompson, *Public Administration* (Knopf, 1950), chap. 7.

a body beholden to them in the top levels of the government. Not only would they expect to acquire strength directly; central agencies also serve as rallying points for previously dispersed pressure groups with overlapping interests.

People will argue over the effect of such differences in structure on efficiency, and over the danger of needless complexity, and will come to different conclusions according to the goals they favor. They will commonly agree, however, that different structures strengthen the hands of some officials and interest groups and reduce the ability of others to get what they want. The effects are not precisely measurable or completely predictable, but their general thrust is usually discernible.

Effects on Policy

Who acquires power and who is deprived of power would be of interest only to the people involved were it not for the implications of such redistributions for governmental policy; what the government *does* is determined by the distribution of influence. For example, if an overarching energy agency is given access to the inner councils of government and power over sister agencies, energy conservation is likely to be stressed even if it slows economic growth, inhibits the rise in the standard of living or even reduces the level of convenience and comfort, and perhaps even increases unemployment. At the same time, intensified striving after increases in energy production might lead to relaxation of environmental safeguards and uncontrolled prices for energy producers that are passed on to consumers. If the energy agency's powers are split up, lodged in hostile parent organizations, placed at low administrative levels, and given scant authority, other values will probably take precedence over energy considerations, with the result that vulnerability to political pressures by oil producing countries, to severe trade imbalances, and to recurrent domestic shortages will increase steadily.

If preferred status is accorded those who believe the economic marketplace is the best promoter of the manifold interests in our society, government regulation of economic activity will be reduced while efforts to break up industry-dominating combinations and competition-suppressing agreements are emphasized. If stronger positions are given to those who believe there are benefits in large-scale operations, and that the way to protect the public interest is to control them rather than to try to dissolve them in a vain quest to preserve a market through government power, then more and more industries will be treated as public utilities and subjected to surveillance and regulation by specialized government agencies.

To take still another example, the Occupational Safety and Health Administration was placed in the Department of Labor and its regulations were addressed heavily to mechanical hazards and to worker comfort. Had it been put under the assistant secretary for health in the Department of Health, Education, and Welfare, there is reason to surmise that chemical and biological dangers to workers probably would have received higher priority in the regulations.

Organizational arrangements in government, in short, affect not only the leaders and members of the organizations established or moved or redesigned; they impinge on the lives of millions of other people in this generation and the future.

Signals

Organizational arrangements are also a means of communicating the government's intentions. They signal people inside the government, people throughout the country, and, indeed, people and governments throughout the world what this government's emphases will be. Such signals often influence the behavior of those who receive them. All too often, they are misconstrued, so the architects of administration would be mistaken to let the symbolic considerations dominate their designs. At the same time, however, administrative designers would be remiss if they did not take into account the interpretations that may be placed on their handiwork. How well their designs work depends in part on the designers' success in selecting organizational patterns that evoke from everyone concerned the kind of behavior the patterns are meant to produce. The symbolic component is a useful and, indeed, a powerful tool.

Thus, a leader who transfers, combines, and splits organizations in government for engineering purposes will usually find that nobody can be sure whether any progress has been made toward those goals. All too often, the effects on efficiency, simplicity, and cost cannot be determined at all. When they can be assessed, what is successful by one standard may be a failure by another; what improves things in one way makes them worse in another. Real political capital is thus consumed in the pursuit of phantom goals. In contrast, a leader who shifts organizations around to confer power on selected people or remove it from others in order to mold government policies, and to impress on everyone what his or her values and priorities are, will more often be rewarded with a sense of having expended political resources for significant accomplishments. The calculus of reorganization is essentially the calculus of politics itself.

A Case in Point

Despite President Carter's emphasis on efficiency, simplicity, and reduction of government size and cost, the first major reorganization step by his administration seemed to be based on the real payoffs rather than on the standard prescriptions. Within six weeks after his inauguration, the President sent to the Congress draft legislation for the creation of a new, cabinet-level Department of Energy in which most of the economic regulatory functions of the government with respect to energy were to be consolidated.

The proposal certainly concentrated power at a high level (and thus made the position attractive to an administrator of stature and drive). It signaled the President's intentions forcefully. It was a longer stride to formulation of a comprehensive energy policy than the government had previously considered. But its consequences for efficiency and simplicity were quite ambiguous.

To be sure, it called for the abolition of three independent agencies (the Federal Energy Administration, the Energy Research and Development Administration, and the Federal Power Commission) and the vesting of their powers in the new secretary. It also provided for the termination of a coordinating body, the Energy Resources Council. It placed under the command of the secretary units transferred from at least eight other departments and agencies with jurisdiction over parts of the energy field. And it centralized in bodies located in the new department the collection and analysis of energy information and the making of rules on economic regulation of energy.

But if it were adopted as formulated, it would stretch the President's span of control, create as many new structures as it abolishes, and generate fresh problems of coordination. The new department would be the twelfth at the cabinet table. In addition to the department itself, two new administrations with heads appointed by the President (the Energy Information Administration and the Energy Regulatory Administration) would be established and housed in the department, and the presidential message accompanying the draft statute expressed the intention of establishing by executive order an interdepartmental coordinating body chaired by the Secretary of Energy to "manage government-wide concerns involving energy." Health, safety, and environmental regulation (as distinguished from economic regulation) were not included within the department's purview; these would remain under the administration of untouched existing agencies. "Because public concerns about the safety of nuclear power are so serious," the President said in his message accompanying the bill, "we must have a strong, independent voice to ensure that safety does not yield to energy supply pressures. Therefore, the Nuclear Regulatory Commission will remain as an independent body. For similar reasons, the Environmental Protection Agency should remain independent to voice environmental concern." Under these arrangements, he acknowledged, "problems of interdepartmental coordination will remain, since virtually all government activity affects energy to some extent."[17] Clearly, the standard prescriptions for reorganization gave the President little helpful guidance, so he set them aside. Power, policy, and symbolic factors were the crucial elements in the decision to recommend the Department of Energy.

The public record contains few clues to other structural options President Carter may have weighed and rejected. Certainly, there are other organizational arrangements that might have been considered. In World War II, for instance, the need to draw together all the resources of the government for the conduct of the war led to the creation of the Office of War Mobilization, a unit with powers second only to the President's. When the war ended, it also took charge of the adjustment to peace under the expanded title, Office of War Mobilization and Reconversion. A comparable pattern might have been adapted for energy problems. OWM, however, was probably suitable for difficulties of relatively short duration, during which all values could be subordinated to one overriding objective. Energy problems, on the other hand, are likely to be with us for a long time. To deal with problems of this nature, the OWM format, had it been considered at all, would doubtless have been ruled out as inappropriate.

Conceivably, the National Security Council might also have served

17. "Energy Reorganization Message," President Carter's Message to Congress, *Congressional Quarterly*, vol. 35 (March 5, 1977), p. 404.

as a model. When a matter is both urgent and interagency in scope, a collegial organ is the logical structure for decisionmaking. Chances are, however, that another deliberative body consisting of the President and key cabinet officers, making demands on the already scarce time of top officials, would also have been judged unlikely to succeed.

Another model that might have been considered is the Office of Economic Opportunity, a command post in the Executive Office of the President to supervise and stimulate existing agencies where coordination and innovation are needed, and to undertake some new operations on its own. But OEO's function did not consist of controlling economic activity and technological exploration. Furthermore, justly or unjustly, OEO became a highly controversial agency. It, too, would not have commended itself as a promising prototype for energy administration.

Thus, none of the immediately evident alternatives to an executive department could have had as much appeal to the President as the Department of Energy. Other options do not seem even to have been in the running at all. But they were not ruled out by the ambiguous conventional lore of reorganization; what defeated them were the hard realities of national needs and power politics.

Organizing the Reorganizers

The hard realities can shape the President's reorganization agenda for him, and perhaps push him in directions he may not want to go. Already in the wings, no doubt heartened by the proposal for a Department of Energy, stand groups seeking (and perhaps, on the basis of their reading of campaign oratory, expecting) elevation of the Office of Education, now in the Department of Health, Education, and Welfare, to full department status. Meanwhile, the secretary of HEW, with presidential approbation, ordered major structural changes in his department, shifting, abolishing, and creating components to handle health care financing, cash assistance payments, student financial assistance, human development and social services programs, and departmental management. Other secretaries have similarly embarked upon, or at least have been contemplating, changes of corresponding magnitude. A consumer protection agency is in the works. How such developments will fit into larger plans for the executive branch remains to be seen; clearly, however, some attractive organizational strategies may be foreclosed unless the administration is prepared to undo a number of ad hoc actions now being taken. If it is, great elements of uncertainty and turbulence would pervade the administrative system. To deal systematically with this risk, and to seize and hold the initiative, the President will doubtless strive to formulate a general scheme of reorganization. If so, he will have to make some hard choices with respect to the approach, scope, and form of the reorganization effort.

As regards the approach, the broad options are to commission a grand design for the whole executive branch and delay all large-scale changes until the design is complete or to begin at once to work on selected problem areas one after the other and introduce changes as each one is resolved. The options on scope are to restrict organizational considerations to existing governmental programs and levels of operation or to direct reorganizers to suggest changes in policy as well as modifications of structure. The options on form are to employ some kind of special committee to draw up recommendations or to use the expertise and resources of existing bodies and units within the government. Within each strategic option, additional choices must be made, but they are just variations on the major themes.

Neither of the broad strategies in each pair is inherently superior to the other. As with everything else, evaluations depend on the objectives sought. But each has consequences associated with it that can be outlined in advance.

Approaches to Reorganization

Commissioning a grand design, for example, gains the President breathing space; waiting for the finished product provides him with a justification for declining to act on proposals from other politicians, from interest groups, from the bureaucracies, and from other sources when his mind is not made up, and it temporarily suspends the complaints about administrative shortcomings from many of his critics. It also permits a comprehensive examination of a system in which everything impinges on everything else, and in which piecemeal remedies for ills in one part may therefore engender even worse ailments in other parts. On the other hand, if the President does wish to change a part of the system, the opponents of his alterations might also plead persuasively for delay until the full design is at hand. And incremental reforms often turn out to be more successful than global efforts.[18] The sword is double-edged.

Strategists also have to estimate what sort of reception each reorganization approach will enjoy. Grand designs frequently mobilize all the defenders of the status quo at once; each defender usually opposes only a small bit of the total plan and is indifferent to the rest, but presenting the whole thing in one package brings all of them out simultaneously and can doom the package before it has a chance to gather support. Taking things one step at a time permits supporters to deal individually, and more effectively, with the opponents. Eschewing the grand design, though, may deprive reorganizers of a banner under which to rally all their backers, a device to build enthusiasm and a sense of accomplishment, and a vision of the way the parts fit together. Thus, supporters may be reduced to a small band rushing from battlefield to battlefield on which numerous special interests protecting their respective sectors of the status quo have the advantage. The choice of approach depends on the President's assessment of the political weather and the breadth of his aspirations.

How Much Scope for the Reorganizers?

With regard to scope, forbidding reorganization planners to suggest changes in policies and in the levels of government activity may reduce them to tinkering with marginal adjustments in the prevailing system. The big opportunities for organizational change are often tied to elimination or contraction of certain services or regulatory functions, and to expansion of others. But linking discussions of reorganization with debates over the role of government in society and other fundamental philosophical issues invites divisions among the structural planners likely to preclude even the limited consensus on administrative arrangements possible in a more circumscribed sphere of responsibility. It imposes on organizational designers obligations as broad as the entire political system. It can involve every proposed organizational change, no matter how innocuous, in bitter controversy. The decision on scope therefore depends on whether the Presi-

18. David Braybrooke and Charles E. Lindblom, *A Strategy of Decision: Policy Evaluation as a Social Process* (Free Press, 1963), esp. chap. 6; Charles E. Lindblom, *The Intelligence of Democracy: Decision Making through Mutual Adjustment* (Free Press, 1965), esp. pp. 303–09.

dent regards reorganization as a means to develop proposals for policy changes or purely as a managerial tool.

Forms of Reorganization Leadership

The options with respect to form diverge widely. Some reorganization plans drawn up under past reorganization acts seem to have been formulated primarily by government officers and employees in the executive branch. When Presidents wanted to make changes in especially sensitive areas or of sweeping effect, however, they usually appointed a body for the specific purpose of offering recommendations. The two Hoover Commissions[19] were the most elaborate, their composition being specified by statute; the President, the Speaker of the House, and the President pro tempore of the Senate each appointed four, two of each group coming from the executive branch, the House, and the Senate, respectively, and two from private life. In the case of the first commission, not more than one of each pair could be from the same major political party, a restriction not imposed on the composition of the second.

In contrast, bodies appointed by Presidents Roosevelt, Johnson, and Nixon were not established by legislation, and their members were the President's personal choices.[20] President Eisenhower also had such a group, in addition to his Hoover Commission.[21] Roosevelt's committee had only three members, none of whom was in full-time federal service at the time, though all were experienced in government. Eisenhower's also consisted of only three members, of whom two were in high government positions and one was from private life.

19. The first of these, officially named the Commission on Organization of the Executive Branch of the Government, was established in 1947 (61 Stat. 246) and reported in 1949. The second, bearing the same name, was established in 1953 (67 Stat. 142) and reported in 1955.

20. Roosevelt's group was the President's Committee on Administrative Management (the "Brownlow Committee," after its chairman, Louis Brownlow). Johnson's first Task Force on Government Reorganization (the "Price Task Force," after its chairman, Don K. Price) was one of eleven task forces on various issues appointed just before Johnson's election; his second, a couple of years later, was also called the President's Task Force on Government Organization (the "Heineman Task Force," after its chairman, Ben W. Heineman). Nixon's was the President's Advisory Council on Executive Organization (the "Ash Council," after its chairman, Roy L. Ash).

21. Eisenhower's group was the President's Advisory Committee on Government Organization (Executive Order 10432, January 24, 1953), consisting of the chairman, Nelson A. Rockefeller (then Under Secretary of Health, Education, and Welfare), Arthur S. Flemming (Director of the Office of Defense Mobilization), and Milton S. Eisenhower.

Each of Johnson's two task forces had ten members, including high federal officials, former officials, state and local officers, and private citizens. Nixon's was composed of five, all from outside the federal government, though one had been a bureau chief and one had been a governor who developed strong Washington ties.

The main reason for setting up special bodies rather than using the regular instrumentalities of government is probably that Presidents are loath to seek advice on change from people with heavy stakes in existing institutions and arrangements. They may also want diversity of viewpoint so that no major problem areas are overlooked and no proposals advanced that are unacceptable to a diverse audience. Moreover, the prestige of the members of a carefully picked body can lend authority to their findings that the same findings put forth from inside the government would not enjoy.[22]

But prestigious committees sometimes bring out reports that a President opposes. Admittedly, the same thing can happen when work is done inside the government. The chances of shaping things more closely to the President's liking, however, are at least a little higher when they are within his own official family. That is probably why Roosevelt and Nixon kept their groups small and nonstatutory, why Johnson treated his task forces' proceedings and reports as submissions to him personally (they still have not been released officially), and why Eisenhower's committee likewise did not produce formal, public studies (even though its recommendations did get into the news from time to time and some were translated into reorganization plans).

Most of the smaller groups brought in relatively short reports and comparatively few recommendations, and concentrated especially on the broad outlines of the executive branch and the problems of the presidency. The larger, more formal commissions delved more deeply into specifics at all levels of management, producing long reports and hundreds of recommendations. It appears that the smaller bodies tended to view the executive branch primarily from the President's standpoint, while the larger ones, reflecting their diversity of origin and interest, ranged more widely.

Of course, it is possible to strengthen and expand the managerial

22. But, according to Mansfield, "Federal Executive Reorganization," p. 335, "The appointment of a mixed public commission is likely to be read as a sign of weakness or irresolution on his [the President's] part."

resources of the Office of Management and Budget and use *them* as the core and driving force in a reorganization campaign. Indeed, the renaming and restructuring of the Bureau of the Budget by President Nixon were intended in part to restore the emphasis on administrative management that many observers felt had been allowed to decline over the years.[23] If this thrust were maintained, it could produce groups of specialists with an ongoing concern for organizational and procedural improvements, a governmentwide view of the implications of individual changes, a steadily accumulating body of experience in planning and administering administrative change, a commitment to administrative change as a continuing process rather than as a single, instantaneous measure, and sufficient detachment from the program responsibilities of line agencies to escape their reluctance to rock any boats. But this mechanism generates a steady stream of incremental adjustments rather than a massive, dramatic rearrangement of the whole executive branch to which leaders can point with a sense of pride and accomplishment. It can gradually acquire the perspectives and values of agencies and programs it was meant to improve, and thus become a high-level impediment to change. If it avoids this pitfall, its continuous proposals for organizational change will be perceived as harassment by many line officers and their constituencies, and as endless niggling by busy legislators. And it lacks the potential prestige and symbolic stature of blue-ribbon panels.

Thus, like everything else associated with reorganization, the options for organizing the reorganizers entail trade-offs. No matter which choices are made, something valuable will be given up as well as gained.

23. Nixon's message accompanying Reorganization Plan Number 2 of 1970 (March 12, 1970) said in part, "creation of the Office of Management and Budget represents far more than a mere change of name for the Bureau of the Budget. It represents a basic change in concept and emphasis, reflecting the broader management needs of the Office of the President.

". . . The budget function is only one of several important management tools that the President must now have. He must also have a substantially enhanced institutional staff capability in other areas of executive management. . . . Under this plan, strengthened capability in these areas will be provided partly through internal reorganization, and it will also require additional staff resources."

This emphasis on better in-house management capabilities had been strongly urged on the President by the Ash Council, which went so far as to recommend that the agency be named simply Office of Management; Richard P. Nathan, *The Plot that Failed: Nixon and the Administrative Presidency* (Wiley, 1975), pp. 59–60, and 77, n. 1. Roy Ash was later named director of the Office of Management and Budget.

414 Herbert Kaufman

Straws in the Wind

Because the advantages of each option are attractive, a new administration may elect to remain as flexible as possible, perhaps experimenting with several options in the course of its period in office. It would therefore be rash to conclude from moves made in the first months of a term that irrevocable commitments have been made, particularly if the initial steps do not preclude shifts and changes later on.

The Carter team has announced that it will proceed in an incremental fashion rather than waiting for the formulation of a comprehensive design before beginning to reorganize. The prompt initiation of legislation for the Department of Energy, the reorganization of the Department of Health, Education, and Welfare, and the announcement that additional "crash programs" are contemplated reflects this choice. Furthermore, the declaration by Harrison Wellford, the executive associate director for reorganization and management of the Office of Management and Budget, that the administration has a long-range perspective on reorganization confirms that it will be handled one step at a time.[24]

There are also signs that the operation will be conducted primarily by regular government staff. A request for $2.6 million for thirty-two added employees for Wellford's reorganization group was submitted to the Congress and advanced smoothly, and Wellford said the effort would depend largely on career personnel in both OMB and other agencies, with the possibility of assistance from volunteers in private business. He told the House Appropriations Committee that the group would be divided into six teams dealing with natural resources and energy, economic development, human development, national security and international affairs, general government, and government regulation.[25] Public pronouncements about reducing the number of federal agencies from 1,900 to 200, made repeatedly during the election campaign, are apparently to be taken as directional guideposts rather than as literal, ironclad guarantees.

Things may change as experience accumulates. For the time being, however, this is the course the administration has set.

24. OMB, "President's Reorganization Authority," pp. 9–14; see also, David S. Broder, *Washington Post*, March 12, 1977.
25. OMB, "President's Reorganization Authority."

Nonsurgical Treatments

Many of the irritations that reorganization of the executive branch is intended to alleviate, however, may not demand anything so drastic to relieve them. Much distress and resentment can be alleviated by relatively limited correctives. Minor remedies can sometimes bring more relief to more people than more radical therapy does.

The federal information centers recently established in three dozen places throughout the country, with toll-free lines to still more places, are an illustration. Set up to guide people needing help through the complexities of the federal administrative system to the officers and documents that can answer their questions or solve their problems, they are still too new to be evaluated definitively. But they could conceivably take care of one problem that accounts for a good deal of the anger and despair and feelings of helplessness and convinces some critics of government that the system has gotten out of hand.

In like fashion, experience with ombudsmen—that is, complaint- and grievance-handling officers with power to investigate citizens' charges against agencies and to initiate redress where warranted—has been building up in various governments throughout the country.[26] Some version of this institution might also salve specific sore points, and thus reduce much discontent, with minimum disruption of existing arrangements at the federal level.

Part of the outcry against government is linked to paperwork thrust on the public by tax-collection agencies and government information-gathering services. The Commission on Federal Paperwork has been working to ease these burdens, taking aim in particular at the individual forms that generate the bulk of the outcries.[27] Perhaps permanent

26. See Walter Gellhorn, *When Americans Complain* (Harvard University Press, 1966), and Gellhorn, *Ombudsmen and Others: Citizens' Protectors in Nine Countries* (Harvard University Press, 1966); Roy V. Peel, ed., "The Ombudsman or Citizen's Defender: A Modern Institution," *Annals of the American Academy of Political and Social Science,* vol. 377 (May 1968); Stanley V. Anderson, ed., *Ombudsmen for American Government?* (Prentice-Hall for The American Assembly, 1968); Alan J. Wyner, ed., *Executive Ombudsmen in the United States* (University of California, Berkeley, Institute of Government Studies, 1973).

27. The Commission on Federal Paperwork began operations in 1975. It will submit its final report in 1977, and has already submitted a number of interim reports and recommendations to the President.

machinery to seek out and lighten specific paperwork burdens can be devised, thereby removing a major source of current dissatisfaction.

Survey research among the clients of agencies could add a dimension to the assessment of administrative performance. Volunteered complaints do not always tell the whole story because the grievously offended or the easily outraged are usually the ones to take the initiative. Their accusations give an inescapably one-sided impression, which is often discounted on these very grounds by the officials to whom they are addressed. Splendid service may go undetected; so may injustices too small individually to justify expense by the victims to correct them, yet numerous enough to amount to significant deprivation in the aggregate. There are possibilities here for altering incentives within the public service in ways leading to higher client satisfaction.

Modest steps of this kind are not substitutes for reorganization, nor do they cut the size and cost of government. But at least some of the demands for reorganization of the executive branch are spawned by hope for relief from the oppressive weight of government requirements and constraints. Often, that weight can be lifted for thousands of citizens by a pinpointed rather than by a blanket remedy. All too often, limited, attainable remedies are neglected when more visible, glamorous, and exciting grand designs tempt reformers.

No Miracle Cures

Those, however, who cling to the belief that any combination of means will instantaneously transform the character, image, or performance of the executive branch, are doomed to disappointment.

The civilian work force of the government grew only modestly over two decades, while the budget as a whole was doubling in constant dollars (increasing fivefold in current dollars).[28] There is not much opportunity for cutbacks here, which is one reason why both the President and the secretary of Health, Education, and Welfare assured civil servants that reorganization would not mean loss of jobs for them. Perhaps the *rate* of growth of federal employment can be

28. From 1956 to 1976, civilian employment in the federal government, including postal workers, went from 2.4 million to 2.8 million, an increase of 17 percent. In the same interval, total federal outlays rose from $70.5 billion to $366.5 billion in current dollars, and from $133.0 billion to $264.4 billion in constant (fiscal year 1972) dollars.

held down (though this rate depends on whether new federal initiatives are undertaken in the years ahead, which is a distinct possibility); even if the rate is limited, however, the effects will be felt in the remote rather than in the near future. In any case, the monetary savings through control of civilian personnel growth cannot be more than a small fraction of federal outlays, since all the compensation and benefits of the civilian work force come to under 11 percent of the total, so that marginal reductions in this area would hardly change the overall budget at all.

Reorganizers have also grown wary of claiming massive savings in operations for their reforms. For the most part, they assert that their changes will produce more output per dollar spent rather than the expenditure of fewer dollars; thus, even if the changes end up increasing total outlays, they contend that the total will be lower than it would have been without the reforms.[29] Whether or not such claims are eventually justified, the *immediate* effect on budgets is almost sure to be indiscernible. In this context, the recent statement by Secretary of Health, Education, and Welfare Califano that the reorganization of his department would yield savings of $2 billion in the first two years and at least $2 billion annually by 1981[30] is surprising. He placed particular emphasis on the elimination of fraud and abuse in various benefit programs, but it is not clear whether the costs of intensified enforcement have been included in his estimates. Furthermore, it is not self-evident how regrouping units in the departments, as opposed to changing procedures or adding auditors and investigators, will contribute to prevention of fraud and abuse.

In short, nobody should expect sudden, swift, dramatic diminishment in the size and cost of the executive branch of the federal gov-

29. See, for example, Harry S. Truman's classic statement accompanying **Reorganization Plan Number 5**, 1950 (March 13, 1950): "The taking effect of the reorganizations included in this plan may not in itself result in substantial immediate savings. However, many benefits in improved operations are probable during the next years which will result in a reduction in expenditures as compared with those that would be otherwise necessary. An itemization of these reductions in advance of actual experience under this plan is not practicable." Similarly, Franklin D. Roosevelt remarked that the transfer of agencies would not save much money. "It is awfully erroneous," he said, "to assume that it is in the reorganization of Departments and Bureaus that you save money;" Richard Polenberg, *Reorganizing Roosevelt's Government: The Controversy over Executive Reorganization, 1936–1939* (Harvard University Press, 1966), p. 8.

30. U.S. Department of Health, Education, and Welfare, *HEW News*, March 8, 1977, p. 2.

ernment as a result of reorganization. Indeed, the upward trend will probably persist for a long time—possibly more gradually than might otherwise have been the case, but upwards all the same.

Even if anticipated structural revisions succeed, they will be slow in coming. The executive branch is very big, and the specific faults that need correcting keep changing. "Our confused and wasteful system that took so long to grow," President Carter told the American people in his first informal address to the nation, "will take a long time to change."[31] His staff member spearheading reorganization testified that it would be "a four-year effort at least."[32] The administration harbors no illusions about the length of the campaign on which it is embarked. The 1977–78 controversies over government organization are only the opening skirmishes in what promises to be a long, hard, and frequently futile endeavor.

31. "The President's Address to the Nation," in *Weekly Compilation of Presidential Documents*, vol. 13 (February 7, 1977), p. 141.
32. Broder, *Washington Post*, March 12, 1977.

APPENDIX A

The Full-Employment Budget

JOSEPH A. PECHMAN

UNTIL RECENTLY, it was generally assumed that the U.S. economy was capable of growing at about 4 percent a year, and that growth rate was widely used to measure the economy's potential output. A number of developments in the last several years seems to have changed the nature of the economy, and economists have had to reevaluate the basic assumptions underlying calculations of the potential gross national product. In the 1977 *Economic Report of the President,* the Council of Economic Advisers presented a revised series that substantially reduced the earlier estimates of potential GNP.[1] The full-employment budget estimates used in chapter 2 are calculated on the basis of a potential GNP series prepared by George L. Perry,[2] which lies between the old and the revised series in most years. Estimates of potential GNP in chapter 11 are based on both the revised CEA series and Perry's estimates. This appendix explains the difference between the three potential GNP series and presents estimates of unified budget receipts, outlays, and surpluses or deficits corresponding to each series for the fiscal years 1955 to 1981 (see table A-1).

The full-employment budget estimates in table A-1 were prepared by Thang Long Ton That and Nancy Osher.

1. See pp. 45–57 of the *Report.*
2. "Potential Output and Productivity," *Brookings Papers on Economic Activity,* *1:1977,* pp. 1–37.

Table A-1. Federal Unified Budget Receipts,[a] Outlays, and Surplus or Deficit, for Three Potential Gross National Product Series, Fiscal Years 1955–81

Billions of dollars

Fiscal year	Series A			Series B			Series C		
	Receipts	Outlays	Surplus or deficit (−)	Receipts	Outlays	Surplus or deficit (−)	Receipts	Outlays	Surplus or deficit (−)
1955	67.2	68.1	−0.9	67.0	68.1	−1.1	66.6	68.1	−1.5
1956	74.9	70.5	4.4	74.4	70.5	3.9	74.2	70.5	3.7
1957	82.2	76.7	5.5	81.5	76.7	4.8	81.5	76.7	4.8
1958	85.2	81.7	3.5	84.4	81.7	2.7	84.4	81.7	2.7
1959	83.3	90.6	−7.3	82.7	90.9	−8.2	82.5	90.6	−8.1
1960	99.9	91.4	8.5	99.3	91.6	7.7	98.6	91.5	7.1
1961	106.9	96.2	10.7	106.4	96.6	9.8	105.5	96.5	9.0
1962	109.2	105.9	3.3	108.8	105.7	3.1	107.8	105.6	2.2
1963	115.7	110.0	5.7	115.1	110.5	4.6	114.3	110.5	3.8
1964	120.7	118.0	2.7	119.5	118.0	1.5	119.3	118.0	1.3
1965	120.8	118.0	2.8	119.3	118.1	1.2	119.6	118.1	1.5
1966	128.6	134.8	−6.2	126.9	134.9	−8.0	127.5	134.9	−7.4
1967	147.7	158.4	−10.7	145.4	158.7	−13.3	146.5	158.7	−12.2
1968	153.6	178.9	−25.3	150.7	179.2	−28.5	152.2	179.2	−27.0
1969	184.6	185.0	−0.4	180.1	185.2	−5.1	182.4	185.2	−2.8
1970	199.1	196.1	3.0	193.0	197.0	−4.0	195.7	197.0	−1.3
1971	213.4	209.2	4.2	206.3	210.2	−3.9	208.4	210.1	−1.7
1972	223.5	228.9	−5.4	216.1	230.7	−14.6	217.0	230.5	−13.5
1973	244.0	245.0	−1.0	236.0	246.8	−10.8	235.8	246.7	−10.9
1974	282.2	267.3	14.9	272.6	269.5	3.1	271.1	269.4	1.7
1975	323.0	317.1	5.9	310.0	321.4	−11.4	307.2	321.4	−14.2
1976	360.3	356.6	3.7	343.5	358.8	−15.3	339.1	358.7	−19.6
1977	409.9	401.0	8.9	396.6	402.9	−6.3	388.5	402.9	−14.4
1978	453.3	457.3	−4.0	439.2	459.3	−20.1	428.3	459.2	−30.9
1979	509.3	489.2	20.1	494.1	490.9	3.2	479.7	490.7	−11.0
1980	567.4	517.5	49.9	550.7	519.1	31.6	533.3	518.8	14.5
1981	632.6	550.3	82.3	614.0	552.2	61.8	593.2	551.8	41.4

Sources: Series A, 1960–75, Office of Management and Budget; other figures are author's estimates. Series A is based on the "old" and series C on the "new" potential GNP estimates in Economic Report of the President, January 1977, p. 54. Series B is based on potential GNP estimates prepared by George L. Perry; see his "Potential Output and Productivity," Brookings Papers on Economic Activity, 1:1977, pp. 1–37.

a. Excludes proposed changes in payroll taxes for social security.

Estimates of Potential GNP

The estimates of potential GNP in the old series assumed that the overall unemployment rate at full employment would average about 4 percent of the labor force. It was also assumed that the nation's fixed capital (including land) would be fully utilized at this level of unemployment. The CEA revised series modifies the full-employment unemployment rate and adjusts productivity downward beginning in 1966.[3] Perry's series also modifies the full-employment unemployment rate and adjusts productivity downward beginning in 1969.

The unemployment rate at full employment was revised because the demographic composition of the labor force has changed significantly since the mid-1950s. The prime-age male is less the predominant labor force participant now than twenty years ago; males twenty years and older constituted 66 percent of the labor force in 1955, but only 55 percent in 1976. This decline reflects a slight reduction in participation among adult males, but it results mainly from a rapid increase in participation among adult women and the growth in the teenage population. Adult women were 28 percent of the labor force in 1955, but 35 percent in 1976; teenagers were 7 percent and 10 percent, respectively. This compositional shift affects the unemployment rate because women and teenagers typically have higher unemployment rates than men. They tend to enter and leave the labor force relatively frequently with changes in family situation, leading to periods of unemployment for job search, and for a variety of reasons they are less likely than men to find jobs worth keeping for long periods of time. Even if the unemployment rate for adult males is held constant, growing participation among adult females and teenagers raises the overall unemployment rate at full employment.[4]

Consequently, the full-employment benchmark in the adjusted potential GNP series is no longer a flat rate. The earlier 4 percent unemployment rate has been replaced by a series that rises from 4.0 percent in 1955 to 4.9 percent in 1976–79 and then declines

3. Peter K. Clark, "A New Estimate of Potential GNP" (Council of Economic Advisers, January 27, 1977; processed), table A-5.
4. George L. Perry, "Changing Labor Markets and Inflation," *Brookings Papers on Economic Activity, 3:1970*, pp. 411–41.

slightly to 4.8 percent in 1980. These adjustments are relatively un-controversial among economists.[5]

A more controversial aspect of the adjusted CEA estimates is a modification of the rate of growth of productivity. According to the council's calculations, productivity in the private sector grew at a lower rate between 1966 and 1973 than it did between 1955 and 1966, and it may even have declined further since 1973 because of the rise in energy prices (which made some capital equipment and some energy-intensive processes inefficient). The adjusted series takes into account the decline in productivity beginning in 1966 but makes no allowance for a possible further decline since 1973.[6]

In his recent reanalysis of the data, Perry concluded that, while productivity growth may have slowed somewhat in recent years, labor force growth and the declining relative importance in the labor force of teenagers will keep the potential GNP growing at a historically rapid rate in the years immediately ahead. His analysis also adjusts the unemployment rate at full employment for demographic changes.

Accordingly, three sets of estimates of potential GNP have been provided as the basis for alternative estimates of the budget at full employment for the years 1955–81. Series A is the old series, which assumes a full-employment unemployment rate of 4 percent and a potential GNP annual growth rate of 3.5 percent from 1955 to 1962, 3.75 percent from 1962 to 1968, and 4 percent from 1968 to 1975. This series was carried forward at a 3.75 percent annual rate beginning in 1976 (to allow for changing the benchmark date for computing real GNP from 1958 to 1972). Series C is the adjusted series as estimated by the Council of Economic Advisers. This series incorporates a full-employment unemployment rate that varies from 4 percent in 1955 to 4.9 percent in 1976–80 and 4.8 percent in 1981, and a reduced rate of productivity growth beginning in 1963. Potential GNP in this series grows at an annual rate of 3.5 percent from 1955

5. This does not mean that the higher unemployment rate at full employment should be accepted as a goal of economic policy. But most economists agree that special programs designed to reduce structural unemployment would be required to reduce the full-employment unemployment rate significantly below 4.8 percent in 1980.

6. A small part of the reduction is attributed to the change in the benchmark year from 1958 to 1972 for the calculation of real GNP. The later base reduces the growth rate because sectors with fast output growth tend to have falling relative prices.

to 1962, 3.6 percent from 1962 to 1976, and 3.55 percent from 1976 to 1981. Series B is Perry's series, which accepts the rise in the full-employment unemployment rate (to 4.9 percent in 1977–78 and 5.0 percent in 1980–81) and makes some reduction in productivity growth beginning in 1969, while using his own projection of labor force growth. In this series, potential GNP growth averages about 3.5 percent annually from 1955 to 1970, 3.95 percent between 1970 and 1976, and 3.9 percent between 1976 and 1981.

The real GNP figures in all three series were converted to current dollar estimates on the basis of the inflation assumptions in the economic projections of the Carter administration for 1977 and 1978 and the House Budget Committee "high growth path" projections for 1979–81.[7]

Unified Budget Receipts and Outlays

Unified budget receipts and outlays for the potential GNP series A were obtained from the Office of Management and Budget for fiscal years 1960–75. Outlays for 1955–59 and 1976–81 were obtained by subtracting from actual outlays estimates of the excess of unemployment compensation benefits at the actual unemployment rate in each year over the 4 percent benchmark.[8] Receipts for 1955–59 were obtained by adding to actual receipts estimates of the additional receipts that would be generated at potential GNP on the basis of the estimated elasticity of federal tax receipts (assumed to be 1.15 for 1955–59). For 1976–81, separate estimates were prepared for the additional receipts at potential GNP from the individual income tax, corporation income tax, and other sources.[9]

7. Office of Management and Budget, "Current Budget Estimates, April 1977" (processed); and House Budget Committee, *First Concurrent Resolution on the Budget—Fiscal Year 1978,* H. Rept. 95-189, 95:1 (Government Printing Office, 1977), p. 98.

8. Actual outlays for fiscal years 1979–81 were obtained from the backup sheets for data in ibid. The adjustment for unemployment compensation benefits was equal to the actual unemployment benefits times the ratio of the difference between the actual unemployment rate and 4 percent to the actual unemployment rate.

9. Elasticity was assumed to be 1.55 for the individual income tax and 1.0 for receipts other than the corporation income tax. For the corporate tax, corporate profits before tax were first estimated on the assumption that they would be 9.5 percent of potential GNP; the amount of tax was then calculated by applying the actual effective rate to estimated corporate profits at potential GNP. A separate adjustment was made to the corporate profits tax figures for fiscal years 1976 and 1977 to allow

Outlays for the potential GNP series B and C were estimated by adjusting actual outlays for the excess unemployment benefits at actual unemployment over the full-employment unemployment rates for each year.[10] Receipts for series B and C were obtained from series A receipts on the basis of assumed elasticity ratios with respect to GNP.[11]

---

for the lag of corporate profits tax payments during periods of sharply rising profits. (This lag occurs because corporations are permitted to pay their estimated tax on the basis of either prior-year or current-year profits.)

10. See note 8 above for method of calculation.

11. The assumed ratios were: 1955–59, 1.15; 1960–69, 1.2; 1970–75, 1.25; 1976–81, 1.3. The increasing elasticity is the result of the rise in the elasticity of the individual income tax as incomes increase. See Joseph A. Pechman, "Responsiveness of the Federal Individual Income Tax to Changes in Income," *Brookings Papers on Economic Activity, 2:1973*, pp. 385–421.

APPENDIX B

Issues In Budget Accounting

ROBERT W. HARTMAN *and* JOSEPH A. PECHMAN

MUCH ATTENTION is now being paid to total outlays and receipts in the federal budget. Yet the accounting conventions that determine on which side of the budget a particular transaction belongs or whether it belongs in the budget at all are matters of considerable disagreement. This appendix considers the issues raised by the budget treatment of off-budget federal entities, tax expenditures, refundable tax credits, and rents and royalties on the Outer Continental Shelf.

Off-Budget Federal Entities

In its January budget submission the outgoing administration proposed that outlays of off-budget federal entities be included in the budget beginning in fiscal year 1979. Off-budget federal entities are like federal agencies in many ways, but their activities have hitherto been excluded from the budget by law.

As shown in table B-1, outlays of the off-budget entities are on the order of 2.0 percent of the unified budget—the customary measure of federal spending—up from a negligible amount before 1974. The most important activity of these agencies is lending, and most of the debate is over whether these activities belong in the budget.[1]

Nancy Osher and Thang Long Ton That prepared the statistical information in this appendix.

1. With regard to the nonlending off-budget federal entities, OMB's comment that "there is no justification for excluding them from the budget total" seems warranted. See the discussion in Office of Management and Budget, *Issues '78: Perspectives on Fiscal Year 1978 Budget* (Government Printing Office, 1977), p. 237.

Table B-1. Outlays of Off-Budget Federal Entities and Relation to Unified Budget Outlays, Fiscal Years 1976–78
Amounts in billions of dollars

Entity	1976 Actual	1977 Estimate	1978 Estimate
Federal Financing Bank[a]	5.9	8.7	5.9
Other lending entities[b]	0.4	1.2	1.4
Nonlending entities[c]	1.0	0.9	1.7
Total	7.2	10.8	9.2
As percent of unified outlays	2.0	2.6	2.1

Source: *The Budget of the United States Government, Fiscal Year 1978*, p. 30. Figures are rounded.
a. Excludes net change in holdings of agency debt issues.
b. Rural electrification and telephone revolving fund, Rural Telephone Bank, housing for the elderly or handicapped fund, United States Railway Association, and (proposed) Energy Independence Authority. The last-mentioned entity, which was dropped in President Carter's budget revisions, accounts for $0.6 billion in 1978.
c. Postal Service fund, Pension Benefit Guaranty Corporation, and exchange stabilization fund.

The largest off-budget lending entity is the Federal Financing Bank, which was created in 1973 to coordinate and reduce the cost of borrowing by federal agencies. It is authorized to purchase or sell any obligation issued, sold, or guaranteed by a federal agency. Since 1975 the U.S. Treasury has been the sole source of funds for the Bank, which, in turn, lends the funds at a rate slightly above the new issue rate of U.S. Treasury securities of similar terms and conditions. As a result of reduced interest costs many federal agencies now borrow through the Federal Financing Bank instead of raising their own funds.

The outlays of the Federal Financing Bank, shown in table B-1, do not include all of its net lending. Purchases by the Bank of the debt of on-budget agencies are already included in the federal budget as outlays by the original lender. Similarly, if off-budget entities were included, purchases of debt of an off-budget entity would be listed in the federal budget under that agency, not under the Federal Financing Bank. What is counted as the outlays of the Bank is its net purchases of loans guaranteed by the federal government and the net purchase of agency assets (such as the U.S. Treasury's holdings of New York City's debt).

The logic of including in the federal budget the change in holdings of guaranteed loans by the Federal Financing Bank is that such transactions are identical in economic impact to direct loans made by a federal agency, which are included in the budget. Although everyone agrees that guaranteed loans ought not to be included in the federal budget because the capital for such loans comes from private sources, the purchase of such loans by the federally owned Federal Financing Bank fundamentally changes the situation. After a purchase by the Bank, the capital for these guaranteed loans has indeed come from federal sources. It does, therefore, seem clear that there is no fundamental difference between direct loans of an on-budget agency, an off-budget agency, or the net change in holdings of loan assets by the Federal Financing Bank. But this argument can just as well support the case that all direct loans ought to be off-budget.

Looked at strictly from the point of view of fiscal policy, the inclusion or exclusion of direct loans and of off-budget entities is irrelevant. Macroeconomists almost always use the federal sector receipts and expenditures in the national income accounts. This budget differs from the unified budget in several respects,[2] one of which is that the national accounts budget excludes all loan[3] and asset transactions of the federal government. Thus if off-budget entity transactions were put in the budget, the national income accounts budget would not be altered.

But the issue of including off-budget entities in the budget rests on considerations other than economic impact, principally that of control over federal lending activity. The primary argument in favor of including the off-budget entities in the budget is that their activities would then be subject to the same discipline as other governmental activities; they would have to compete against other agencies for outlays in the congressional budget resolutions. Moreover, a direct loan by an off-budget entity would no longer have an unfair advantage compared to a direct loan of an on-budget agency.

While not denying the sense of making off-budget entities compete more with other government activities, opponents of including them in the budget stress how such inclusion is at best a half-way measure. They contend that the activity that is in need of greater control—in need of a policy, in fact—is the whole spectrum of federally assisted credit. While the off-budget entities are an important factor in total lending under U. S. government auspices, their inclusion in the budget would still leave about 60 percent of federally assisted credit *out*

2. See "Special Analysis A," in *Special Analyses, Budget of the United States Government, Fiscal Year 1978*, for a full accounting of the differences.

3. One major exception is nonrecourse agricultural loans, included on the grounds that these are more like an ordinary government purchase than a loan.

Table B-2. Lending under Federal Auspices, Fiscal Year 1976

Type of lending	Amount (billions of dollars)	Percent of total lending under federal auspices
Direct loans		
On-budget	4.2	15.8
Off-budget	6.7	25.2
Guaranteed loans	10.3	38.7
Sponsored agency loans	5.4	20.3
Total	26.6	100.0

Source: *Special Analyses, Budget of the United States Government, Fiscal Year 1978*, p. 89.

of the budget (see table B-2). These other lending activities—guaranteed loans and the lending of government-sponsored agencies[4]—would become more attractive lending sources if off-budget entities were moved onto the budget. For example, one of the off-budget entities is the housing for the elderly or handicapped fund, which provides direct loans for new construction of rental units for moderate-income persons. If this fund's net lending were to go on-budget, the Secretary of Housing and Urban Development might direct the Federal National Mortgage Association, a government-sponsored off-budget agency that purchases mortgages, to acquire mortgages of units for moderate-income elderly and handicapped people. Whether this is a better or worse deal for the federal government compared to direct loans is not clear, but the budgetary status of an agency ought not to determine the best financing arrangement for housing the elderly. Thus, putting on the budget entities that primarily engage in lending would tend to reduce the advantage they now have over currently on-budget direct lenders, but it would make other federally assisted lending even more attractive.

The issue of control over federally assisted lending cannot be resolved by any simple changes in the inclusiveness of the federal budget. Some of the existing off-budget entities are already fairly tightly regulated by the executive branch and Congress, as are some

4. Government-sponsored agencies are privately owned but were established by the federal government and are given special preferences, resulting in generally low interest costs. Some examples are the Federal National Mortgage Association (Fannie Mae), the National Railroad Passenger Corporation (AMTRAK), and the Student Loan Marketing Association (Sallie Mae). For a description of these organizations, see Senate Committee on the Budget, *Off-Budget Agencies and Government-Sponsored Corporations: Factsheets*, 95:1 (Government Printing Office, 1977).

government-sponsored agencies that no one wants to include in the budget. But other entities seem to escape full-scale federal review; judging by their growth, guaranteed loans are probably the category of federally assisted lending most out of control.[5] There is no easy way to incorporate guaranteed loans into the federal budget.

One way to integrate lending and budgeting activity is to divide government-assisted lending into two parts. The first part would be the subsidy implicit in the government loan as a result of the lower interest rate paid by the borrowers. Such subsidies, which usually occur over several years, could be measured at their present value in the year the loan is made. These present values would be calculated for all government-assisted loans and counted in the unified budget, thereby making agencies carefully evaluate the best technique of lending. The second part of the proposal would be to tally the "pure loan" component[6] of all loans as a separate loan or credit "budget." Such a budget—which might have to include the Federal Reserve System's accounts—would be used as a planning document by the executive branch, and some apparatus for congressional review would have to be established.[7] This proposal has the merit of dealing with the major federal credit issues: control over the total and efficient choice of lending techniques.

In summary, the case for including off-budget entities in the budget is primarily one of consistency in the treatment of direct lending. But establishing a well-coordinated credit policy involves much broader measures and cannot be solved by simple changes in budget coverage.

Tax Expenditures

Many private activities are financed by special provisions of the income tax laws that subsidize individuals or businesses who make

5. The net volume of guaranteed loans in fiscal year 1976 was nearly five times its level in fiscal year 1967. Federal direct loans—on- or off-budget—approximately doubled in the same period. See *Special Analyses, 1978*, p. 89.

6. If the government makes a one-year loan for $1,000 at 2 percent interest when the market rate of interest is 10 percent, $80 would represent the subsidy component and the remaining $920 is the pure loan.

7. For a discussion of issues relating to loan subsidies and budgets, see *Report of the President's Commission on Budget Concepts* (Government Printing Office, 1967), and President's Commission on Budget Concepts, *Staff Papers and Other Materials Reviewed by the Commission* (GPO, 1967).

payments or receive incomes in certain designated forms. The effect of these tax subsidies is, in most instances, virtually indistinguishable from direct federal expenditures. For example, the Tax Reform Act of 1976 provides a tax credit for child care of 20 percent of amounts paid by working parents, up to a maximum of $400 for one child and $800 for two or more children. Approximately the same result could have been achieved by making direct payments to parents, instead of giving them a tax credit.[8] The direct payment would be counted as an expenditure, whereas the tax credit is reflected in the federal budget only as a reduction in income tax receipts. The Congressional Budget Act of 1974 applies the term "tax expenditures" to tax subsidies to emphasize the similarity between them and direct outlays. The law requires a listing of tax expenditures in each budget and directs all congressional committees to identify any changes made in tax expenditures by new legislation.

Tax expenditures are defined by the 1974 budget act as "revenue losses attributable to provisions of the Federal tax laws which allow a special exclusion, exemption, or deduction from gross income or which provide a special credit, a preferential rate of tax, or a deferral of tax liability." To identify a tax expenditure, it is necessary first to define a normal tax structure, any deviation from which is a tax expenditure. The law does not give a definition of a normal tax structure, but it is generally regarded to imply a tax base as close to "economic income" as possible. Thus, the term "income" includes capital gains in full, but does not include such imputed incomes as the rental value of owned homes, because they are difficult to measure. The normal structure includes the current personal exemption, standard deduction, and rate schedules.

The major tax expenditures are: (1) personal deductions under the individual income tax (for state and local income, sales, property, and gasoline taxes, charitable contributions, medical expenses, and interest paid); (2) the exclusions for state and local bond interest, employee benefits, and transfer payments (social security, unemployment compensation, and welfare payments); (3) the preferential

8. The tax credit and the direct payment would be identical if the tax credit were "refundable," that is, if people with little or no tax liability were given a payment for the excess of a credit over their liability. For the treatment of refundable credits in the budget accounts, see the following section.

Table B-3. Major Tax Expenditures, Fiscal Year 1978
Millions of dollars

Tax expenditure	Individuals	Corporations	Total
Deductibility of state and local nonbusiness taxes	13,460	...	13,460
Deductibility of charitable contributions	6,040	685	6,725
Deductibility of mortgage interest and interest on consumer credit	8,595	...	8,595
Deductibility of medical expenses	2,870	...	2,870
Excess of percentage standard deduction over low-income allowance	1,410	...	1,410
Exclusion of employer contributions to pension, health, and welfare plans	18,650[a]	255	18,905[a]
Exclusion of benefits and allowances to armed forces personnel	1,260	...	1,260
Additional exemption for over sixty-five and blind	1,300	...	1,300
Credit for the elderly	440	...	440
Exclusion of veterans' disability compensation and veterans' pensions	725	...	725
Transfer payments	8,300	...	8,300
Parental personal exemptions for students nineteen and over	770	...	770
Credit for child and dependent care expenses	870	...	870
Capital gains	15,980[b]	905	16,885
Exclusion of interest on state and local debt	2,090	3,925	6,015
Corporate surtax exemption	...	4,250	4,250
Investment credit	2,205	9,670	11,875
Excess first-year depreciation and depreciation on buildings in excess of straight line	745	345	1,090
Excess of percentage over cost depletion and expensing of exploration and development costs	450	1,660	2,110
Deferral of income of domestic international sales corporations	...	1,190	1,190
Excess bad debt reserves of financial institutions	...	645	645
Other	9,495	5,210	14,705
Total[c]	95,655	28,740	124,395

Sources: *Special Analyses, Budget of the United States Government, Fiscal Year 1978*, pp. 128–30; Congressional Budget Office, *Five-Year Budget Projections, Fiscal Years 1978–1982: Supplemental Report on Tax Expenditures* (GPO, 1977).

a. Includes Keogh plans for the self-employed and contributions to individual retirement accounts.

b. Includes revenue effect of deferral of tax on capital gains transferred by gift or at death.

c. The totals are the arithmetic sums of the columns. Individual estimates in this table are based on the assumption that no other changes are made in the tax law; consequently, the aggregate revenue effect will not equal the sum of the revenue effects of the individual items shown.

treatment of long-term capital gains; and (4) tax incentives to promote investment (such as the investment credit) and other activities
(such as accelerated depreciation for child care facilities). A list of
the major tax expenditures is given in table B-3.

The major purpose of requiring the inclusion of information on
tax expenditures in the budget request is to encourage the administration and the Congress to take into account tax, as well as direct,
expenditures in budget decisions. Total tax expenditures constitute
26 percent of budget outlays (see table B-4), and in recent years the
rate of growth of tax expenditures has been higher than the rate of
growth of regular outlays. For some budget functions tax expenditures exceed the amount of outlays: for example, commerce and
transportation and revenue sharing. The distributional effects of tax
expenditures are often quite different from those of direct expenditure programs, however. For example, homeowner tax preferences
provide little benefit to the poor, while housing allowances are concentrated at the lower end of the income scale.

The energy program developed by the Carter administration includes several new tax expenditures to encourage insulation, increase
use of solar energy, and induce business investment in energy-
conserving equipment and conversion of oil- and gas-using facilities
to coal. If enacted, these tax expenditures will be costly and of little
benefit to low- and middle-income people (unless they are made
refundable), and they will complicate the income tax laws. The tax
expenditure approach requires that such tax devices be compared
with alternative methods of dealing with the same problem, either
through direct federal expenditures or by regulation.

While it is too early to evaluate the effectiveness of the tax expenditure approach,[9] how the Congress deals with these energy proposals
will be a good test of the effect that the tax expenditure approach has
had on the tax legislative process.

Treatment of Refundable Tax Credits

The idea of a refundable tax credit has been discussed for a long
time, but it is only recently that such a credit found its way into

9. A tax expenditure table appeared in the President's budget for the first time in
the *Special Analyses* for the fiscal year 1976 budget, which was issued in January
1975.

Table B-4. Estimated Federal Budget Outlays and Tax Expenditures, by Budget Function, Fiscal Year 1978
Billions of dollars

		Tax expenditures	
Budget function	Total budget outlays	Amount	As percent of budget outlays
National defense	112.8	1.4	1.2
International affairs	7.2	1.8	24.4
General science, space, and technology	4.7	0.0	0.0
Natural resources, environment, and energy	20.9	2.8	13.4
Agriculture	4.4	1.2	27.2
Commerce and transportation	19.9	54.4	273.5
Community and regional development	9.9	*	0.3
Education, training, employment, and social services	27.0	9.0	33.4
Health	44.6	9.8	22.0
Income security	148.7	27.7	18.6
Veterans' benefits and services	18.8	1.0	5.1
Law enforcement and justice	3.8	0.0	0.0
Interest	40.9	0.6	1.5
General government	4.0	*	0.9
Revenue sharing and general purpose assistance	9.7	14.6	151.0
Total	477.3ᵃ	124.4ᵇ	26.1

Sources: *Special Analyses, Budget of the United States Government, Fiscal Year 1978*, pp. 128–30; Congressional Budget Office, *Five-Year Budget Projections, Fiscal Years 1978–1982: Supplemental Report;* and Office of Management and Budget, "Current Budget Estimates, April 1977" (processed). Figures are rounded.
* $0.05 billion or less.
a. Excluding undistributed offsetting receipts and allowances.
b. The totals are the arithmetic sums of the columns. Individual estimates in this table are based on the assumption that no other changes are made in the tax law; consequently, the aggregate revenue effect will not equal the sum of the revenue effect of the individual items shown.

federal tax law. In 1975, when the earned income tax credit of 10 percent of the first $4,000 of earned income (phasing down to zero between $4,000 and $8,000) was adopted, Congress decided that the amount of the credit exceeding an individual's income tax liability should be paid or refunded to him. The $50 rebate proposed, and later withdrawn, by President Carter would also have been refundable for persons who were eligible for the earned income credit.

In accounting for the refundable earned income tax credit, the budgets prepared by Presidents Ford and Carter treated the part of the credit that resulted in payments to individuals as a budget outlay (like any other transfer payment) and the part that was subtracted from taxpayers' liabilities as a reduction in budget receipts (like ordinary tax refunds). The House Budget Committee has followed this practice, but at the insistence of the Senate Budget Committee, the first concurrent budget resolution for fiscal year 1978 treated the refunded as well as the credited part of the earned income credit as a reduction in receipts. The two methods of accounting yield the same budget deficit, but budget outlays and receipts are higher when the refundable part of tax credits is treated as an expenditure.[10]

This difference is not entirely a matter of appearance. If the absolute amount of budget outlays acts as a constraint on expenditure decisions, any action that inflates budget outlays will tend to reduce the amount available for other government expenditures.[11] Moreover, if welfare reform were to emphasize negative income taxes, the exclusion of the refundable portion of such a plan from outlays would mean that one of the largest transfer payment programs would not appear as federal spending.

No simple budget accounting rule can accommodate all the various possibilities of administering a negative income tax. For example, suppose a welfare or negative income tax payment is set up as an allowance that is offset by a tax on any earnings of the recipient. If the beneficiary receives only the net payment after the tax offset, the sum of such net payments will be counted, under present procedures, as outlays. However, if the system provided for disbursing the full allowance to all families and recovering the offset through the tax system, budget outlays and receipts would be higher by the amount of the tax offset.[12]

This example illustrates the point, often made by economists, that transfer payments are merely negative taxes. Clearly, the decision on whether to adopt, and how to administer, a negative income tax should be made on its merits, and should not be affected by budgetary accounting conventions.

10. The refundable part of the earned income credit will amount to an estimated $1 billion in fiscal year 1978. The refundable part of the $50 tax rebate would have amounted to an estimated $1.4 billion in fiscal year 1977.

11. President Carter has stated repeatedly that he intends to limit federal budget outlays to 21 percent of GNP in fiscal year 1981. His ability to finance new programs may be reduced, however, by the accounting treatment of the earned income credit. Offsetting this, of course, is the possibility of replacing direct expenditures with tax expenditures, which lowers budget outlays.

12. A major criticism of Senator George McGovern's $1,000 demogrant plan proposed during the 1972 presidential campaign was that federal expenditures would rise by several hundred billion dollars, even though the net cost of the plan was only a fraction of gross payments.

Rents and Royalties on the Outer Continental Shelf

Federal outlays in the unified budget reflect a considerable amount of "netting" of receipts against disbursements in various budget accounts. For example, in fiscal year 1976 there were $53.2 billion in deductions for offsetting receipts made in reaching the $366.5 billion total outlays of that year.

Most such offsetting receipts are not controversial. Some are purely bookkeeping entries to keep straight the accounting for outlays when one government fund makes a payment to another (such as a payment from general funds to a trust fund). Other offsetting receipts arise when the government charges fees for performing a service or realizes receipts from a sale of assets. These "proprietary receipts from the public" are subtracted from disbursements in the agency or program account in which the service is performed or the good sold to arrive at outlays for that account. Such an accounting convention probably reasonably reflects the net activity in the account.

In one case a major receipt from the public is not offset against any program or agency budget, yet it is treated as a "negative outlay" rather than as a receipt. That exception is the receipt of rents and royalties from the Outer Continental Shelf lands. These receipts amounted to $2.7 billion in fiscal 1976 and were estimated by the Ford administration to rise to over $3 billion in fiscal 1978. Since these receipts are not tied to the ongoing activity of any government program—which is the rationale for netting out other proprietary receipts from their agency's account—there is no reason to treat income from the Outer Continental Shelf as an offset to outlays.

The effect of converting rents and royalties on the Outer Continental Shelf lands into receipts is to raise both total outlays and total receipts of the federal government (by about 0.7 percent in fiscal 1978). In addition, such a reclassification would transfer one of the accounts that is most difficult to estimate to the receipts side of the budget. This switch may be desirable in that it would remove the temptation for the President or the Congress to manipulate the Outer Continental Shelf income estimates in order to hit a desired target level for total outlays.

Index

Administrative Procedure Act of *1946*, 399

Administrative process: decentralization of, 394, 398, 401; executive authority and, 393, 395–97; grouping of functions in, 393, 400–01; limitation of line subordinates in, 392–93, 395, 401; policy formulation and, 399–400; politics and, 393–94, 397–98, 401, 402; public participation in, 394, 399; staff assistance and, 393, 395, 402; suggestions for correcting, 415–16

AFDC. *See* Aid to families with dependent children

Aid to families with dependent children (AFDC) program: coverage of, 257; errors in, 260; proposed changes in, 267, 268, 269, 276; provisions of, 255–56

Aircraft. *See* Military aircraft

Airlift program for Europe, 112–13

Antitrust laws, 66

Arab-Israeli conflicts, 85, 86, 114

Army ground forces: NATO, 106–07; Soviet, 89–90, 92–93; U.S., in Korea, 123, 124; Warsaw Pact, 109

Automobile tax, 20, 350–51

Balanced budget. *See* Budget

Benefits, social security: calculation of, 208–09; decoupling of, 229–35, 236; earnings test for, 243–46; extension of retirement age for, 235–36; inequities in, 238–40; minimum, 237–38; overindexing, 213, 227–35, 246; spouse's, 238–43

Benefits, welfare, 252; in-kind, 254, 270; minimum, 269

Block grants, 19, 36, 294, 299, 302, 304–05

Breeder reactors, 341–43

Budget, 2–7, 29–54, 355–89; assumptions underlying projection of, 366–74; balanced, 2, 5, 6–7, 356, 368, 371, 372, 374; built-in stabilizers for, 30, 36; Carter *1978*, 47–50, 359–60; Carter stimulus program for *1977*, 43–44, 361; congressional *1977*, 42–43; deficit, 36, 37; Ford *1977*, 40–42, 43; Ford *1978*, 1, 46, 47, 360; full-employment, 37–39, 50–53, 419–24; procedures for formulating, 377–89; procedures for projecting, 364–66; projected *1981*, 5–6, 355–56, 359–60, 364–66; proposed *1979*, 374–77; surplus, 37; trends in, 29–39

Budget accounting, 425–35

Certificate-of-need laws, 13, 200–01

437

vice employment, 9, 11, 18, 49, 152–54, 161, 163–65, 171, 173–74; for public works employment, 9, 156, 159, 161, 162–63; role in coping with unemployment, 148–50; under welfare reform, 173–74, 263–64, 274–75

Energy, 20–22, 66–67, 317–53; environmental quality and, 318, 321, 332; exploration and development, 327, 333, 351, 353; inflationary effects of, 66–67, 321–22; prices, 321–23, 327–32; problems relating to, 20, 317–21, 351–53; rising cost of, 318–20, 330–31; strategic reserves of, 335–38; subsidies to control use of, 327, 347; tax policies relating to, 347–51

Energy, Department of, proposed, 26, 406–08

Energy policies: for conservation, 20, 317, 327, 333–34; effect on budget, 335–51; effect on inflation, employment, and income distribution, 321–23; natural gas supply and, 323–26; for research and development, 338–47

Energy Policy and Conservation Act of *1975*, 335

Energy taxes, 327; on consumption, 348; on imports, 347; rebate on, 350–51; transportation, 349–50; wellhead, 348–49

Environmental quality, 21, 318, 321, 332

Europe: airbase facilities proposed for, 113–14; airlift capability proposed for, 112–13; efforts to stabilize military balance in, 138–40; NATO–Warsaw Pact military balance, 106–09; *1978* budget to strengthen U.S. forces in, 111–14; risk of surprise attack by Warsaw Pact forces in, 109–11; role of armed forces in protecting U.S. interests in, 105

Executive branch. *See* Reorganization of executive branch

Federal aid to cities and states, 18–20, 35–36. *See also* Cities; Federal grants; Revenue sharing

Federal expenditures, 29; Carter proposals for, 44, 68; countercyclical, 44, 311; curtailment of, 1, 2; effect of inflation on, 31–32; Ford proposals for, 40–42, 67–68; projected increase in, *1978–81,* 377–79; shortfall in, 53–54; to stimulate economy, 36, 67–70

Federal grants: allocation of, 298; budget for, 35, 296–97; for capital purposes, 301–02; categorical, 312–13; community development block, 19, 294, 299, 302; dual-formula, 299, 304; effect on public versus private sector, 314–15; employment and training block, 304–05; housing, 300–01; manpower block, 36, 294; for mass transportation, 305–06; multiple-formula, 312; for selected functional areas, 313; shift from project to formula, 294–95; supplemental "action," 19, 300, 302. *See also* Revenue sharing

Fertility rate, 223–26

Fiscal policy, 36–39, 55–79, 372–73

Fiscal stimulus program, 2–3, 5, 19, 43–44, 48–50, 55–79, 156–60; affecting employment, 156–60; Carter versus Ford, 67–68, 77–79; factors leading to need for, 57–59; through government spending, 36, 67–70; growth rate and, 60–61; inflation and, 59–60; main features of, 43–44, 48–50; through tax reductions, 70–76

Food stamp program, 30, 35; in Carter budget, 49; coverage, 256–57; errors in, 260; proposed changes in, 267, 269–70, 276

Fossil fuel program, 343–44

Full employment: budget outlays and receipts, 37–39, 50–53, 423–24; controversy over, 60; GNP, 357–58, 421–23; likelihood of, by *1981,* 369–71

Fusion program, 343

Gasoline tax, 21, 349–50

TYPESETTING *Monotype Composition Company, Inc., Baltimore*
PRINTING & BINDING *R. R. Donnelley & Sons Company, Chicago*